TEXT ENCODING INITIATIVE

Text Encoding Initiative
Background and Context

Edited by
Nancy Ide
Department of Computer Science, Vassar College, Poughkeepsie, NY, USA

AND

Jean Véronis
Laboratoire Parole et Langage, CNRS & Université de Provence, Aix-en-Provence, France

Reprinted from *Computers and the Humanities*, Volume 29, Nos. 1, 2 & 3 (1995), *edited by* Glyn Holmes
(With the addition of an SGML/TEI Bibliography)

Kluwer Academic Publishers
Dordrecht / Boston / London

Library of Congress Cataloging-in-Publication Data

Text encoding initiative : background and contexts / edited by Nancy Ide and Jean Véronis.
p. cm.
"Reprinted from Computers and the humanities 29:1-3, 1995."
ISBN 0-7923-3689-5 (hardcover : alk. paper)
1. Text processing (Computer science) 2. Coding theory. I. Ide, Nancy M. II. Véronis, Jean. III. Computers and the humanities.
QA76.9.T48T47 1995
005.7'2--dc20 95-31289

ISBN 0-7923-3689-5

Published by Kluwer Academic Publishers,
P.O. Box 17, 3300 AA Dordrecht, The Netherlands.

Kluwer Academic Publishers incorporates
the publishing programmes of
D. Reidel, Martinus Nijhoff, Dr W. Junk and MTP Press.

Sold and distributed in the U.S.A. and Canada
by Kluwer Academic Publishers,
101 Philip Drive, Norwell, MA 02061, U.S.A.

In all other countries, sold and distributed
by Kluwer Academic Publishers Group,
P.O. Box 322, 3300 AH Dordrecht, The Netherlands.

Printed on acid-free paper

Printed in the Netherlands

Table of Contents

PART IV: SPECIAL ENCODING MECHANISMS

Preface

Charles F. Goldfarb
Saratoga, California

If asked for a sure recipe for chaos I would propose a project in which several thousand impassioned specialists in scores of disciplines from a dozen or more countries would be given five years to produce some 1300 pages of guidelines for representing the information models of their specialties in a rigorous, machine-verifiable notation. Clearly, it would be sociologically and technologically impossible for such a group even to agree on the subject matter of such guidelines, let alone the coding details. But just as clearly as the bumblebee flies despite the laws of aerodynamics, the Text Encoding Initiative has actually succeeded in such an effort.

The TEI Guidelines are extraordinary. Even if they were never adopted they would stand as a significant contribution to scholarship for their detailed analysis of the information sets of a huge range of complex text types. But in fact they have already been implemented, both by scholars for research and interchange and by commercial publishers for the publication of linguistic and humanistic works.

I am delighted that my invention, the Standard Generalized Markup Language, was able to play a role in the TEI's magnificent accomplishment, particularly because almost all of the original applications of SGML were in the commercial and technological realms. It is reasonable, of course, that organizations with massive economic investments in new and changing information should want the benefits of information asset preservation and reuse that SGML offers. It is gratifying that the TEI, representing the guardians of humanity's oldest and most truly valuable information, chose SGML for those same benefits.

The vaunted "information superhighway" would hardly be worth traveling if the landscape were dominated by industrial parks, office buildings, and shopping malls. Thanks to the Text Encoding Initiative, there will be museums, libraries, theaters, and universities as well.

Introduction *

Nancy Ide
Department of Computer Science, Vassar College, Poughkeepsie, New York 12601, U.S.A.
e-mail: ide@cs.vassar.edu

and

Jean Véronis
Laboratoire Parole et Langage, CNRS & Université de Provence 29, Avenue Robert Schuman, 13621 Aix-en-Provence Cedex 1, France
e-mail: veronis@univ-aix.fr

The Text Encoding Initiative (TEI) *Guidelines for Electronic Text Encoding and Interchange* (Sperberg-McQueen and Burnard, 1994), known familiarly as TEI P3 (i.e., "TEI Proposal number 3") or just "the Guidelines", appeared in May, 1994. The Guidelines are the result of over six years' work by dozens of scholars from all over the world who were involved in TEI working groups, providing their conclusions concerning the optimal way to consistently and comprehensively encode a vast range of text types and features. As such, TEI P3 represents a pioneer effort in an area where only occasional and isolated attempts had been made before, and will certainly serve as the primary basis for encoding texts in electronic form for the foreseeable future.

As a reference manual, TEI P3 necessarily contains only the final result of the sometimes lengthy and occasionally heated discussions within the TEI working groups that produced the final recommendations. Contextual information, lengthy explanations, and extensive exemplary materials could obviously not be included in the Guidelines, which comprise two volumes spanning over 1300 pages. Most importantly, many of the challenges of text encoding that the TEI working groups had to face are not obvious in what was eventually included in TEI P3. This collection of papers is intended to fill this gap, by providing a background and context for the contents of TEI P3.

The idea for this collection came primarily as a result of our experience in one of the working groups in which we participated, concerned with encoding dictionaries. At the end of our work it was clear to us that much of the intellectual process that went into the final decisions is not apparent in reading the chapter of the Guidelines concerned with dictionaries alone, or, for that matter, any other part of TEI P3. In fact, within the dictionary working group there was considerable debate, and a number of extremely interesting ideas and insights for a dictionary encoding scheme were proposed. Obviously, many of these ideas were ultimately not included in the final scheme; but readers of TEI P3 alone will not be aware of these ideas nor, more importantly, the reasons why some were rejected in the final recommendations. However, this information is valuable for users of the dictionary encoding guidelines, both to answer their questions about the choices we eventually made and to highlight the fundamental problems for encoding this text type. We felt strongly that readers of the dictionary chapter of TEI P3, and in fact any chapter of TEI P3, would benefit from a discussion of the rationale behind what the working groups finally produced. We therefore put together this collection of papers, comprising contributions from

* Nancy Ide is Associate Professor and chair of Computer Science at Vassar College, and Visiting Researcher at CNRS. She is president of the Association for Computers and the Humanities and chair of the Steering Committee of the Text Encoding Initiative. Jean Véronis is Maître de Conférences in Computer Science at the Université de Provence and head of the Natural Language Processing Group of Laboratoire Parole et Langage.

members of virtually all TEI committees and working groups.

There is an even more compelling reason for collecting this series of papers. The TEI is a pioneering effort; the TEI working groups were the first to comprehensively address the substantial intellectual problem of representing textual data in electronic form. They were faced with a vast array of new problems: it became immediately apparent that the development of a text encoding scheme demanded much more than assigning tag names to features, and included looking at the conceptual structure of texts and determining the commonalities across different text types. It also demanded finding the most consistent and effective ways to encode texts using the Standard Generalized Markup Language (SGML), which provides only the fundamental machinery for marking texts and provides for many alternative means to encode texts. Therefore, the work of participants in the TEI not only involved consideration of problems of text encoding that are likely to be with us for decades to come, but also required the development of a methodology, from scratch, for approaching these problems. These pioneering efforts, while likely to be refined and extended, should not be lost; they provide the intellectual basis upon which text encoding practices will build in the future. This collection is therefore also an attempt to document the course of these efforts.

The papers in this collection are grouped in four sections. The first section provides background material for the remainder of the papers, by outlining the motivation for establishing the TEI together and the development of its overall goals and philosophy, giving a summary of the overall design of the TEI scheme, and providing a brief tutorial on SGML. The authors of papers in the remaining sections of this collection have assumed a basic familiarity with TEI P3 and SGML that is, for the most part, provided by the papers in section one. The second section treats encoding problems present in all text types, particularly character representation and bibliographic documentation of electronic materials. The third section of the collection provides a survey of the encoding concerns for a range of important specific text types, including all of those treated in TEI P3. This section not only looks at specific text types in isolation, but also serves to highlight many of the fundamental encoding problems across text types – such as recoverability of original source materials, the representation of different "views" of a text, etc. – and demonstrates how they were approached by different groups with often very different problems and concerns. The final section is concerned with mechanisms for a few special encoding problems not particular to any text type, including cross-reference and linkage, alignment of non-contiguous elements, and dealing with text elements which do not conform to SGML's basic requirement for an entirely hierarchical, nested internal structure. Many of these papers have repercussions for SGML use in general, and constitute valuable contributions to some of the more technical discussions concerned with problems of text encoding.

This collection is the result of much effort and enthusiasm by everyone over the past two years, but most of all the authors, who worked hard to fit their papers into the larger whole. Our thanks to them and to Glyn Holmes, the editor of *CHum*, for their efforts. We hope that this collection will prove to be as valuable a companion to the TEI Guidelines as we envisioned at the outset, and that it will contribute to the on-going development of text encoding research and practice.

Reference

Sperberg-McQueen, C.M. and L. Burnard, eds. *Guidelines for Electronic Text Encoding and Interchange*. Chicago and Oxford, 1994.

Computers and the Humanities **29:** 5–15, 1995.

The TEI: History, Goals, and Future *

Nancy M. Ide
Department of Computer Science, Vassar College, Poughkeepsie, New York, 12601, U.S.A.
e-mail: ide@cs.vassar.edu

and

C.M. Sperberg-McQueen
Computer Center, University of Illinois at Chicago, Chicago, Illinois 60680, U.S.A.
e-mail: u35395@uicvm.uic.edu

Key words: TEI, electronic texts, text encoding, encoding standards, SGML, tagging

Abstract

This paper traces the history of the Text Encoding Initiative, through the Vassar Conference and the Poughkeepsie Principles to the publication, in May 1994, of the *Guidelines for the Electronic Text Encoding and Interchange.* The authors explain the types of questions that were raised, the attempts made to resolve them, the TEI project's aims, the general organization of the TEI committees, and they discuss the project's future.

1. Overview

Before they can be studied with the help of computers, texts must be encoded in computer-readable form. Standard data processing practice provides convenient solutions for basic text representation problems, but many texts of interest to scholarly research present difficulties not resolved by industrial standards. Therefore, over the years scholars have developed a variety of methods for representing special characters, encoding logical divisions of a text, representing analytic or interpretative information, and reducing text-critical apparatus to a single linear sequence. Because of the lack of a unified, standard format, scores of such encoding schemes were developed from scratch or adapted from existing schemes in the 1960s, '70s, and '80s. These schemes typically reflected the specialized interests of their originators and were, by and large, incompatible; the end result was that a text encoded for one purpose or piece of software often required substantial editing to be used for another purpose or with other software, if it was reusable at all. Recognizing this, the humanities computing community attempted very early to launch efforts to develop encoding standards for computer-readable texts intended for scholarly research (San Diego 1977, Pisa 1980). However, these efforts failed to generate consensus on how, or even whether, such a standard should be developed, and thus they were aborted at the outset.

In November of 1987, the Association for Computers and the Humanities (ACH) convened a meeting at Vassar College in Poughkeepsie, New York, of over 30 representatives from archives, humanities computing centers, and professional organizations, to consider once again the standardization question.[1] This group agreed not only on the need for common practice but also on a set of basic principles to guide the development of guidelines for the encoding and exchange of literary and linguistic data, now commonly referred to as the "Poughkeepsie Principles":[2]

* Nancy Ide is Associate Professor and chair of Computer Science at Vassar College, and Visiting Researcher at CNRS. She is president of the Association for Computers and the Humanities and chair of the Steering Committee of the Text Encoding Initiative. C. M. Sperberg-McQueen is a Senior Research Programmer at the academic computer center of the University of Illinois at Chicago; his interests include medieval Germanic languages and literatures and the theory of electronic text markup. Since 1988 he has been editor in chief of the ACH/ACL/ALLC Text Encoding Initiative.

1. The guidelines are intended to provide a standard format for data interchange in humanities research.
2. The guidelines are also intended to suggest principles for the encoding of texts in the same format.
3. The guidelines should
   a. define a recommended syntax for the format
   b. define a metalanguage for the description of text-encoding schemes
   c. describe the new format and representative existing schemes both in that metalanguage and in prose
4. The guidelines should propose sets of coding conventions suited for various applications.
5. The guidelines should include a minimal set of conventions for encoding new texts in the format.
6. The guidelines are to be drafted by committees on
   a. text documentation
   b. text representation
   c. text interpretation and analysis
   d. metalanguage definition and description of existing and proposed schemes

   coordinated by a steering committee of representatives of the principal sponsoring organizations.
7. Compatibility with existing standards will be maintained as far as possible.
8. A number of large text archives have agreed in principle to support the guidelines in their function as an interchange format. We encourage funding agencies to support development of tools to facilitate this interchange.
9. Conversion of existing machine-readable texts to the new format involves the translation of their conventions into the syntax of the new format. No requirements will be made for the addition of information not already coded in the texts.

The success of the Vassar conference had several sources. First, at the time of the conference more was known about encoding problems and basic principles were clearer than at the time of the earlier efforts already mentioned. Second, the Vassar group included a far more robust representation of key organizations and active research centers than had been gathered before. Third, the recently developed Standard Generalized Markup Language (SGML)[3] provided a tool for developing a simple, flexible, and extensible encoding scheme capable of satisfying the widely varying needs of textual research. Finally, the consensus reflected the growing urgency of the need. At earlier meetings, it was predicted that if the humanities computing community did not adopt a common practice, chaos would ensue. At the Vassar meeting, no one needed to predict chaos; it was, as several speakers observed, the status quo.

Following the Vassar conference, the ACH was joined by the Association for Literary and Linguistic Computing and the Association for Computational Linguistics in driving the standards effort, thus forming the Text Encoding Initiative (TEI). The three organizations pledged to guide the effort and seek funding to support the TEI as an international, multi-lingual project to develop guidelines for the preparation and interchange of electronic texts for scholarly research.[4] Very quickly, it was recognized that the TEI's goals served not only humanities scholarship, but were critical for a broad range of applications by the language industries more generally. It has become crucial for both research and industry to ensure that any text that is created can be used and, more importantly, reused for any number of applications, including applications which have not yet been imagined or developed. Thus, since its inception, the work of the TEI has achieved increasing importance for text-based work across disciplines and applications.

In May 1994, the TEI issued the first full version of its *Guidelines for Electronic Text Encoding and Interchange*.[5] This report, which provides encoding conventions for a large range of text types and features relevant for research in language technology, the humanities, and computational linguistics, represents a major milestone: never before the TEI was it possible to achieve such broad consensus among the research community about encoding conventions.

In developing its Guidelines, the TEI identified the encoding needs for interchange and for the varied processing and analysis needs of the research community, laid out on this basis the encoding principles demanded for a general purpose scheme, and identified key text types and features for which encoding conventions needed to be developed. In most cases there were no pre-existing encoding conventions. In almost as many cases, there had not even been any usable prior analysis of the required categories and features and their relations for a given text type, in the light of real and potential processing and analytic needs. The TEI motivated and accomplished the substantial intellectual task of completing this analysis for a large number of text types and provided encoding conventions based upon it. The TEI's achievements include:

1. determination that the Standard Generalized Markup Language (SGML) is the appropriate framework for development of the Guidelines;

2. specification of restrictions on and recommendations for SGML use that serve the needs of interchange among unlike systems, while retaining the generality and flexibility that make SGML suitable for a broad range of needs in research, development, and applications;
3. analysis and identification of categories and features for encoding textual data, at many levels of detail;
4. specification of a set of general text structure definitions that is effective, flexible, and extensible;
5. specification of a method for in-file documentation of electronic texts that is compatible with library cataloging conventions and can be used to trace the history of the texts and thus can assist in authenticating their provenance and the modifications they have undergone;
6. specification of encoding conventions for special kinds of texts or text features:
   a. character sets
   b. language corpora
   c. general linguistics
   d. dictionaries
   e. terminological data
   f. spoken texts
   g. hypermedia
   h. literary prose
   i. verse
   j. drama
   k. historical source materials
   l. text critical apparatus.

The TEI Guidelines are the result of this work. They provide encoding conventions for describing the physical and logical structure of many classes of texts, as well as features particular to a given text type or not conventionally represented in typography. They treat common text encoding problems, including intra- and inter-textual cross reference, demarcation of arbitrary text segments, alignment of parallel elements, and overlapping hierarchies. In addition, they provide conventions for linking texts to acoustic and visual data. As such, the TEI Guidelines answer the fundamental needs of a wide range of users: researchers in the humanities, sciences, and social sciences, publishers, librarians, and those concerned generally with document retrieval and storage. They also answer many of the needs of the growing "language technology" community, which is amassing substantial multi-lingual, multi-modal corpora of spoken and written texts and lexicons in order to advance research in human language understanding, production, and translation.

In what follows, we discuss in more depth the goals of the TEI and its overall organization.

2. Rationale for an Encoding Scheme

2.1 *Scope and intent*

2.1.1 *Definition of "text"*

The concern of the group who met at the Vassar conference was "texts intended for humanities scholarship". The range of texts included under this definition was not entirely clear; very generally, such texts can be said to include pieces of extended natural discourse, ancient or modern, in any language. We can for the most part think of texts existing in written form, although transcripts of spoken language may be included. It was not clear that concordances, word lists, results of linguistic surveys, and other items lacking the inter-relational coherence and co-referentiality of continuous discourse meet the implicit criteria for textuality assumed at the Vassar conference. Dictionaries, which are not composed of pieces of continuous text but whose co-referentiality is extensive, clearly exist on a borderline and were eventually taken by the Vassar group to be included under the rubric "text".

Whatever the boundaries, the needs of humanities research were not fully addressed by schemes such as the Association of American Publishers' standard for encoding materials for eventual typesetting.[6] Computer-readable texts intended for research occasionally use mark-up to describe potential physical layout, but typically include very different types of information, such as bibliographic information, physical description of an existing form or forms of the text (not necessarily with the intention of reproducing it in this form), information concerning the logical structure, and interpretive or analytic information concerning semantic or linguistic elements within the text.

Over time the range of text types to be covered by the TEI and the community it intended to serve was broadened, as it became clear that the needs of any textual research within or outside the humanities, as well as the growing number of researchers and users of text in industry, were largely overlapping. The growing diversity of applications for electronic texts includes not only humanities research but also natural language processing (machine translation, language understanding, etc.), information retrieval, hypertext, and electronic publishing. An early TEI emphasis on encoding linguistic information, such as morphology and syntax, reflects the recognition that such encoding was fundamental to scholars and researchers across a broad range of disciplines and applications.

2.1.2 *Guidelines vs. standards*

The TEI made an early commitment to formulating its encoding scheme as a set of *guidelines*, rather than as a *standard*, for encoding literary and linguistic materials. This reflects first of all a commitment to preserving the intellectual autonomy of researchers who encode texts electronically: by constraining the allowable forms and intellectual content of electronic texts, a strictly normative standard would risk constraining their ability to reflect the particular intellectual commitments of individual researchers, and thus in some ways the types of intellectual work which can conveniently be undertaken. A wholly permissive encoding scheme, on the other hand, risks failing to provide a usable basis for the sharing and reuse of expensive textual resources. It also encourages pointless variation in encoding methods arising not from different intellectual approaches to textual research, but from merely random differences in the use of the scheme.

The TEI has attempted to steer a middle course:

1. Rather than generalities and non-binding advice on the use of SGML in text encoding, the TEI has developed a specific SGML document type definition, which allows the encoding of a specific (and thus finite) set of textual features. Explicitly normative language is used to define this DTD, with systematic gradations in the modal verbs used to describe the use of each SGML element and attribute. Distinctions among required, recommended, and optional practice are common in standards documents; the TEI Guidelines differ from most such documents in the much smaller relative weight of its requirements, and the much larger weight attached to the definition of purely optional practices.

2. In the body of the Guidelines, alternative methods of recording specific textual features are provided wherever the choice is felt to reflect important aspects of the encoder's understanding of the text, or the kind of processing to be performed; variations which do not reflect such important issues of opinion have been suppressed as far as possible, with one significant exception. Common applications of some extremely general SGML elements have been given shorter expressions which are, by definition, exactly synonymous with a longer expression using a more general element; examples of such "syntactic sugar" include the provision of specialized elements for indications of grammatical gender, number, inflectional type, and the like, which are specializations of the more general (and hence at once more flexible and more verbose) element for grammatical information of any type.

3. An explicit and precise definition of *TEI conformance* is given, which should allow clear distinctions to be made between conforming and non-conforming uses of the TEI scheme.

4. Explicit mechanisms for modifying and extending the encoding scheme are defined, and the definition of conformance guarantees that documents using such extensions can be strictly TEI-conformant. Thus, even if the TEI scheme is adopted as normative in some contexts, the intellectual freedom of researchers to modify the scheme however they see fit remains guaranteed. This does not prevent funding agencies or other bodies from imposing requirements beyond those of TEI conformance, nor software developers from electing to support only the subset of TEI-conformant documents which use no extensions – but it does ensure that the notion of TEI conformance cannot itself be used to enforce intellectual conformity.

5. Finally, since the TEI scheme has been developed not by any standards agency, funding body, or other authority, but by and for the research community, researchers who do not find it useful remain free to ignore it entirely and to develop their own encoding scheme whenever they see fit.

The description of the TEI scheme as a set of guidelines rather than a standard is one way of attempting to avoid imposing unwelcome and counterproductive burdens on the text computing community. A second is the explicit distinction, reflected in the Poughkeepsie Principles, between the use of the Guidelines for local storage and processing and their use in *interchange*.

The participants at the Vassar conference included several representatives of major archives, who were anxious to promote the idea of a common format for text encoding. At the same time they were loath to incur the costs of converting their existing holdings into a new format, or to abandon their substantial investments in local expertise, software, and systems built around other encoding schemes, often schemes developed for the individual archive. Such archives have no need to adopt the TEI scheme for local storage and processing, since they already have schemes satisfactory for those purposes, but they may still find it useful as an *interchange format*. Many existing archives pursue an active program of exchange of data with other archives in their field; such exchanges, however, typically require the reformatting of texts from one archive's format to the other's. Direct translation from one format to the other requires a new pair of translation programs for each pair of archives exchanging material – ninety such programs, for ten archives all exchanging data. Indirect translation by means of a common interchange format like the TEI requires fewer programs, only two per archive (for ten distinct archival formats, twenty programs: ten to import data from the TEI interchange format to the archival formats, and ten to export data from the archival format into the interchange format). Archives also supply texts to individual users; distributing archival texts in a single, familiar, publicly documented format supported by commercially available SGML software would represent a significant convenience for the individual and a serious reduction in the consulting load on the archive.

The concern over the specter of enforced retrospective conversion led first to the specification, in the ninth Poughkeepsie Principle, that such conversion must not require the addition of new information to existing material, which has been fulfilled by keeping the set of required elements very small. It also led to the recommendation, in the third Principle, that the TEI should develop a formal metalanguage for the description of existing encoding schemes and their mapping into the TEI scheme. This recommendation – alone among those of the Vassar meeting – was explicitly abandoned by the TEI later on in the project, for several reasons. First, anxiety over the translation of existing schemes into TEI markup subsided as the TEI scheme took shape and it became clear that for the majority of existing research texts, the mapping was normally straighforward. Second, since the Vassar conference SGML has gained much wider acceptance in both the research and industrial communities, and many archives and projects are adopting SGML for both internal and external use. Finally, the volume of new texts being encoded since 1987 has shifted the balance of concern significantly away from the problems of converting pre-1987 legacy data. It was explicitly foreseen at the Vassar Conference that the then existing resources would ultimately be only a small proportion of the available electronic texts, but the speed with which this prophecy was fulfilled has surprised some of the prophets themselves. Hundreds of millions of words of newly encoded text, in many languages, are becoming available now, a large proportion of them – perhaps even most – encoded with at least an eye toward SGML and the TEI.

The Guidelines were of course also intended to provide recommendations for newly-encoded texts – specifically, to assist scholars and research centers with no commitment to an existing encoding format in deciding both *what* text features to encode and *how* to encode them. Recognition of this goal led to three desiderata for the Guidelines:

1. The Guidelines should specify a *recommended* minimum set of tags to be included in every newly-encoded text, including descriptive and bibliographic information as well as information concerning the encoding itself.
2. The Guidelines should define the textual features relevant to specific disciplines or text types, and define tag sets to enable marking these features within a text.
3. Because the varieties and needs of both textual materials and research defy exhaustive classification, the Guidelines should include a mechanism to enable users to extend the scheme.

2.1.3 *Polytheoreticity*

It is easy to define the textual features relevant to a specific discipline, when there is unanimity within the discipline as to what they are and how they behave. In general, however, no such unanimity prevails, and different theories of the subject contend within a discipline for adherents, each postulating different kinds of features in the text and different behavior of those features. In linguistics, for example, different schools postulate different parts of speech – and some assign no meaning at all to the category "parts of speech". Other disciplines are divided less visibly by overt differences of theory than by differences of opinion on the best approach to some particular practical question.

Such diversity of opinion poses a difficult problem for the definition of a general-purpose encoding scheme suitable for research work, for which different solutions are possible. At one extreme, the encoding scheme might adopt the viewpoint of a specific single theory (e.g. the one apparently commanding widest belief) – a tag set for encoding syntactic structure, for example, might use the theory of generalized phrase structure grammar, with no consideration of the major theories in the field. Needless to say, those who subscribe to the theory in question will find the resulting tag set useful, while those who find the theory uncongenial will find the tag set a positive hindrance in their work.

Other approaches are also possible. The tag set may pluralistically allow the user to adopt any of several competing theories. It may eclectically mix the concepts of many theories (thus allowing, at least in principle, encodings reflecting hybrid mixes of theories which might be disowned by purists on either side). In the extreme case, an encoding scheme might formulate a common ground among the competing theories, a theoretically neutral or polytheoretical tag set which enables a text to be encoded according to any one of several viewpoints, and which captures any commonalities among the theories, in the same way that a database schema captures the commonalities among the various views of the data and allows each view to be derived systematically from the underlying database. However, the formulation of such a polytheoretical view can often involve considerable research, and may prove impossible within the current theoretical climate.

In the TEI, work groups attempted to formulate, as well as they could, the consensus of the particular discipline in question. Where consensus was clearly not to be had, a number of alternative approaches were adopted. In some cases (e.g. in the encoding of dictionary entries and term-bank entries), two different encoding schemes have been formulated (in these cases, one reflecting a relatively tightly prescribed entry structure, the other reflecting a much looser structure). In other cases (e.g. the treatment of quotation marks or end-of-line hyphenation), a number of alternatives have been formally defined, and the choice of alternatives may be declared formally in the TEI header. In the case of linguistic annotation, a feature structure notation and feature system declaration have been developed, which allow the theoretical postulates governing a particular set of annotations to be documented formally and explicitly.[7]

2.2 *Syntactic issues*

2.2.1 *SGML*

The participants in the Vassar conference agreed unanimously that the TEI Guidelines should specify a concrete syntax for the recommended and suggested tags. No final decision about the syntactic basis for the new encoding scheme was made at the conference, but it was agreed that if possible, the syntax should be borrowed from an existing scheme, be relatively simple to use, and be capable of expressing the fine distinctions and occasionally complex overlapping hierarchical structures required in textual data. In addition, the conference mandated that the syntax of the Guidelines should be designed to ensure device independence within the data stream. A third goal was compatability with existing standards. Consequently, the Standard Generalized Markup Language (SGML) was seen as the most likely candidate to provide a syntactic basis for the Guidelines.

SGML, which is a meta-language for the specification of tag sets rather than a tag set itself, was early adopted as the basis for the Electronic Manuscript Project of the Association of American Publishers.[8] A survey of encoding problems at Queens University in 1986 concluded that SGML offers a better basis for research-oriented text encoding than other schemes,[9] in large part because of its orientation toward *descriptive* markup (markup which describes function rather than form – e.g., "emphasis" or "foreign word" rather than "italics").[10] Since 1987, SGML has been widely adopted by government, industry, and academic groups world-wide. Thus the TEI Guidelines, by adopting SGML, have achieved de facto compatability with a large number of other encoding schemes in addition to that of the AAP.

2.2.2 *Software and application independence*

The TEI scheme was from the outset intended to be hardware-, software-, and application-independent. Software independence has meant that the current capabilities and limitations of SGML-processing software have not played a determining role in choices made in the design of the TEI scheme. The TEI Guidelines are intended to serve for many years to come, and it would be foolish to design them solely to accommodate existing software.

Application-independence has meant that the TEI has not, in particular, been driven by the notion of electronic text as a stage in the production of paper documents. Like the publishing industry, the academic community is rapidly coming to realize that its stock-in-hand is not words on the page, but information, independent of its physical realization. Thus, in its design the TEI has also embraced a view of electronic text as an end in itself, whether as a research database or a component in non-paper publications.

Application-independence, coupled with the TEI's commitment to serve the full range of research interests, also means accomodating different views of a text. In different contexts, texts may be regarded as:

- physical objects (volumes or loose leaves of paper, parchment, or papyrus with ink in specific places; or acoustic signals occurring at a particular time and place; or clay tablets or stones with a three-dimensional writing surface);
- typographic objects (series of characters in specific fonts, laid out and justified in a particular style);
- linguistic objects (series of graphemes or phonemes, or at a higher level series of morphemes or lexical items or phrases or sentences);
- formal objects (series of stanzas, cantos, acts, chapters, sections, etc., in turn subdivided into smaller formal units);
- rhetorical objects (series or hierarchies of speech acts, rhetorical figures, tropes);
- propositional objects (referring to specific persons, things, places, and events, real or imaginary, in ways subject to paraphrase and abstract representation);
- historical and cultural objects (with strands and layers of witnesses to the textual transmission, interpretation, re-interpretation, and commentary).

The TEI Guidelines define a general-purpose encoding scheme which enables encoding any of these views. Further, it enables the simultaneous encoding of multiple views, which is important for both research and industrial text applications. For example, the scholar reconstructing the lexicon of an ancient language from surviving parchment fragments or an industrial application for document translation must constantly switch between the levels of physical and linguistic description; the historian or anthropologist testing a theory of social interactions or customs by an investigation of textual records relating to them must switch between linguistic and propositional perspectives. No absolute recommendation to embody one specific view of text can apply to all texts and all approaches to it. The TEI scheme therefore provides multiple ways to encode the same feature in many cases.[11]

3. Organization of the Project

3.1 *General organization*

A small central organization coordinates the work of the TEI. Two representatives from each of the three sponsoring organizations (ACH, the Association for Computational Linguistics, and the Association for Literary and Linguistic Computing) form a Steering Committee which oversees the project. An editor-in-chief and an associate editor have been responsible for the centralized work and for elaborating the basic design produced at the Vassar meeting.

To help ensure that the TEI Guidelines reflect the needs of scholarly research, an Advisory Board representing professional groups for literary, linguistic, and historical research and teaching as well as computing, library, and publishing organizations is responsible for approving the content of the Guidelines at various stages in their development. These organizations are:

- Modern Language Association
- Association for History and Computing
- American Historical Association
- Association for Documentary Editing
- American Philological Association
- American Philospohical Association
- Association Internationale de Linguistique Appliquée
- Linguistic Society of America
- American Society for Information Science
- Association Internationale Bible et Informatique

3.2 *Committees*

Most standards-development efforts are voluntary, and the effort to develop the TEI Guidelines has been more voluntary than most. From the outset it has been clear that the Guidelines must reflect the consensus of those interested and at the same time take into account the special needs and special desires of everyone who is to use them. It was therefore important to involve many different people, with differing areas of expertise including discipline-specific expertise as well as technical and SGML-specific expertise, in the design process. The success of the TEI is in particular the result of the donation of time and expertise by the many members of the wider research community who served on the TEI's Committees and Working Groups.

Four committees were initially responsible for producing appropriate sections of the Guidelines; in most cases, several specialist Working Groups within these committees worked on developing schemes for specific areas.

3.2.1 *Committee on text documentation*

The committee on text documentation was given primary responsibility for the "prolog" or "header" section of a TEI-conformant document. They defined tags for the information *about the text* which encoders are encouraged, or may wish, to provide. This metatextual information falls into four classes:

1. identification of the text itself, in sufficient detail that the user can locate either the original copy text or some other edition of the text encoded);
2. identification of the encoding itself sufficient to allow library cataloguers or text archivists to catalog the files;
3. description of features of interest to archivists and their borrowers;
4. declaration of special features of the encoding, so that programs can process the text properly. The text documentation committee must provide a location for this information and prevent conflicts among various declarations, but the syntax and content of the declarations will be determined by the other committees.

This committee was competent in bibliographic description and archive management. Fortunately, there existed when they began their work a well-developed discipline for bibliographic description, both for texts on paper and for machine-readable data files. The committee worked from the International Standard Bibliographic Descriptions for most text types, supplementing them from other sources were necessary. Experienced data archivists recommended tags for the kinds of information (apart from a good bibliographic description) that they find most useful and important in dealing with their borrowers. Other work groups also forwarded suggestions to this committee, when their work indicated the need for items in the header.

The result of this committee's work was the TEI header, described in Giordano, and treated extensively in Dunlop, both in this volume.

3.2.2 *Committee on text representation*

The committee on text representation provided for the adequate representation of printed or manuscript versions of the text. This includes:

1. the "physical" description of the copy text;
2. the "logical" description of the text, with tags for the textual features conventionally represented by typography in a printed edition (whether present in the copy text or not), including:
   a. special characters, symbols, and non-Latin alphabets;
   b. the structural hierarchy of the text (e.g. book, chapter, verse);
   c. common typographically realized text features (e.g. emphasis, quotation, tabular layout, etc.);
   d. less common or special text features (e.g. notes, marginalia, commentary, parallel texts, editorial emendations, and critical apparatus).

Scholars have already devised solutions for most of the problems faced by this committee, notably character set issues[12] and the delineation of text structure.[13] With these and the AAP tag set as a starting point, the committee formulated a single coherent solution, including recommendations for common cases, procedures for documenting deviations if the recommendations are not followed, and procedures for declaring character sets or structural tags in the cases to which the recommendations do not apply.

In the first phase of this committee's work, the focus was on the logical description of the text, reserving detailed physical description for later phases. The tag set proposed is intended to be adequate to the fundamental needs of unillustrated literary texts (poetry, plays, novels and short stories) in both critical and popular editions. Codes are provided only for alphabetic languages; methods of encoding multidirectional text will be treated in future version of the Guidelines. The tag set was later extended to handle problems presented in less common text types, more general cases of reference works, and more complex tabular and mathematical material.

More complex types of apparatus and commentary for text critical work have since been covered based on experiences with the initial set of tags.[14] In addition, a mechanism which effectively constitutes an extension of SGML, called the Writing System Declaration, has been developed to enable the encoding of every language in which computer-assisted work is known to be underway in Europe or North America.[15]

3.2.3 *Committee on text analysis and interpretation*

This committee was charged with providing tags for textual features not conventionally represented typographically in a text. For several scholarly fields and research areas, it provided specific tag sets for recording textual features (objective or subjective, given or achieved as the result of analysis or study) of interest to researchers in that field.

The work of this committee can be broken down into the problems presented by various types of textual study:

1. problems common to many fields (e.g. intratextual and intertextual cross reference, demarcation of arbitrary text segments with pointers to commentary or other related material, tags for indexing text items or segments with arbitrary terms of interest to the scholar, etc.);[16]
2. linguistic analyses (e.g. tags for corpora, dictionaries, syntax, morphology, and lexical analysis);[17]
3. literary study (e.g. tags for thematic study, identification of allusions, marking for traditional narrative materials like myths, meter, prosody, and the structural analysis of narrative).[18]

As noted earlier, the committee was forced to decide, within any field, whether to provide separate or overlapping tag sets for any competing theoretical approaches, to attempt a union of the various sets of textual features they tag, to delimit the areas of difference as they affect the tagging of the text and allow the encoder to declare the use of specific positions or practices in the areas of difference, or to unify the various positions in a theory-neutral or poly-theoretical tag set. Similarly, for each area it was necessary to decide upon the degree of generality of the scheme provided – that is, whether the recommended encoding strategy would be general enough to enable representation of even the most exotic of structures for a given text type, or whether it would provide a more constrained but more exact scheme describing the structure of the majority of texts of that type but possibly not accomodating the few extreme variants. This problem and one committee's solution are treated extensively in Ide and Véronis, in this volume.

3.2.4 *Committee on metalanguage issues*

The committee on metalanguage issues was responsible for providing a syntax for the tag set of the Guidelines.

The syntax of the international standard SGML was adopted as the basis for all work on the tag set of the Guidelines themselves. The committee also legislated on the features of SGML which would be generally adopted by the TEI in its recommendations for an interchange format, as well as on specific syntactic solutions to problems encountered within various work groups (see Barnard *et al.* in this volume for a discussion of some of these).

3.3 *Affiliated projects*

It was recognized from the outset that the Guidelines will be successful only if they prove useful to those who are actually encoding texts. While the working committees will encode texts and text fragments in the course of their work, it was seen necessary to try the Guidelines out on larger bodies of material if possible. This required the cooperation of current encoders of significant bodies of material.

The TEI established liaison with several large encoding projects over the course of the development of the Guidelines. The TEI provided drafts of portions of the Guidelines (including drafts and internal copies) to each affiliated project as soon as they were available, and provided consulting on the TEI scheme. In exchange, the TEI requested that these affiliated projects review TEI materials, provide feedback on their utility and clarity, report all problems they encounter in applying the encoding scheme, give permission to use extracts of their work as examples in our documentation, and (as appropriate) serve on working committees.

The degree of involvement naturally varied among the various projects; among the affiliated projects most active during the development of the Guidelines are:

- Nietzsche Nachlaz Project (Stanford, later Dartmouth)
- Brown University Women Writers Project
- Vassar/CNRS Electronic Dictionaries Project
- Perseus Project (Harvard University)
- Middleton Edition Project (Brandeis University)
- Global Jewish Database (Bar-Ilan)
- Leiden Armenian Database
- Stockholm-Umea Corpus of Modern Swedish
- British National Corpus
- Network of European Corpora

3.4 *End products*

In July, 1990, the TEI produced the first public draft of its Guidelines, and made them freely available under the document number TEI P1 ("proposal 1"); a corrected reprint (version 1.1) was distributed in November, 1990. Starting in April 1992, the TEI began publishing in electronic fascicles various chapters of the second public draft, TEI P2.

The initial development phase of the TEI ended in early 1994 when the TEI formally published its Guidelines for electronic text encoding and interchange as document TEI P3. The Guidelines describe methods of text encoding corresponding, in their level of technical detail, to a reference manual for a major software package. TEI P3 also includes the formal SGML declarations for the tag sets it describes. It is available in both paper and electronic form.[19]

4. Future of the Project

The TEI has achieved a major milestone in establishing an intellectual foundation for text encoding and a set of encoding conventions substantial enough to serve the fundamental needs of most encoding projects, both large and small. However, much of this development has necessarily taken place in advance of experience. It is essential to continue the work if the TEI by extending the Guidelines more broadly and providing materials and facilities for user support. In addition, now that the core of a coherent set of encoding practices has been established, it is critical to provide for extensive evaluation and testing in large-scale use, and to implement mechanisms for continued extension and modification of the Guidelines in response.

The best way to promote a standard is to develop resources and software that embody it. Therefore, the primary focus of the TEI must shift to the wide-spread and large-scale implementation of the Guidelines. Actual use of the Guidelines will become the major force driving the development of extensions and modifications to it. Activity within the TEI will focus on user support, instruction, consulting, etc. One of the primary roles of the TEI will be to form a liaison with and provide consultancy for users, as appropriate, to ensure compatibility with the Guidelines as they currently exist, and to incorporate the results eventually into future versions. Another central concern of this phase will be systematic evaluation and review, again accomplished on the basis of actual experience using the Guidelines, the results of which will also guide the further development of the Guidelines.

Extension of the Guidelines will continue to incorporate modifications, revisions, and extensions suggested or required on the basis of user responses; to provide refinements and further developments of chapters in the current version; and to form or to encourage work groups for areas that have only been outlined – for example, physical description (manuscripts, papyri, inscriptions, etc.), literary analysis and interpretation, alignment mechanisms for multilingual corpora and for coordinating speech with speech transcriptions, multimedia processing, etc.

5. Conclusion

The TEI is satisfying a need recognized by the research community, by industry, and by government funding agencies – in North America, in Europe, and in Japan.[20] The TEI is well established internationally, and its role in international coordination is critical for the future development of standards for tagging electronic texts. The TEI has established or is working to establish relations with a variety of related efforts and projects, including standardization efforts (e.g., ISO, HyTime, the Expert Advisory Group on Language Engineering Standards [EAGLES]), text collections (e.g., the ACL Data Collection Initiative, the European Corpus Initiative, the Network of European Research Corpora, the Consortium for Lexical Research), evaluation and development efforts (EAGLES), text access efforts (the Coalition for Networked Information, the Center for Electronic Texts in the Humanities), and software developers (commercial SGML discipline-specific academic and research efforts, the Text Software Initiative). Through these collaborations and through the continued contributions of the research community to its further elaboration, the TEI scheme should provide the basis of the uniform encoding scheme envisaged at Vassar.

Notes

[1] This meeting was funded by the U.S. National Endowment for the Humanities.

[2] These basic principles are expounded in various internal documents of the Text Encoding Initiative, notably TEI EDP1 and TEI EDP2, available from the TEI central office at the academic computer center of the University of Illinois at Chicago.

[3] ISO (International Organization for Standardization). ISO 8879:1986 / A1: 1988 (E). *Information Processing–Text and Office Systems–Standard Generalized Markup Language (SGML), Amendment 1*. Published 1988-07-01. [Geneva]: International Organization for Standardization, 1988.

[4] Major support for the TEI has been provided by the U.S. National Endowment for the Humanities (NEH), an independent federal agency; Directorate General XIII of the Commission of the European Communities (CEC/DG-XIII); the Andrew W. Mellon Foundation; and the Social Science and Humanities Research Council of Canada.

[5] Association for Computers and the Humanities (ACH), Association for Computational Linguistics (ACL), and Association for Literary and Linguistic Computing, *Guidelines for Electronic Text Encoding and Interchange* (TEI P3), ed. C. M. Sperberg-

McQueen and Lou Burnard (Chicago, Oxford: Text Encoding Initiative, 1994).

[6] Association of American Publishers, *Reference Manual on Electronic Manuscript Preparation and Markup*, The Association of American Publishers Electronic Manuscript Series (Washington, D.C.: Association of American Publishers, 1986). Association of American Publishers, *Author's Guide to Electronic Manuscript Preparation and Markup*, The Association of American Publishers Electronic Manuscript Series (Washington, D.C.: Association of American Publishers, 1986). Association of American Publishers, *Markup of Mathematical Formulas*, Association of American Publishers Electronic Manuscript Series (Washington, D.C.: Association of American Publishers, 1986). Association of American Publishers, *Markup of Tabular Material*, The Association of American Publishers Electronic Manuscript Series (Washington, D.C.: Association of American Publishers, 1986). This encoding scheme was adopted by the National Information Standards Organization as standard ANSI/NISO Z39.59; a revised version has recently been adopted as ISO 12083.

[7] See Langendoen and Simons, in this volume.

[8] See note 1, above.

[9] Cheryl A. Fraser, "An Encoding Standard for Literary Documents", M.S. thesis, Queen's University, Ontario, 1986. See also D.T. Barnard, C.A. Fraser and G.M. Logan, "Generalized Markup for Literary Texts", *Literary and Linguistic Computing*, 3, 1 (1988), 26–31.

[10] James H. Coombs, Allen H. Renear, and Steven J. DeRose, "Markup Systems and the Future of Scholarly Text Processing", *Communications of the Association for Computing Machinery*, 30, 11 (Nov. 1987), 933–47.

[11] At the outset of the TEI, it was not clear that SGML could adequately handle multiple overlapping hierarchies which often result from the encoding of multiple views (e.g., *canto, stanza, line* on the one hand and *poem, sentence, word* on the other). It had been shown that overlapping hierarchies can be defined over a text but not that they could be processed simultaneously (see D. Barnard, R. Hayter, M. Karababa, G. Logan and J. McFadden, "SGML-Based Markup for Literary Texts: Two Problems and Some Solutions", *Computers and the Humanities*, 22 [1988] 265–76). This problem received considerable attention within the TEI, the results of which are described in Barnard *et al.* in this volume.

[12] See Gaylord in this volume.

[13] See forx instance Johannson, Lavagnino and Mylonas, and Chisholm and Robey in this volume.

[14] See Cover and Robinson in this volume.

[15] See chapter 25 of TEI P3; see also Gaylord in this volume.

[16] See DeRose and Durand in this volume.

[17] See Dunlop, Ide and Véronis, and Langendoen and Simons in this volume.

[18] For meter, see Chisholm and Robey in this volume. Other areas of literary analysis are not treated in TEI P3, due to serious problems arising from so far unresolvable differences of opinion concerning fundamental questions of the appropriateness of marking such items at all within the literary critical community. Work in this area will continue within the TEI.

[19] TEI P3 is available by anonymous ftp from ftp-tei.uic.edu (in pub/tei and its subdirectories), sgml1.ex.ac.uk (in tei/p3 and its subdirectories), TEI.IPC.Chiba-u.ac.jp (in /TEI/P3), and ftp.ifi.uio.no (in pub/SGML/TEI). Paper copies are available from offices in the U.S., England, and Japan. For more information contact C. M. Sperberg-McQueen at the University of Illinois at Chicago, Computer Center (M/C 135), 1940 W. Taylor St., Chicago IL 60612–7352, tei@uic.edu.

[20] The Japanese have formed a TEI committee to encourage TEI use in Japan and to coordinate Japanese input to the Guidelines.

Computers and the Humanities **29:** 17–39, 1995.

The Design of the TEI Encoding Scheme *

C. M. Sperberg-McQueen
Computer Center, University of Illinois at Chicago, Chicago, Illinois 60612-7352, U.S.A.
e-mail: u35395@uicvm.uic.edu

and

Lou Burnard
Oxford University Computing Services, 13 Banbury Road, Oxford OX2 6NN, U.K.
e-mail: lou@vax.ox.ac.uk

Key words: TEI, text encoding, encoding schemes, electronic text, markup language, tagging, SGML

Abstract

This paper discusses the basic design of the encoding scheme described by the Text Encoding Initiative's *Guidelines for Electronic Text Encoding and Interchange* (TEI document number TEI P3, hereafter simply *P3* or *the Guidelines*).[1] It first reviews the basic design goals of the TEI project and their development during the course of the project. Next, it outlines some basic notions relevant for the design of any markup language and uses those notions to describe the basic structure of the TEI encoding scheme. It also describes briefly the "core" tag set defined in chapter 6 of P3, and the "default text structure" defined in chapter 7 of that work. The final section of the paper attempts an evaluation of P3 in the light of its original design goals, and outlines areas in which further work is still needed.

1. Design Goals and Development Process

1.1 *Design goals*

At the outset of its work, the overall goals of the TEI were defined by the closing statement of the planning conference held in Poughkeepsie, N.Y., in November, 1987; these "Poughkeepsie Principles" are reproduced and discussed in Ide and Sperberg-McQueen, elsewhere in this issue. These goals were elaborated and interpreted in a series of design documents (TEI ED P1, ED P2, and ED P3) which formulated specific design goals for the work of specifying the TEI markup scheme. The Guidelines, say document TEI ED P1, should:

- suffice to represent the textual features needed for research;
- be simple, clear, and concrete;
- be easy for researchers to use without special-purpose software;
- allow the rigorous definition and efficient processing of texts;
- provide for user-defined extensions;
- conform to existing and emergent standards.

We address each of these issues in more detail below.

1.2 *Research adequacy*

The TEI, as an undertaking of the research community, felt itself responsible primarily to that community for creating encoding practices adequate to research

* C. M. Sperberg-McQueen is a Senior Research Programmer at the academic computer center of the University of Illinois at Chicago; his interests include medieval Germanic languages and literatures and the theory of electronic text markup. Since 1988 he has been editor in chief of the ACH/ACL/ALLC Text Encoding Initiative. Lou Burnard is Director of the Oxford Text Archive at Oxford University Computing Services, with interests in electronic text and database technology. He is European Editor of the Text Encoding Initiative's Guidelines.

needs. Since researchers also use commercial software and publish their results, the practices and needs of commercial software developers and publishers also needed to be considered, but they were not to outweigh the needs of textual research. In fact, commercial and research interests do not necessarily conflict. Both are best served by an intellectually adequate analysis of textual problems and their representation. Moreover, very few problems in the research area lack analogues in commercial areas, though in research the problems may occur more often, or in more extreme forms, and it may be less possible to proceed without a full solution. The interest taken by many members of the commercial SGML community in the work of the TEI has shown clearly that they are well aware of its potential relevance to their work.

Research work requires above all the ability to define rigorously (i.e. precisely, unambiguously, and completely) both the textual objects being encoded and the operations to be performed upon them. Only a rigorous scheme can achieve the generality required for research, while at the same time making possible extensive automation of many text-management tasks. The TEI scheme addresses the need for a rigorous description of textual objects, by using SGML to define a formal grammar for TEI-encoded documents; it does not, however, attempt to define a set of primitive operations on textual objects.

Research work may also require relatively esoteric sets of tags for marking up phenomena of interest in specialized areas. This requirement has led the TEI to develop tags for a variety of research interests not served well by other extant encoding schemes.

Because the TEI tag sets are intended to be usable by any researcher, it has been necessary to exercise caution in defining such specialized tag sets, to ensure that they avoid theoretical presuppositions which would make them unacceptable to researchers in the specialty who do not share those presuppositions. It is not possible to define a tag set – at least, not a useful one – in a purely atheoretical way, but it is possible, given a specific set of sufficiently explicit theoretical approaches to a field, to define a tag set which allows adherents of competing theories to encode the textual features they find of interest. This problem is analogous to that of generating a common database schema from a variety of views, all of which must be equally well supported. In practice, there is often difficulty in formulating such a "poly-theoretical" tag set, but the difficulty arises most frequently either because one or more of the theories to be accommodated may not be sufficiently explicit, or because the adherents of individual theories, not content with a tag set which supports their view of the problem domain, may insist also that other views be unencodable (i.e. forbidden).

1.2.1 *Simplicity and concreteness*

A scheme must be clear, concrete, and easy to use in order to be adopted by the research community. It has naturally been difficult to keep the TEI encoding scheme small, simple and easily explained in its entirety while simultaneously including in it facilities for every specialized area of research covered by P3. A strenuous effort has therefore been made to make the encoding modular, so that the parts of P3 not of interest to a given researcher might safely be ignored. The goal of clarity and concreteness also led the TEI to specify a full SGML DTD (document type definition), rather than contenting itself with either a set of general recommendations as to how such a thing might be constructed or an abstract model or meta-DTD for such a thing. The discipline of defining a concrete DTD, and testing it on real texts, has had (we believe) a beneficial effect on the robustness and precision of the TEI scheme, as well as enabling us to present scholars with a usable product requiring no prior knowledge of DTD construction or the building of abstract models.

The pursuit of simplicity has led to two conflicting patterns in the development of the TEI tag set. First, the TEI has tried wherever possible to apply Occam's Razor – the principle, named for the medieval philosopher William of Occam, of seeking the simplest possible solution to any problem. Occam's formulation was "non sunt multiplicanda entia praeter necessitatem", which may be loosely translated "plurality should not be assumed without necessity". As applied by the TEI, Occam's Razor leads to the merger of similar elements into single elements, possibly differentiated with a *type* attribute. Thus, where many markup languages distinguish three or four types of list (e.g. with bullets, with numbers, or unadorned) and three or more types of note (e.g. footnotes, endnotes, and in-line block notes), the TEI defines a single <**list**> and a single <**note**> element. The systematic application of Occam's Razor has significantly reduced the number of distinct elements of the TEI tag set, compared with other markup schemes.

A countervailing pressure, however, has led to some apparent violations of Occam's principle. In several instances, a very powerful general notation which proved cumbersome in some common simple cases has been supplemented by specialized tags which handle those common cases in a simpler notation. Simplifying tags of this kind, being defined as synonymous with the more cumbersome general notation, are not strictly necessary. For example, the general tags for text-critical apparatus defined in chapter 19 of TEI P3 could certainly be used to encode all forms of editorial intervention in a text, but simple editorial emendations or normalizations can be recorded much more simply by using the simpler tags defined for such purposes in section 6.5. Occam's Razor, strictly applied, would require the removal of all such redundancy.

Certainly, excessive use of such redundant constructs (or "syntactic sugar") can lead to an excessive number of elements and excessive complication of the markup language as a whole; in moderation, however, such devices can ensure that the markup language handles simple cases with a simple notation, reserving more complex notations for situations which really require them. In this and other ways, the TEI has sought to devise a markup language which *scales* gracefully. That is, the TEI scheme can be used both for very light markup of texts and for extremely dense markup encoding detailed analysis of texts on multiple linguistic and interpretive levels.

1.2.2 *Extensibility*

Since research necessarily involves the asking of questions that have not been asked before, a research-oriented encoding scheme must also be extensible. Some measure of extensibility, then, was from the beginning an absolute requirement for the TEI markup scheme, rather than a design goal. The extent to which the various portions of the scheme might be extended, and the degree to which the various possible kinds of extensions can be easily created and integrated do, however, form important design goals. TEI P3 attempts to support convenient extension and modification of the TEI DTD by modularizing the DTD into base and additional tag sets, by standardizing the interface among tag sets so as to allow new modules to be introduced easily, and by the extensive use of SGML parameter entities to allow the suppression of individual declarations, the ability to rename elements, and the addition of new elements to existing element classes, as described further below.

1.2.3 *Compatibility with standards*

Compatibility with "existing and emergent standards" and practice was to be sought, but (as its rank suggests) not at the expense of the other design goals. From the start, the standards perceived as most relevant to the work of the TEI were SGML and existing applications of SGML; the TEI therefore decided that its Guidelines should, if possible, use the formalisms of SGML, with the caveat that, if the needs of research required constructs unavailable in SGML, research was to take precedence over the standard. It is a tribute to the expressive power and generally good design of SGML that no extensions to SGML were in practice found to be necessary. P3 can thus require all TEI-encoded documents to be conforming SGML documents; in addition, the TEI Interchange Format adds some simple restrictions beyond those of SGML proper, intended to ensure that documents in that format can be parsed by software simpler than full SGML parsers.[2]

The TEI was not committed to using the full range of constructs available with SGML; a meta-language committee was responsible for assessing the guidelines' compatibility with commonly available software. That committee formulated a subset of SGML which used few enough constructs to allow users without SGML-conformant software to construct ad hoc processors for the TEI Interchange Format.

1.3 *Additional design issues*

The design goals discussed so far relate for the most part to *how* the TEI scheme would be defined. This section discusses some important aspects of the scheme's coverage – *what* it is intended to address.

1.3.1 *Guidance for new encodings – and new encoders*

The Poughkeepsie Principles mandated that the Guidelines should simplify the task of encoding texts in machine-readable form for the first time by making it unnecessary for projects creating such resources to design an encoding scheme from scratch. The Guidelines recommend a standard minimum set of textual features, derived from (but not limited by) common existing practice. The widespread use of this tag set will, we hope, contribute to an improvement in both the quality and the re-usability of newly-created encoded texts. In addition, the specialized tag sets described in chapters 14 to 23 of TEI P3 should make it easier for projects working in those specific discipline areas to exchange data and results.

The Guidelines are also intended to provide *guidance* for researchers who are uncertain as to which textual features are likely to be of maximal usefulness in an encoding. They should reduce, not increase, the perplexity of deciding what to encode.

At present, only the full reference documentation of TEI P3 is available. Since it is the task of a reference manual to describe every detail and arcane subtlety of a system, P3 is only imperfectly suited to the role of a reassuring introduction to the TEI encoding scheme. It is therefore a matter of some priority for the TEI to produce a set of introductory manuals for the Guidelines. In an introduction, only a portion of the TEI scheme will need to be introduced, and many details can be postponed until they are needed; only such introductions will make it possible to achieve the goal of providing suitable guidance to the perplexed novice.

1.3.2 *Interchange format for existing material*

The Poughkeepsie Principles also directed that the Guidelines must be suitable for the interchange of encodings among sites using different schemes. As a definition of an interchange format, the Guidelines will be of assistance to data archives, their borrowers, and even to software developers who can rely on this interchange format, whether as a documented interface between their software and the textual data they may import or export, or as a reference point with which their format can be compared.

For interchange, it must be possible to translate from any existing scheme for text encoding into the TEI scheme without loss of information. All distinctions present in the original encoding must be preserved. Any conventions used in the original encoding but not made explicit by its encoding format should be documented within the interchange format.

When the TEI scheme is used as an interchange format for pre-existing encodings, only those textual features expressed explicitly in the pre-existing encoding format can be converted into their TEI equivalents. If the original encoding lacks, for example, information about paragraph breaks in the original source, so will the TEI version, even though marking this particular feature is strongly recommended to those creating new electronic texts. As the final item in the Poughkeepsie Principles makes clear, translation into the TEI scheme should not be construed as requiring the addition of any new information not present in the original encoding.

1.3.3 *Prescription and description*

An SGML document type definition specifies a set of formal rules which define the set of "valid" documents. The formal definition of document validity is one of SGML's great practical strengths, because it allows automatic mechanical checking for markup errors. It also allows the designer of the document type to make the expected structure of documents much more explicit than would be possible without such a formal specification. As described in more detail in section 2 of this paper, such a formal specification may be regarded as a "document grammar", which accepts a certain subset of the set of all possible documents.

Grammars, however, may be used for two quite different purposes. One may use a grammar to prescribe the legal forms of some language. The formal grammar for the programming language Pascal, for example, prescribes the syntactically legal forms of Pascal programs. And old-fashioned prescriptive grammars of natural languages like English similarly attempted to prescribe certain grammatical constructions, and proscribe others. A prescriptive grammar is a recipe for the construction of documents which conform to a specification expressed by that grammar.

SGML is frequently used for the specification of document grammars which are prescriptive in just this way. A publisher of technical documentation, for example, may use an SGML DTD to prescribe a standard structure for introductory manuals, and a different structure for user manuals, and to enforce rules such as "There must never be an example without a preceding paragraph introducing it, and a paragraph following it which describes what the example means". The SGML parser cannot enforce the prescribed contents of the introductory and following paragraphs, but it can ensure that an object tagged as an **<example>** is invariably preceded by an **<introPara>** and invariably followed by at least one **<discussionPara>**. Memoranda can be required to have a date, a subject line, and a confidentiality status. Dictionary entries can be required to have an etymology section at the beginning. And so on. When a document fails to conform to such a prescriptive grammar, the document typically has some flaw which requires correction.

Grammars may also be used, however, to *describe* some set of independently existing objects. Since the objects already exist, the function of the grammar is not to specify how they may be constructed but to explain how they were constructed in the first place, or to identify the differences between the objects in the set and the objects outside the set. It is characteristic of descriptive grammars that when an object fails to conform to the grammar, the flaw is usually sought not in the object itself, but in the grammar. In descriptive linguistics, grammars are used in this way to explain, or at least to identify, differences between the sets of grammatical and ungrammatical sentences in a language. If a sentence fails to conform to the grammar, but is felt acceptable by native speakers or occurs in a corpus, it is not the sentence but the grammar which needs correction.

Before the advent of the TEI, SGML had not been widely used for the specification of descriptive document grammars for existing texts. When pre-existing texts were converted to SGML, the texts involved were frequently reference works or technical documentation being converted by the publishers or corporate authors. Prescriptive grammars were used, and discrepancies between the grammars and the documents were normally resolved in favor of the grammars: i.e., the documents were changed to conform to the grammar. In cases where no such changes were to be contemplated – as in the creation of the electronic version of the first edition of the Oxford English Dictionary – SGML-like encodings have sometimes been used, but without the formulation of any DTD. (See further the description of the "Waterloo syntax" below in section 2.)

The TEI thus explored new territory in attempting to formulate a descriptive grammar for existing documents using the formalisms of SGML. In the course of this exploration, it faced a critical problem which often arises in the development of descriptive grammars. When the population being described by the grammar is sufficiently various and complex, it is often the case that no grammar can readily be written which exactly matches the population. Either the grammar *overgenerates* for the population, that is, it accepts some items which are not actually present in the target population, or it *undergenerates,* that is, it rejects as invalid some items which actually occur. In a grammar of English, overgeneration would mean accepting as grammatical some sentences which no native speaker accepts as English, or which never occur in practice; undergeneration would mean rejecting as ungrammatical some sentences which actually occur in practice and are accepted by native speakers. In a document grammar, overgeneration means allowing as a valid document some sequence of text which never occurs and can never occur in the set of texts studied by researchers; undergeneration means rejecting as invalid some actual existing document.

For the TEI, the target population includes, in principle, any document written in any language during the entire span of written history – a population certainly various and complex enough to defy any attempt at a rigidly prescriptive grammar. In this situation, we chose consciously to err on the side of overgeneration, rather than undergeneration, whenever the choice presented itself. An overgenerating document grammar has the drawback that it accepts nonsensical documents as valid ones; it will thus fail to catch some errors of markup which a less generous grammar would detect mechanically. An undergenerating grammar, on the other hand, will detect many markup errors which would slip past an overgenerating grammar; unfortunately, it will also detect as markup errors some constructs which are not markup errors at all but merely unusual document structures not foreseen in the grammar. An undergenerating descriptive grammar thus behaves like a prescriptive grammar which has strayed into the wrong arena. When an SGML document grammar overgenerates, researchers who would prefer that the SGML parser perform a tighter validation of their documents will be inconvenienced: to achieve the tighter validation, they will have to restrict the document grammar to reduce or eliminate the overgeneration. When it undergenerates, the inconvenience will befall any researcher who is working on a document with structures other than those foreseen in the grammar: to allow the document to be parsed, they will have to loosen the document grammar to allow their document's eccentricities to be accepted as legitimate. Since the skills needed for modifying the document grammar seem more likely to be found among researchers who want to exploit SGML's document validation powers to the full than among researchers who happen to be working with eccentric document structures, it is clearly preferable for the TEI to err by overgenerating, rather than by undergenerating. In order to minimize the baleful effects of such overgeneration, the TEI tag sets sometimes define two alternative forms of markup: a somewhat prescriptive form for use when validation is highly desired, and a very loose alternative form for use in transcribing items which simply do not fit the more prescriptive form. The elements **<bibl>** (loose) and **<biblStruct>** (prescriptive) for bibliographic citations, and **<entry>**

and <**entryFree**> for dictionary entries, exhibit this approach.

1.3.4 *Descriptive markup*

In the TEI encoding scheme, descriptive markup has in general been preferred to presentational markup. TEI tags typically describe structural or other fundamental textual features, independently of their representation on the page. In some cases, however – e.g. for codicologists, paleographers, or analytical bibliographers – the physical appearance of the original text carrier can be the primary object of interest. In others, there may be no consensus as to the meaning of all aspects of the text's physical appearance; it must therefore be possible to represent them as explicitly as possible, without being forced to speculate as to their meaning. For use in such cases, the TEI defines elements (e.g. <**hi**>, for highlighted phrases of any type) which simply record some salient fact about the appearance of the source text, without requiring any overt interpretation on the part of the encoder. A great deal of work remains to be done, however, to ensure that students of a text's transmission or physical presentation can conveniently record the relevant information in a precise, readily processable form.

1.4 *Development process*

The work of developing an encoding scheme consistent with these goals devolved initially upon a set of four working committees. Committee TD had responsibility for issues of text documentation and produced the TEI header described in chapter 5 of P3. Committee TR, responsible for text representation, produced the bulk of the material now in chapters 4, 6, and 7. Committee AI addressed issues of text analysis and interpretation, producing the work now described in chapters 12, 15, and 16. Committee ML, mentioned earlier, studied issues of metalanguage and formal syntax; it was responsible for the usage of SGML in the TEI scheme and provided formal definitions of the TEI Interchange Format and of TEI conformance. The committees ranged in size from seven to fourteen members, with approximately equal representation from Europe and North America.

Following publication of the first draft of the Guidelines (TEI P1) in July, 1990, the extension and revision of the work of committees TR and AI was entrusted to about twenty small, specialized work groups, each reporting either to TR or to AI; committees TD and ML, which had somewhat more tightly circumscribed areas of responsibility, continued their work without formal subcommittees. These specialized work groups, typically numbering three or four members, were charged with extending or revising the recommendations of TEI P1 in some specific field in which the members of the group had expertise. Areas addressed by the work groups, many of which resulted in drafts for the appropriate chapter of P3, were wide-ranging, including character set issues, text criticism, hypertext, mathematical formulae, language corpora, manuscripts, verse, drama and literary prose, spoken texts, literary and historical studies, print dictionaries, computational lexica and terminological databases.

2. Features, Identifiers and Tags

2.1 *Feature sets, identifier sets, and tag sets*

A marked-up document is one in which specific textual features are identified by tags or other mechanisms. More abstractly, markup in electronic text serves simply to predicate the existence of some quality or feature in some specific passage of the text being marked up. In simple presentational markup, the feature involved may be simply that the passage is intended to be printed in italics; in the analytic or descriptive markup characteristic of SGML-based encoding schemes, the features made explicit by markup tend to be slightly more abstract: the passage is a quotation or an emphatic phrase.

We distinguish sharply between the textual *feature* marked and the string of characters or other device used to mark it in the electronic text. That string of characters is conventionally referred to as a *tag*. Formally, we regard a tag as a specific piece of markup in a text, which signals the occurrence or location of a given textual feature. We will use the term *identifier* to refer to the string of characters itself, without reference to any feature associated with it.[3]

The TEI tag <**figure**>, the Formex tag <**pic**>, and the ISO "starter set" tag <**artwork**>, for example, are used to signal occurrences of the same textual feature, namely that at the given position in the document a graphic of some sort is to be located.[4] A page formatter might leave space on the page for the artwork; a galley formatter might print a marginal note calling attention to the expected artwork; a text database might embed a special symbol indicating that the original document had material not included in the database.

Note that a tag must refer to a feature, but a feature need not be tagged. The same feature can be denoted by many identifiers in different encoding schemes. Thus in the TEI tag set, the element <**div1**> may be used to identify occurrences of the feature *chapter.* In other tag sets the same feature might be tagged with <**chapter**>, <**Kapitel**>, <**chapitre**>, or <**caput**>. We use the term *feature* precisely in order to stress what would be common among all these tags and ignore what varies (the name or identifier associated with the feature: in SGML terms, its *generic identifier* or *gi*). Users of the TEI Guidelines may for example wish to abbreviate identifiers or translate them into another language; the TEI provides mechanisms for such substitutions; with them, the generic identifiers may be changed without altering either the definition of the features themselves or the syntax which governs their occurrences.

The association of a given identifier with a given feature in a given encoding system is an SGML *element.*[5] Instances of a particular element type are indicated by SGML start- and end-tags in the document, and so in informal discussions elements are often referred to metonymically as "tags". In TEI documentation, the term *element* is normally used to refer either to the abstract type denoted by a tag, or to a particular instance of that type, while *tag* is used to refer to a specific start-tag or end-tag in the document which delimits a given element instance.[6] By definition each element associates a single (though not necessarily an atomic) textual feature with a specific identifier. As just noted, different encoding schemes may readily mark the same feature using different identifiers (the TEI, for example, marks an International Standard Book Number with the tag *idno type=isbn*, while ISO 12083 uses the tag *isbn* for the same feature). They may also use the same identifier for quite different features; the TEI and the Formex tag set both use the identifier *body,* the former for the body of the text as distinct from the front or back matter, the latter for the name of a corporate body or entity.

Different encoding schemes may resemble each other in the sets of features they mark, while differing completely in the sets of identifiers they use, and vice versa. Tag sets which mark the same set of features, moreover, may differ in the document grammar they define for those features, and thus in the sets of documents they accept.

We can distinguish, for any given encoding scheme:

– the set of features it marks;
– the set of identifiers it uses;
– the mapping from identifiers to features;
– the grammar it imposes on documents.

Encoding schemes which mark the same set of features may be said to use the same *feature set*; those which use the same set of identifiers have the same *identifier set* or *name set*. Those which additionally impose the same formal restrictions on the allowable combination of features or identifiers may be said to share the same *feature grammar* or *identifier grammar*, respectively. When two tag sets are identical in all four characteristics above (feature set, identifier set, document grammar, and mapping from identifiers to features), they have an identical *element grammar*, which defines the full set of rules and conventions governing the use of a particular document type, referred to in SGML as a *document type definition* or DTD.

Since SGML provides no formalisms for the declaration of semantics, the formally expressible part of the DTD (i.e. the set of all applicable element, attribute-list, and related declarations) captures only the identifier grammar of an SGML-based encoding scheme, the *document type declaration* in SGML parlance. The full scheme requires natural-language documentation, of the sort provided in the TEI Guidelines, to qualify as a document type *definition*.

Comparing the identifiers used by two encoding schemes is of course simpler than comparing the feature sets they mark, since textual features are typically identified only by natural-language descriptions which are difficult to compare mechanically. Natural-language descriptions are notorious for vagueness and ambiguity; their only advantage appears to be that no other method of defining textual features appears to exist, or is likely to exist soon. If despite the difficulties of documenting their meanings, the feature sets of two encoding schemes can be identified, then translation from one scheme to the other may be relatively simple. If the feature sets and feature grammars are identical, or if the source's feature grammar is a subset of the target's feature grammar, then translation from one of the associated tag sets to the other becomes very simple.

More formally, we define:

feature: a characteristic of some segment of text or of some location in a text, considered independently of any identifier used to denote it. In SGML terms, a segment of text possessing the feature may be marked up as an SGML *element*, though the presence of the feature may also be indicated by other SGML constructs, as described below in the section on "Methods of Predication".

element: a component of an encoded text corresponding with an occurrence of a specific textual feature. An element has both a *tag* and a textual *feature* associated with it.

tag: the use of a specific identifier to signal the boundaries of an element.

identifier: the string of characters used in a tag to identify an element, considered as a string of characters and independent both of any particular instance of the tag used to mark the feature and of the feature itself. The SGML equivalent term is *generic identifier*.

We can also identify sets (that is, unordered collections) of features, elements, and identifiers.

To define the allowable relationships among elements and features, document markup languages define *syntaxes* for the elements of the language. The formal syntax is necessarily defined in terms of the identifiers used by the language; the semantics of the elements (their links to specific features) are not usually specified formally. If the distinction between *element* and *identifier* is rigorously maintained, then, formal syntaxes like those expressed by the element declarations of an SGML DTD must be viewed strictly speaking as governing only identifiers, not elements. If we wish to speak of rules governing elements rather than identifiers, we must include both the formal declarations and the semantic specifications of the markup scheme: in SGML terms, we must talk of the document type *definition*, rather than its *declaration*. This distinction is preserved in the following discussion.

To express the ways in which sets of features or elements may be combined, we may define the following:

feature syntax: a set of rules specifying the allowable combinations of feature occurrences within a given type of text, considered independently of the identifiers used to identify them;

tag syntax, element syntax: a set of rules defining the allowable sequences of tags and textual data in a markup language;

DTD (document type definition): a tag syntax defined according to the rules of SGML;

identifier syntax: a syntax governing the allowable combinations of identifiers in a markup language (without regard to their association with particular features).

From any document type definition, one may derive a *tag set*, which is precisely all and only the tags defined in the DTD.[7] The *element syntax* of a DTD is expressed by the content models of its constituent elements. If we modify a DTD by changing the syntax rules expressed in its content models, the tag set (and the associated set of identifiers) and feature set remain unchanged. We may say that the tag set is what remains constant when the syntax is changed without introducing new tags or deleting old ones.

We may change a DTD by translating all the identifiers into another language (as is done with the labels for the ISO starter set in ISO TR 9573, for example). The legal relationships among features remain the same, the features described remain the same; the DTD changes only because the identifiers used to define the syntax change. The term *feature syntax* is coined to denote what does not change if one translates all the generic identifiers into another vocabulary.

2.2 *Important types of document grammar*

While for any given DTD or element syntax there exists a unique corresponding tag set, the converse is not true: for any given tag set, one may formulate a very large number of possible element syntaxes. Several types of such grammars can be readily identified, which are useful for discussion purposes even if they are not all often used in practice.

The first of these types of document grammar is of particular importance, because it comes close to being a null grammar, imposing no requirements on the document beyond those of SGML itself. This is the grammar which, for any given set of elements, requires merely that all elements nest and allows any element to nest within any other. We call this the *Waterloo grammar* (or, in SGML, the *Waterloo DTD*), because its most visible exponents in recent years have been located at the University of Waterloo's Centre for the New Oxford English Dictionary, which designed a tag set with this type of document grammar for the encoding of the *Oxford English Dictionary*.[8] In SGML terms, a pure Waterloo DTD is one in which each element has an element declaration of the form

```
<!ELEMENT blort - - ANY>
```

For details of the element-declaration syntax, see Burnard, elsewhere in this issue. This example declares an element with a generic identifier of *blort*. The two minus signs indicate that neither the start-tag nor the end-tag may be omitted (even if the omitted markup could be unambiguously inferred). The keyword ANY signifies that a *blort* can contain a mix of character data and any element declared in the DTD, in any sequence.[9]

The obvious advantage of the Waterloo grammar is that it radically simplifies the task of data capture and translation from other tag sets, since all that is necessary is the identification and marking of textual features, without concern for grammatical restrictions on their repetition or nesting. The obvious disadvantage is that, as a grammar, it vastly overgenerates for its population. The Waterloo DTD for the *Oxford English Dictionary* will accept dictionary entries in any of the many forms they take in the actual text, without complaining that some are ill-formed. This is a distinct advantage. But this DTD will also accept entries which are not merely eccentric, but purely nonsensical – in which citations appear within sense numbers or sense numbers within date elements, for example. (In the OED project, such nonsensical tagging was detected and controlled, but by means of specially written checking routines rather than through the grammatical formalism of a DTD.)

A second type of grammar provides a useful contrast to the extreme permissiveness of the Waterloo grammar by prescribing a rigid hierarchical relationship among the SGML elements it defines. As an example, consider the definition of the TEI header:

```
<!ELEMENT teiHeader - - (fileDesc, profileDesc?,
                         encodingDesc?, revisionDesc?) >
```

This declaration specifies that a **<teiHeader>** element must invariably begin with a **<fileDesc>** element, which may be followed by **<profileDesc>**, **<encodingDesc>**, and **<revisionDesc>** elements. Each of these three is optional, but if they appear they must do so in sequence.

This prescriptive form of content model is often found in the definition of elements with clear internal structure; in TEI working papers these are often referred to as *crystals*. Crystals often represent textual features which are themselves compounds of other, usually simpler, features: lists, personal names, addresses, and bibliographic citations may all be defined as crystals in a sufficiently prescriptive tag set. In SGML terms, a crystal is an element defined as having *element content* rather than *data content* or *mixed content*: that is, an element whose children are invariably other elements, rather than strings of characters, possibly with other elements mixed in. In the TEI scheme, "pure" crystals are found almost exclusively in the TEI header, since within the body of the text, it is not feasible to require that encoders always capture the internal structure of items like personal names, addresses, or bibliographic citations.

The third type of grammar to be identified here combines the flexibility of the Waterloo grammar with the notion of crystals, to produce a document grammar which overgenerates slightly less than would an equivalent Waterloo grammar. This type, known to the authors as a *Belgian grammar* in honor of Jean-Pierre Gaspart, who introduced us to it, uses the SGML mechanism of inclusion exceptions to control the appearance of crystals and their parts. In a "pure" Belgian grammar:

- crystals will be defined using some form of prescriptive grammar;
- overall text structure will typically be defined using a prescriptive grammar;
- elements which may directly contain text will have a content model of "(#PCDATA)";
- top-level text-containing elements such as paragraphs will also have an inclusion exception which allows all crystals, but not their constituent parts, to appear anywhere within the text-containing element.

The following simple DTD, for example, allows personal names and lists to appear anywhere in any paragraph, but allows **<surname>**, **<forename>**, and **<item>** to appear only within appropriate contexts:

```
<!-- overall text structure: belgiandoc is series of P     -->
<!ELEMENT belgiandoc  - - (p+)                              >
<!-- Text-container -->
<!ELEMENT p           - - (#PCDATA) +(name | list)          >

<!-- 'Crystals' -->
<!ELEMENT list        - - (item+)                           >
<!ELEMENT name        - - (forename+, surname)              >

<!-- parts of crystals -->
<!ELEMENT item        - - (#PCDATA)                         >
<!ELEMENT forename    - - (#PCDATA)                         >
<!ELEMENT surname     - - (#PCDATA)                         >
```

The declaration for the **<p>** element above demonstrates the power of a Belgian syntax. Its use of inclusion exceptions ensures that names and lists can appear within any element within a paragraph, including within names and lists; items and parts of names, however, can appear only within the relevant enclosing crystal (i.e. within lists or names, respectively).

As this example shows, Belgian constructs can be restricted to some elements, allowing the rest of the document grammar to be defined using other constructs.

The final type of grammar which must be described uses declarations of the form:

```
<!ELEMENT blort - - (#PCDATA | blort | foo | bar | fubar)* >
```

This construct, which we will call a *starred alternation*, can be used to mimic the effects of Waterloo and Belgian grammars, but also allows slightly easier control over nesting.[10] By avoiding the use of inclusion exceptions, it makes clearer precisely what sub-elements are legal within elements of a given type. Its primary disadvantage is that it requires each phrase-level element to name explicitly all the other phrase-level elements which may appear within it, thus exploding the size of the DTD. Compare, for example, the Belgian DTD above with this equivalent DTD in starred-alternation form:

```
<!ELEMENT starreddoc   - - (p+)                      >
<!-- Text-container -->
<!ELEMENT p            - - (#PCDATA | name | list)*  >
<!-- 'Crystals' -->
<!ELEMENT list         - - (item+)                   >
<!ELEMENT name         - - (forename, surname)       >
<!-- parts of crystals -->
<!ELEMENT item         - - (#PCDATA | name | list)*  >
<!ELEMENT forename     - - (#PCDATA | name | list)*  >
<!ELEMENT surname      - - (#PCDATA | name | list)*  >
```

The growth in the grammar, small but perceptible here, may prove a practical hindrance when, as in the main TEI DTD, the number of phrase-level elements, which can occur within paragraphs or within other phrase-level elements, rises above fifty. Despite this fact, the starred alternation is probably more common in existing standard DTDs than the constructs of either the Belgian syntax or the Waterloo syntax.

One advantage of the starred alternation version of this document grammar over the Belgian version given above is that the content model for each element describes its legal contents in full. In the Belgian syntax, the legal contents of *item* are determined not only by the content model for that element, but by the inclusions on the *p* element given elsewhere. If lists can occur both within and outside of paragraph elements, then the legal contents of items may differ, depending on location, in ways which are not immediately obvious, even from a careful reading of the DTD. The starred alternation makes it possible to eschew inclusion and exclusion exceptions in a DTD, thus ensuring that the legal contents of an element do not vary depending on its context; this is important for the validation of SGML fragments in isolation, and for the convenient decomposition of documents into fragments suitable for retrieval and maintenance using standard database techniques.

2.3 *Methods of predication*

If we view markup languages merely as means of predicating the existence of particular qualities or features in particular passages or locations of a text – ignoring for the moment the other functions of a markup language, such as ensuring system independence of data or securing useful mechanisms for document management – then it is useful to ask exactly how we may legitimately infer, from a marked up text, the existence of a given feature at a given location. We assume in this discussion that the feature in question is marked explicitly, ignoring the problems of inferring the occurrence of features not marked from those which have been marked. Such inference is possible when the implication relations of different features are made explicit, as may be done in formal feature-system declarations (FSDs), but it is quite difficult for the most part, and has not as far as we know been undertaken for any markup language intended for general use.

In a TEI-encoded text, the predication of a given feature at a given location may be accomplished by any combination of several mechanisms. For any location, the features predicated by the markup as applicable to that location are signaled by:

- the generic identifiers of open elements;
- attribute value specifications on open elements;
- the structural position of the location in the document (a TEI **<head>**, for example, marks a chapter title if and only if it is the first child of a text division which is itself marked as a chapter);
- pointers to some open element from a **<join>** element, an encoded feature structure, note, **<span>**, or **<interp>** element;
- the position of the location between a location pointed to as the start, and a location pointed to as the end, of a passage pointed at by an encoded feature structure, note, or **<span>** element;
- an *ana* attribute on an open element pointing to a feature structure or interpretation element;
- the position of the location between two milestone elements (e.g. **<pb>**, **<cb>**, **<milestone>**, etc.).

Note that the pointers in each case may be indirect, by means of one or more links in a chain of extended pointers.

These methods for predicating features in a text are particularly important for search and retrieval applications, which often involve finding instances of particular features in a document; they are relevant for other software as well, in cases where correct processing depends on what features are present in a given passage. The implementation of software sensitive to generic identifiers, attribute values, and structural location in the document is relatively simple and thus quite common. At the time TEI P3 was published, however, software capable of treating virtual elements like <**join**>, or of following predications across links like those given by the <**link**> element or by the *inst* and *ana* attributes, remained relatively rare. These markup techniques are nevertheless widely used in the TEI Guidelines, primarily because they make it possible, and indeed convenient, to represent multiple possibly conflicting interpretations of the same passage, without requiring that one be privileged vis à vis the others.

3. The TEI Document Type Definition

Other contributions to the present volume describe in more detail different aspects of the various parts of the TEI scheme. Here, we provide a general overview of the DTD itself, and a very brief summary of the textual features and default text structures defined by its core components.

3.1 *Core, base, additional, and auxiliary tag sets*

TEI P3 describes several distinct document type definitions: a single main DTD for the transcription of texts, and several auxiliary DTDs for the encoding of meta-information relevant to the transcription of one or more texts. The main DTD is described further below; the auxiliary DTDs include:

- the independent header, which documents the identity of a particular electronic text and its source, as further described below;
- the writing system declaration, which documents the alphabet or writing system used by a given text, and the character sets, transliteration schemes, and SGML entity sets used to record it in machine-readable form;
- the feature system declaration, which defines the set of features nameable within a given feature system, the domains over which their values may range, their default values, and co-occurrence constraints upon sets of feature values;
- the tag set documentation, which defines tags for systematic documentation of SGML tag sets.

Although formally it defines only a single document type, the TEI main DTD may vary dramatically in different invocations, to reflect the varying needs of the document and encoder. By specifying a particular view of the DTD, the user may tailor it to the needs of a particular application in a way difficult or impossible with most other general purpose DTDs so far developed. The user of the TEI scheme is offered the opportunity of building a DTD which matches his or her requirements, but constrained to do so in a way that facilitates interchange.

The main TEI DTD thus resembles a complex database schema from which different views may be derived for different applications. The main DTD is defined as a set of tag sets, which may be used in a variety of combinations. Each view of the main DTD selects one or more of these tag sets, thus making the tags in those sets available for use in the encoding; different views of the main DTD differ because they select different tag sets and thus make different elements available. Three types of tag sets are distinguished:

- the core and header tag sets; these include elements which must be included in any view of the main DTD;
- base tag sets; these define textual components specific to particular text types;
- additional tag sets; these define elements of interest for particular types of analysis or processing, which may conceivably be tagged in texts of any type.

This classification of tag sets reflects what is jocularly known as the *Chicago pizza model* of DTD construction. In Chicago, as elsewhere in the U.S. (though not in Italy), all pizzas have some ingredients in common (cheese and tomato sauce); the consumer may specify, however, a choice of one style of crust (thin crust, deep-dish or pan, or stuffed) and an arbitrary selection of toppings to be strewn on the top of the pizza. In the same way, the user of the TEI scheme constructs a view of the TEI DTD by combining the core tag sets (which are always present), exactly one "base" tag set, and any selection of "additional" tag sets, which play the part of the toppings.

The core tag set is described in more detail further below; it includes elements which are specific neither to particular genres or types of text, nor to particular types of application or research.

The TEI header allows the provision of documentary or bibliographic information about electronic texts. Such information is essential for any satisfactory interchange of texts coming from multiple sources, or for which long term uses are envisaged. As with software, leaving the documentation of an electronic text to the last moment is a recipe for disaster all too commonly followed. The TEI header is one of the few mandatory elements in a TEI document. It has four major divisions which together provide a detailed framework for the documentation of:

- the electronic document itself and the sources from which it was derived;
- the encoding system which has been applied;
- non-bibliographic aspects of the document (e.g. the demographic characteristics of its author and readers, its subject matter, or its classification in some scheme of text types);
- the revision history of the electronic document.

The TEI header may vary widely in its size and complexity. At one extreme, an encoder may provide nothing more than a bibliographic identification of the text. At the other, encoders wishing to ensure that their texts can be used for the widest range of applications, will want to provide the kind of detailed documentation most often found in a detailed user's manual. Most headers will lie somewhere between these extremes; textual corpora in particular will tend more to the latter extreme. A collection of TEI headers can also be regarded as a distinct document, and an auxiliary DTD is provided to support interchange of headers alone, for example between libraries or archives, as noted above.

The greater part of the TEI main DTD is taken up, however, not by the core and header tag sets, but by the base and additional tag sets which may be selected by the user in various combinations.

To construct a view of the TEI DTD, the user must always choose one of eight base tag sets. Six of these are intended for documents which are predominantly composed of one type of text; the other two are provided for use with texts which combine these basic tag sets:

- prose;
- verse;
- drama;
- transcriptions of spoken material;
- printed dictionaries;
- terminological data;
- a "general" base for anthologies, etc.;
- a "mixed" base for anarchic mixtures of text types.

In addition to one base tag set, the user of the TEI main DTD may select any combination of the following additional tag sets; these typically define elements relevant for particular types of processing, or for particular types of research, or text components which may occur in many different types of text, but are not so widespread as to belong in the core tag set. The additional tag sets define SGML elements for:

- hypertext linking, text segmentation, and alignment of multiple texts or multiple passages;
- simple analysis and interpretation of the text;
- markup of feature structures;
- recording the certainty or uncertainty of markup and responsibility for markup;
- transcription of primary sources (principally manuscripts);
- text-critical apparatus;
- detailed analysis of names and dates;
- graphs, networks, and trees;
- tables, formulae, and graphics;
- demographic information about authors or speakers, and text-classification elements, of types particularly useful in language corpora.

Aspects of most of the above tag sets are described in more detail elsewhere in this issue.

3.2 *Selection of tag sets*

The pizza model is implemented by means of parameter entities in the TEI DTD, as further discussed below. To illustrate the basic mechanism we present here the outline of a TEI-conformant document in which the base tag set for prose has been selected together with the additional tag set for linking:

```
<!DOCTYPE tei.2 [
<!ENTITY % TEI.prose "INCLUDE">
<!ENTITY % TEI.linking "INCLUDE">
]>
<tei.2>
<!-- content of document here -->
</tei.2>
```

As may be seen, the user selects a particular tag set by declaring a parameter entity with a particular name as having the value "INCLUDE". Because tag sets are selected explicitly by means of declarations within the DTD subset, as shown above, any recipient of a TEI document can tell which TEI tag sets are required to process it. Any deviations or modifications of the TEI definitions (for example, the renaming of elements, or the addition of new ones) are made visible in a similarly declarative manner. In the following example, all modifications to the TEI scheme are contained in the files *project.ent* and *project.dtd*:

```
<!DOCTYPE tei.2 [
<!ENTITY % TEI.prose "INCLUDE">
<!ENTITY % TEI.linking "INCLUDE">
<!ENTITY % TEI.extensions.ent SYSTEM "project.ent">
<!ENTITY % TEI.extensions.dtd SYSTEM "project.dtd">
]>
<tei.2>
<!-- content of document here -->
</tei.2>
```

3.3 *Implementation of the pizza model*

In implementing the pizza model so as to work with any conforming SGML parser, several problems must be solved:

- preventing logical or syntactic conflict among tag sets;
- embedding the correct files, i.e. only those which define the tag sets selected by the user;
- ensuring that the elements defined in each tag set appear in the appropriate content models in the effective DTD;
- allowing for user-defined extensions to the DTD.

The first problem has a relatively simple solution. To avoid name clashes among elements, and to ensure that tag sets may be used in any combination, we adopt the simple rule that elements may in general appear in only one tag set. Special handling must provided for the tags of the default text structure, which are used by all bases.

The second problem has a slightly more complex, but still rather straightforward solution. The individual tag sets are defined and referred to by the main driver file of the TEI DTD, *tei2.dtd,* in such a way that they will be embedded in the DTD if and only if the user has selected them. Simplified slightly, the general pattern followed is as follows:

```
<!ENTITY % TEI.prose "IGNORE">
<![ %TEI.prose [
<!ENTITY % TEI.prose.dtd SYSTEM "teipros2.dtd">
%TEI.prose.dtd;
]]>

<!ENTITY % TEI.verse "IGNORE">
<![ %TEI.verse [
<!ENTITY % TEI.verse.dtd SYSTEM "teivers2.dtd">
%TEI.verse.dtd;
]]>

<!-- ... etc. -->
```

As can be seen, the entity containing each tag set's declarations is declared and referred to within a conditional marked section controlled by a parameter entity with a default value of IGNORE, which the user can override to INCLUDE. If the user has selected the tag set for prose, for example, then upon interpretation of the parameter entities *TEI.prose* and *TEI.verse,* the fragment above will resolve to the following:

```
<![ INCLUDE [
<!ENTITY % TEI.prose.dtd SYSTEM "teipros2.dtd">
%TEI.prose.dtd;
]]>

<![ IGNORE [
<!ENTITY % TEI.verse.dtd SYSTEM "teivers2.dtd">
%TEI.verse.dtd;
]]>

<!-- ... etc. -->
```

and then, upon parsing of the marked sections, the declaration of the verse tag set will disappear entirely:

```
<!ENTITY % TEI.prose.dtd SYSTEM "teipros2.dtd">
%TEI.prose.dtd;

<!-- ... etc. -->
```

The third problem requires even more extensive use of parameter entities and conditional marked sections, as well as a set of shared conventions in the definition of content models.

Each TEI base tag set determines the basic structure of all the documents with which it is to be used. More exactly, it defines the constituents of **<text>** elements. In practice, so far, though means exist for them to vary, all the TEI bases defined use the same "default" text structure, described in detail below, which allows a text to contain nested text divisions (chapters, sections, etc.). The bases do however differ greatly in the components which may appear within those divisions: the sections of a dictionary (for example) will contain dictionary entries, while the scenes of a play will contain speeches and stage directions, and the subdivisions of a speech transcript will contain utterances and descriptions of non-verbal activity. The sets of components, moreover, may overlap: prose paragraphs may occur within conventional prose texts, and in (the front matter of) dictionaries, and in plays. To cater for this variety, the constituents of all divisions of a TEI **<text>** element are defined indirectly in terms of a parameter entity named *component,* which is in turn defined differently in each base tag set. Once more, marked sections are used to control which declaration is effective, as shown in this simplified example:

```
<!ENTITY % TEI.prose "IGNORE">
<![ %TEI.prose [
<!ENTITY % component "p | list | note" >
]]>

<!ENTITY % TEI.dictionaries "IGNORE">
<![ %TEI.dictionaries [
<!ENTITY % component "entry | p | list | note" >
]]>

<!ENTITY % TEI.spoken "IGNORE">
<![ %TEI.spoken [
<!ENTITY % component "u | vocal | pause | event | p | list |
note">
]]>
<!-- ... etc. -->

<!-- This definition is always in force -->
<!-- Its effect is to define component.seq as one or more of -->
<!-- whatever definition of component is currently in force -->
<!ENTITY % component.seq "(%component)+">
```

Within the body of the DTD, elements are defined using these parameter entities, for example:

```
<!ELEMENT div - - (head?, (%component.seq), div*) >
```

When a base tag set is selected, one or the other of the optional entity declarations will be "activated" by the user's selection of a base DTD.

The components of a text are thus invariably defined by entities whose values vary with the particular base in use. All textual divisions are defined with the same content model, which includes a reference to the parameter entity *component.seq;* the value of this parameter entity will however be different in different bases. In this way it is possible for the divisions of a text using the drama base (for example) to consist of speeches and stage directions, while those of a text using the dictionary base will consist of lexical entries.

In the distributed DTD, the definitions of *component* and other parameter entities for use in content models are found in a separate file, *teiclas2.ent,* which also defines the structure of the TEI element-class system described below in more detail.

The final problem of implementing the pizza model, ensuring easy introduction of user-specified extensions to the DTD, is accomplished once more by use of parameter entities. Because most user modifications will be effected by overriding the default declarations of parameter entities, it is essential that any user-modified parameter-entity declarations be processed before the default declarations are encountered. (In SGML, the first declaration of an entity is the only one which counts.)

In simple cases, it would be enough for the user to insert the desired new parameter-entity declarations in the DTD subset of a document; since the DTD subset is processed before the external DTD entity, this would ensure the necessary priority of declaration. In practice, however, this would have several disadvantages. A project which consistently used the same modifications of the TEI DTD would have to include all of the modifications in the DTD subset of every document; this is inconvenient and would lead to confusion when the local modifications were themselves revised. Moreover, elements declared within the DTD subset are unable to refer to the parameter entities normally used in element declarations; because *component*, for example, has not yet been declared, an element declaration in the DTD subset cannot refer to that parameter entity anywhere within its content model.

It is more convenient if user-supplied element declarations can refer to the same parameter entities as are found in the standard TEI declarations. This is possible if they are encountered in the DTD not before but after the TEI-supplied parameter-entity declarations. The TEI's method of embedding user-supplied defaults ensures precisely this. The main driver file of the TEI DTD embeds two entities, within which local modifications can be conveniently enclosed. First, before declaring the standard TEI parameter entities, it embeds any local modifications of those declarations:

```
<!ENTITY % TEI.extensions.ent ''>
%TEI.extensions.ent;
<!-- ... default entity declarations ... -->
```

As shown, the default declaration of *TEI.extensions.ent* is the null string, so by default the reference to that entity has no effect. When the user overrides that declaration, as shown in the previous section, the user's modifications will be embedded before the TEI declarations of standard parameter entities are encountered.

After all standard parameter entities such as *component* have been declared, the driver file embeds any local element declarations:

```
<!ENTITY % TEI.extensions.dtd ''>
%TEI.extensions.dtd;
```

Again, the default expansion of the entity is to the null string.

4. Other Formal Aspects of the TEI Scheme

Several other characteristics of the TEI DTD should be described briefly here, as they may be relevant to understanding the other articles in this issue, and may also be of interest to others developing general-purpose SGML tag sets. This section describes in particular

- the global attributes defined for every TEI element;
- the TEI class system, which allows attributes and structural characteristics to be declared for classes of elements and inherited by all elements which are members of those classes;
- the full range of mechanisms for extension and modification of the TEI DTD;
- the notion of the *derived DTD*, which is important for the understanding of TEI conformance.

4.1 *Global attributes*

Several attributes are so widely useful that they have been defined as applying to every element in the TEI DTD. These are:

id: provides an SGML identifier for an element; SGML requires this identifier to be unique within the document, and it may therefore be used as the target of cross-references and other pointers.

n: provides a possibly non-unique number, label, or name for an element; this is particularly useful when it is desired to specify explicitly the number of a section, or of a list item, without transcribing the number as data content.

lang: specifies the language of the content of an element; this is an indirect pointer to a TEI Writing System Declaration, which identifies the natural language and writing system and the character set used to transcribe them.

rend: provides information about the rendering of an element where this is desirable.

The *id* and *n* attributes allow for the identification of any element occurrence within a TEI-conformant text. Elements carrying an *id* attribute value may be the object of a link or cross-reference, or any of the other re-structuring mechanisms proposed by the TEI for circumventing the rigidly hierarchic structure of a simple SGML DTD. The fact that the requirement for such links is usually unpredictable is one reason for making this attribute global.

Values on *id* attributes must be unique (their declared value is ID). Values on the *n* attribute however need not be; they may be used to carry a TEI canonical reference. A method for defining the structure of such canonical reference schemes is also provided, so that documents using it can be processed automatically.

The *lang* attribute indicates both the language and hence the writing system applicable to the element's content, thus providing explicit support for polyglot or multi-script texts. If no value is given, that of the element's direct parent is inherited. (A number of TEI attributes use inheritance of this type; in the DTD, it is indicated by the use of the TEI-defined keyword %INHERITED to specify the attribute's default value.) The value of this element identifies a special purpose <**language**> element which documents the language in use, optionally associating it with an external entity in which a formal *writing system declaration* may be given.

The TEI writing system declaration (WSD) attempts to help encoders come to terms with a world in which, for one reason or another, documents may not always use the same universal character set, whether from ignorance, perversity, or the sheer impossibility of finding one large enough to represent all the glyphs they contain. It provides for the systematic documentation of a writing system, in terms of existing international or other standards, public or private entity sets, ad hoc transliteration schemes or explicit definitions, as well as combinations of all four.

Finally, the global *rend* attribute may be used to give information about the physical presentation of the text in the source, where this is not otherwise given. A default rendition may be specified for all elements of a given type. No specific set of values is defined for this attribute in the current text, though it is possible that some suitable set of DSSSL primitives may be proposed in a later version.[11]

It should be stressed that the *rend* attribute does *not* specify procedurally how an element is to be formatted. It does associate the element with a particular form of presentation, but does so in a purely declarative way. Its normal meaning is that the element in question was rendered as indicated *in the source* – it says nothing in itself as to how the element is to be rendered in later processing, except insofar as it may be desired to mimic the approximate appearance of the source edition. In document production applications, where there is no physical source, some users may be tempted to use the *rend* attribute to guide a formatting process, but external style sheets will normally provide a better method of handling this task.

4.2 *Inheritance of attributes from element classes*

Other attributes, while not so widely useful as those defined globally, do apply to more than one element type, and need to be kept consistent among all elements which use them. In the TEI scheme, such attributes are defined as belonging to a particular *class* of elements; attributes of a class in turn are inherited by all members of that class.

For example, all TEI elements which represent links or associations between one element and another do so using a common set of attributes. To express this visibly in the DTD, all such elements are defined as members of an *attribute class*, to which the TEI gives the name *pointer.* Since SGML has no explicit concept of element classes, class inheritance is implemented by parameter entities. The attributes of a class are defined in a parameter entity, the name of which is the string *a.* followed by the name of the class itself. Members of the class refer to that parameter entity in declaring their own attributes. In the following simplified example, the element <**ref**> is a member of the class *pointer,* while <**xref**> is a member of the subclass *xPointer*:

```
<!ENTITY % a.pointer '
          type       CDATA             #IMPLIED
          resp       CDATA             #IMPLIED
          targType   NAMES             #IMPLIED
          evaluate   (all|one|none)    #IMPLIED' >
<!ENTITY % a.xPointer ' %a.pointer
          doc        ENTITY            #IMPLIED
          from       CDATA             "ROOT"
          to         CDATA             "DITTO"' >
<!ATTLIST ref        %a.global
                     %a.pointer
          target     IDREFS            #IMPLIED>
<!ATTLIST xref       %a.global
                     %a.xPointer>
```

After expansion of the parameter entities, it is as though <**ref**> had been declared with the attributes *id, n, lang, rend, type, resp, targType, evaluate,* and *target.* The element <**xref**> has further inherited the attributes of the *xPointer* class. It is as though the following declarations had been in the DTD:

```
<!ATTLIST ref
          id         ID                #IMPLIED
          n          CDATA             #IMPLIED
          lang       IDREF             %INHERITED
          rend       CDATA             #IMPLIED
          type       CDATA             #IMPLIED
          resp       CDATA             #IMPLIED
          targType   NAMES             #IMPLIED
          evaluate   (all |one|none)   #IMPLIED
          target     IDREFS            #IMPLIED  >
<!ATTLIST xref
          id         ID                #IMPLIED
          n          CDATA             #IMPLIED
          lang       IDREF             %INHERITED
          rend       CDATA             #IMPLIED
          type       CDATA             #IMPLIED
          resp       CDATA             #IMPLIED
          targType   NAMES             #IMPLIED
          evaluate   (all|one|none)    #IMPLIED
          doc        ENTITY            #IMPLIED
          from       CDATA             "ROOT"
          to         CDATA             "DITTO"   >
```

As may be seen:

- The global attributes themselves are declared as the attributes of a class named *global* – all elements are members of this class.
- The subclass *xPointer* inherits attributes from its superclass *pointer,* and thus its members do, too; inheritance is thus transitive, as it should be.
- The attributes of a class can readily be modified by the user, who need merely provide an alternative declaration for the appropriate parameter entity.

4.3 *Model classes*

Inherited class membership is also used in defining content models. Members of a *model class* share the same structural properties: that is, they may appear at the same position within the SGML document structure. For example, the class *phrase* includes all elements which can appear within paragraphs but not between them, while the class *chunk* includes all elements which can appear between but not within paragraphs (such as paragraphs, for example). A class *inter* is also defined, for elements such as lists which can appear either within or between chunk elements. Similarly, the class *divtop* contains all elements (headings, epigraphs, etc.) which can appear at the start of a textual division.

As well as these general purpose classes, some *functional* or *semantic* classes are defined: for example, all elements used to mark editorial corrections or omissions are members of the class *edit;* elements marking bibliographic citations, etc., are members of the class *bibl* and so on.

Elements may of course be members of more than one class. Classes may have super- and sub-classes, and properties are inherited. For example, reflecting the needs of many TEI users to treat texts both as documents and as input to databases, a sub-class of phrase called *data* is defined to include "data-like" features such as names of persons, places or organizations, numbers and dates, abbreviations and measures. These behave in exactly the same way as phrase elements, and so the *data* class is a sub-class of the *phrase* class.

The formal definition of these classes in the SGML syntax used to express the TEI scheme makes it possible for users of the scheme to extend it in a simple and controlled way: new elements may be added into existing classes, and existing elements renamed or undefined, without any need for extensive revision of the TEI document type definitions. The class is defined by two parameter entities: one contains a list of class members, in a form suitable for use within a content model; it is given a name constructed by adding the prefix *m.* (*m* plus full stop) to the name of the class itself, and is thus termed an *m-dot*. The *m-dot* entity also contains a reference to an *x-dot* entity, which by default is declared as the empty string. (N.B. the use of m-dot and similar prefixes is a naming convention followed consistently by the TEI; it is not an SGML construct, and for an SGML processor, the m-dot and x-dot entities for a class are simply two distinct parameter entities. The formal relationship between them is detectable only by TEI-aware software, not by generic SGML systems.)

For example, the element class *divtop* is defined as follows:

```
<!ENTITY % x.divtop "">
<!ENTITY % m.divtop "%x.divtop head | byline | epigraph">
```

To add a new element (say, <**keywords**>) to this class, enabling it to appear anywhere in the content model that other members of the class do, all that is needed is to re-define the x-dot entity within the DTD subset:

```
<!ENTITY % x.divtop "keywords |">
```

Note the trailing vertical bar, which is required. As it happens, the element <**keywords**> is already defined in the TEI scheme (within the header); if it were not, an element declaration would also be necessary here.

The m-dot entity is used in content models wherever members of the class can appear. The *divtop* class, for example, appears in the declaration of text-division elements:

```
<!ELEMENT div - - ((%m.divtop)*, (%component.seq), div*) >
```

4.4 *Extension and modification mechanisms*

The TEI takes the following steps to ensure that the TEI DTD can be readily extended or modified where necessary; some have already been described:

- modularization of the DTD, to allow individual components, which are referred to by using external parameter entities, to be replaced by modified components;
- pre-defined entities for TEI extensions, embedded by the driver at appropriate points, as described above;
- the provision of x-dot entities for all model classes, to allow convenient addition of new elements to the model-class system;
- the expression of attribute classes using parameter entities, allowing them to be modified easily;
- use of parameter entities for common content models, to allow easy modification;
- use of parameter entities for the generic identifier of each element, so that elements may be renamed simply by overriding the default declaration of the element's *n-dot* entity;
- declaration of each element within a conditional marked section controlled by a parameter entity, to allow individual elements to be suppressed at will.

The first few points have already been explained; the latter two can be illustrated with a simple example. In the non-modifiable form of the TEI DTD, the declarations for <**ptr**>, for example, are given in the following form:

```
<!ELEMENT ptr      - O EMPTY                >
<!ATTLIST  ptr          %a.global
                        %a.pointer
           target       IDREFS    #REQUIRED >
```

In the modifiable-form version of the same file, however, the declarations take the following form (again, we simplify slightly):

```
<!ENTITY    % n.ptr 'ptr' >
<!ENTITY    % ptr 'INCLUDE' >
<![ %ptr; [
<!ELEMENT %n.ptr;  - O EMPTY                >
<!ATTLIST  %n.ptr;      %a.global
                        %a.pointer
           target       IDREFS    #REQUIRED >
]]>
```

The <**ptr**> element can be renamed <**crossref**> by simply redefining the entity used for its generic identifier:

```
<!ENTITY % n.ptr 'crossref'>
```

It can be suppressed entirely by redefining that used to control the marked section within which it is declared:

```
<!ENTITY % ptr 'IGNORE'>
```

4.5 *Derived DTDs*

The TEI DTDs may be used as they stand; it is expected, however, that many users will modify them slightly, if only by selecting a particular set of tag sets and suppressing the declaration of elements which they expect never to tag in their documents. The Oxford Text Archive, for example, has for some time been distributing documents encoded with a small subset of the TEI DTD, in which the main difference from the standard DTDs has been the elimination of many elements of the core and header. The OTA DTD can be expressed purely as a set of modifications of the standard TEI DTD, in the manner shown earlier, in which the *TEI.extensions.ent* file contains a large number of declarations of the following forms:

```
<!ENTITY % sic 'IGNORE'>
<!ENTITY % corr 'IGNORE'>
<!-- etc. -->
<!ENTITY % n.titleStmt 'titlStmt' >
<!ENTITY % n.editionStmt 'edStmt' >
<!ENTITY % n.publicationStmt 'pubStmt' >
<!-- etc. -->
```

Rather than parse the entire TEI DTD each time a document needs to be parsed, however, it is more convenient to define a free-standing OTA DTD, which defines exactly the same element grammar as that of the TEI DTD as modified by OTA; this derived DTD is smaller than the TEI DTD, makes no reference to suppressed elements, and is thus more readily comprehensible on its own terms than it would be if it had to be read only in conjunction with the full TEI DTD. Its disadvantage, from the point of view of document interchange, is that it is difficult to disentangle the parts which represent modifications of the TEI DTD from the parts which are exactly the same; a recipient who wanted to know exactly what changes would be required to process an OTA text with a standard TEI-aware processor would have difficulty finding out. It will be most convenient, in general, if the derived DTD is provided in two forms: both as a free-standing DTD and as a pair of extension files which are to be used as the *TEI.extensions.ent* and *TEI.extensions.dtd* entities.

Documents conforming to a derived DTD are also TEI conformant, as long as the element grammar expressed by the derived DTD can also be expressed by a set of legal modifications to the TEI DTD. For ease of maintenance, it will be convenient to maintain the DTD as a set of modifications, and to generate the free-standing derived DTD by processing the DTD with a program which generates, from the modified TEI DTD, a free-standing derived DTD which expresses the same element grammar.

As pointed out in chapter 29 of TEI P3, any modification of a DTD changes the set of documents accepted by that DTD. The set of documents accepted by a derived DTD may be:

- a subset of the documents accepted by the unmodified TEI DTD;
- a superset of those documents;
- neither a subset nor a superset.

If either of the first two cases applies, the changes may be said to be "clean" modifications; clean modifications, however, are not a condition of TEI conformance, and a combination of clean modifications is not itself guaranteed clean.

5. Elements of the Core Tag Set

It remains to describe at least briefly the elements defined in the core tag set and in the default text-structure tag set, which are not described elsewhere in this volume. The core tag set defines elements common to many different types of text, which are commonly enough used that it seemed inconvenient to separate them out into additional tag sets. The elements defined in the core can be grouped into:

- those which can appear directly within a text division ("paragraph-level" elements – to avoid a bias toward prose, P3 defines these as *component-level* elements);
- those which can appear at character, word, or phrase level, i.e. within paragraphs or other component-level elements – and also within other phrase-level elements; these elements are members of the class *phrase*;

– those which can appear both at phrase-level and at component-level; these are members of the class *inter*.

There are few documents which do not exhibit some of these features; and none of these features is particularly restricted to any one kind of document. In some cases, additional more specialized tag sets are provided for those wishing to encode aspects of these features in more detail (e.g. in chapter 14, which provides a more elaborate tag set for cross references and hypertext linking, or chapter 20, which allows for detailed analysis of the components of names, dates, and measures), but the elements defined in this core are believed to be adequate for most applications most of the time.

5.1 *Paragraph-level elements*

The only items defined as strictly component-level elements by the core tag set are:

– paragraphs (tagged <**p**>);
– verse lines (<**l**>);
– verse stanzas or other line groups (<**lg**> – an <**lg**> contains one or more <**l**> elements);
– dramatic speeches (<**sp**>), which contain an optional speaker indication (<**speaker**>) and a series of paragraphs, lines, or line groups.

Paragraphs are included in the core, rather than in the base tag set for prose, because prose materials regularly appear in texts of all types, including dictionaries and term banks, if only in the front and back matter. SGML elements for verse and dramatic speeches are included in the core tag set, rather than in the base tag sets for verse and drama, on similar grounds: they appear frequently in texts of all sorts, either directly, in the case of mixed-genre materials, or indirectly through quotations and epigraphs. Any attempt to segregate these elements into the respective base tag sets would have rendered it so frequently necessary to combine base tag sets that the utility of separating the bases would have been seriously impaired.

5.2 *Phrase-level elements*

The phrase-level elements of the TEI core serve a variety of uses. They include:

– Typographically highlighted phrases, optionally distinguishing among emphasis (<**emph**>), technical terms (<**term**>), foreign words (<**foreign**>) or words otherwise regarded as linguistically distinct or anomalous (<**distinct**>), titles of books (<**title**>), etc. When such distinctions are not to be made, the phrase may be tagged simply as "highlighted" (<**hi**>); the global *rend* attribute can be used in either case to specify how the phrase is highlighted in the source.
– Quoted phrases, optionally distinguishing quotation or direct discourse (<**q**> – strictly speaking, <**q**> is an inter-level element), glosses (<**gloss**>), cited phrases (<**mentioned**>), "scare quotes" (<**soCalled**>), or not so distinguishing (<**hi**> again).
– Semantically distinct and important items like names (<**name**>), references to people, places, or things (<**rs**>, for 'referring string'), numbers and measures (<**num**> and <**measure**>), dates and times (<**date**>, <**time**>, <**dateRange**>, <**timeRange**>), abbreviations and their expansions (<**abbr**>, <**expan**>), etc.
– Simple editorial changes such as correction of apparent errors (<**corr**>) or faithful reproduction of errors (<**sic**>), regularization and normalization or the reproduction of unnormalized forms (<**reg**> or <**orig**>), additions (<**add**>), material transcribed despite being deleted (<**del**>), and omissions (<**gap**>); material not reliably transcribed because the original is illegible or inaudible may be marked <**unclear**>.
– Simple links and cross references (<**ptr**> and <**ref**>), providing basic hypertextual features; <**ptr**> is an empty element, used as in a document-production system which generates the appropriate cross reference; <**ref**> encloses a phrase which expresses a cross reference.
– Pre-existing or generated indexing (<**index**>).
– Simple or complex referencing systems, not necessarily dependent on the existing SGML structure (<**pb**>, <**lb**>, <**cb**> for page, line, and column breaks, <**milestone**> for other reference units).

5.3 *Inter-level elements*

The core tag set defines a number of elements which can appear at either the phrase or the component level:

– Annotation, whether pre-existing or added by the encoder (<**note**>); the *place* and *type* attributes can be used to distinguish notes by place of appearance in the source (footnotes, endnotes, marginal notes, etc.) or by type (source, parallel passage, etc.).

– Lists of all kinds (<**list**>, <**item**>, and <**label**> for item labels; <**listBibl**> for lists of bibliographic citations).
– Quotation, whether actual or pretended (e.g. dialog in a novel or narrative history); these are not always reliably distinguishable and may both be tagged <**q**>. Where it is possible and desirable to draw a distinction between the two, <**q**> should be used for dialog or direct discourse, and <**quote**> for actual quotations from other authors. Attributed quotations may be associated with their bibliographic references by enclosing both within a <**cit**> element.
– Bibliographic citations, adequate for most commonly used bibliographic packages, in either a free or a tightly structured format (<**bibl**> for unstructured, <**biblStruct**> for tightly structured, bibliographic citations, <**listBibl**> for lists of bibliographic entries).
– Stage directions, which can occur either within or between speeches (<**stage**>).
– Embedded texts (tagged <**text**>).

6. Elements of the Default Text Structure Tag Set

The default text structure, which is currently embedded by all TEI base tag sets, divides each text into a body, surrounded by optional front and back matter. These three top-level units are tagged, respectively, <**front**>, <**body**>, and <**back**>.

6.1 *Text body and text divisions*

While different text types exhibit a bewildering variety of names for their component parts (chapters, sections, subsections, acts, scenes, entries, parts, books, cantos, adventures, staves, fittes, etc. – to mention only English-language terms), nevertheless the components and subcomponents of text typically behave in the same way whatever their name: typically each such is incomplete in itself, and typically smaller ones nest within larger ones. In the TEI scheme, therefore, all such objects are regarded as the same fundamental kind of element, which the TEI calls a <**div**> (or text division).

A *type* attribute may be used to give the name associated with a particular text division in the source; chapters may thus be tagged <**div type='chapter'**>, cantos may be tagged <**div type='canto'**>, and so on. In this way, the encoder can distinguish different types of division. It will frequently be possible to distinguish them also by their hierarchical position: when plays are consistently divided into acts, and acts into scenes, then the top-level division of a text body will consistently be a <**div type='act'**> and the next level a <**div type='scene'**>. Like others of its kind in the TEI scheme, the *type* attribute has no standard set of values, precisely because no such standard set of terms exists, or is likely to exist. A set of legal values may however be defined for a given application, either in the TEI Header or by a user-defined modification to the DTD.

Following the example of such markup languages as Scribe, LaTeX, GML, and the SGML tag set developed for the Association of American Publishers (now ISO 12083), the TEI defines a set of text-division elements each labeled with its hierarchical depth (<**div0**>, <**div1**>, etc., down to <**div7**>). This style of tagging is intuitively clear to many users, allows convenient markup omission techniques, and can sometimes assist in the detection of errors in the markup. Since such a style of markup can make it hard to reuse text unless it is embedded at exactly the same level in the hierarchy of text divisions, however, a second style of markup is sometimes preferred; this too is provided by the TEI, in the form of an un-numbered or "vanilla" <**div**>. Either numbered or un-numbered division elements may be used in TEI documents, but they may not be mixed in the same <**front**>, <**body**>, or <**back**> element.

In the normal case, the components of all divisions in a particular base are homogeneous – they all use the same value for *component.seq*. However, the scheme also allows for two kinds of heterogeneity. If the *general* base is selected, together with two or more other bases, then different divisions of a text may have different constituents, though each division must itself be homogeneous. A *mixed* base is also defined, in which components from any selection of bases may be combined promiscuously across division boundaries. The way in which this is done is beyond the scope of this article; full details are, however, given in the appropriate chapter of the TEI Guidelines.

At the beginning of each text division, a division title (tagged <**head**>) may appear, as may several other items (<**epigraph**>, <**argument**>, <**byline**>, <**dateline**>, <**salute**> – the salutation at the opening of a letter, or the signoff at its closing – , <**signed**> – the signature of a letter). A number of these may also appear at the end of a division. To avoid ambiguity in the document grammar, the ambiguous items (<**byline**>, <**dateline**>, <**salute**>, and <**signed**>) must be enclosed within the grouping elements <**opener**> or <**closer**>.

For example:

```
<div><head>A LETTER TO THE PUBLISHER
Occasioned by the present
Edition of the DUNCIAD</head>
<p>It is with pleasure I hear that you have procured a correct
edition of the <title>Dunciad</title>, ...
<!-- ... -->
<p>I shall conclude with remarking ...
I am
<closer>
<salute>Your most humble Servant,</salute>
<dateline><name type=place>St. James's</>
<date>Dec. 22, 1728</date></dateline>
<signed>William Cleland.</signed>
</closer>
</div>
```

6.2 *Front and back matter*

In general front and back matter are tagged in TEI documents using the same elements as the text body; a few specialized elements are defined for specialized elements found only there. No specialized elements are defined for items like prefaces, acknowledgements, etc., since these may conveniently be tagged <**div type='Preface'**>, etc. The title page, however, is given a tag of its own (<**titlePage**>), and a number of specialized elements are defined for it, to make it easier to extract salient information like the title and author of the document in question.

6.3 *Groups*

Textual divisions pose no problems in many conventional texts. In some cases, however, it is impossible to find a satisfactory method of handling the internal structure of a text, using only the elements <**text**>, <**body**>, and <**div**>. In encoding an anthology, for example, one might well balk at tagging a poem or short story as a division of some larger whole, ignoring the fact that it too is a text in its own right. One could, of course, tag the entire anthology as a corpus of texts, enclosing each item in the anthology within its own <**tei.2**> and <**text**> elements; but only at the cost of losing the ability to regard the entire collection as a text in its own right. For anthologies prepared by later editors, this might not be an unacceptable cost, for some encoders, but it is intolerable for poem cycles and other elaborately structured works.

For cases of this sort, the TEI scheme defines an alternative to <**body**> and <**div**>. In an anthology, the front and back matter surround a <**group**> element, which contains either a series of <**text**> elements, or a series of smaller <**group**> elements, or some combination thereof. A group can have the same kind of header and trailer elements at its beginning and end as can a text division; texts enclosed within a group have the normal structure and can thus have their own front matter, body, and back matter – or may themselves be compound texts, containing groups of their own.

In addition, <**text**> is declared as a component-level element, so that embedded texts quoted in full can be tagged as free-standing texts.

7. Conclusion

It is too early to tell with certainty, and the authors are not the judges called to decide, whether the TEI scheme has wholly justified all the hopes placed in it at its inception. But it is possible to make a brief survey of the original design goals and see where the TEI now stands in relation to them.

We believe that the scheme defined in TEI P3 does suffice, thanks to the generous work of scores of specialists, for the immediate needs of the majority of scholars working with electronic text. Without user-defined extensions, it does not suffice, and no finite vocabulary can ever suffice, for all the future needs of all researchers; by providing extensive facilities for user extensions, however, we believe the TEI does the best job possible of meeting the future needs of research which cannot be foreseen today, as well as making the existing DTD usable for those with specialized needs today. The extensive facilities for analysis and interpretation are designed to allow a great deal of extension to the native semantics of the TEI tag sets to occur without requiring any formal modification to the SGML DTD.

The scheme is, however, far more complex and daunting than either of us thought likely when the project began. In part, this reflects the project's efforts to meet the existing documented needs of researchers; in part, no doubt, it reflects shortcomings in the editorial work for which we must shoulder responsibility. In our own defense we will offer only the observation that a markup language truly capable of reflecting in detail the research results of work of scholars and researchers in very diverse fields will necessarily take on some of the complexity inherent in advanced work in those fields; a very simple markup scheme will hardly provide the kind of support for research work which P3 provides. We do hope to have kept the explanations in TEI P3 reasonably clear, and we do claim that TEI P3 is reasonably concrete: it is not a meta-DTD but a real markup language which can be used without further ado, and for every element there are concrete examples, almost always from real texts.

We can also certify that it is possible to use the TEI markup language without special-purpose software; we have used earlier versions of it ourselves for several years, with no editors or word processors other than the standard ones on our systems. The goal, of course, was that the scheme should be not just "possible", but *easy* to use without special-purpose software. And here we must admit that while it has not been very onerous to edit TEI documents in standard editors, the task is made much easier by the use of SGML-aware editors. And while it has been possible to write our own software to process our own SGML documents (with which the printed version of TEI P3 was generated), the task of processing SGML documents becomes incomparably simpler when SGML software is used.

The final items in the initial list of design goals call for the TEI scheme to allow user-defined extensions, and to conform to existing and emergent standards. The list of facilities given above for simplifying the task of extending the TEI DTD has, we hope, persuaded the reader that such extension is adequately catered to. And the final goal has been met by erecting the Guidelines on the foundations provided by SGML. The task of conforming to emerging standards, of course, has no end, and future revisions of the Guidelines will have to take explicit account of HyTime, DSSSL, and other standards which accompany and extend SGML.

Some work remains for the future. Several existing chapters would benefit from further elaboration; several missing areas (analytic bibliography of early printed books, computational lexica, detailed description of page layout and design, letters and memoranda, and numerous others) should be included in some future revision. The most pressing need, however, remains that of developing simple introductory manuals for teaching the Guidelines to practitioners and students – a task to which we now turn our attention, and that of the community as a whole.

Notes

[1] Association for Computers and the Humanities (ACH), Association for Computational Linguistics (ACL), and Association for Literary and Linguistic Computing (ALLC), *Guidelines for Electronic Text Encoding and Interchange*, ed. C. M. Sperberg-McQueen and Lou Burnard (Chicago, Oxford: Text Encoding Initiative, 1994).

[2] Although it requires SGML conformance of all TEI-encoded documents, the TEI encoding scheme is not strictly speaking a "conforming SGML application" within the definition given in ISO 8879, because of the additional restrictions it imposes on the SGML constructs to be used in the TEI Interchange Format, and because P3 sometimes replaces standard terminology used in ISO 8879 with terminology which was felt to be less stilted and thus, we hope, clearer.

[3] In Saussure's terminology, we are distinguishing here between the *signified* and the *signifier.* The association we postulate between the tag and a specific feature, however, means that a *tag,* as we use the term, is not a signifier but a *sign.* Since in common usage, the term *tag* is used both to refer to signifiers and to refer to signs, we use *identifier* when it is important to refer unambiguously to the signifier, and *element* (see below) when it is desired to refer unambiguously to the sign.

[4] For Formex, see C. Guittet, ed., *Formex: Formalized Exchange of Electronic Publications* (Luxembourg: Office for Official Publications of the European Communities, 'New Technologies – Project Management' Department, 1984; for the starter set see ISO 8879–1986 *Information Processing – Text and Office Systems – Standard Generalized Markup Language (SGML)* ([n.p.]: ISO, 1986), Annex E.1, pp. 136–139. The starter set is discussed and various national-language versions defined in ISO technical report ISO/TR 9573–1988(E) *Information Processing – SGML Support Facilities – Techniques for using SGML.*

[5] In our usage, an SGML *element* is thus a *sign:* an association between a *signifier* (the identifier) and a *signified* (the feature).

[6] It is therefore perhaps rather inconsistent to refer to the sets of elements described in chapters 5 to 23 of P3 as *tag sets*, but the usage is now established.

[7] More rigorously, the formal portion of the DTD directly determines only a set of identifiers. Taken in conjunction with the semantic rules of the encoding scheme, however, this set uniquely determines the tag set defined by the DTD.

[8] See, for example, Frank Wm. Tompa, "What is (Tagged) Text?" in *Dictionaries in the Electronic Age: Fifth Annual Conference of the UW Centre for the New Oxford English Dictionary* (Oxford: [n.p.], 1989).

[9] A content model of ANY is defined as equivalent to a *starred alternation* of #PCDATA and all the elements declared in the DTD. For further discussion of starred alternations, see below.

[10] For example, in a DTD containing declarations for <**foo**>, <**bar**>, <**fubar**>, and <**blort**>, the declaration given here is the exact equivalent of the Waterloo-style declaration for <**blort**> given earlier.

[11] DSSSL, the Document Style Semantics and Specification Language, is a draft ISO standard for specifying the processing or layout of SGML documents; it is formally defined in *ISO DIS 10179 – Information Technology – Text Composition – Document Style Semantics and Specification Language* ([Geneva]: ISO, 1994).

References

Association for Computers and the Humanities (ACH), Association for Computational Linguistics (ACL), and Association for Literary and Linguistic Computing (ALLC). *Guidelines for Electronic Text Encoding and Interchange*. Eds. C. M. Sperberg-McQueen and Lou Burnard. Chicago, Oxford: Text Encoding Initiative, 1994.

Guittet, C., Ed. *Formex: Formalized Exchange of Electronic Publications*. Luxembourg: Office for Official Publications of the European Communities, 'New Technologies – Project Management' Department, 1984.

International Organization for Standardization (ISO). ISO 8879-1986 *Information Processing – Text and Office Systems – Standard Generalized Markup Language (SGML)*. [Geneva]: ISO, 1986.

International Organization for Standardization (ISO). ISO/TR 9573–1988(E) *Information processing – SGML support facilities – Techniques for using SGML*. [Geneva]: ISO, 1988.

International Organization for Standardization (ISO). *ISO DIS 10179 – Information Technology – Text Composition – Document Style Semantics and Specification Language* [Geneva]: ISO, 1994.

Text Encoding Initiative. TEI ED P1 "Design Principles for Text Encoding Guidelines". [Chicago, Oxford]: TEI, 1989.

Text Encoding Initiative. TEI ED P2 "Charges to the Working Committees". [Chicago, Oxford]: TEI, 1989.

Text Encoding Initiative. TEI ED P3 "Theoretical Stance and Resolution of Theory Conflict". [Chicago, Oxford]: TEI, 1989.

Tompa, Frank Wm. "What is (Tagged) Text?" In *Dictionaries in the Electronic Age: Fifth Annual Conference of the UW Centre for the New Oxford English Dictionary*. Oxford: [n.p.], 1989.

Computers and the Humanities **29:** 41–50, 1995.

What Is SGML and How Does It Help? *

Lou Burnard
Oxford University Computing Service, 13 Banbury Road, Oxford OX2 6NN, U.K.
e-mail: lou@vax.ox.ac.uk

Key words: TEI, SGML, markup, metalanguage

Abstract

SGML is an abbreviation for "Standard Generalized Markup Language". This language, or rather metalanguage, was first defined by an International Standard in 1986. [1] To complement the many detailed technical descriptions of SGML now available,[2] this paper[3] briefly describes the purpose and scope of the standard, aiming to persuade non-technically minded readers that it has something to offer them.

1. What Is SGML for?

The objectives of those who designed SGML were simple. Confronted with an increasing number of so called "markup languages" for electronic texts, each more or less bound to a particular kind of processing or even to a particular software package, they sought to define a single language in which all such schemes could be re-expressed, so that the essential information represented by such texts could be transferred from one program or application to another. I begin, therefore, by giving a slightly more formal definition of what is meant by the term "markup language". A universal language necessarily presupposes some basic concepts or semantic primitives in which the notions of all other languages can be expressed: the semantic primitives of SGML are simple and few in number, and their definition forms the bulk of the rest of this paper. I begin however with a few remarks about what SGML is *not*.

Newcomers to SGML often think of it as a special case of the kind of markup language with which they may be familiar. They expect it to define a universal set of tags or to define exactly what tags mean, in terms of how the items identified by tags are to be processed. But the semantics of a markup language are precisely what SGML does not concern itself with: it describes only the formal properties and inter-relations of the components of a document. It does not tell you what it means to define part of a text as belonging to some category (say, "blort"); it simply tells you how things-called-blort can legally appear within texts –whether they can be decomposed into "blortettes", or whether more than one can appear at the start of a document, and so on. Determining what a thing-called-blort actually may be is inextricably entangled with how the text is to be processed, and the function of SGML is to define the content of a document in terms that are entirely independent of its processing.

It follows from this that it is nonsensical to think of SGML as a kind of text formatting system (although its origins can be readily traced in the world of electronic text formatting), or as a competitor for such languages as TeX or PostScript. These are languages which define how ink (or its equivalent) is to be placed onto paper (or its equivalent); they are not primarily concerned with the formal structure of the language represented by those placements of dark-on-light. SGML by contrast is decidedly unhelpful about how texts are to be reproduced, since this is but one of the many applications for which a text may be placed into electronic form. Its strength is that by separating the notion of what the text actually *is* from how the text *is rendered*,

* Lou Burnard is Director of the Oxford Text Archive at Oxford University Computing Services, with interests in electronic text and database technology. He is European Editor of the Text Encoding Initiative's Guidelines.

it makes possible the use of the same text by many different kinds of processor.

As a simple example, consider the headings used to introduce the subdivisions of the present document. These need to be separated from the body of the text so that they can be formatted in a particular way. However, I have not yet decided how they should be formatted–and it is more than likely that those responsible for printing this text will prefer to format them in some other way in any case. If therefore I use the facilities available on my word processor for the display of headings – say a change of font size, a margin indent and a switch to bold font – I will not be helping the typesetter's task very much. Moreover, should I wish to prepare a list of the subheadings in my text to serve as an index, I will very probably find it quite difficult to distinguish occasions where bold font indicates headings from cases where it indicates (say) emphasized phrases in the text. By the same token, I will find it difficult to check that each subsection has one and only one subheading, that any numbers included in the subheadings are in the right sequence and so forth. And when, in the fullness of time, this text enters the great database of late twentieth century prose, future linguists and historians will have comparable difficulties in assessing the linguistic properties of text used as sub-headings as distinct from those of the main text. If, however, I simply tag each sub-heading as such, using some unique string of codes to say "here begins the text of a sub-heading" and some other to mark its end, then the same input text can be used unchanged by any formatter, any indexing program and any linguistic analysis program. Each one will be able to decide for itself what it wants to do with the subheadings – how it would like to process them, if at all.

While indexing the subheadings in a document of this nature is clearly of somewhat limited importance, it should be apparent that the solution proposed for that problem is an entirely generalizable one. Consider historical source materials for example. Which is likely to be of more use in compiling a list of the names in an electronic transcription of the records of an ecclesiastical court – a version in which the names are simply italicized (as are, for example, Latin phrases, running titles, annotations, etc.) or one in which each name is marked off clearly by a tag such as **<name>** ? Which is likely to be of more use in extracting statistical data for input to a spreadsheet analysis of the average age of offenders – a version in which birth dates are clearly marked as such, perhaps incorporating some normalized version of the date concerned, or one in which all dates are simply intermingled with the running text?

2. Markup and Markup Languages

The word "markup" was originally used to describe annotation or other marks within a text intended to instruct a compositor or typist how a particular passage should be printed or laid out. Examples, familiar to proofreaders and others, include wavy underlining to indicate boldface, special symbols for passages to be omitted or printed in a particular font and so forth. As the production of texts was automated, the term was extended to cover all sorts of special "markup codes" inserted into electronic texts to govern formatting, printing, or other processing. Generalizing from that sense, we define markup, or (synonymously) "encoding", as any means of making explicit an interpretation of a text. At a banal level, all printed texts are encoded in this sense: punctuation marks, use of capitalization, disposition of letters around the page, even the spaces between words, might be regarded as a kind of markup, the function of which is to help the human reader determine where one word ends and another begins, or how to identify gross structural features such as headings or simple syntactic units such as dependent clauses or sentences. Encoding a text for computer processing is, in principle, like transcribing a manuscript from "scriptio continua", a process of making explicit what is conjectural or implicit, a process of directing the user as to how the content of the text should be interpreted.

A "markup language" may be no more than a loose set of markup conventions used together for encoding texts. A markup language must specify what markup is allowed and whereabouts, what markup is required, how markup is to be distinguished from text, and what the markup means. As noted above, SGML provides the means for doing the first three of these only; it allows you to describe a markup language independently of what the markup is intended to do. To understand and act upon the markup, additional semantic information is needed, which will differ in different situations. Documentation like that enshrined in the TEI's "Guidelines" provides such information. In just the same way as one may be able to parse the syntactic structure of a Latin unseen without having the least idea what it is about, so an SGML-aware processor can analyze the structure of an SGML-encoded document with no sense of its meaning. This independence is necessary, given the open-ended nature of electronic textual applications. It does not, of course, imply that the intentions of the encoder of a text are unimportant or vacuous; only that they are formally distinct from the encoding itself.

Three basic concepts are fundamental to an understanding of all markup languages, when described in SGML terms. These are the notions of a markup "entity", a markup "element", with its associated "attributes", and a "document type". At the most primitive level, texts are composed simply of streams of symbols (characters or bytes of data, marks on a page, graphics, etc.): these are known as "entities" in SGML. At a higher level of abstraction, a text is composed of representations of objects of various kinds, linguistically or functionally defined. Such objects do not appear randomly within a text: coherence demands that particular types of object appear in specifiable relationship to other objects – they may be included within each other, linked to each other by reference or simply presented sequentially, for example. This level of description sees texts as composed of structurally defined objects, known as "elements" in SGML. The grammar defining how elements may be legally combined in a particular class of texts is known as a "document type". (This view of the nature of text has been nicely defined by DeRose [1990] as an "ordered hierarchy of content objects".) These three fundamental concepts together are, it is claimed, adequate to describe all the complexities of marked-up texts, of whatever kind and for whatever purposes. Each is discussed in turn in the next three sections.

3. Entities

The word "entity" is used in SGML rather differently from its use elsewhere, notably in database design methodology. An SGML entity is simply a named bit of text, considered entirely independently of any structural or categorical classification it might have. A document may be an SGML entity, as may any arbitrary sequence of characters within it, or any symbol it contains. The definition of an entity associates a name with a particular string of bytes, which may be the representation of some characters in a particular computer encoding or held in a system-defined container of some kind (such as a file). Within an SGML document, entities are represented by reference, using the defined name. This mechanism has a number of important uses, specified further below, primarily in making it possible to encode textual features such as special characters or symbols which are unique to a particular environment or application in a way that is independent of that particular environment.

Everyone who has communicated by electronic mail, or even tried to move a file from a Macintosh computer to a PC, knows that some of the symbols of which texts are composed are less portable than others. With the best will in the world, computer manufacturers and standards bodies alike will never be able to represent all the possible symbols occurring in written texts in a single universally agreed code set, simply because these symbols do not form a closed set: the task is as hopeless as that of enumerating all the words in a language. Moreover, it is a fact of life that different computing environments adopt different methods of representing the same symbols, disregard entirely the existence of some and insist on distinguishing others.

A notorious consequence of this state of affairs is that some letters which appear perfectly normal when typed at a keyboard in Odense, Paris, Stockholm, or Berlin will either be mysteriously transmuted into a percent sign, or lost completely when transmitted over the network to the UK. How, then, are words to be stored in a computer file in such a way as to ensure that they can be satisfactorily processed by any computer, not just those which have the decency to be aware of the Danish, French, Swedish or German national character sets?

Exactly the same problem arises, in a more acute form, when considering the range of symbols likely to required in transcribing manuscript texts or spoken language. There is no computer character set in which the long form of "s" is distinguished from the short, still less for distinguishing ligatured forms of the same letters, or for representing all scribal abbreviations, astrological symbols, non-vocalic grunts, pauses etc. Nor, UNICODE notwithstanding, do I think it likely that there ever will be.

The SGML solution is to encode characters not available in the particular character set used for document transmission[4] by means of entity reference. If Hans J/ø/rgen is represented as Hans Jørgen, I can associate the unlovely acronym "ø" with whatever particular stream of bytes is necessary on my computer to produce the slashed-o in the Danish national set.[5]

Some have objected to the apparent verbosity of such mnemonics, by comparison with the variety of encoding tricks or ad hoc solutions customarily resorted to. The advantage of the entity reference solution is simply that it forms part of a single and consistent convention, comprehensible without resort to special purpose documentation (which is generally absent). Sets of standard mnemonics for all the accented letters and special symbols of modern European languages are to be found in ISO 8879 and elsewhere.

The same mechanism can be applied more widely for any stream of bytes to be included within a document. The use of a single short abbreviation for a much repeated or particularly complex phrase is a simple way of ensuring consistency and reducing effort; it is worth noting in this context that the value of an entity reference can include other mark-up, such as tags or other entity references, provided that any element opened within a given entity is also closed within it. This method has been adopted, for example, by the TEI committee responsible for defining linguistic annotation. Another use is for identifying objects which cannot be directly represented in a text, for example non-textual entities like graphics or formulae. More mundane uses are not difficult to identify.

It should be stressed that entities have no structural properties: they are simply shortcuts enabling an SGML-aware processor to substitute a system-defined string of bytes for a name identified as such by special SGML delimiters. As such they are merely a special (if well thought out) way of doing the kinds of things which transcribers and encoders of text have already been doing for many years.

4. Elements and Their Content

The level of description at which texts are composed solely of entities in the SGML sense defined above is not, however, a very satisfactory one. All markup schemes to a greater or lesser extent attempt to identify and to distinguish components of texts at a more ambitious level of description. Texts are not simply sequences of words, still less of bytes; they contain instances of objects, such as paragraphs, titles, names, dates etc. represented by such sequences. All markup schemes, to a greater or lesser extent, attempt to describe these components. A consideration of such schemes indicates at least three important aspects of textual objects which need to be recognized: their "extent" – that is, the points in the textual stream at which object instances begin and end; their "type" – that is, the category to which object instances are assigned; and their "context" – that is, their relationship to other object instances within the document. SGML addresses each of these concerns: everything in an SGML document is delimited explicitly in some way; a document is decomposed into elements of a named type; and a kind of textual grammar can be defined.

4.1 *A note on syntax*

Most discussions of SGML mention if only in passing that the particular characters and conventions used to represent SGML markup in a particular document can be redefined. This is of course a necessary consequence of the fact that SGML is not itself a markup language, but a method of describing such languages. However, in order to stay sane, this document will follow customary practice in using the "reference concrete syntax" to represent SGML markup. This rebarbative phrase is actually quite a precise description of what it denotes: it is a "concrete" syntax, because it represents by particular characters (the characters ">", "<", "!" and other delimiters) distinctions required by the SGML model of how markup should be described (its "abstract" syntax); it is provided for "reference" purposes, as an example of one generally useful way of representing the constructs of the language.

The SGML reference concrete syntax has two great advantages over most other ways of making concrete a view of the abstract structure of a markup language: everything is delimited (bracketed) explicitly, and very few special characters are needed. As we have already seen, entity references are delimited explicitly by the ampersand character and the semicolon.[6] In the same way, element occurrences within an SGML document are explicitly delimited in the reference concrete syntax by named "tags". There are two kinds of tag: "start-tags", which indicate the beginning of an element, and "end-tags", which indicate its end. The tags themselves are delimited by special characters: "<" to mark the beginning of a start-tag, and "</" to mark the beginning of an end-tag. In either case, the character ">" is used to indicate the end of a tag. Between these delimiters is given a name identifying the type of element delimited by the start and end tag pair. For example, an embedded name element in a text might be tagged as follows:

Call me <name>Ishmael</name>.

This is by no means the only way of indicating the presence of an SGML element within a text; it is, however, the most explicit, and hence that into which other representations are most generally mapped.

4.2 *Content models*

As suggested earlier, the primary function of the start and end tags within a marked-up text is to indicate the extent of a particular object or textual component (the SGML term is "element") within it. In addition, the tags identify the category or type of the element which they delimit, by supplying a name for it ("name" in the example above). An SGML-aware processor can thus easily identify the start and end of all elements of a given type within a document – it can identify all names, all sentences, all paragraphs (etc) and process them in a way appropriate for such objects.

The content of a document element of a particular type (that is, the portion between the start and end tags) may consist simply of running text, perhaps including entity references. More usually, it will contain other embedded document elements; occasionally it may have no content at all. The ability of SGML to specify rules about how elements can nest within other elements is one of its chief strengths and is discussed further below. Here we simply note that elements of one type typically contain elements of another: for example, a parish register consists of a mixture of birth, marriage and death records, each of which contains elements such as names, dates and details of an event. We might thus expect to find such records encoded in SGML with different tags for **<birth>**, **<marriage>** and **<death>** elements, within each of which might be found **<name>** and **<date>** elements. In exactly the same way, a document such as this one might be encoded as a series of **<paper>** elements, each of which begins with a **<title>**, followed optionally by an **<abstract>**, and at least one (and probably several) **<section>**s, each composed of **<paragraph>**s.

An empty element (one which has no content) may seem like a contradiction: what use can it be simply to tag a specific point in a text, especially if there is no way of associating information with it? At the very least, it should be possible to supply a name or other identifier to distinguish one such empty point in a text from another. Fortunately, SGML does provide a mechanism for adding such "extra-textual" information to the elements of a text: that of "attributes", discussed in the next section.

4.3 *Attributes and cross-references*

Like "entity", the word "attribute" has a specific technical sense when used in the SGML context, which differs somewhat from its sense when used in the database design context. An SGML attribute is a category of information associated with a particular type of element, but not contained within it. Attributes are associated with particular element occurrences by including their name and value within the start-tag for the element concerned. For example:

```
Call me <name type=Biblical>Ishmael</name>.
```

Here *type* is the name of an attribute associated with any occurrence of the **<name>** element; *Biblical* is the value defined for this attribute in the case of the example **<name>** shown above.[7]

Attributes are used for two related purposes: they enable an identifying number or name to be associated with a particular element occurrence within a text (which might otherwise be missing), and they enable additional information missing from a text to be added to it without violating its integrity.

As an example of the first usage, consider the page or folio numbering of a historical source. There is a sense in which the individual pages of a source might be regarded as distinct elements within it. This is not however generally the primary focus of interest for those using it: in most cases, the number of the page is of importance only as a means of documenting where the other elements of the text occur. Moreover, the page numbers may not appear at all in the original source. In such cases, a tag **<pb>** (for "page break") may conveniently be used to mark the point in the text at which a new page begins. An attribute (say, *n* for "number") would then provide a convenient means of indicating the number of the page just begun: thus

```
text of page 3 ends here
<pb n=4>
text of page 4 starts here
```

As an example of the second usage, consider the common need for normalization in prosopographical studies. One way of achieving this might be to associate an attribute such as *key* with each occurrence of **<name>** elements in a text, the value of which would be a regularized and encoded form of the name, which could also serve as an identifying key in a database derived from the text. For example:

```
<name key='SMITJ04'>Jack Smyth</name>
```

Attribute values may be defaulted, taken from a controlled list or specified freely, the only constraint being that they cannot contain markup.

The most common use for attributes in the TEI and other SGML schemes is not, however, to categorize element occurrences in this way, but to identify them. In the TEI scheme, for example, every element is defined to have an *id* attribute, which supplies a unique identifier for that particular textual element within the text. This makes possible the encoding of links between individual elements of a text in a simple and economical way. This facility is very commonly used in document preparation systems (such as TeX or Scribe) in order to link cross-references (such as "see section 3 above") within a text with the sections of a text to which they refer, when the section number is not known or may be dynamic. In SGML, such a system is completely generalizable. For example, let us suppose that we wish to encode a register of names in which the following passage occurs:

John Smith, baker.
Mary Smith, seamstress, wife of the above.

In this example we have two **<entry>**s, each containing a **<name>** and a **<trade>**. The second entry however contains an additional clause which states a relationship between it and another element. We begin by tagging the elements so far identified:[8]

```
<register>
   <entry>
      <name>John Smith</name>
      <trade>baker</trade>
   </entry>
   <entry>
      <name>Mary Smith</name>
      <trade>seamstress</trade>
      <relation>wife of the above</relation>
   </entry>
   ...
</register>
```

Clearly "wife of the above" is meaningless as a relation unless we have some way of pointing to the entry with which it is linked. Let us assume that the referent of "the above" is the whole of John Smith's entry rather than just the name within it; the assumption does not affect the argument. What is needed is some way of identifying that entry uniquely; that identifying number can then be supplied as the target of the relationship. In other words, we need an identifying attribute (call it *id*) that can be attached to any **<entry>** and a pointer attribute (call it *target*) which can be attached to any **<relation>**. Using these, and inventing an arbitrary value for the identifier, we can encode the link implicit in the above text as follows:

```
<register>
   <entry id=E1234>
      <name>John Smith</name>
      <trade>baker</trade>
   </entry>
   <entry>
      <name>Mary Smith</name>
      <trade>seamstress</trade>
      <relation target=E1234>wife of the above</relation>
   </entry>
```

Here we have allocated the arbitrary name or identifier "E1234" to the Baker's entry. By supplying that same identifier as the value for the target attribute associated with the **<relation>** element of the Seamstress' entry, we assert both the existence of the relationship itself, and also its target. This simple solution to a well-known problem has several attractive features, but perhaps the most attractive is that it makes explicit the fact that the target of the relationship is an interpretation brought to bear on the text by the encoder of it, leaving the text itself unchanged. Other attributes (say, *certainty* or *authority*) may also be imagined which might carry additional interpretative information associated with the link.

5. Ensuring Consistency

While a rose might smell just as sweet by any other name, every computer user knows that names intended for automatic processing must be spelled exactly and defined precisely. The human reader might tolerate paragraphs sometimes labelled **<p>**, sometimes labelled **<para>**, and sometimes not labelled at all, but the computer is less forgiving. Slightly less obviously, perhaps, the user of an SGML aware software system needs to know what elements have been defined for a given text (or group of texts) and what their possible contents are. He or she needs to know not just whether personal names should be tagged **<persName>** or **<name>**, but also in what contexts personal names may reasonably be expected to appear (for example, if something tagged as a name appears "within" a name, it is probably an error). He or she also needs to know what attribute names have been defined for particular elements and their legal values, and also what entity names should be used for particular symbols. The formal specification of these names and their usage is enshrined in a separate component, unique to SGML, known as a "Document Type Definition" or DTD.

5.1 *Defining a document: The content model*

A DTD performs a function analogous to that of a grammar: it formally defines what are the legal productions of a given markup language. Of course, DTDs can be as lax or as restrictive as any other kind of grammar: the designer of a DTD generally has to trade off generality of use with accuracy of error detection. The simplest kind of DTD would be one which did no more than specify a set of tag names, requiring only that every element tagged in a document use one of them. Such a DTD would of course be unable to detect errors such as **<name>**s occurring within **<name>**s or within **<date>**s, nor to prohibit such errors as register entries appearing other than inside registers. Creating correctly encoded texts with such a DTD would be rather like trying to speak a foreign language with the aid of a lexicon of the language, but no idea of its syntax.

More usually, however, the transcribers and creators of electronic texts wish to control how elements can meaningfully appear within a given class of texts, so that processors intended to act on them can do so more intelligently. The specification of what is legal within any one kind of textual component or element is known in SGML as its "content model", because it provides a model for its content. Here, for example, is a hypothetical DTD fragment for the register example given above.

```
<!ELEMENT register - - (entry+)>
<!ELEMENT entry - - o (name, trade, relation?)>
<!ELEMENT name - - o (#PCDATA)>
```

These three lines are examples of SGML "declarations": each defines or declares a name for an element and what its content should be. The details of the syntax need not detain us; note only that each declaration (like everything else in SGML) is explicitly delimited, in this case by a symbol marking the start of a declaration (the "<") and its end (the ">"). The content model part of each declaration is given in parentheses at the end. Between the name of the element (*register* in the first case) and the content model are two characters which specify whether or not both start- and end-tags are required to mark off occurrences of the element. The hyphen character indicates that a tag is required, the letter O that it is optional. Thus, in this example, **<register>**s must have both a start and an end tag, whereas **<entry>**s and **<name>**s can be specified using start-tags only.

The content model for register states that a **<register>** consists of one or more **<entry>**s, the plus sign indicates that the element before it can be repeated one or more times. Thus a register containing no entries, or one containing something other than an entry would be regarded as an error by this DTD. The content model for an entry states that an **<entry>** must begin with a **<name>**, followed by a **<trade>** and then optionally by a **<relation>**. The commas between the components of this content model indicate that the elements must all appear in the order given. The question mark following the **<trade>** indicates that this element need not be present. Thus, an entry with no name, or one where the trade preceded the name, would both be regarded as erroneous by this DTD, whereas entries are equally acceptable, either with or without **<relation>**s. Finally, the content model for a **<name>** states that it may contain only text, that is, simply data with no embedded tags. (The word "#PCDATA" is a special SGML symbol standing for "parsed character data" – which must be "parsed" because it may contain entity references as well as raw characters.)

SGML syntax allows for other variations, which will be necessary if we are to refine this model to reflect more accurately the probable content of register entries in the real world. We will begin by relaxing the restriction on the number of **<trade>**s an entry may contain:

```
<!ELEMENT entry - - o (name, trade*, relation?)>
```

The asterisk following the word "trade" indicates that an entry may contain zero or more **<trade>**s. An entry such as the following

```
<entry>
    <name>John Smith</name>
    <trade>butcher</trade>
    <trade>baker</trade>
    <trade>candle-stick maker</trade>
</entry>
```

would be legal according to this second definition, as would one like this:

```
<entry>
    <name>John Smith</name>
</entry>
```

Suppose, however, that entries are mixed, sometimes containing names and trades, sometimes only one or the other. One possible content model for this situation would be:

```
<!ELEMENT entry - - o (name|trade|relation)+>
```

The vertical bar symbol may be read as "or". This content model states that an **<entry>** must contain at least one component, which may be a **<name>**, a **<trade>** or a **<relation>**, and may contain more than one of any of them, in any order. (The inner set of parentheses is needed to indicate that the plus sign is to be applied to the whole group of alternated names.) The following entries would all be legal according to this definition:

```
<entry>
   <name>John Smith</name>
   <trade>Baker</trade>
   <trade>Chandler</trade>
</entry>
<entry>
   <relation>wife of the above</relation>
   <name>Mary Jones</name>
</entry>
<entry>
   <name>John Smith</name>
   <name>Henry Jones</name>
   <trade>smith</trade>
</entry>
```

As the last example indicates, such laxity of definition may lead to difficulties of interpretation – our syntax now cannot help us determine whether it is Smith or Jones who is the smith. But presumably in that respect we are being true to the source!

A more realistic situation would be that names, trades and relationships are found promiscuously intertwined in any order within any amount of other text. SGML offers two ways of dealing with this. One is simply to add #PCDATA as a fourth alternate to the example above, to give a declaration like this:

```
<!ELEMENT entry - - (name|trade|relation|#PCDATA)>
```

This solution is that generally preferred in the TEI Guidelines, for the general case, where elements consist of small identifiable elements (names, trades etc.) swimming about in an arbitrary mixture or "primal soup". Note that with this content model it is no longer possible to leave out end-tags.

Another approach achieving a similar effect is to use what is known as an "inclusion exception", as in this example:

```
<!ELEMENT entry - - (#PCDATA) +(name|trade|relation)>
```

Either of the above definitions states that items tagged as names, trades or relations may appear anywhere within an entry, an arbitrary number of times, interspersed with arbitrary sequences of character data. The following example would be regarded as legal according to both the above definitions:

```
<entry>
   Also<name>John Smith</name>
</entry>
<entry>
   <name>John Smith</name> and<name>Adam
      Smith</name>
   <relation>his brother</relation>
</entry>
<entry>
   <relation>Second cousin</relation>of
      the<trade>blacksmith </trade>
</entry>
<entry>
   Old<relation>Uncle</relation>
   <name>Tom Cobbley</name> and all
</entry>
```

The difference between the two element declarations is that the second allows names, trades, or relations to appear arbitrarily not only within entries, but also within anything that entries contain. Unless further modified, this definition allows (for example) names to occur within trades (or vice versa), or even within other names. Entries such as the following would be legal by the second definition, but not the first:

```
<entry>
   <name>John
      <trade>Smith</trade> Jones
   </name>
   <relation>Brother of
      <name>Henry
         <trade>Potter</trade>Jones
      </name>
   </relation>
</entry>
```

Of course, entries such as the following would also be acceptable by either definition:

```
<entry>Any old string of characters you care to type in
```

To complete the content models for our simple register example, we need to define the sub-components of an entry. For the sake of argument, we will assume that

<name>, **<trade>** and **<relation>** are to contain only text, with no further embedded elements. Since they all share the same content model a single declaration will suffice:

```
<!ELEMENT (name|trade|relation) - - (#PCDATA)>
```

5.2 *Defining a document: Attribute lists*

We now turn to the definition of attributes for each of the elements discussed so far. As with elements, SGML requires that all attributes likely to be used within a document must be defined in advance. It also offers a variety of features to control the values that specific attributes may take.

An example attribute declaration might look like the following:

```
<!ATTLIST name  id    ID        #IMPLIED
                key   CDATA     #IMPLIED
                type  (personal|honorific)  personal>
```

This declaration associates three different attributes with the element **<name>**. The first attribute is called *id*, the second *key* and the third *type*. Note that all the attributes for a given element are defined together in a single ATTLIST declaration. For each attribute named, two additional pieces of information are required for its declaration. The first, following the name of the attribute, defines what type of value may be supplied for it, while the third, following the type specification, indicates what value should be assumed if the attribute is not specified for any element occurrence.

In this example, three different kinds of value are specified. The *id* attribute may take as its value only a string[9] which the SGML processor will treat as an identifier for the associated element: this is indicated by the keyword "ID". An ID-value need not be supplied, and if it is not, then a processor may take whatever default action it chooses; this is indicated by the keyword "#IMPLIED".

The *key* attribute may take as its value any string of characters; this is indicated by the keyword CDATA. The SGML processor will not check the value of this attribute in any way, except, of course, that it may not contain any form of markup.[10] Again, there is no requirement to supply a value for this attribute.

More exact checking is provided for in the case of the *type* attribute: here we have specified that only two values are legal for this attribute – the type of a name must be marked as either *personal* or *honorific*. If no value is specified, the processor is to assume that the intended value is *personal*.

To illustrate some of the other possibilities for attribute specifications, we conclude with a declaration for the attribute list to be attached to the **<relation>** element:

```
<!ATTLIST relation  target     IDREF    #REQUIRED
                    certainty  NUMBER   0          >
```

This states that the relation element may have two attributes, called *target* and *certainty*. The former takes as its value an "IDREF", that is a string which has been used as the value for an ID-type attribute somewhere within the current document. The SGML parser will check that the value actually identifies some other element, as is the case in our example. The keyword "#REQUIRED" means additionally that no **<relation>** can exist in the document unless the element to which it points is specified in this way; this keyword is used to specify that a value *must* be supplied for every occurrence of the attribute to which it is attached (the examples of relations given above are thus all illegal by this definition!). Finally, the *certainty* attribute is defined as taking a numeric value, which defaults to zero.

6. Why Should I Use a DTD?

It should be emphasized that the preceding brief discussion is by no means comprehensive and is intended only to give a flavour of the kinds of tools at the disposal of the SGML document designer. The interested reader is referred to one of the introductory texts cited in the bibliography for more comprehensive information. It should also be noted that designing a DTD is not something which every user of an SGML system needs to do afresh. On the contrary, it is the objective of endeavours such as the Text Encoding Initiative to define general-purpose DTDs which can be used for a wide variety of purposes.

Why, however, should anyone transcribing a historical source for analysis care about the existence of such endeavours? How can a knowledge of SGML help in understanding a text, in placing it into its proper context? It should be relatively uncontentious that the mechanical drudgery of transcribing, editing and reproducing texts is enormously simplified by the uncoupling of the tasks of data *interpretation* (tagging) and data *reproduction* (formatting). The former is an essentially hermeneutical and scholarly act, while the latter is not. Coombs, Renear *et al.* have persuasively argued that the proliferation of sophisticated tools for desktop publishing have effectively seduced scholars from their true vocation (Coombs, 1987) and that SGML offers a chance to regain the high ground.

Suppose that you have obtained, or created, a DTD which adequately describes the kind of source texts you wish to process. How will it be of use to you? You will use it firstly as a means of checking that each individual document you process conforms to the model you have defined. As well as providing you with a diagnostic check on the accuracy of your keyboarding, this will also provide what the Americans call a "reality check" on your interpretation of the sources concerned: you may be forced to confront aspects of your sources to which an initial, possibly over-hasty, assessment has blinded you. Moreover, because each part of an electronic text (or at least, each part that has been tagged) is equally accessible, equally processable, you can analyze the contents of your sources with a far higher degree of accuracy and sophistication than either a simple transcription or a database of derived observations would provide.

Historical sources do not belong to one individual, however. More, perhaps, than other kinds of resource, they must be shareable, whether from economic or ethical considerations. An electronic text encoded in SGML, with its associated document type definition and appropriate documentation, is a permanent asset, independent of time, place and personality.

Notes

[1] International Organization for Standardization, "ISO 8879: Information Processing – Text and Office Systems – Standard Generalized Markup Language (SGML)", ([Geneva]: ISO, 1986).

[2] Examples include Bryan (1988), van Herwijnen (1990) and Goldfarb (1991).

[3] Originally published as part of Greenstein, D.I. (ed), *Modelling Historical Data* (Goettingen: Max-Planck-Institut für Geschichte, 1991).

[4] I do not discuss here the possibility of using variant character sets within an SGML document; though possible this does not of course solve the general case.

[5] The use of the ampersand and semicolon to delimit the acronym is an example of the SGML "reference concrete syntax", discussed briefly below. It is not a necessary part of the SGML solution; merely a conventional one.

[6] The semicolon is not in fact strictly necessary in all situations: the end of an entity reference is signalled by the first character encountered which cannot form part of a name. A space is therefore sufficient; since however entity references are often found within words, rather than between them, the semicolon is often necessary to indicate where the entity name ends and the word within which it is embedded resumes.

[7] Categorization of this kind could of course equally well be achieved by using a different tag – say **<biblicalName>**. The decision as to whether to use an attribute or a distinct element type is often a difficult one, involving more detailed technical and design skill than it is appropriate to consider here.

[8] For clarity of discussion, more specific element names have been used here than those proposed in the TEI scheme.

[9] More exactly, a "name token", that is a sequence of alphanumeric characters of which the first is a letter.

[10] It must also be enclosed in quotation marks if it is not a name token.

References

This bibliography lists some useful further reading for general information about SGML and markup languages. A full and very detailed SGML bibliography edited by Robin Cover and David T. Barnard is also available as TEI document MLW14.

Bryan, Martin. *SGML: An Author's Guide to the Standard Generalized Markup Language*. Addison-Wesley, 1988. [Detailed text book giving full treatment of the standard, but primarily from the publishing perspective.]

Coombs, James H., *et al.* "Markup Systems and the Future of Scholarly Text Processing". *Communications of the ACM*, 30, 11 (1987), 933–47. [Classic polemic in favour of descriptive over procedural markup presented from the scholarly perspective.]

DeRose, Steven J., *et al.* "What is Text, Really?" *Journal of Computing in Higher Education*, 1, 2 (1990).

Goldfarb, Charles. *The SGML Handbook*. Oxford University Press, 1991. [Authoritative and exhaustive presentation of all aspects of ISO 8879, including annotated and cross referenced full text of the standard itself.]

International Organization for Standardization. "ISO 8879: Information Processing – Text and Office Systems – Standard Generalized Markup Language (SGML) (ISO,1986)". [Annexes A and B to the Standard provide a formal but readable summary of its most important features.]

International Organization for Standardization. "ISO/TR 9573: Information Processing – SGML Support Facilities – Techniques for Using SGML" (ISO,1988). [Tutorial discussion of main features of the standard with some interesting examples.]

van Herwijnen, Eric. *Practical SGML*. 2nd edition. Dordrecht: Kluwer, 1994). [Second, much improved, edition of an excellent introductory textbook with emphasis on how SGML is currently being used.]

Computers and the Humanities **29:** 51–73, 1995.

Character Representation[1,*]

Harry E. Gaylord
Vakgroep Alfa Informatica, Rijksuniversiteit Groningen, POB 716, Groningen 9700 AS, The Netherlands
e-mail: galiard@let.rug.nl

Key words: character sets, special characters, national character sets, standards, international standards organization, ISO, TEI

Abstract

This paper describes ISO standard character sets currently in use, the use of SGML entity sets, and the TEI writing system declaration.

1. Introduction

Computer character sets are not adequate for encoding texts in any language, even in modern English. In all likelihood this will remain the case for some time to come, though a major improvement in the situation is approaching with the implementation of the new ISO 10646 universal coded character set. Because of the present limitations, the standards committee which drew up SGML included one type of general entity for this purpose and included entity sets for a number of fields – for European languages, mathematics, and publishing – in an appendix of the SGML standard. This work is being expanded by the ISO committee and TEI.[2]

This article addresses the following topics: 7-bit coded character sets, 8-bit coded character sets, the Universal coded Character Set (UCS), SGML and TEI entity sets, the SGML declaration, the TEI writing system declaration, coded characters and glyphs, standards work, and a conclusion.[3]

The focus in this article will be upon international and national standards on this subject. Therefore, we are discussing primarily the work of the International Organization for Standardization (ISO) whose headquarters is in Geneva and national standardization bodies, e.g. NNI (The Netherlands), AFNOR (France), ANSI (U.S.A.), BSI (U.K.), DIN (Germany), JIS (Japan) etc.

2. Coded Character Sets

Coded character sets[4] is the name standards bodies give for character sets. Within ISO the production of these sets takes place in ISO/IEC JTC1/SC2 (Joint Technical Committee 1/ Subcommittee 2) and ISO TC 46 (Technical Committee 46). The former is largely made up of people from computer and software companies and focuses upon sets with the widest groups of users. The latter committee is largely made up of librarians and archivists and focuses upon their shared problems. Of course, the latter body's resources are much more restricted than the former as is the use of their standards. The only TC 46 standard discussed here in detail is ISO 5426. There are a number of other standards and draft standards which they have produced. They have had a substantial contribution toward the character inventory included in ISO 10646.

---

* Harry Gaylord is a senior lecturer in the Department of Humanities Computing at Groningen University, Groningen, The Netherlands. He is Chair of the SC 18 committee of the Dutch Standards Institute (NNI), and member of ISO SC 2 (Coded Character Sets) and ISO SC 18/WG8 (Document Processing and Related Communication). He is the author of *TEI TR1 W4 Character Entities and Public Entity Sets* and co-author with John Esling of "Computer Codes for Phonetic Symbols", *Journal of the International Phonetic Association* (1993), 23, 2, 85–97.

2.1 *Control and graphic characters*

The first work on standardization of computer character sets was done jointly by ANSI and ISO. Before that work each computer spoke its own language, so to speak. The resulting standards were ANSI 3.4 (better known as ASCII) and ISO 646. The first agreement in these standards was that control and graphic characters should each have their separate sections in the coded character set.

2.1.1 *Control characters*

Control characters are coded characters which perform a processing, rather than a graphic, function. At the time that ISO 646 was being defined, the control functions envisaged were used during the processing of data on punch cards or paper tape and in communication between telex machines on a communication line. Their names reflect this situation. They include SOH (start of header), STX (start of text), ACK (acknowledge), BEL (bell), NAK (negative acknowledge), and EOT (end of transmission). Some of them are drawn from typing machines of the time, e.g. telex machines. These include BS (backspace), HT (horizonal tab), LF (line feed), VT (vertical tab), FF (form feed), and CR (carriage return). Two others are based upon the model of a typewriter: SO (shift out) and SI (shift in), designed to shift the character set as the caps lock does on a keyboard.[5]

Standards bodies are very reluctant to remove these characters or change their names for fear of incompatibilities. For one thing, obsolescent machinery that needs them may still be used. More important for us, no present-day machine or process needs all of these control functions, so people have used for other purposes those code positions that became free. The control-character columns (now columns 0–1, 8–9) are still reserved for control characters alone.[6]

We must include some discussion of Record Boundaries here. Two characters in ISO 2022 are LF (line feed decimal 10) and CR (carriage return decimal 13). Different operating systems use 13 10 or 13 or 10 to mark record boundaries. We would not be surprised to find yet another OS which uses 10 13 just to complete the set.[7] SGML has a way of inserting RS (record start) as line beginning and RE (record end) as line end to avoid this problem. This is an improvement, but there are still problems in so-called mixed content models.[8] A useful technical report on the subject has been issued by Exoterica (1992a) and proposals are in discussion within JTC1/SC18/WG8 about revisions in the standard on this issue. Goldfarb's first law of text processing still holds. "If a text processor has bugs, at least one of them will have to do with the handling of input line endings".[9]

2.1.2 *Graphic characters*

Graphic characters are defined negatively in the first instance, i.e. they are not control characters. Secondly, they have a visible representation. These characters have names in standards, though the standards explicitly do not define the exact meaning of graphic characters or their particular style or font design.

In ISO 646 most of the graphic characters designate unique characters; 2 others have two alternatives, and 10 others are subject to national standard definition (see Figure 1). The two with alternatives are number sign('hash')/pound sign (02/03) and dollar sign/ currency sign (02/04).

2.1.3 *Control or graphic characters*

Two characters in the standards discussed have an interesting history. In the older versions of standards, they are shaded blocks.[10] Position 02/00 is reserved for SP (space) and position 07/15 for DEL (delete).[11] However, in more recent versions[12] these are explicitly placed in these positions which logically would mean they are now viewed as graphic characters.

2.2 *7-Bit standards*

A computer can make use of one or more coded character sets. International standards for coded character sets often describe not a single coded character set, but rather the set of rules according to which a national standards body can establish a new standard which conforms to the international standard's requirements. This is the case with the most widely used standard (ISO 646). First issued in 1967, this was a standard which designated a 7-bit coded character set with a total of 128 coded characters or code points. This standard was developed by the International Organization for Standardization (ISO) in Geneva, together with a number of the national standards bodies. It was developed over a period of several years and changes were made at three points in its developments, as agreement about various aspects was achieved.[13]

The first agreement was to distinguish two types of characters, i.e. control characters and graphic characters, and special sections of the code page were reserved for the two types of characters. If we divide, as is conventionally done, the 128 characters into 8 columns of 16 coded characters each, the first two columns were reserved for control characters and the rest could contain graphic characters. This decision was made in 1963. It was not until 1967 that the ISO framework was published, and a year later the U.S. standards body issued its national standard within this framework. This national standard containing 128 coded characters is what is referred to as ASCII. It differs from all other national standards within this ISO standard, and only in 1991 was there an ISO character set which had all the same graphic characters of the U.S. national standard. This is referred to as ISO 646-IRV:1991 (International Reference Version).[14]

2.2.1 *National standards conforming to iso 646*

The U.S. and U.K. quickly registered their national standard character sets within ISO 646, as did a number of other countries. In the non-unique character positions, Germany, Denmark, and Norway and other countries placed letters with diacritics and extra characters of their national alphabets. As a result, text encoded according to one national character set conforming to the ISO 646 principles will produce anomalies if processed using another national standard also conforming to ISO 646. Thus, there is the likelihood of conflicting characters in different national 7-bit standards in the following positions:[15]

<table>
<tr><th></th><th>US</th><th>DE</th><th>NO</th></tr>
<tr><td>05/11</td><td>[</td><td>Ä</td><td>Æ</td></tr>
<tr><td>05/12</td><td>\</td><td>Ö</td><td>Ø</td></tr>
<tr><td>05/13</td><td>]</td><td>ü</td><td>Å</td></tr>
<tr><td>07/11</td><td>{</td><td>ä</td><td>æ</td></tr>
<tr><td>07/12</td><td>|</td><td>ö</td><td>ø</td></tr>
<tr><td>07/13</td><td>}</td><td>ü</td><td>å</td></tr>
<tr><td>07/14</td><td>~</td><td>ß</td><td>|</td></tr>
</table>

Even the British national standard conforming to ISO differs in one character position. The British standard has the pound sign (£) at the coded character position containing the hash mark (#) in ISO 646 IRV.

Since some Western European languages, such as French, contain more than 10 extra combinations, another technique was accepted for encoding accented letters within ISO 646. A composite graphic character could be formed by using a control character so that a BS <grave> or <grave> BS a could be coded to produce *à*. BS is the control character BACKSPACE.[16]

2.2.2 *ISO 646 IRV*

Not until 1991 was this version of 646 made identical with ASCII. The last change from the 1983 version was to place $ in position 02/04. Until then this position was filled by the currency sign. The references in ISO 8879 to ISO 646:1983 are at least ambiguous in this respect as are the SGML declarations governing nearly all SGML software which uses ASCII.[17]

2.3 *8-Bit international character standards*

2.3.1 *ISO 5426*

A wider range of diacritics was needed for transliterations in bibliographical circles and a suitable standard was set up for this purpose.[18] This standard makes use of non-spacing characters preceding spacing characters.[19] This is in use in international bibliographical circles, and a similar national standard is in wide use in the U.S.A. Their exact inventories are not precisely the same, nor are the code positions.

This standard has not been more widely accepted because no limits are placed upon how many characters can be composed.[20] Since any non-spacing character can be combined with any spacing character, a very large repertoire could be encoded. Since the positioning of non-spacing characters depends upon the width, height, and shape of its spacing letter, using an unbounded range of possibilities makes it difficult to represent the composite characters graphically. For this reason, work was begun on a new series of international 8-bit coded character sets in the early 1980s, with the 8859 series below as the result.

2.3.2 *ISO 6937*

Because of the inadequacy of ISO 646 for encoding Latin-based European texts, a new standard was developed for data transmission purposes. It has been used in two modes, one of which is discussed here. This mode uses an 8-bit character set, in which Columns 0–1 and 8–9 are reserved for control characters. Columns 2–7 contain the coded characters of ISO 646, and extra coded characters are placed in columns 10–15. Accented letters could be encoded by combinations of non-spacing and spacing characters (i.e. <grave>a is the encoding for à as in 5426). The non-spacing character must precede the character which it changes. This standard has been used in data transmission for over a decade and is very servicable. With it one can encode all Latin-script European languages.[21] The concept of a character repertoire was introduced, differing from simply the number of characters themselves. Now the repertoire included a specific number of characters or combinations of characters and not every non-spacing character can be used with every character. 333 characters are explicitly defined and encoded as spacing graphic characters (some of which were non-spacing character + spacing character). This number of characters is in contrast with the limits of the 192 maximum of graphic characters within an 8-bit standard character set.

2.3.3 *ISO 8859 series*

Like ISO 646, ISO 8859 is not a single coded character set. It includes a series of character sets, each of which is adequate for representing more than one language. Ten have been issued so far, two of which have recently been withdrawn.

Three principles govern their organization:

- Characters from older standards (international, national, and vendor specific) are included as far as possible.[22]
- Characters which are included in more than one set should be encoded in the same code position as much as possible.
- Only pre-composed characters are permitted.

The first principle means that there can be a mapping between older character sets, including some of the EBCDIC IBM mainframe standards, to this new series. This was not the case with earlier international standards.

Furthermore, since non-spacing characters are explicitly forbidden, the graphic quality of accented letters would be improved. More importantly, the rendering of texts in non-English European languages would be as simple as that for English text. Of course, sorting (alphabetizing) in these languages is more complicated. The following list indicates the part number of ISO 8859, the equivalent ECMA document, and the languages it claims to support.[23]

ISO	ECMA	Languages
8859–1	94	Latin 1. modern Danish, English, Faroese, Finnish, French, German, Icelandic, Irish, Italian, Norwegian, Portuguese, Spanish, and Swedish
8859–2	94	Latin 2. modern Albanian, Czech, English, German, Hungarian, Polish, Rumanian, Croatian, Slovak, and Slovene
8859–5	113	modern Bulgarian, Byelorussian, English, Macedonian, Russian, Serbian, and Ukrainian.[24]
8859–6	114	Arabic and English
8859–7	118	modern Greek and English
8859–8	121	modern unpointed Hebrew and English
8859–9	128	Latin 5. modern Danish, Dutch, English, Faroese, Finnish, French, German, Irish, Italian, Norwegian, Portuguese, Spanish, Swedish, and Turkish.
8859–10	144	Latin 6. Danish, English, Estonian, Finnish, German, Greenlandic, Icelandic, Sami, Latvian, Lithuanian, Norwegian, Faroese, and Swedish.

The most lasting influence of the 8859 series, as of the standards 5426 and 6937, is that their inventories have been included in ISO 10646. In addition, 8859–1 has been assigned the first 256 positions in this new standard.

2.3.4 *Non-standard 8-bit code pages*

The sins of one's youth, *nostra culpa*.[25] Many of us who have contributed to this article have created local code pages in the past. The data created with them will have to be re-encoded if it is to have any future use. Vendors also have constructed code pages for their users. Examples of this are the EBCDIC code pages produced by IBM, PC code pages 437 and 850 etc. by IBM and Microsoft, and the various Apple character sets for their users. Character sets have been created by many users of PCs and Apples as well.

Apple is particularly guilty in this respect because it has tended to view character sets and fonts as the same thing, which they are not. There is no space in this article to explore the differences. Briefly a font is something which produces a discrete number of images and their code position is not of fundamental importance. The code position of coded characters in a set is important. In the series 646-IRV:1991, 8859, 10646 the first 127 positions are identical. The first 256 positions of 8859–1 and 10646 are identical.

3. UCS: ISO 10646/Unicode

This standard was approved in 1992 and is currently being implemented by a number of vendors within operating systems and applications. The work on UCS was originally started in the ISO JTC1/SC2 and the Unicode consortium; their work was merged to a single standard in 1992 and issued by ISO. Presently it is a 16-bit set, but it is highly likely that a future version will be 32-bit. We refer to the documents which define the standard for further information (ISO 10646:1992; The Unicode Consortium, 1991). There can be no doubt that this standard will form the basis for all character sets and subsets in the future.[26]

4. Public Entity Sets

A number of public entity sets were published in Appendix D of ISO 8879 (SGML). These include many characters[27] for European languages, modern Greek, modern Cyrillic, and math and publishing symbols. This work is being expanded by the TEI TR1 W4 and ISO JTC1/SC18/WG8. The TEI sets are being published electronically on the Internet SGML servers. That of ISO will appear as TR 9573-15.[28] The material already available from TEI at this writing is:

- TEIgreek.ent includes Classical Greek;[29]
- TEIphon.ent includes the current IPA symbol set;[30]
- TEIarab.ent includes basic modern Arabic;[31]
- TEIcop.ent includes a full set of Coptic with dialect variants.[32]

Work is progressing in subcommittees on a number of other sets. These include a full set for Hebrew (including alternative vocalization systems), Runes, Cuneiform, and Early Slavic. We are planning to include Syriac, Ethiopic, Old Icelandic, IndoEuropean transliteration, a full set for Arabic, and Hieroglyphics in the future. Suggestions for other sets and cooperative work on them are welcome.[33]

5. The SGML Declaration

Information about the character set(s) used should be placed in the SGML Declaration, which is processed before a DTD (Document Type Declaration) and a DI (Document Instance). Together they constitute an SGML Document. If it is omitted, a default will be chosen by the SGML system, usually that of the Reference Concrete Syntax, described in ISO 8879.[34]

To begin this discussion on declarations, we include a short sample of a mapping of an EBCDIC character set.[35]

```
CHARSET
BASESET "ISO 646-IRV:1991 //CHARSET International
    Reference Version (IRV)//ESC 2/8 4/2"
DESCSET  0    5   UNUSED
         5    1   9        - TAB (EBCDIC HT) -
         6    7   UNUSED
         13   1   13       - RE (EBCDIC CR) -
```

In this example the EBCDIC character set is being mapped to ISO 646-IRV:1991. The first 5 characters in EBCDIC are unused. The EBCDIC character at decimal 5 is mapped to decimal 9 in 646.

In a declaration, one can give information about the character set and how it is used. TEI has published sgmldecl.tei with the electronic form of its DTD. We continue the discussion using ISO 646 itself.

Two portions of a declaration give information about the character sets. The first section of the declaration is CHARSET in which the information for the character set is related to ISO 646 IRV. This information can be supplemented in a fourth section on SYNTAX (see below). The declaration of CHARSET and character set SYNTAX of ISO 646 IRV can be defined in this way:

```
CHARSET
BASESET "ISO 646-IRV:1991 //CHARSET International
    Reference Version (IRV)//ESC 2/8 4/2"
  DESCSET  0    9    UNUSED
           9    2    9
           11   2    UNUSED
           13   1    13
           14   18   UNUSED
           32   95   32
           127  1    UNUSED
```

The public identifier is first given for BASESET of CHARSET. DESCSET describes the character use. The numbers are the decimal number of the character position in the coded character set. On the first line starting with character 0 the first 9 characters (of the character set used, not the baseset) are not used. On the second line starting with character 9 in the character set two characters are used and mapped to the character set used beginning with character 9 of the baseset (in this case ISO 646-IRV:1991).[36] The SYNTAX section can contain information on shunned characters and CHARSET.

```
SYNTAX
SHUNCHAR CONTROLS 0 1 2 3 4 5 6 7 8 9 10 11 12 13 14
    15 16 17 18 19 20 21 22 23 24 25 26 27 28 29 30 31 127
BASESET "ISO 646-IRV:1991 //CHARSET International
    Reference Version (IRV)//ESC 2/8 4/2"
```

```
DESCSET 0     9    UNUSED
        9     2    9
        11    2    UNUSED
        13    1    13
        14    18   UNUSED
        32    95   32
        127   1    UNUSED
FUNCTION RE        13
        RS         10
        SPACE      32
        TAB   SEPCHAR 9
```

In the SYNTAX declaration SHUNCHARS declares which control characters are excluded. Errors will be generated if any of these characters are used in the SGML document other than those explicitly named in the FUNCTION section below.

A sample declaration for a character set in the ISO 8859 series would look in part like the following:

```
CHARSET
BASESET "ISO 646-IRV:1991 //CHARSET International
   Reference Version (IRV)//ESC 2/8 4/2"
   DESCSET 0     9    UNUSED
           9     2    9
           11    2    UNUSED
           13    1    13
           14    18   14
           32    95   32
           127   1    UNUSED
BASESET "ISO Registration Number 109 //CHARSET
   ECMA-94 Right Part of Latin Alphabet Nr. 1//ESC
   02/13 04/01"
   DESCSET 128   32   UNUSED
           160   96   "Supplementary Set"
CAPACITY PUBLIC "ISO 8879:1986//CAPACITY
   Reference//EN"
SCOPE       DOCUMENT
                        SYNTAX
SHUNCHAR CONTROLS 0 1 2 3 4 5 6 7 8 9 10 11 12 13 14
   15 16 17 18 19 20 21 22 23 24 25 26 27 28 29 30 31 127
   128 129 130 131 132 133 134 135 136 137 138 139 140
   140 142 143 144 145 146 147 148 149 150 151 152 153
   154 155 156 157 158 159
BASESET "ISO 646-IRV:1991 //CHARSET International
   Reference Version (IRV)//ESC 2/8 4/2"
   DESCSET 0     9    UNUSED
           9     2    9
           11    2    UNUSED
           13    1    13
           14    18   UNUSED
           32    95   32
           127   1    UNUSED
BASESET "ISO Registration Number 109 //CHARSET
   ECMA-94 Right Part of Latin Alphabet Nr. 1//ESC
   02/13 04/01
   DESCSET 128   32   UNUSED
           160   96   "Supplementary Set"
   FUNCTION RE                 13
           RS                  10
           SPACE               32
           TAB   SEPCHAR       9
```

In the positions 128–159 (columns 8 and 9) in this series these code positions are reserved for control characters.[37] The SHUNCHAR declaration could be shortened to SHUNCHAR CONTROLS (Exoterica, 1992, p. 17). Our committee has serious doubts about the extent to which SGML software actually supports the CHARSET and SYNTAX of SGML declarations. It is our contention that it should if it claims conformity to SGML and we support the revision of the section of 8879 on this towards simplicity and clarity in the current review taking place.

For IBM PC and Apple 8-bit a declaration might include:

```
CHARSET
BASESET "ISO 646-IRV:1991 //CHARSET International
   Reference Version (IRV)//ESC 2/8 4/2"
   DESCSET 0     9    UNUSED
           9     2    9
           11    2    UNUSED
           13    1    13
           14    18   14
           32    95   32
           127   1    UNUSED
           128   128  "Supplementary Set"
   CAPACITY PUBLIC "ISO 8879:1986//CAPACITY
   Reference//EN"
SCOPE      DOCUMENT
     SYNTAX
SHUNCHAR NONE
BASESET "ISO 646-IRV:1991 //CHARSET International
   Reference Version (IRV)//ESC 2/8 4/2"
   DESCSET 0     9    UNUSED
           9     2    9
           11    2    UNUSED
           13    1    13
           14    18   UNUSED
           32    95   32
           127   1    UNUSED
           128   128  "Supplementary Set"
   FUNCTION RE        13
           RS         10
           SPACE      32
           TAB   SEPCHAR 9
```

without additional SHUNCHARS, because in these character sets these positions are occupied by graphic characters.

6. The Writing System Declarations and Language Attribute

In each document instance a *lang* attribute should appear at least once. An example of this is the following:

```
<s>The sins of one's youth,<s lang=la>nostra culpa</s>
```

If the whole document is in a single language, the indication is on the TEI3 element. The value of the *lang* attribute should be the two or three letter code in ISO 639.[38] If more than one writing system is used for a single language, then the codes should be supplemented for the multiple writing systems, and multiple writing systems should be specified. Each language change should be noted in the document instance with a *lang* attribute.

The *id* of the appropriate writing system must contain the same value as the *lang* attributes in the document instances. How this works can be seen in the TEIen.wsd (for English) and TEIla.wsd (for Latin). These are brief and indicate the base character set they use (IS 8859–1).

The writing system declaration (wsd) has been developed for several purposes. It defines the way each symbol has been represented in its documents. Furthermore, this information is related to standard encodings in a structural way. This means that the document can be imported and exported between local and interchange formats algorithmically. Information is included for transformations to international standards which are presently being implemented for future use. A few examples will clarify this. On a machine using the ISO 8859–1 coded character set the local wsd would include the declaration:

```
<character class=lexical>
<form string="&#225" entityStd="aacute" ucs-4="00E1"
   afiicode="00E1">
<desc>Small letter a with acute </desc></form>
   </character>
```

Its interchange wsd would contain the declaration

```
<character class=lexical>
<form string="" entityStd="aacute" ucs-4="00E1"
   afiicode="00E1">
<desc> Small letter a with acute </desc></form>
   </character>
```

The transducer for import/export would use the entity name and entity reference value for all references within all elements containing the language attribute connected to this wsd to translate between local and interchange format.

Another local system using the IBM PC code page 437 or 850 might contain in its local wsd the declaration

```
<character class=lexical>
<form string=" " entityStd="aacute" ucs-4="00E1"
   afiicode="00E1">
<desc>Small letter a with acute </desc></form>
   </character>
```

A third local system on an IBM mainframe using EBCDIC code page 500 v.1 might have as its local wsd declaration

```
<character class=lexical>
<form string="&#69" entityStd="aacute" ucs-4="00E1"
   afiicode="00E1">
<desc> Small letter a with acute </desc></form>
   </character>
```

The local declaration for an Apple using Apple's Extended Roman set might contain

```
<character class=lexical>
<form string="&#135" entityStd="aacute" ucs-4="00E1"
   afiicode="00E1">
<desc> Small letter a with acute </desc></form>
   </character>
```

In this way each user is able to use the full facility of his local character set and to exchange documents with colleagues using their different local character sets without interchange corruption.

An alternative approach is available, in which the documents are maintained in the interchange character set but processed with local character sets. In this case a single wsd would be maintained for local and interchange, but two entity sets would be used. The local DTD modification on the IBM PC machine would contain the entity declaration

```
<!ENTITY aacute " " – small Latin a with acute –>
```

and the interchange DTD modification would contain

```
<!ENTITY % ISOlat1 PUBLIC "ISO 8879–1986//ENTITIES
   Added Latin 1//EN">
%ISOlat1;
```

If other entities of ISO Added Latin 1 were used locally these would be declared after the local modifications in the local DTD.

If at some point the local system is updated to the ISO 10646 coded character set, then a table is available to create a new version using that coded character set algorithmically.

6.1 *Currently available writing system declarations*

The following wsds are available on the Internet SGML servers:

- ISO 646 IRV
- ISO 646ss[39]
- ISO 8859 series
- TEIphon for IPA[40]
- TEIgreek for Classical Greek
- TEIen for English using the base character set 8859–1
- TEIla for Latin using the base character set 8859–1

A large number of other writing system declarations are planned or in progress.

7. Coded Characters and Glyphs

Coded character sets is an area of work in which JTC1/SC2 establishes standards. From the work of JTC1/SC18/WG8 on fonts a central registration point has been established for glyph registry. This is AFII (Association for Font Information Interchange).[41] The distinction of what is a glyph and what is a character is fuzzy. At the present time a working committee is trying to formulate a clear answer.[42]

The problem can be illustrated from ISO 10646. Each of the "common" characters of Chinese, Japanese, and Korean is given only one code position in that standard. Three glyphs are provided in the AFII registry. This means that for any application using 10646, information on the language in which the text is written must be added from outside. We have done this with the lang attribute of TEI. When we have wsds for these languages, the ucs-4 attribute values will be the same in the three wsds for these common characters, but their afficode attribute values will be different.

8. Standards Work

This section is relevant not only to character representation, but to the work of TEI as a whole. Until TEI was created, there was little input in standards circles by the humanities community. TEI has changed this, we suspect. By working on the problems of electronic text in all its complexity for people studying documents in electronic form, we have developed ways in which business and government offices, libraries and archives will be able to perform their work better in the future. It is our next responsibility to convince them of this. This is something which Don Walker[43] felt very strongly about. In matters of documents the expression "industrial strength" needs to be replaced with "academic industrial strength".

The traditional circles who have been active in ISO committees are largely made up of people who are not active humanities scholars, but many have had a liberal arts education and some even hold PhDs. They are not always aware of recent changes in the scholarly world. TEI has been able to make two concrete contributions to ISO in the last three years. JTC1/SC2 and the Unicode consortium had decided to include IPA in the new coded character set ISO 10646 before we became involved. However, they had used the 1949 inventory of phonetic symbols. With the intervention of TEI and IPA together we were able to ensure that the inventory of 1989 was included. Secondly, at a meeting of our Hypertext committee in Providence in 1991 the members decided to compose a commentary on the committee draft for the HyTime standard. Fundamental improvements were made in the HyTime standard as a result. Both of these interventions were officially contributions of the Nederlands Normalisatie Instituut. If TEI were a permanent organization, we could seek liaison status with JTC1/SC2, JTC1/SC18, and TC46. This would be far superior to relying on the incidental position of a few members of TEI.

We began working on ISO standards work in the academic year 1988/89 before we were formed into a technical committee of TEI in 1990. Communication between humanities scholars and standards people had been patchy at best before then. Quite often the two groups have not understood each others' needs and problems. We have seen confused ideas of scholars presented as proposals by technical experts in ISO official meetings. These have been rejected rightly by the other technical experts there. If someone had properly formulated them, as TEI could have done if asked, these scholarly needs would have been met in ISO 10646 already. We of the TEI team are fortunate in being able to combine our background in the whole breadth of humanities and linguistics and our knowledge about developing and implementing computing systems. It would be a pity if this opportunity were lost and we were disbanded as a group.

The international archive and library community has its organization for its voice to be heard; this is TC46. Yet their concerns are not always precisely the same as those of scholars. They have some standards which give simplifying transliteration schemes. These are not reversible to the original form of text and therefore not appropriate for a scholar to use if he works in the given field. For example, such a standard will be sufficient for the non-Arabist to look at a reference in Arabic, but unacceptable to an Arabist. We need to make that point in the standards committees and to make our contributions.

Our scholarly needs are not sufficiently a part of the concerns of all the members of the standards committees. That does not mean that they are not willing to take these needs seriously. In our experience we have only encountered one person who refused to take our contributions seriously and that was because of special personal circumstances–in other words, a minor exception. When we have been able to formulate clear proposals, they have been accepted if possible. In fact, ISO needs the TEI contributions as does TEI need ISO standards.[44] Secondly, adequate provision for the history of documents in languages would be included rather than only post World War II practices.[45]

On the other hand, there is a lack of understanding on the part of many humanities scholars of what we do in standards activities. We get no officially acknowledged credit in an ISO standard. TEI is not mentioned in ISO 10646 nor in ISO 10744 (HyTime) and those who made the TEI contributions have no way of indicating their contributions in the standards work. We were too late to influence ISO 8879 (SGML) in its formulation. If we had not been, we might have tried to make CONCUR a requirement of all conforming systems, rather than a largely unimplemented optional feature. We might have lost the vote, but it would have been worth the effort of explaining to standards engineers the need for such a feature in humanities computing. In the near future, on a computer conforming to ISO 10646, many scholars will be able to use IPA symbols for phonetic notation, but many will do so blissfully unaware of the arduous standardization work which was required to make this possible.

The scholarly community will be heard in ISO only when it is a recognizable interest group. There is no need to form another ISO subcommittee or technical committee, but we have an identity as TEI which is presently recognized and which we can use within ISO. We hope that this will be continued.

This would help us in our scholarly work worldwide. Present coded character sets for Japanese include about 6,000 characters, publishing houses in Japan print about 20,000 characters. Yet it is claimed that the inventory which scholars in Japanese need to encode includes more than 40,000. Those scholars are in a unique position to contribute to a coded character set which is adequate for the Japanese language. The same is true of Early Slavic, Hieroglyphics, and Cuneiform, to only mention a few areas. Only when scholars develop well-thought out solutions for these problems in electronic text and propose them in international standards meetings, will the standards committees be able to standardize them and implementers make them reality. It may be thought that this is unrealistic, because ISO 10646 is a 16-bit standard without much extra space for more characters. The ISO committee knows that it is filling up and made provision for a future version which is 32-bit. As a mental exercise the reader should calculate 2^{32} to see how much space there will be for more coded characters. Space will not be the problem. Hard work by scholars is required.

9. Conclusion

Much technical information has been presented in this article. Not all of it is necessary for every reader. This is inherent in an article for a variety of audiences. It is sufficient that the readers know that there are people working for standardization in their interest, and that they should examine hardware and software to see that they conform to the standards that have been developed internationally. When a vendor deviates from standards, he does it at his and your risk if you purchase his product. It is a short-sighted decision.

No time and space have been permitted to set out how you, the reader, can supplement or revise the decisions taken in TEI on character representation. That will have to be the subject of another article in the near future.

For those working in ancient and medieval documents, one word of caution is necessary. It is costly to encode electronic documents and they should be encoded with the maximal amount of information the first time. If manuscript documents in a given language have 5 forms of o, it may well be important to encode them separately in the TEI scheme. For a concordance it is not difficult to join them up under a common o in lemmas within an SGML application. If they are represented by a single character, one prevents the information about the 5 forms from being used. The forms may not be important for a text edition, but they may be important in establishing the relation of manuscripts in a stemma or carry information about copyists' pronunciation, orthographic schools, or something totally different.

The work of TEI itself, at least the first phase, is complete with the publication of the Guidelines. The work of our technical committee is far from finished. We will continue to develop and publish entity sets, writing system declarations, and documentation in cooperation with standards bodies and scholarly organizations as fields become ripe for standard solutions to character representation.

Notes

[1] The Chair of our technical committee submitted a draft of this article. Comments were received from David Birnbaum, Bert Bos, Steve DeRose, Berend Dijk, and Michael Sperberg-McQueen for which we thank them. The committee made revisions before submitting the final version to the editors of this issue of CHUM. In recognition of longstanding contributions to our work, the committee has elected the above mentioned contributors as honourable members, which increases our numbers five-fold. We also wish to thank the secretary general of ISO, L.D. Eicher, for permission to publish portions of the ISO standards and Jan van den Beld, secretary general of ECMA, for furnishing a complete copy of its official register of all known character sets and current versions of the ECMA standards. We also thank Edwin Smura, registrar of AFII, for supplying a copy of much of their font registry.

[2] Some languages, such as Chinese and Japanese, require a coded character set of more than 128 or 256 characters. There are national character standards for these languages and unfortunately a number of encoding methods are in use. These languages are excluded from the discussion here. It is a separate subject and should have an article devoted to it.

[3] Extracts from ISO 646:1991 and ISO 8859 parts 1 to 10 have been reproduced with the permission of the International Organization for Standardization, ISO. The complete standards can be obtained from your national standards organization or from the ISO Secrétariat Central, Case Postale 56, CH-1211 Geneva 20, Switzerland. Copyright remains with ISO. European Computer Manufacturers Association (ECMA) standards are available free from ECMA, 114 Rue du Rhône, CH-1204 Geneva.

[4] Technically defined, a coded character set is a set of characters, each associated with a unique pattern of bits, for use in representing character data on an electronic digital binary computer. The term *coded character set* is the preferred term in national and international standards, but elsewhere the term *code page* is often used. (The term *character set* is sometimes used for *coded character set*, and *character repertoire* for the set of characters included in a coded character set, without regard to any mapping from character to bit pattern.) It may be clarifying to think of this in terms of Morse code in the radio and telegraphic world. This has dots and dashes. Each sequence is unique and unambiguous.

[5] The left 2 columns of all figures are empty. These are positions for control characters. They are subjects for standards themselves. The oldest standard for these is ISO 2022. It was designed by computer specialists. A new version is expected this year. Two standards which are based on 2022 are ISO 6429:1991 and 10538:1991, which is specificly aimed at text. To what extent these standards are or will be fully implemented is not clear. Each manufacturer or developer is free to use whatever parts they need. ASCII and early versions of ISO 646 included these control characters, but the 1991 version of ISO 646 only makes reference in an appendix to ISO 2022.

[6] This distinguishes standard coded character sets from many vendor and home-brew ones in which graphic characters are placed in this area. Documents, encoded in such non-standard characters cannot be exchanged among users of different machines or over a network without modification or prior agreement and testing.

[7] We are told by Erik Naggum that there was an OS with that sequence.

[8] See Goldfarb (1990), pp. 321ff. This is the first difficulty in SGML that students usually encounter and the error messages are not clarifying usually.

[9] Goldfarb (1990), p. 321, n. 2. The collary to this concerning operating systems is the Gaylord law of operating systems. If OS create problems for users using multiple platforms, one of them is the directory separator character (/ or \).

[10] See Figures 11 and 12.

[11] David Birnbaum adds an explanation for the DEL function, now obsolete. "There is no way to erase a hole in punch tape, but if the convention for erasing is that one reverse the tape and punches out all the holes in the row, one can erase any mistake the same way. And 127 punches seven holes." This explains its position here. The functionality in recent times is performed by a del key on the keyboard or a key sequence in an editor.

[12] See Figures 1 and 2.

[13] There is a sort of pragmatism in this approach which has been a hallmark of ISO. North America and the U.K. uses inches and feet and considers them a sacred measure. They are also accepted in Japan. Continental Europe, since Napoleon, considers the metric system sacred. Both systems have their advantages. ISO has defined a "metric inch" which happens to be 2.54 cm. As long as one is not dealing with hundreds or thousands of them, this is a useful fiction.

[14] See Figure 1 for the form for national coded character sets of ISO 646:1991 and Figure 2 for ISO 646-IRV:1991. The fascinating story of how ASCII and ISO 646 were developed in the standards bodies is told in Mackenzie (1980).

[15] As long as computer data does not cross national borders, this causes no problems. Note especially the potential problem which can be caused by the Norwegian decision to place vertical bar in position 07/14 while it is in position 07/12 in most national standards if it is used. The Norwegian national body no longer holds to the position given. Their standard NS 4551 – Version 1 gives 07/14 as overline. It also changed currency sign to $ at 02/04.

[16] The use of BS followed by accent after the letter was sanctioned in some earlier version of ISO 646.

[17] This is a personal rant of our chair. He contends that the escape sequence ESC 2/5 4/0 is unambiguous, but it refers to a coded character set that has currency sign in position 02/04, not a $. The sequence should be ESC 2/5 4/2. Before that time the two possible references to ISO 646:1983 contain currency sign at position 02/04 or optional $ or currency sign. Earlier versions of ISO 646 contained overline at 07/14 instead of tilde as in ASCII, see Figure 11. The 8859 series has been alligned with ASCII, not the ISO 646 versions current before IRV:1991.

[18] This is currently being supplemented in DIS 5426–2. A closely related, but not identical, U.S. standard is ANSI/NISO Z39.47–1992.

[19] In 5426 and 6937, the non-spacing character precedes the spacing one unlike 646 and now 10646.
[20] The North American library community uses terminals with built-in composite characters to view data using this character set. It is not recommended for use without such devices.
[21] Draft versions including modern Cyrillic and Greek have been voted on, but no IS (International Standard) has ever been issued.
[22] Note that examples of this in 8859–1 include 10/04 (currency sign), 10/06 (broken vertical line from early IBM PC keyboards), 10/12 (logical not from EBCDIC and elsewhere) and 10/15 (overline from earlier versions of ISO 646 in position 07/14.
[23] See Figures 3–10. These claims are not necessarily justified in practice and the appropriate inventory should be checked for its adequacy before a project should use it for encoding. 8859–3 and 8859–4 are not included here for reasons of space.
[24] This is the second edition. It does not include all characters for every language using Cyrillic: e.g. the Ukrainian "g" which is not included.
[25] In fact it was not a sin, since there were no adequate character sets or ways of coding characters not in the standard character sets for our requirements at the time. That is not the situation today.
[26] This does not mean that scholars and especially scholars working on ancient texts won't need characters outside the coded character set. They will be able to add what they need in the so-called Private Zone in 10646. They can also supplement it with SGML character entities.
[27] Or glyphs. See Section 7: Coded Characters and Clyphs, p. 58.
[28] Public entity sets for non-Latin based alphabets are being edited by Dr. Anders Berglund with input from the TEI character representation committee.
[29] Developed by HEG with comments from Elli Mylonas.
[30] Developed by John Esling of IPA and HEG. This is the International Phonetic Association's character inventory for phonetic transcriptions.
[31] Developed by Alaa Ghoneim of IBM Cairo and HEG.
[32] Developed by Stephen Emmel of the International Association for Coptic Studies and HEG.
[33] Please send them to galiard@let.rug.nl.
[34] The most useful source for elucidation of the SGML declaration is Exoterica (1992b).
[35] This example is taken from Exoterica (1992b), p. 29.
[36] In many older editors character 26 is used as EOF (end of file) at the close of a file. This can cause problems if files are appended to another file. Some editors will not read past the first character 26, possibly falsely assuming that this is the end of the file. However, if a file has character 26 as the end of file, an error will be generated by conforming SGML software unless it is declared in the SGML declaration. Therefore, it is worth considering adding this character in one's declaration, which would look as follows:

14	11	UNUSED
26	1	EOF
27	5	UNUSED

[37] The one issue which needs resolution is the function of coded character 10/00 (NBSP no-break space) and 10/13 (SHY soft hyphen). These appear to be control characters in the view of our committee, contrary to the philosophy of SGML, and should be shunned.
[38] This standard is currently being revised within ISO. An electronic listing of the abbreviations under discussion is available from TEI. Political events are affecting it. The proposed 1992 revisions included removing Serbian and Croatian and inserting Serbo-croatian. The influence of national bodies on ISO standards is considerable. The national body of the Soviet Union kept the letters unique to Ukrainian and BeloRus out of standards for Cyrillic. The representative of Greece at the final meeting of JTC1/SC2 on IS 10646 attempted to have the word "Macedonian" removed from the standard.
[39] This is the safest subset of ISO 646.
[40] Of course this is not strictly speaking a language, but here it is regarded as a closed set of symbols.
[41] 2961 Copa de Oro, Los Alamitos, CA 90720, U.S.A.
[42] The latest document on this issue is JTC1/SC2/WG2 N 915.
[43] Don died in November, 1993. He is much missed by all at TEI and ACL. Without his work and support TEI would not have been produced.
[44] If TEI had been involved in JTC1/SC2 decisions at the time Œ and œ would have remained in 8859–1 at 07/13 and 07/15 so that it could be used for French, rather than being replaced by × and ÷ respectively. Since it was changed, 8859–1 is inadequate to encode many French documents.
[45] This issue is beginning to be dealt with in ISO and not only on the basis of TEI influence. At the final meeting on ISO 10646 the long s was added without our presence.

References

Birnbaum, David J. "Issues in Developing International Standards for Encoding Non-Latin Alphabets". *Proceedings of the Fourth International Conference on Symbolic and Logical Computing.* 1989, pp. 41–54.

Esling, John and Harry Gaylord. "IPA and TEI encoding for Phonetic Symbols". *Journal of the International Phonetic Association.* (1993), 23, 2.85-97.

Exoterica. *Record Boundary Processing in SGML.* Exoterica Corporation, 1992a. (1545 Carling Avenue, Suite 404, Ottawa, Ont., CA K1Z 8P9.) ECM13–1092.

Exoterica. *Understanding The SGML Declaration.* Exoterica Corporation, 1992b. (1545 Carling Avenue, Suite 404, Ottawa, Ont., CA K1Z 8P9.) ECM03–1092.

Gaylord, Harry E. "Character Entities and Public Entity Sets". Technical Report TEI TR1 W4, Text Encoding Initiative, 1992. Available on internet SGML servers. On sgml1.ex.ac.uk it is in tei/tech/tr1w4.tei1.

Goldfarb, Charles F. *The SGML Handbook.* Clarendon Press, Oxford, 1990. Edited and with a foreword by Yuri Rubinsky.

Edwin Hart, ed. *ASCII and EBCDIC: Character Set and Code Issues in Systems Application Architecture.* SHARE Inc., 1989. (111 East Wacher Drive, Chicago, Ill 60601, U.S.A.)

ISO. *ISO 8879:1986, Standard Generalized Markup Language.* Geneva: ISO, 1986.

ISO. *ISO 10646:1992 Universal Coded Character Set (UCS).* Geneva: ISO, 1992.

ISO. *ISO 10744:1992 Hypermedia/Time-based Structuring Language (HyTime).* Geneva: ISO, 1992.

Mackenzie, Charles E. *Coded Character Sets: History and Development.* The System Programming Series. Reading, MA: Addison-Wesley, 1980. ISBN 0-201-14460-3.

The Unicode Consortium. *The Unicode Standard: Worldwide Character Encoding.* Vol. 1. Addison-Wesley, 1.0 edition, 1991. ISBN 0-201-56788–1.

Wingen, Johan W. van. *Manual: standards for the electronic exchange of personal data. Part 5: character sets.* The Hague: Ministry of the Interior, 1995. ISBN: 90-5414-019-4.

				b7	0	0	0	0	1	1	1	1
				b6	0	0	1	1	0	0	1	1
				b5	0	1	0	1	0	1	0	1
b4	b3	b2	b1		0	1	2	3	4	5	6	7
0	0	0	0	0			SP	0	②	P	②	p
0	0	0	1	1			!	1	A	Q	a	q
0	0	1	0	2			"	2	B	R	b	r
0	0	1	1	3			# / ① £	3	C	S	c	s
0	1	0	0	4			¤ / ① $	4	D	T	d	t
0	1	0	1	5			%	5	E	U	e	u
0	1	1	0	6			&	6	F	V	f	v
0	1	1	1	7			'	7	G	W	g	w
1	0	0	0	8			(	8	H	X	h	x
1	0	0	1	9			)	9	I	Y	i	y
1	0	1	0	10			*	:	J	Z	j	z
1	0	1	1	11			+	;	K	②	k	②
1	1	0	0	12			,	<	L	②	l	②
1	1	0	1	13			-	=	M	②	m	②
1	1	1	0	14			.	>	N	②	n	②
1	1	1	1	15			/	?	O	_	o	DEL

C0 Set

Fig. 1. ISO 646:1991. Basic code table. Extracts from ISO 646:1991 and ISO 8859 parts 1 to 10 have been reproduced with the permission of the International Organization for Standardization, ISO. The complete standard can be obtained from any ISO member or from the ISO Central Secretariat, Case Postal 56, 1211 Geneva 20, Switzerland. Copyright remains with ISO.

b4	b3	b2	b1	b7	0	0	0	0	1	1	1	1
				b6	0	0	1	1	0	0	1	1
				b5	0	1	0	1	0	1	0	1
					0	1	2	3	4	5	6	7
0	0	0	0	0			SP	0	@	P	`	p
0	0	0	1	1			!	1	A	Q	a	q
0	0	1	0	2			"	2	B	R	b	r
0	0	1	1	3			#	3	C	S	c	s
0	1	0	0	4			$	4	D	T	d	t
0	1	0	1	5			%	5	E	U	e	u
0	1	1	0	6			&	6	F	V	f	v
0	1	1	1	7			'	7	G	W	g	w
1	0	0	0	8			(	8	H	X	h	x
1	0	0	1	9			)	9	I	Y	i	y
1	0	1	0	10			*	:	J	Z	j	z
1	0	1	1	11			+	;	K	[	k	{
1	1	0	0	12			,	<	L	\	l	|
1	1	0	1	13			-	=	M	]	m	}
1	1	1	0	14			.	>	N	^	n	~
1	1	1	1	15			/	?	O	_	o	DEL

Fig. 2. ISO 646IRV:1991.

				b8	0	0	0	0	0	0	0	0	1	1	1	1	1	1	1	1
				b7	0	0	0	0	1	1	1	1	0	0	0	0	1	1	1	1
				b6	0	0	1	1	0	0	1	1	0	0	1	1	0	0	1	1
				b5	0	1	0	1	0	1	0	1	0	1	0	1	0	1	0	1
b4	b3	b2	b1		00	01	02	03	04	05	06	07	08	09	10	11	12	13	14	15
0	0	0	0	00			SP	0	@	P	`	p			NBSP	°	À	Ð	à	ð
0	0	0	1	01			!	1	A	Q	a	q			¡	±	Á	Ñ	á	ñ
0	0	1	0	02			"	2	B	R	b	r			¢	²	Â	Ò	â	ò
0	0	1	1	03			#	3	C	S	c	s			£	³	Ã	Ó	ã	ó
0	1	0	0	04			$	4	D	T	d	t			¤	´	Ä	Ô	ä	ô
0	1	0	1	05			%	5	E	U	e	u			¥	µ	Å	Õ	å	õ
0	1	1	0	06			&	6	F	V	f	v			¦	¶	Æ	Ö	æ	ö
0	1	1	1	07			'	7	G	W	g	w			§	·	Ç	×	ç	÷
1	0	0	0	08			(	8	H	X	h	x			¨	¸	È	Ø	è	ø
1	0	0	1	09			)	9	I	Y	i	y			©	¹	É	Ù	é	ù
1	0	1	0	10			*	:	J	Z	j	z			ª	º	Ê	Ú	ê	ú
1	0	1	1	11			+	;	K	[	k	{			«	»	Ë	Û	ë	û
1	1	0	0	12			,	<	L	\	l	|			¬	¼	Ì	Ü	ì	ü
1	1	0	1	13			-	=	M	]	m	}			SHY	½	Í	Ý	í	ý
1	1	1	0	14			.	>	N	^	n	~			®	¾	Î	Þ	î	þ
1	1	1	1	15			/	?	O	_	o				¯	¿	Ï	ß	ï	ÿ

Fig. 3. ISO 8859-1 Latin 1.

b8					0	0	0	0	0	0	0	0	1	1	1	1	1	1	1	1
b7					0	0	0	0	1	1	1	1	0	0	0	0	1	1	1	1
b6					0	0	1	1	0	0	1	1	0	0	1	1	0	0	1	1
b5					0	1	0	1	0	1	0	1	0	1	0	1	0	1	0	1
b4	b3	b2	b1		00	01	02	03	04	05	06	07	08	09	10	11	12	13	14	15
0	0	0	0	00			SP	0	@	P	`	p			NBSP	°	Ŕ	Đ	ŕ	đ
0	0	0	1	01			!	1	A	Q	a	q			Ą	ą	Á	Ń	á	ń
0	0	1	0	02			"	2	B	R	b	r			˘	˛	Â	Ň	â	ň
0	0	1	1	03			#	3	C	S	c	s			Ł	ł	Ă	Ó	ă	ó
0	1	0	0	04			$	4	D	T	d	t			¤	´	Ä	Ô	ä	ô
0	1	0	1	05			%	5	E	U	e	u			Ľ	ľ	Ĺ	Ő	ĺ	ő
0	1	1	0	06			&	6	F	V	f	v			Ś	ś	Ć	Ö	ć	ö
0	1	1	1	07			'	7	G	W	g	w			§	ˇ	Ç	×	ç	÷
1	0	0	0	08			(	8	H	X	h	x			¨	¸	Č	Ř	č	ř
1	0	0	1	09			)	9	I	Y	i	y			Š	š	É	Ů	é	ů
1	0	1	0	10			*	:	J	Z	j	z			Ş	ş	Ę	Ú	ę	ú
1	0	1	1	11			+	;	K	[	k	{			Ť	ť	Ë	Ű	ë	ű
1	1	0	0	12			,	<	L	\	l	|			Ź	ź	Ě	Ü	ě	ü
1	1	0	1	13			-	=	M	]	m	}			SHY	˝	Í	Ý	í	ý
1	1	1	0	14			.	>	N	^	n	~			Ž	ž	Î	Ţ	î	ţ
1	1	1	1	15			/	?	O	_	o				Ż	ż	Ď	ß	ď	˙

Fig. 4. ISO 8859-2 Latin 2.

				b8	0	0	0	0	0	0	0	0	1	1	1	1	1	1	1	1
				b7	0	0	0	0	1	1	1	1	0	0	0	0	1	1	1	1
				b6	0	0	1	1	0	0	1	1	0	0	1	1	0	0	1	1
				b5	0	1	0	1	0	1	0	1	0	1	0	1	0	1	0	1
b4	b3	b2	b1		00	01	02	03	04	05	06	07	08	09	10	11	12	13	14	15
0	0	0	0	00			SP	0	@	P	`	p			NBSP	А	Р	а	р	№
0	0	0	1	01			!	1	A	Q	a	q			Ё	Б	С	б	с	ё
0	0	1	0	02			"	2	B	R	b	r			Ђ	В	Т	в	т	ђ
0	0	1	1	03			#	3	C	S	c	s			Ѓ	Г	У	г	у	ѓ
0	1	0	0	04			$	4	D	T	d	t			Є	Д	Ф	д	ф	є
0	1	0	1	05			%	5	E	U	e	u			Ѕ	Е	Х	е	х	ѕ
0	1	1	0	06			&	6	F	V	f	v			І	Ж	Ц	ж	ц	і
0	1	1	1	07			'	7	G	W	g	w			Ї	З	Ч	з	ч	ї
1	0	0	0	08			(	8	H	X	h	x			Ј	И	Ш	и	ш	ј
1	0	0	1	09			)	9	I	Y	i	y			Љ	Й	Щ	й	щ	љ
1	0	1	0	10			*	:	J	Z	j	z			Њ	К	Ъ	к	ъ	њ
1	0	1	1	11			+	;	K	[	k	{			Ћ	Л	Ы	л	ы	ћ
1	1	0	0	12			,	<	L	\	l	|			Ќ	М	Ь	м	ь	ќ
1	1	0	1	13			-	=	M	]	m	}			SHY	Н	Э	н	э	§
1	1	1	0	14			.	>	N	^	n	~			Ў	О	Ю	о	ю	ў
1	1	1	1	15			/	?	O	_	o				Џ	П	Я	п	я	џ

Fig. 5. ISO 8859-5 Latin/Cyrillic.

b4	b3	b2	b1		00	01	02	03	04	05	06	07	08	09	10	11	12	13	14	15
				b8	0	0	0	0	0	0	0	0	1	1	1	1	1	1	1	1
				b7	0	0	0	0	1	1	1	1	0	0	0	0	1	1	1	1
				b6	0	0	1	1	0	0	1	1	0	0	1	1	0	0	1	1
				b5	0	1	0	1	0	1	0	1	0	1	0	1	0	1	0	1
0	0	0	0	00			SP	0	@	P	`	p			NBSP	°	ΐ	Π	ΰ	π
0	0	0	1	01			!	1	A	Q	a	q			ʽ	±	Α	Ρ	α	ρ
0	0	1	0	02			"	2	B	R	b	r			ʼ	²	Β		β	ς
0	0	1	1	03			#	3	C	S	c	s			£	³	Γ	Σ	γ	σ
0	1	0	0	04			$	4	D	T	d	t				΄	Δ	Τ	δ	τ
0	1	0	1	05			%	5	E	U	e	u				΅	Ε	Υ	ε	υ
0	1	1	0	06			&	6	F	V	f	v			¦	Ά	Ζ	Φ	ζ	φ
0	1	1	1	07			'	7	G	W	g	w			§	·	Η	Χ	η	χ
1	0	0	0	08			(	8	H	X	h	x			¨	Έ	Θ	Ψ	θ	ψ
1	0	0	1	09			)	9	I	Y	i	y			©	Ή	Ι	Ω	ι	ω
1	0	1	0	10			*	:	J	Z	j	z				Ί	Κ	Ϊ	κ	ϊ
1	0	1	1	11			+	;	K	[	k	{			«	»	Λ	Ϋ	λ	ϋ
1	1	0	0	12			,	<	L	\	l	|			¬	Ό	Μ	ά	μ	ό
1	1	0	1	13			-	=	M	]	m	}			SHY	½	Ν	έ	ν	ύ
1	1	1	0	14			.	>	N	^	n	~				Ύ	Ξ	ή	ξ	ώ
1	1	1	1	15			/	?	O	_	o				―	Ώ	Ο	ί	ο	

Fig. 6. ISO 8859-7 Latin/Greek.

				b8	0	0	0	0	0	0	0	0	1	1	1	1	1	1	1	1
				b7	0	0	0	0	1	1	1	1	0	0	0	0	1	1	1	1
				b6	0	0	1	1	0	0	1	1	0	0	1	1	0	0	1	1
				b5	0	1	0	1	0	1	0	1	0	1	0	1	0	1	0	1
b4	b3	b2	b1		00	01	02	03	04	05	06	07	08	09	10	11	12	13	14	15
0	0	0	0	00			SP	0 ٠	@	P	`	p			NBSP			ذ	ـ	ِ
0	0	0	1	01			!	1 ١	A	Q	a	q					ء	ر	ف	ّ
0	0	1	0	02			"	2 ٢	B	R	b	r					آ	ز	ق	ْ
0	0	1	1	03			#	3 ٣	C	S	c	s					أ	س	ك	
0	1	0	0	04			$	4 ٤	D	T	d	t			¤		ؤ	ش	ل	
0	1	0	1	05			%	5 ٥	E	U	e	u					إ	ص	م	
0	1	1	0	06			&	6 ٦	F	V	f	v					ئ	ض	ن	
0	1	1	1	07			'	7 ٧	G	W	g	w					ا	ط	ه	
1	0	0	0	08			(	8 ٨	H	X	h	x					ب	ظ	و	
1	0	0	1	09			)	9 ٩	I	Y	i	y					ة	ع	ى	
1	0	1	0	10			*	:	J	Z	j	z					ت	غ	ي	
1	0	1	1	11			+	;	K	[	k	{				؛	ث		ً	
1	1	0	0	12			,	<	L	\	l	|			،		ج		ٌ	
1	1	0	1	13			-	=	M	]	m	}			SHY		ح		ٍ	
1	1	1	0	14			.	>	N	^	n	~					خ		َ	
1	1	1	1	15			/	?	O	_	o					؟	د		ُ	

Fig. 7. ISO 8859-6 Latin/Arabic.

				b8	0	0	0	0	0	0	0	0	1	1	1	1	1	1	1	1
				b7	0	0	0	0	1	1	1	1	0	0	0	0	1	1	1	1
				b6	0	0	1	1	0	0	1	1	0	0	1	1	0	0	1	1
				b5	0	1	0	1	0	1	0	1	0	1	0	1	0	1	0	1
b4	b3	b2	b1		00	01	02	03	04	05	06	07	08	09	10	11	12	13	14	15
0	0	0	0	00			SP	0	@	P	`	p			NBSP	°			א	נ
0	0	0	1	01			!	1	A	Q	a	q				±			ב	ס
0	0	1	0	02			"	2	B	R	b	r			¢	²			ג	ע
0	0	1	1	03			#	3	C	S	c	s			£	³			ד	ף
0	1	0	0	04			$	4	D	T	d	t			¤	´			ה	פ
0	1	0	1	05			%	5	E	U	e	u			¥	µ			ו	ץ
0	1	1	0	06			&	6	F	V	f	v			¦	¶			ז	צ
0	1	1	1	07			'	7	G	W	g	w			§	·			ח	ק
1	0	0	0	08			(	8	H	X	h	x			¨	¸			ט	ר
1	0	0	1	09			)	9	I	Y	i	y			©	¹			י	ש
1	0	1	0	10			*	:	J	Z	j	z			×	÷			ך	ת
1	0	1	1	11			+	;	K	[	k	{			«	»			כ	
1	1	0	0	12			,	<	L	\	l	|			¬	¼			ל	
1	1	0	1	13			-	=	M	]	m	}			SHY	½			ם	
1	1	1	0	14			.	>	N	^	n	~			®	¾			מ	
1	1	1	1	15			/	?	O	_	o				‾			‗	ן	

Fig. 8. ISO 8859-8 Latin/Hebrew.

				b8	0	0	0	0	0	0	0	0	1	1	1	1	1	1	1	1
				b7	0	0	0	0	1	1	1	1	0	0	0	0	1	1	1	1
				b6	0	0	1	1	0	0	1	1	0	0	1	1	0	0	1	1
				b5	0	1	0	1	0	1	0	1	0	1	0	1	0	1	0	1
b4	b3	b2	b1		00	01	02	03	04	05	06	07	08	09	10	11	12	13	14	15
0	0	0	0	00			SP	0	@	P	`	p			NBSP	°	À	Ğ	à	ğ
0	0	0	1	01			!	1	A	Q	a	q			¡	±	Á	Ñ	á	ñ
0	0	1	0	02			"	2	B	R	b	r			¢	²	Â	Ò	â	ò
0	0	1	1	03			#	3	C	S	c	s			£	³	Ã	Ó	ã	ó
0	1	0	0	04			$	4	D	T	d	t			¤	´	Ä	Ô	ä	ô
0	1	0	1	05			%	5	E	U	e	u			¥	µ	Å	Õ	å	õ
0	1	1	0	06			&	6	F	V	f	v			¦	¶	Æ	Ö	æ	ö
0	1	1	1	07			'	7	G	W	g	w			§	·	Ç	×	ç	÷
1	0	0	0	08			(	8	H	X	h	x			¨	¸	È	Ø	è	ø
1	0	0	1	09			)	9	I	Y	i	y			©	¹	É	Ù	é	ù
1	0	1	0	10			*	:	J	Z	j	z			ª	º	Ê	Ú	ê	ú
1	0	1	1	11			+	;	K	[	k	{			«	»	Ë	Û	ë	û
1	1	0	0	12			,	<	L	\	l	|			¬	¼	Ì	Ü	ì	ü
1	1	0	1	13			-	=	M	]	m	}			SHY	½	Í	İ	í	ı
1	1	1	0	14			.	>	N	^	n	~			®	¾	Î	Ş	î	ş
1	1	1	1	15			/	?	O	_	o				¯	¿	Ï	ß	ï	ÿ

Fig. 9. ISO 8859-9 Latin 5.

				b_8	0	0	0	0	0	0	0	0	1	1	1	1	1	1	1	1
				b_7	0	0	0	0	1	1	1	1	0	0	0	0	1	1	1	1
				b_6	0	0	1	1	0	0	1	1	0	0	1	1	0	0	1	1
				b_5	0	1	0	1	0	1	0	1	0	1	0	1	0	1	0	1
b_4	b_3	b_2	b_1		00	01	02	03	04	05	06	07	08	09	10	11	12	13	14	15
0	0	0	0	00			SP	0	@	P	`	p			NBSP	°	Ā	Đ	ā	ð
0	0	0	1	01			!	1	A	Q	a	q			Ą	ą	Á	Ņ	á	ņ
0	0	1	0	02			"	2	B	R	b	r			Ē	ē	Â	Ō	â	ō
0	0	1	1	03			#	3	C	S	c	s			Ģ	ģ	Ã	Ó	ã	ó
0	1	0	0	04			$	4	D	T	d	t			Ī	ī	Ä	Ô	ä	ô
0	1	0	1	05			%	5	E	U	e	u			Ĩ	ĩ	Å	Õ	å	õ
0	1	1	0	06			&	6	F	V	f	v			Ķ	ķ	Æ	Ö	æ	ö
0	1	1	1	07			'	7	G	W	g	w			§	·	Į	Ũ	į	ũ
1	0	0	0	08			(	8	H	X	h	x			Ļ	ļ	Č	Ø	č	ø
1	0	0	1	09			)	9	I	Y	i	y			Đ	đ	É	Ų	é	ų
1	0	1	0	10			*	:	J	Z	j	z			Š	š	Ę	Ú	ę	ú
1	0	1	1	11			+	;	K	[	k	{			Ŧ	ŧ	Ë	Û	ë	û
1	1	0	0	12			,	<	L	\	l	|			Ž	ž	Ė	Ü	ė	ü
1	1	0	1	13			-	=	M	]	m	}			SHY	―	Í	Ý	í	ý
1	1	1	0	14			.	>	N	^	n	~			Ū	ū	Î	Þ	î	þ
1	1	1	1	15			/	?	O	_	o				Ŋ	ŋ	Ï	ß	ï	ĸ

Fig. 10. ISO 8859-10 Latin 6.

				b_7	0	0	1	1	1	1
				b_6	1	1	0	0	1	1
				b_5	0	1	0	1	0	1
b_4	b_3	b_2	b_1		2	3	4	5	6	7
0	0	0	0	0		0	@	P	`	p
0	0	0	1	1	!	1	A	Q	a	q
0	0	1	0	2	"	2	B	R	b	r
0	0	1	1	3	#	3	C	S	c	s
0	1	0	0	4	¤	4	D	T	d	t
0	1	0	1	5	%	5	E	U	e	u
0	1	1	0	6	&	6	F	V	f	v
0	1	1	1	7	'	7	G	W	g	w
1	0	0	0	8	(	8	H	X	h	x
1	0	0	1	9	)	9	I	Y	i	y
1	0	1	0	10	*	:	J	Z	j	z
1	0	1	1	11	+	;	K	[	k	{
1	1	0	0	12	,	<	L	\	l	|
1	1	0	1	13	–	=	M	]	m	}
1	1	1	0	14	.	>	N	^	n	‾
1	1	1	1	15	/	?	O	_	o	

Fig. 11. Norway standard NS 4551.

				b_7	0	0	1	1	1	1
				b_6	1	1	0	0	1	1
				b_5	0	1	0	1	0	1
b_4	b_3	b_2	b_1		2	3	4	5	6	7
0	0	0	0	0		0	@	P	`	p
0	0	0	1	1	!	1	A	Q	a	q
0	0	1	0	2	"	2	B	R	b	r
0	0	1	1	3	#	3	C	S	c	s
0	1	0	0	4	$	4	D	T	d	t
0	1	0	1	5	%	5	E	U	e	u
0	1	1	0	6	&	6	F	V	f	v
0	1	1	1	7	'	7	G	W	g	w
1	0	0	0	8	(	8	H	X	h	x
1	0	0	1	9	)	9	I	Y	i	y
1	0	1	0	10	*	:	J	Z	j	z
1	0	1	1	11	+	;	K	[	k	{
1	1	0	0	12	,	<	L	\	l	|
1	1	0	1	13	-	=	M	]	m	}
1	1	1	0	14	.	>	N	^	n	~
1	1	1	1	15	/	?	O	_	o	

Fig. 12. ANSI standard X3.4:1968 (ASCII).

Computers and the Humanities **29:** 75–84, 1995.

The TEI Header and the Documentation of Electronic Texts *

Richard Giordano
Information Systems, Department of Computer Science, University of Manchester, Manchester M13 9PL, U. K.
e-mail: rich@cs.man.ac.uk

Key words: text encoding initiative, TEI header, header, electronic documentation, cataloging, SGML

Abstract

The article gives a general introduction to the form and function of the TEI header, points out some of the reasoning of the Text Documentation Committee that went into its design, and discusses some of its limitations. The TEI header's major strength is that it gives encoders the ability to document the electronic text itself, its source, its encoding principles, revisions, and characteristics of the text in an interchange format. Its bibliographical descriptions can be loaded into standard remote bibliographic databases, which should make electronic texts as easy to find for researchers as texts in other media, including print. Its major weakness is that it does not yet provide the ability for retrieval across texts in a networked environment, which users may want now or in the future.

1. Introduction

The documentation of encoded texts – the text itself, its source, its encoding practices and its revision history – is necessary for people using texts, for software processing them, and for catalogers and archivists collecting them. No text encoded for electronic interchange is identifiable or usable unless it is accompanied by documentation. This article will introduce humanities scholars to the TEI header, which is the means by which TEI-conformant texts are documented. [1]

In 1988, when the TEI began its work, the task of the Text Documentation Committee was to design a set of descriptions and declarations to provide the electronic equivalent to the title page attached to a printed book. Additionally, the TEI header was to constitute the equivalent to code books or introductory manuals customarily accompanying electronic data sets (Ide & Sperberg-McQueen, 1995). These declarations form the TEI header, which fully documents a TEI-encoded text, and which is prefixed to every TEI-conformant text. No encoded text, even if it follows P3 religiously in every other respect, is TEI-conformant unless a TEI header prefixes it.

The Text Documentation Committee was initially composed of archivists and librarians from both Europe and North America who had experience in cataloging, collecting and describing electronic sources. This committee was composed chiefly of members of the library and related professions, and their work was guided by documentation principles related to their discipline for describing texts both on paper and as machine-readable data files. Additionally, their work was also influenced by other TEI work groups unrelated to the library and archival professions, specifically the work group on spoken language which did much of the work on the profile description part of the TEI header (Johansson, in this volume). As a consequence of input from other work groups, the TEI header describes both bibliographic and non-bibliographic information, and supports, in addition to the identification and retrieval of an encoded text, the machine analysis of encoded text.

Before discussing the significance of combining both descriptive and analytical information in a single

* Richard Giordano was a member of the Text Documentation Committee since it was established in 1988. He has held positions at Butler Library of Columbia University, Computing and Information Technology at Princeton University, and the Laboratory for Research in Academic Information at the Johns Hopkins University Medical School. His teaching positions have included Barnard College, Princeton and, since 1990, the Computer Science Department at the University of Manchester.

unified structure, and the reasons why that came about, we shall briefly describe the TEI header and its functions.

2. Brief Overview of the TEI Header

In general terms, the TEI header has three major constituencies: those creating an electronic text who must supply at least some form of documentation; users of that text, such as librarian catalogers who would supply full cataloging information, and researchers. It can be safely assumed that people in the business of creating electronic texts do not feel comfortable creating headers (in much the same way that authors or publishers do not feel that they can create full cataloging information of their works) for the simple reason that they believe that they do not understand the intricacies of library cataloging. This overview is therefore meant to explain to the humanist the main features of the TEI header, what it is and what it does. It will not attempt to document it fully. If researchers are neither able nor willing to provide a full structured header, this article should make them aware of the sorts of information required by librarians who will fully catalog their electronic texts. Because this article will be most readers' first point of contact with the TEI header, it will of necessity be a minimal description rather than a full discussion or formal analysis. (For a detailed discussion of the Header, especially as it relates to corpora, see Dunlop [in this volume].) The elements of the TEI header are described here only to give an introduction to what they are and how they could be used, but they are not a guide to constructing headers. The reader should consult TEI P3 for detailed and full information and recommended practices. P3 provides readers with advice on creating minimal headers as well as guidance on constructing headers which far exceed documentation standards found in most libraries or repositories.

The TEI header, or <**teiHeader**>, is composed of four functional major parts that document the bibliographic description of the electronic text and its source, the encoding of the text, non-bibliographical information that characterize the text, and a history of updates and changes made to the electronic texts. These major elements are referred to as *descriptions*.

The bibliographic description of the encoded text and its source, which is essential for the retrieval of an item, forms the *File Description*, or <**fileDesc**>; documentation on the relationship of the encoded text to its source – for instance, a documentation of editorial decisions or procedures – is provided in the *Encoding Description*, or <**encodingDesc**>; non-bibliographic information characterizing various descriptive aspects of a text, and which are useful for the human or machine-assisted analysis of text, form the *Profile Description*, or <**profileDesc**>; and, the history of updates and changes to the machine readable text comprise the *Revision Description*, or <**revisionDesc**>. Together, these elements allow people to identify an encoded text, understand the editorial decisions when the text was encoded, have documentation of the characteristics of the text, and maintain a history of any revisions to the transcription of the text.

3. The File Description

The <**fileDesc**> is best thought of as an electronic analogy to the title page of a book. It provides users of an encoded text with at least the information normally found on a title page of a printed work. In addition to providing bibliographic information about the encoded text itself, it provides citation information of the source (or sources) from which the encoded text was derived.

Because any work without a title page is difficult or impossible to identify accurately, the <**fileDesc**> is thus the sole required element of the TEI header. The <**fileDesc**> should not be confused with a cataloging record but, like a title page, can be used by a librarian cataloger for the creation of a cataloging record, or be used by anyone to derive the correct bibliographic citation for the encoded text.

Because the bibliographic description of a machine-readable text resembles the bibliographic description of a book or manuscript, the <**fileDesc**> has been closely modelled on existing descriptive standards in library cataloging. Elements of the <**fileDesc**> have been given explicit names that are familiar to librarians. The three elements that are required in every header are the title statement <**titleStmt**>, the publication statement <**publication Stmt**>, and the source description <**sourceDesc**>. The title statement groups information about the title of the work and those responsible for its intellectual content, the publication statement groups information concerning the publication or distribution of an electronic or other text, and the source description supplies a bibliographic description of the copy text(s) from which an electronic text was derived or generated. These three required elements will allow a user to identify a unique electronic text, access it from a publisher or distributor, and provide a reference to the source from which the electronic text was derived.

This information can be grouped formally, or expressed in prose. For example, consider a TEI header attached to an encoded version of Thomas Paine's *Common Sense* derived from a collection of Paine's work edited by Phillip Foner. The following minimal **<fileDesc>** would look something like this:

```
<teiHeader>
   <fileDesc>
      <titleStmt>
         <title>Common sense, a machine-readable
            transcript</title>
      <respStmt><resp>compiled by</resp><name>Jon
         K. Adams</name>
      </respStmt>
      </titleStmt>
      <publicationStmt>
         <distributor>Oxford Text Archive</distributor>
      </publicationStmt>
      <sourceDesc>
         <bibl>The complete writings of Thomas Paine,
            collected and edited by Phillip S. Foner
            (New York: Citadel Press, 1945)</bibl>
      </sourceDesc>
   </fileDesc>
<teiHeader>
```

If a researcher chooses to create minimal headers, notice that one needs to know very little cataloging. For instance, the minimal header does not call for an explicit **<author>** sub-element as there would be in, say, a traditional library citation. The **<titleStmt>** encompasses the "statement of responsibility", (or **<respStmt>**), which holds author information, or, to be more precise, information on everyone who has any intellectual responsibility for the encoded work. This is to say, *everyone whom the encoder considers to be responsible for the intellectual content of an encoded text* can be included within the **<respStmt>**. Though this practice is at variance with standard cataloging procedure, we chose this course primarily because the creator of a TEI header should not be cataloging an encoded text when constructing a header, but simply documenting the electronic text in an electronic equivalent to the title page. Further, by requiring an encoder to include an **<author>** element, the Text Documentation Committee feared that this might give the unintentional impression that encoders would have to decide blindly the author of an encoded text. As many librarians know only too well, deciding on the author is not always a simple matter, especially when there are cases of multiple authorship or organizations as authors or where arcane cataloging rules apply in deciding authorship. As if these rules were not enough, there is always the vexing question of the form of the author's name once the author is determined. For instance, it is unreasonable to think that an encoder would know the correct form for the name, T. S. Eliot. Would it be *Eliot, T. S.* , or *Eliot, Thomas Stearns*, or *Eliot, T. S. (Thomas Stearns), 1888–1965*? If the Text Documentation Committee had included an explicit **<author>** element, some encoders might construe this to mean that the correct author and the correct form of entry must be given. The most likely outcome in this circumstance, of course, is that encoders would give nothing.

The Text Documentation Committee believed that if it were possible for an encoder uninitiated or uninterested in the rules of cataloging to include everyone in the statement of responsibility who was seen to be responsible for the intellectual content of a work, and the role made clear (such as compiler, editor or, perhaps, person who sent for pizzas) then a cataloger, not an encoder, could apply both standard AACR2 rules and local practice to determine the appropriate author and others responsible for the work, and the form of their names. Our intention was thus not to place the burden of documentation squarely on the shoulders of the encoder, but to share the work, if need be, with librarians and others in the documentation community.

4. The Encoding Description

The relationship between the encoded text and its source or sources is described in the Encoding Description, or **<encodingDesc>**. The **<encodingDesc>** documents editorial rationales, decisions and practices made both before and during the transcription of a source text into encoded machine readable form. Such documentation can include a prose description of the aim or purpose for which the file was encoded, the method or rationale used in sampling texts in the creation of a corpus or collection, editorial principles and practices, including whether or how the text was normalized during transcription, how the encoder resolved ambiguities in the source, what levels of encoding or analysis were applied, how canonical references are constructed, and definitions of any classification codes, if any, introduced in the text by the encoder. Such information is related to code book information that one would normally find accompanying computerized datasets. Our decision to include such "codebook" information in a unified structure was, in part, guided by library experience with collecting social science datasets and their associated codebooks that document variable names, value labels, record structures, sampling procedures and other editorial and documentary evidence. [2]

A minimal **<encodingDesc>** might look something like this:

```
<encodingDesc><p>Blank lines and multiple blank spaces,
   including paragraph indents, have not been preserved.</p>
</encodingDesc>
```

The **<encodingDesc>** can, moreover, hold structured information in its sub-elements. If different editorial practices were applied to different parts of the text (for instance, sampling procedures may differ throughout a large corpus [Dunlop, in this volume]), one can repeat the **<encodingDecl>** element in the TEI header to reflect different editorial practices, and assign an *id* attribute to each one. The value of the *id* attribute can then be linked to the specific part of the text (which would have the same *id* value) where those editorial principles apply.

A simple, but structured, example of the **<encodingDesc>** for a typical project that converts texts from sources of American history for use in a course on historical methodology might look something like this:

```
<encodingDesc>
   <projectDesc><p>Transcription of the US Constitution
      for the teaching of a first-year course in historical
      methodology at Barnard College, Columbia
      University.</p>
   </projectDesc>
   <editorialDecl>
      <correction><p>Errors in scanning and transcription
         controlled by using the Microsoft Word, v. 5. 0,
         spell checker.</p></correction>
   </editorialDecl>
</encodingDesc>
```

5. The Profile Description

The **<profileDesc>** is an optional element that provides a detailed description that characterizes various descriptive non-bibliographic aspects of the text, such as language usage, the situation in which the text was produced, and the participants and their setting. The purpose of the **<profileDesc>** is to enable descriptive aspects which do not identify the work, as bibliographic elements would, and which go beyond information typically found in codebooks, to be recorded within a single unified framework. The **<profileDesc>**, which resulted largely from input from the Spoken Language workgroup, is of most use to linguistic-based spoken text projects, although many of its features can be applied to written text, such as drama, or to those projects that desire to track multiple speakers, or voices, through prose. (See Johannson and Dunlop in this issue for a fuller discussion.)

The core **<profileDesc>** element has three optional components, represented by the following sub-elements:

- **<creation>**: contains information about the creation of a text. This may vary from the publication date in the bibliographic description in that it gives the date and place of composition, and may be of acute relevance to studies of linguistic variation across space and time.
- **<langUsage>**: describes the languages, sublanguages, dialects, etc. represented within the text.
- **<textClass>**: groups information which describes the nature of the text in terms of a standard classification scheme.

A brief profile description might look like this:

```
<profileDesc>
   <creation><date value='1989-08'>August 1989</date>
      <place>Brooklyn, New York</place>
   </creation>
   <langUsage><language id=EN wsd=wsd.en>[3]<language
      id=SP wsd=wsd.sp><p>Approximately 95% of the
      text is in American English with quotations from first
      and second generation Italian immigrants to Brooklyn;
      the remainder is in transcribed Spanish spoken by first
      and second generation Puerto Rican immigrants to
      Brooklyn.</p>
   </langUsage>
   <textClass>
      <keywords scheme=LCSH>
         <list>
            <item>Brooklyn (New York, N. Y. ) - -
               Biography.</item>
            <item>Brooklyn (New York, N. Y. ) - - Social
               life and customs.</item>
         </list>
      </keywords>
```

```
    <classCode scheme=LC>F129. B7</classCode>
  </textClass>
</profile Desc>
```

Such a classification system, while useful to most projects may be too coarse when applied to the analysis of language in spoken text, or when applied to some written text (such as drama), collections or corpora. In these cases the **<profileDesc>** allows the encoding of a high degree of classificatory information about the text itself, the voices of characters or participants within it, and the setting within which a language interaction takes place. This information can be recorded using the optional extensions to the **<profileDesc>**: The Text Description or **<textDesc>**; the Participants Description or **<particDesc>**; and the Setting Description or **<settingDesc>**.

Formal situational information may be included in the **<textDesc>** to support the analysis of speech or written text. Such information – the medium by which the text is delivered or experienced, the internal composition of a text or of a text sample (for instance, documenting a complete text, a fragment, a composite text), the nature and extent of indebtedness or derivation of the text to others, the social context for which the text was realized or intended (for instance, as entertainment, or religious and ceremonial purposes, etc.), the interaction between those producing and experiencing the text, whether or not a text was prepared or spontaneous, and the purpose of the text – can be referred to as situational parameters. [4]

Situational parameters are a description of the situation within which the text was produced or experienced, and thus characterize it in a way relatively independent of any *a priori* theory of text types. Rather than insisting on a system of discrete text types, which in practice would be impossible to formulate, TEI P3 recommends the use of situational parameters that can be used in combination to supply distinguishing descriptive features of individual texts. When text types are used in combination with situational parameters, the internal structure of each text type can be specified in terms of the parameters proposed. This allows for the relatively continuous characterization of texts, in contrast to discrete categories based on type or topic, supports meaningful comparisons across corpora, allows analysts to build their own text types based on the particular parameters of interest to them, and may be equally applicable to both spoken and written texts.

An informal domestic conversation might be characterized as follows:

```
<textDesc id=t1 n='Informal domestic conversation'>
  <channel mode=s>informal face-to-face conversation
  </channel>
  <constitution type=single>each text represents a
     continuously recorded interaction among the specified
     participants
  </constitution>
  <derivation type=original>
  <domain type=domestic>plans for coming week, local
     affairs</domain>
  <factuality type=mixed>mostly factual, some
     jokes</factuality>
  <interaction type=complete active=plural passive=many>
  <preparedness type='spontaneous'>
  <purpose type=entertain degree=high>
  <purpose type=inform degree=medium>
</textDesc>
```

We have noted that situational parameters may be applied to texts other than to spoken texts. Consider this example of situational parameters applied to a novel:

```
<textDesc n='novel'>
  <channel mode=w>print</channel>
  <constitution type=single>
  <derivation type=original>
  <domain type=art>
  <factuality type=fiction>
  <interaction type=none>
  <preparedness type=prepared>
  <purpose type=entertain degree=high>
  <purpose type=inform degree=medium>
</textDesc>
```

It is possible, in addition, to document information about the participants in a spoken text or persons named or depicted in written text, including demographic and descriptive information about their individual characteristics and the relationships among them. The **<particDesc>** element is used for this purpose. Individual speakers, or groups of speakers, can be named and identified by a code (or *id* attribute), which can then be used to identify the speaker throughout the text. This allows an analyst to identify multiple speakers or voices in the text, provide detailed information about them, and then to track the participants' speech throughout the text. [5]

An individual appearing in a text might be described either informally or formally. For instance, consider the following informal prose description of a character:

```
<participant id=P1 sex=M age=39><p>Male, well-educated,
   born in Newark, NJ, 28 September 1953, son of toolmaker
```

```
      and seamstress, speaks pitiful but passable Italian taught to
      him by his maternal grandmother, good French, lived on
      Upper West Side of Manhattan for past fourteen years,
      Social-Economic status high white collar (HWC) from
      Thernstrom's classification scheme, works as an
      endocrinologist.</p>
</participant>
```

Although a prose description may be sufficient for most projects, demographic information may be described formally, and lend itself to machine capture and analysis. For example, consider the formal description of the same character:

```
<participant id=P1 sex=M age=39>
   <birth date='1953–09–28'<date>28 Sep 1953</date>
      <place>Newark, NJ</place>
   </birth>
   <firstLang>English</firstLang>
   <langKnown>Italian</langKnown>
   <langKnown>French</langKnown>
   <residence>New York City</residence>
   <education>medical school</education>
   <occupation>Endocrinologist</occupation>
   <socecstatus source=Thernstrom code=HWC>
</participant>
```

Finally, the setting or settings in which the language interaction takes place can be described in the <**settingDesc**> element. The information here may contain prose or it may be grouped in a series of sub-elements, depending on the level of analysis required by the encoder. For instance, the setting can be described informally as follows:

```
<settingDesc>
   <p>The time is early summer, 1993. P1 is doing the dishes.
      P2 is in the living room chair reading an unidentified
      newspaper. P3 is watching the news on television. P4 (a
      television news broadcaster) is in a broadcasting
      studio in New York.</p>
</settingDesc>
```

This description is useful as codebook information, may be sufficient for the purposes of most projects, but it would be difficult for use in machine analysis. The following formal setting description may make computer processing tractable.

```
<settingDesc>
   <setting who="P1">
      <place>New York City</place>
      <date value=1993>early summer, 1993</date>
      <locale>kitchen sink of New York apartment</locale>
      <activity>washing dishes</activity>
   </setting>
   <setting who="P2">
      <place>New York City</place>
      <date value=1993>early summer, 1993</date>
      <locale>living room chair of New York
         apartment</locale>
      <activity>reading newspaper</activity>
   </setting>
   <setting who="P3">
      <place>New York City</place>
      <date value=1993>early summer, 1993</date>
      <locale>living room of New York apartment</locale>
      <activity>watching news on television</activity>
   </setting>
   <setting who="P4">
      <place>New York City</place>
      <date value=1993>early summer, 1993</date>
      <locale>broadcasting studio, New York City</locale>
      <activity>reading news</activity>
   </setting>
</settingDesc>
```

The <**profileDesc**> can thus provide researchers with a powerful tool to identify and track each participant throughout the text by the use of a formal description, or can be used solely for documentation by using informal prose descriptions.

6. The Revision Description

The final part of the TEI header the Revision Description or <**revisionDesc**> provides a detailed change log in which each change made to a text can be recorded. This log is very similar to logs kept of data files in the social sciences. It is an especially important element for recording changes to a file as that file is passed from system to system or from researcher to researcher.

The revision description consists of the following tags:

- <**revisionDesc**>: summarizes the revision history of a file.
- <**change**>: summarizes a particular change or correction made to a particular version of an electronic text which is shared among several researchers.
- <**date**>: contains a date in any format.
- <**respStmt**>: supplies a statement for someone responsible for the intellectual content of text, edition, etc., where specialized elements for authors, editors, etc. do not apply.
- <**item**>: contains one component of a list.

An example of a change log might look like this:

```
<revisionDesc>
   <change><date>6/4/93</date>
      <respStmt><name>RG</name><resp>ed.</resp>
         <respStmt>
         <item>proofread SJW's work</item>
            <change><date>6/2/93</date>
      <respStmt><name>SJW</name><resp>data
         entry</resp></respStmt>
         <item>Changes to pretty-up printed
            version</item>
</revisionDesc>
```

7. The Size and Complexity of the TEI Header

From the above overview, it is easy to see that the TEI header can become quite large, and in some cases may even exceed the size of the text it is documenting! The size of the TEI header, however, depends on the nature of the project and the amount of documentation that encoders wish to attach to a text. On the other hand, it is not intended that all of the elements recommended in TEI P3, nor even the formal structures illustrated in this article, be present in every TEI header. At one extreme, an encoder may expect that the TEI header will be needed only to provide minimal bibliographic information of the text adequate to local needs, or to be shared with a small number of close colleagues. Similarly, encoders may wish to describe their texts only in detailed prose, leaving it to catalogers, archivists and others to create structured sub-elements that are tractable by machine. At the other extreme, wishing to ensure that their texts can be used for the widest range of applications, encoders may want to document both bibliographic and descriptive information as explicitly as possible such that no prior or ancillary knowledge about the text is needed in order to process it. The TEI header, in the latter case, will be very full, approximating to the kind of documentation often supplied in the form of a manual. Most texts will lie somewhere between these extremes; large corpora and linguistics-based research projects in particular will tend toward the latter. TEI P3 makes no recommendations how a particular project must encode a TEI header other than to require that an informal **<fileDesc>** be included for all encoded texts. Having said that, P3 does offer guidance on creating minimal and recommended headers, [6] as well as creating freestanding or independent headers that can be sent libraries and other sites without text attached to them. [7] Contingent resources such as time, staff and money, as well as the intended purposes of the encoded texts, should determine the level of encoding, not printed guidelines. Once the participants in a project decide which information is to be encoded, TEI P3 will give guidance on ways to do it.

Some elements of the TEI header may be difficult to understand to those unfamiliar with bibliographic description, and potential users may be wary of even attempting to construct a TEI header. It is not the TEI's intention that everyone who creates a TEI header take a course in cataloging in order to know which elements to include. Rather than grappling with the intricacies of bibliographic description, one approach for those uninterested in spending a lot of time and effort on the TEI header would be to make as large a prose description as possible in the **<fileDesc>**, and to leave it to a librarian cataloger at a text repository to structure the information into appropriate sub-elements, or to input that information into a local bibliographic system. What matters when encoders construct a TEI header is not so much the structure of the information, but rather its completeness and fidelity to the encoded text.

Highly structured and accurate bibliographic information contained in the header, however, will greatly ease the burden of catalogers because such information can be loaded directly into online catalogs with relatively little human intervention. If Header information is already contained on a database, it might be a matter of generating a TEI header automatically from that database, as was done with the British National Corpus (Dunlop, in this volume), and transferred to a bibliographic file.

8. Use of the TEI Header to Support Document Retrieval and Analysis: Prospects and Problems

TEI headers can be distributed and published in paper or electronic form as Independent headers (that is, the TEI header is physically separated from the text it describes), and distributed to libraries and other repositories to support online bibliographic retrieval. Two advantages of this approach, mentioned by (Dunlop, 1995) are that users save local storage by not needing the full text in order to make selections, and users need not undertake any copyright responsibilities defined in end-user agreements. Most important, TEI headers loaded into or referenced from standard bibliographic databases will provide users with the same abilities to identify electronic texts as easily as texts in other formats, including print. Linked with easily assessable bibliographic databases, the Independent TEI header should, in the near future, engender widespread use of electronic texts, and encourage people to encode texts for distribution, rather than simply for local use. There are limitations, however, with the current TEI header's ability to provide fine-grained retrieval that might be important for some applications. TEI P3 provides encoders with a relatively fixed set of tags and attributes (which, of course, can be extended by the user), but the values given to those tags and attributes are, for the most part, open. For instance, one encoder might encode **<locale>**New York City**</locale>** while another might encode **<locale>**Manhattan**</locale>** while yet another might encode **<locale>**Upper West Side**</locale>** to designate the same place. This uncontrolled vocabulary, and its form, may seriously affect retrieval.

This lack of specificity in TEI P3 is the result of twin circumstances. First, the Text Encoding Initiative was concerned primarily with providing users with a set of recommended tags and guidelines for using them instead of rules for determining the values that encoders would use with those tags. Second, and more significantly, the encoders themselves and relevant international and professional bodies are best positioned to address the syntactic and semantic questions of standardized content formats and values because the specific form of values is very much related to the intended use of the encoded texts, the purposes of a project, and the "language" of the discipline to which the text or encoding project is connected. The TEI could not issue specific guidelines or make recommendations that would apply across a range of disciplinary or professional orientations. TEI P3 therefore assumes that encoders will refer to the work of professional organizations, such as the Library of Congress, the International Standards Organization, or discipline-specific organizations, such as art documentation associations, for guidance. Encoders who wish to distribute their texts to others in their discipline, or across disciplines, are strongly encouraged to make use of standard subject thesauri in their fields, for the quality of retrieval may otherwise suffer.

The model of "documentation" that guided much of the work of the Text Documentation Committee was informed by standard library and archival practice, and this resulted in the default structure of the TEI header which is adequate to the needs of many applications. The reliance on standard library practice is both a strength and a weakness. Typically, documentation in the library community involves providing enough descriptive information to users so that a text itself can be uniquely identified among many. The Text Documentation Committee thus made reference to an existing working model as defined in the *Anglo-American Cataloging Rules* (AACR, 1988) for the cataloging and description of machine-machine readable data files. Consequently, the Committee began work under the assumptions embedded in those rules which implied that users would need information in the form of an index and codebook to identify a text for retrieval, and in general they would use that index and codebook information the same way as one would when identifying a social science machine readable data file stored on tape in a data archive. This assumption led to the construction of the **<fileDesc>**, **<encodingDesc>**, and **<revisionDesc>** which document the bibliographic aspects of texts, their encodings and revisions, and serve as pointers to encoded texts. This is to say, the mental model of documentation presupposed the traditional notion of an index, which is a physical object – such as a catalog – that points users to another physical object – such as a book (Gorman, 1992). The problem is that this model of an index points to the electronic text, and assumes that electronic texts exist only as separate unified physical objects, and therefore assumes that users are interested in retrieving only the entire physical object, rather than, say, only parts of it. Thus, in many ways the TEI header at present functions as little more than an electronic analogy of the catalog card; one can retrieve the encoded text with information from the **<fileDesc>**, but there is no mechanism in the default header to navigate through the text, or to retrieve portions of it that fit some analytic criteria.

As readers of this volume will no doubt recognize from the other articles on the TEI, the work of the Text Encoding Initiative in general has been to support multiple view of texts, (as physical objects, typographic objects, linguistic objects, rhetorical objects, etc.), and recognizes that in many situations more than one view of text is needed. It should then come as no surprise to observers that outsiders to library science, notably the Spoken Language work group and members of the Corpus Linguistics community, made recommendations to the **<profileDesc>** which are extremely useful to researchers for the retrieval and analysis of portions of texts (for instance, linguistic objects such as phonemes) which fall outside the traditional boundaries of retrieval one normally associates with librarianship. The **<profileDesc>**, for instance, gives encoders the ability to track participants and voices through a text, and extensions to the TEI header that support corpora allow users to isolate sub-portions of the text (Dunlop, in this volume).

Such features, though useful, can be seen to be under-specified. Although voices can be traced through a text using the TEI header, no unified structure exists at present in the default header to track the occurrences of intellectual or editorial responsibilities throughout the text. Take a case where there are multiple editors in a text, each responsible for different parts of the text, perhaps edited at different times. The default TEI header does not at present give encoders the ability to identify each editor, isolate which parts of the texts were edited by them, and retrieve them. There are, of course, ways of encoding intellectual interventions, but none are to be found in the default TEI header without extending its content model.

Further, the default TEI header at present does not provide tools for the tracking of editors, voices, or participants *across* texts. For example, it does not give encoders the ability to isolate an editor in a text, retrieve those parts of the text for which s/he is responsible, and to retrieve parts from other texts for which that editor is also responsible. Such a facility would give researchers the ability to compare editorial styles across works of, for example, one genre to another. It can be used, also, to investigate the effects of different situations on the register of the speech of a given speaker.

The potential solutions to these problems are deceptively simple: there is no reason why one might not re-define the TEI header so that those listed in the **<respStmt>** are given an *id* attribute, and their 'interventions' isolated in the text using much the same mechanism that isolates speech by participants in spoken text. However, the Text Documentation Committee did not take this approach because it demands that the **<respStmt>** do something which the library community never intended, and the Guidelines would therefore be at variance with standard library practice. Such information can be carried in the **<profileDesc>**, but encoders then run the risk of encoding redundant information in the **<respStmt>** (by listing editors of a text) and again in the **<profileDesc>** (by pointing to areas of the text that they had indeed edited).

One can hazard the proposition, however, that once textual collections are in an electronic environment, in particular a networked electronic environment where texts in arbitrary locations can easily be combined in a screen buffer, the rules that guide the identification and retrieval of texts are altered, for it is important for users not only to have the ability to retrieve texts in a traditional sense (as one would retrieve a book), but some standard mechanisms are needed as well for the fine-grained retrieval and analysis to support multiple views of texts.

Although the international library and documentation community will sooner or later have to focus on this problem, there are mundane issues that will need to be addressed soon. The difficulty, however, is that no one really knows yet what those mundane issues are. There is no large-scale empirical field experience with the TEI header, only a set of guidelines and a lot of good will. How people will make use of the TEI header; if people make use of the TEI header; whether the TEI header can provide the documentation that researchers and scholars need; whether encoders will be willing to create accurate TEI headers . . . only time will tell.

Notes

[1] This article is intended primarily for humanities scholars who create electronic texts, but should also be of interest to librarian catalogers and archivists. An article on the TEI header for the library and documentation community appears in Library Resources and Technical Services, October, 1994.

[2] An encoded text, however, is not just another electronic file that can be categorized like a data set of numbers. For this reason, the Profile Description, which is discussed later in this article, was developed for the TEI header largely through the efforts of the Spoken Language and Corpus Linguistics workgroups.

[3] The *wsd* attribute must give the name of an entity containing a writing system declaration. Typically, this will be an external file in the document type declaration. See P3, p. 129 for details.

[4] See P3, pp. 648–58 for more details.

[5] TEI P3 provides a set of elements to identify the name of the speaker, place of birth, residence, education, occupation and so on, but in practice such details will vary enormously for different forms of analysis, and users of TEI P3 are encouraged to customize them to fit the needs of their projects.

[6] See P3, pp. 134–35.

[7] See P3, pp. 667–78.

References

AACR. *Anglo-American Cataloging Rules*. Ed. Michael Gorman. Chicago, IL: American Library Association, 1978, 1988 rev.

Burnard, Lou and Michael Sperberg-McQueen. *TEI P3: Guidelines for Electronic Text Encoding and Interchange*. Oxford, Chicago: The Text Encoding Initiative, 1994.

Crawford, Walt. *MARC for Library Use: Understanding USMARC*. Boston: G. K. Hall, 1989.

Dunlop, Dominic. "Practical Considerations in the Use of TEI Headers in a Large Corpus". In this volume.

Gorman, Michael. "After AACR2: The Future of the Anglo-American Cataloging Rules". In *Origins, Content and Future of AACR2*. Revised. Ed. Richard Smiraglia. Chicago: American Library Association, 1992.

Ide, Nancy M. and Michael Sperberg-McQueen. "The Text Encoding Initiative: Its History, Goals and Future Development". In this issue.

International Federation of Library Associations. *Working Group on the General International Standard Bibliographic Description, ISBD(G): General International Standard Bibliographic Description*. London: IFLA International Office for UBC, 1977.

Johansson, Stig. "The Encoding of Spoken Texts". In this volume.

Library of Congress. *USMARC Format for Bibliographic Data, Including Content Designation*. Washington, D. C.: Library of Congress, 1987.

Computers and the Humanities **29:** 85–98, 1995.

Practical Considerations in the Use of TEI Headers in a Large Corpus*

Dominic Dunlop
Oxford University, Computing Services, 13 Banbury Road, Oxford OX2 6NN, U. K.
e-mail: Dominic@natcorp.ox.ac.uk

Key words: bibliographic records, electronic texts, electronic title page, large corpora, standard generalized markup language, SGML, text encoding initiative, TEI

Abstract

Many aspects of the guidelines of the Text Encoding Initiative (TEI) are applicable to corpora and text collections, and to the texts that these contain. As the first large corpus developed using mark-up conforming to the guidelines, the British National Corpus (BNC) is a test-bed for many TEI-developed mechanisms. This is particularly true in the case of the TEI header, which has three intended applications – to describe a corpus, to describe an individual text, and as a free-standing bibliographic record – all of them used by the BNC. This paper describes the application of the TEI header to the BNC. It is intended that this information should, through a description of experience on a practical project, serve as a guide for those wishing to use TEI headers in the documentation and management of other corpora and collections of texts.

1. Introduction

The Text Encoding Initiative (TEI) header, described by Giordano (1993), is required in all TEI-conformant texts. While its default structure is adequate to the needs of many applications, there are two groups of optional additions or considerations. These cover the needs of language corpora, and of the electronic exchange of bibliographic information. The British National Corpus (BNC) project is currently constructing a 100 million word corpus of modern British English for use in linguistic research. It is a collaborative, pre-competitive initiative carried out by Oxford University Press (OUP), Longman Group UK Ltd., W. R. Chambers, Lancaster University's Unit for Computer Research in the English Language (UCREL), Oxford University Computing Services (OUCS), and the British Library. The project receives funding from the UK Department of Trade and Industry and the Science and Engineering Research Council within their Joint Framework for Information Technology, and from the British Library.

Burnage and Dunlop (1993) discuss the constitution of the BNC, provide examples of the application of TEI-conformant mark-up to written and spoken texts, and discuss the processing steps necessary to transform a source text into a form which may be included in the corpus. These issues are not developed, except where they bear on the contents of text and corpus headers. The current paper, taking examples from the practical application of the TEI header in the BNC, is intended to serve as a model for the application of TEI headers to further corpora and their component texts by other workers in the field.

The overall SGML (Goldfarb, 1990) structure of the header and its immediate descendants are shown in Figure 1. Sections 4–7 of this paper discuss each part of the header as it applies to the corpus header and to three example text headers. Section 8 briefly describes applications of free-standing headers in the British National Corpus.

* Dominic Dunlop is project manager for the British National Corpus at Oxford University Computing Services. Prior to assuming this position, he worked in a variety of positions related to development and support of the UNIX operating system, and was active in the POSIX initiative for the standardization of UNIX.

```
<teiHeader>
    <fileDesc>
        Mandatory description of electronic text and any source
        texts
    </fileDesc>
    <encodingDesc>
        Optional description of the means by which the source
        texts have been rendered into electronic form
    </encodingDesc>
    <profileDesc>
        Optional description of the characteristics of an
        electronic text or the of the texts in a corpus
    </profileDesc>
    <revisionDesc>
        Optional text or corpus revision history
    </revisionDesc>
</teiHeader>
```

Fig. 1. Content model for TEI header.

1.1 *Notes on the figures*

The Figures in this paper consist of fragments of a preliminary version of the BNC corpus header and three example text headers. Their contents are subject to change prior to publication of the corpus. Indentation is used to show structure, and, with the exception of **</p>**, end-tags are shown, even where their omission is allowed. Ellipses (...) show where material has been omitted from some of the Figures for reasons of brevity.

2. General Issues

2.1 *Portability*

TEI P3 allows conformant materials to exist in two forms: a local storage format and an interchange format. The former will typically use a richer character set than the latter, and may use SGML options such as end-tag omission (Goldfarb, 1990). In the interests of portability across networks and between computer architectures, an interchange format often uses a restricted character repertoire and, making few assumptions about the capabilities of processing software, does not use end-tag omission or other SGML options. The promotion of portability in this manner makes for larger files, and may compromise intelligibility to humans.

Because a primary goal of the BNC is that it should easily be interchangeable between archive and user sites, no local storage format has been specified: the corpus exists only in an interchange format which uses the character repertoire of the International Reference Version of ISO (1991). All examples given in this paper are presented in this form. Those building corpora for which interchange is a less important consideration may wish to specify a richer, more compact, local storage format.

2.2 *Language*

TEI P3 accommodates texts and corpora which intermix languages and the writing systems used to represent them. The language of the British National Corpus is modern British English. As no other language is explicitly accommodated, and because the corpus does not provide information about, for example, prosody, which might require a repertoire of special characters, a single writing system declaration (TEI P3) suffices. This declaration is comparatively simple, as differences between the character repertoire of the interchange format (see previous subsection) and that of the source text for the corpus can, for the most part, be handled by means of SGML public entity sets (Goldfarb, 1990). The BNC writing system declaration is not discussed further here.

Compilers of corpora of source texts written in languages requiring a richer character repertoire than English, compilers of multi-lingual corpora, and those using special marks for annotation will need to devote greater effort to the writing system and language usage declarations (see 4.3) than has been necessary for the BNC.

3. Issues Specific to Large or Modern Corpora

3.1 *Accommodating practical SGML processors and computing platforms*

Conceptually, a TEI-conformant corpus is a single SGML-compliant document. In the case of the BNC, this document would contain some two gigabytes of data. As such, it should be possible to submit it as a whole to SGML-aware software in order to accomplish user-specified processing. In practice, current SGML-aware software and computing hardware cannot handle such a large corpus as if it were a single document. Further, ISO (1986) specifies that conforming software must meet or exceed capacity limits which are very low: in some cases limits are unavoidably exceeded by individual texts in the BNC. Consequently, the BNC must be decomposable into manageable pieces in order to be processed at all, and steps must be taken to ensure that capacity limit requirements placed on processing software are not gratuitously inflated.

The likely needs of users of the corpus suggest that such a manageable piece should consist of the corpus header, other global structures such as the writing system declaration (see 2.2), and a sub-corpus selected according to arbitrary user criteria from the totality of texts in the corpus. Such a scheme implies that no text in the corpus may require the presence of any other text (for example because of a cross-reference using the TEI <**ptr**> element) in order that it can be processed: such requirements would constrain the composition of user-specified sub-corpora. Instead, a text may reference only information in its own header or in the corpus header.

While TEI P3 requires a greater value for the name length limit – thirty-two – than the minimum specified in ISO (1986), the BNC has elected to stay with a lower limit so as to be usable with current SGML-aware applications, some of which do not allow name lengths to be increased above eight characters. This has two consequences. Firstly, those TEI element and attribute names longer than eight characters are renamed in the BNC. TEI P3 describes how this may be done. This paper uses TEI names for attributes and elements, rather than the shortened versions. Secondly, the identifiers through which one SGML element may reference another are limited in length to eight characters, and so are necessarily terse. The scheme used is described in the next subsection.

3.2 *Ensuring the uniqueness of identifiers*

Identifiers are heavily used in the BNC, and are likely to be so in any large corpus. As stated in the previous subsection, they are limited in length to eight characters. Rather than pick names at random, a name-generation scheme is used. Identifiers for corpus header elements have two fields encoding the element name and its instance; identifiers in a text prepend a third field unique to that text. Table 1 describes the scheme.

Table 1. Structure of identifiers in BNC.

Positions	Function	Notes
1–3	Uniquely identify text in which ID is defined	Derived from 6-character text name by a mapping or hash. First character alphabetic; others alphanumeric. Mapping given explicitly by text header <**idno**>s – see figure 15. Omitted in corpus header.
4–5	Uniquely identify the element type (GI) to which the ID belongs	Somewhat mnemonic.
6–8	Make the identifier unique across the entire BNC	Effectively a separate base-33 counter per GI and per text.

3.3 *Minimizing file size*

Some aspects of the interchange format of TEI P3 are likely to increase file size. For example, the limited nature of the interchange character set means that entity references, rather than single character codes, must be used to encode accented letters; and the requirement that minimized SGML is transmitted means that files must contain end-tags which could otherwise be omitted. This size increase is unfortunate since, other things being equal, it is easier to transport a smaller file than a larger over a network or on some physical medium.

Happily, SGML provides a means by which files can be shortened through the replacement of repeated sequences of text by entity references which expand when processed to the replaced sequence. As subsequent sections show, several parts of a typical text header consist of "boilerplate" which may conveniently be replaced with entity references. This paper points out such situations as they occur, but the Figures show the full text in such cases, rather than abbreviating it to an entity reference.

A second means of reducing file size is to ensure that text headers contain a minimum of redundant information. This means that, where identical information would otherwise be be repeated in a number of text headers, the information is instead moved into the corpus header and simply referenced by the text headers concerned. Again, the following sections draw the reader's attention to situations in which this mechanism is used by the BNC. Taken together, these mechanisms help to compensate for the increase in file size engendered by the interchange format.

3.4 *Copyright*

While some corpora may consist entirely of historical material which may be freely used and distributed, all the material in the BNC is modern and, as such, generally subject to copyright considerations.

After a text has been selected for inclusion in the BNC, but before it is converted to electronic form, con-

```
<sourceDesc>
    <p> The corpus, considered as a text in its own right, has
        no source: it was originated in electronic form.
    <p> See the source descriptions to component texts in order
        to trace the sources of those texts.
</sourceDesc>
```

Fig. 2. Corpus header source statement.

siderable effort is put into tracing copyright holders and obtaining permission for a number of types of world-wide use. In order that users of the corpus are reminded of the responsibilities set out in BNC (1992b), copyright information is included in the header of each text and of the corpus itself. The information appears as plain text so as to be human-readable, in spite of the duplication this engenders. (See also 5.1.)

4. The Corpus Header

4.1 *The file description*

The TEI file description has two main functions: firstly, it serves as a bibliographic record of an electronic text as a work in its own right; and secondly, it describes the source text or texts from which an electronic text was derived. While the corpus header could be used to list the sources for all the texts in the corpus, the source description in the BNC corpus header – shown in Figure 2 – instead contains a short note directing users to examine individual text headers for details of the sources of particular texts. The source description is the final element of the file description. The elements which precede it give a bibliographic description of the corpus as a whole. The first such element is the title statement, shown in Figure 3. It gives the name of the corpus, and lists those responsible for its intellectual content. It is followed by the edition statement, which gives the release identifier of the corpus. This will change as the corpus is revised, with the initial published version being release 1.0. The Figure also shows the extent statement, which describes the size of the corpus.

The final element of the bibliographic record provided by the file description is the publication statement, shown in Figure 4. Since no organization can strictly be identified as the publisher, distributor or release authority of the corpus, these TEI-suggested elements have been discarded in favour of using the general-purpose **<resp>** element to identify an archive site. The publication statement also contains availability information. The description shown is an

```
<titleStmt>
    <title>The British National Corpus
    </title>
    <resp>
        <role> Consortium member </role>
        <name> The British Library Board </name>
    </resp>
    ... details of five futher partners omitted
    <resp>
        <role> Consortium member </role>
        <name> The University of Oxford </name>
    </resp>
</titleStmt>
<editionStmt n=0.1>
    0.1 (initial alpha test version)
</editionStmt>
<extent>
    One hundred million words &mdash; ninety million from
    written sources, ten million from spoken sources.

    Occupies approximately two gigabytes (eight-bit bytes) of
    computer storage.
</extent>
```

Fig. 3. Corpus header title statement.

```
<publicationStmt>
    <resp>
        <role>
            Archive site
        </role>
        <name>
            Oxford University Computing Services
        </name>
    </resp>
    <address>
        13 Banbury Road, Oxford OX2 6NN U.K.
        Telephone:   +44 491 273280
        Facsimile:   +44 491 273275
        Internet mail: natcorp@ox.ac.uk
    </address>
    <idno type=bnc>
        bnc0.1
    </idno>
    <availability status=restricted>
        <p> Available at nominal charge for academic research
            purposes throughout the EC subject to a signed
            permissions agreement having been received by
            Oxford University Computing Services, from which
            blank forms and supporting materials are available.
        <p> Availability for commercial research and
            exploitation only where terms have been agreed with
            the BNC Consortium Exploitation Committee. Apply in
            the first instance to Oxford University Computing
            Services.
    </availability>
    <date>
        1993-04-17
    </date>
</publicationStmt>
```

Fig. 4. Corpus header publication statement.

example only: ultimate constraints on availability may differ.

4.2 *The encoding description*

The encoding description describes the manner in which a text or corpus has been rendered into electronic form. The description in the corpus header may be used simply to give those parts of the description which apply to all texts in the corpus. If it does only this, text-specific information must appear in the headers of affected texts, with the result that it will be duplicated if particular encoding practices apply to several texts, but not to every text in the corpus. This duplication may be eliminated by moving descriptions of such practices to the corpus header, and using the TEI's declarable ele-

```
<projectDesc id=PD000>
    <p> The British National Corpus project is a pre-
        competitive collaboration between commercial and
        academic partners in the U.K. running from 1991 to
        1994.

        further descriptive material omitted...

    <p> Funding for the British National Corpus has been
        provided by ...
</projectDesc>
```

Fig. 5. Corpus header project description.

```
<samplingDecl id=SD000 default=Y>
    <p> Where a source text is a book, no more than 40,000
        words are sampled. This is true even where the book
        contains a collection of works from a selection of
        authors ...
    <p> No more than 120,000 words from any one author, whether
        individual or corporate, and whether writing
        individually or collaboratively, appear in the corpus
        ...
    </p>
</samplingDecl>
<samplingDecl id=SD001>
    <p> Where a source text is a book shorter than 40,000
        words, the whole text is captured, and ten per cent is
        then excised ...
    <p> No more than 120,000 words from any one author, whether
        individual or corporate, and whether writing
        individually or collaboratively, appear in the corpus
        ...
</samplingDecl>
<samplingDecl id=SD002>
    <p> Where the source text is a magazine or newspaper, the
        whole of the editorial text is captured ...
</samplingDecl>
<samplingDecl id=SD003>
    <p> The length of demographically-sampled spoken samples is
        limited by recording technology to ninety minutes. No
        word-count limit is applied.
</samplingDecl>
<samplingDecl id=SD004>
    <p> Samples of context-governed spoken material are
        truncated to no longer than 40,000 words ...
    </samplingDecl>
```

Fig. 6. Corpus header sampling declarations.

ment mechanism to associate particular practices with particular texts. This methodology is heavily used in the BNC, leaving only encoding information specific to single texts to appear in specific texts' headers.

The first element of the encoding description is the project description. Shown in Figure 5, it gives a prose description of the British National Corpus project.

A single project description covers the corpus and all texts in it. This is not the case with the sampling declarations which follow: there are five of these, covering respectively: books longer than 40,000 words; books shorter than 40,000 words; written material from sources other than books; demographically-sampled spoken material; and context-governed spoken material. Figure 6 shows them all. Two features are of note. Firstly, each declaration has an *id* attribute in order that it may be referenced from those texts to which it applies; secondly, descriptions which apply to more than one sampling method are repeated in each declaration to which they apply. (The limit on the number of words from any one author is a case in point.) This duplication is necessary because each

```
<editorialDecl>
    <correction status=medium method=tags id=CN000>
        <p> When noticed during encoding, errors or suspected
            errors in the original text are tagged with sic.
    </correction>
    <normalization method=silent id=NN000 default=y>
        <p> No normalization applied.
    </normalization>
    <normalization method=silent id=NN001>
        <p> Transcription uses standard English spelling,
            except for a control list of dialectal forms and
            vocalized pauses and does not reflect
            pronunciation.
    </normalization>
    ...
    <analysis id=AN000 default=y>
        <p> Part-of-speech information corresponding to the
            CLAWS C5 tag set is appended to each word ...
        <p> Overlapping speech is marked when two or three
            speakers are speaking simultaneously. The fourth
            and subsequent simultaneous utterances are not
            marked.
    </analysis>
    <analysis id=AN001>
        <p> Part-of-speech information corresponding to the
            CLAWS C5 tag set is appended to each word ...
    </analysis>
    ...
</editorialDecl>
```

Fig. 7. Corpus header editorial declarations.

text must refer to exactly one sampling declaration; it is not possible to factor common parts of two declarations into a third declaration, and then point from each text to two declarations. Duplication of this type occurs at several points in corpus and text headers, and, while it may be shown in the Figures, will not generally subsequently be mentioned in the text of this paper.

TEI P3 specifies a defaulting mechanism for declarable elements. This allows texts described by a default declaration to omit an explicit reference to that declaration. Although each sampling declaration applies to roughly equal numbers of texts, a default has been specified because BNC policy is that defaults should always be provided, thus allowing a little space to be saved in each text to which the default applies – see for example 5.5. (Designers of other corpora may wish to pursue a different policy.)

TEI P3 allows multiple declarations. This is useful in the case where a corpus contains a number of distinct text types, and uniform editing conventions have been applied to all texts of a particular type. In such a case, a text need only reference the single declaration which applies. A single declaration describing a variety of editorial conventions, as shown in Figure 7, is more appropriate to the BNC, in which different practices apply to different texts of the same type. For example, written texts obtained from existing electronic archives are treated in a manner different from those captured specifically for the BNC.

A consequence of the use of a single editorial declaration is that each text must reference exactly one of each type of child element of **<editorialDecl>**.

```
<refsDecl doctype=CDIF>
    <step gi=tei.2 att=n length=6 delim='-'>
    <step gi=seg att=n length=5>
</refsDecl>
```

Fig. 8. Corpus header reference declaration.

This reference may be implicit if there is only one such element – as is the case with **<correction>** in the Figure – or if a default declaration is supplied and is applicable. In other cases – **<analysis>**, for example – explicit references are required. The example texts (sections 5–7) show these references. They also also show that, while TEI P3 gives editorial declarations in an individual text's header higher precedence than those in the corpus header, no BNC text has such declarations in its header; the declarations in the corpus header always apply.

The encoding description continues with a reference declaration. That for the BNC is shown in Figure 8. The BNC reference scheme provides for a unique reference to any segment in the corpus. (A segment is broadly analogous to an orthographic sentence. All parts of each text in the corpus, whether conventionally sentential or not, are divided into segment elements.) These references should be used when material in the corpus is cited. The reference declaration specifies an algorithm for constructing such references by concatenating a hyphen separator and a five-character segment name with a six-character text name using the stepwise method described by TEI P3. (Segment names consist of five digits, and are unique within a particular text; text names consist of six alphanumeric characters, and are unique across the corpus.) Sample references to segments in the example texts discussed in sections 5–7 are Wingss-01009, GaWldA-00035 and 026211-0005. The reference declaration for the released BNC may have an extra element in order that a particular revision of the corpus may be specified. TEI P3 allows a single header to contain more than one reference declaration. This could be useful if some texts in the corpus had a reference mechanism applying to their source form – by page and line number, for example – and this information was preserved in the corpus. The BNC, however, does not heed its sources' reference schemes (in general, they have none), so a single reference declaration suffices.

The corpus header encoding description ends with the classification declaration, which contains one or more taxonomy elements. These define the dimensions along which texts in the corpus are classified, and legal values along each dimension. Figure 9 shows fragments of taxonomies relating to text type; to the medium and domain of written texts; and to the medium of spoken texts. As the Figure suggests, the necessary declarations can be lengthy, but the result is that the specification of the profile of a particular text relative to a taxonomy can be very compact. (See sections 5.3 and 7.3.)

The taxonomy of the BNC is complex, with each text being classified along many dimensions, although, while TEI P3 provides for a single text to assume multiple values in a given dimension, values assumed by a BNC text are always single. Some dimensions are important in balancing the content of the corpus relative to its design criteria. For example, BNC (1991a) specifies that the numbers of spoken texts recorded in the north, middle and south of Britain should be approximately equal. Such criteria are known as balance criteria. Other dimensions, while not used in balancing the content of the corpus, classify texts in manners which may be useful to corpus users. An example here is author sex for written works: while the design documents for the corpus do not specify a ratio of female to male authors (or, indeed of single-sex to mixed-sex collaborations), BNC (1991b) provides for such information to be recorded, although the examples in this paper do not show these classification criteria. Either balance or classification criteria may apply only to particular text types. For example, interaction type – monologue or dialogue – applies only to spoken texts.

A complex taxonomy can be specified in a number of ways. It may be specified as a single large taxonomy in which not all the dimensions specified apply to each text; or it may be split into a number of taxonomies where, if one dimension in a particular taxonomy applies to a particular text, then all the dimensions in that taxonomy apply. The BNC follows the latter course. Figure 9 shows a selection of the taxonomies defined in the corpus header.

4.3 *The profile description*

The profile description in the header of an individual text serves mainly to classify that text against criteria specified in the corpus header encoding description and elsewhere. The corpus header profile description might be expected to contain only profile information common to all texts in a corpus, and hence to be quite short. The language usage element, shown in Figure 10 is a case in point: it states that all texts in the BNC are examples of modern British English. It references a

```
<taxonomy id=TA000>
    <category>
        <catdesc> Text type </catdesc>
        <category id=CA000>
            <catdesc> Written published </catdesc>
        </category>
        <category id=CA001>
            <catdesc> Written unpublished </catdesc>
        </category>
        <category id=CA002>
            <catdesc> Spoken </catdesc>
        </category>
    </category>
</taxonomy>
<taxonomy id=TA001>
    <category>
        <catdesc>Medium (written published only) </catdesc>
        <category id=CA002>
            <catdesc> Books &amp periodicals </catdesc>
        </category>
        <category id=CA003>
            <catdesc> Miscellaneous </catdesc>
        </category>
        <category id=CA004>
            <catdesc> Written to be spoken </catdesc>
        </category>
    </category>
    <category>
        <catdesc>Domain (written published only) </catdesc>
        <category id=CA005>
            <catdesc> Imaginative <catdesc>
        </category>
        <category id=CA006>
            <catdesc> Applied science </catdesc>
        </category>
        ...
    </category>
</taxonomy>
<taxonomy id=TA006>
    <category>
        <catdesc> Medium (spoken only) </catdesc>
        <category id=CA00V>
            <catdesc> Demographic </catdesc>
        </category>
        <category id=CA00W>
            <catdesc> Context-governed </catdesc>
        </category>
    </category>
    ...
</taxonomy>
```

Fig. 9. Corpus header classification declaration.

```
<langUsage id=LU000>
    <language wsd=wsd.en id=EN>
        Modern British English
    </language>
    <p> The language of the British National Corpus is modern
        British English. Words, fragments, and passages from
        many other languages, both ancient and modern, occur
        within the corpus where these may be represented using
        a Latin alphabet. Long passages in these languages, and
        material in other languages, are generally silently
        deleted. In no case is the LANG attribute used to
        indicate the language of a word, phrase or passage, nor
        are alternate writing system definitions used.
</langUsage>
```

Fig. 10. Corpus header language usage declaration.

writing system declaration. As a modern, monolingual, corpus using a single alphabet, the BNC requires only a simple definition of its language usage: other types of corpus would be likely to require greater complexity in this area. (See 2.2.)

In addition to giving information applying to all texts in a corpus, the profile description can group information which describes aspects of particular texts or, more usefully, groups of texts. The types of information provided for by TEI P3 are more useful for grouping spoken material than for written, and it is for this purpose that the remainder of the profile description is used in the BNC.

```
<particDesc>
    <participant sex=m age=77 id=PA000>
        <person> Fred </person>
        <firstLang> British English; East Midlands dialect
        </firstLang>
        <residence> Northants, England </residence>
        <education> To age 14 </education>
        <occupation> Retired </occupation>
    </participant>
    <participant sex=f age=71 id=PA001>
        <person> Florence </person>
        <firstLang> British English; Midlands dialect
        </firstLang>
        <occupation> Retired </occupation>
    </participant>
    ...
    <participant sex=m age=37 id=PA006>
        <person> Steven </person>
        <firstLang> British English; East Midlands dialect
        </firstLang>
        <occupation> Office manager </occupation>
    </participant>
    ...
    <particLinks>
        <relation desc=husband active=PA000
            passive=PA001>
        <relation desc=father active=PA000
            passive=PA006>
        <relation desc=grandfather active=PA000
            passive='PA007 PA009'>
        <relation desc=father-in-law active=PA000
            passive=PA008>
        ...
    </particLinks>
</particDesc>
```

Fig. 11. Corpus header participant descriptions.

```
<revisionDesc>
    <change>
        <date> 1993-05-17 </date>
        <by> DFD </by>
        <what> Internal alpha test version </what>
    </change>
</revisionDesc>
```

Fig. 12. Corpus header revision description.

Figure 11 shows information which is common to a number of spoken texts in the corpus, and which consequently is encoded in the corpus header. It details the participants in a series of written texts, and the relationships between those participants. Texts in which these participants appear reference the descriptions by means of the *who* attribute on the **<u>** (utterance) tag, as shown in section 7.3.

4.4 *The revision description*

Figure 12 shows the corpus header revision description, which documents changes to the corpus header itself, and to the corpus as a whole. (Changes to individual texts in the corpus are described in the texts' own headers – see section 5.4.)

While the revision description in the initial released corpus may be expected to be larger than the stub shown in the Figure, it is not likely to be greatly expanded. Future revisions of the corpus, should there be any, will have more detailed revision descriptions which describe the global and corpus header changes made between successive revisions.

5. Text Header for a Non-Composite Written Text

This section is the first of three dealing with sample headers for three texts from the BNC. The subsections of this section discuss all parts of the text header; subsections for the second and third examples discuss only those aspects of the header which are of interest in connection with particular types of text.

The first example text is *Wings* (Pratchett, 1991), a novel. Because the source text contains more than 40,000 words, a whole number of chapters starting at the beginning of the book and totalling a little less than 40,000 has been captured. This example is a sample from the beginning of the source text; the BNC contains approximately equal numbers of beginning, middle and end samples.

As with all written published texts in the BNC, Pratchett (1991) was chosen by applying selection criteria to a number of lists of publications. BNC (1991a) describes the methodology. Half the texts in the corpus are chosen at random using the method described in BNC (1992a); the remainder are chosen from lists which suggest that a publication is influential in some manner (frequently borrowed from libraries; recommended reading on courses ...). Pratchett (1991), which has sold well, is an example of the latter class.

The header for the text is introduced by the markup shown in Figure 13. The name of the text, given by the *n* attribute of the <**TEI.2**> element, is for use in constructing references. (See 4.2.) This attribute is provided for the convenience of users of the BNC: its value duplicates information to be found in the edition statement. (See next section.)

```
<TEI.2 n=Wingss>
<teiHeader type=text n=1.0
        creator=OUCS status=new
        date.created=1993-05-17 id=A7CTH000>
```

Fig. 13. Header start for non-composite written text.

5.1 *The file description*

The file description of an electronic text begins with a statement of the title of the text, and of those responsible for its intellectual content as an electronic text. Thus, as shown in Figure 14, the title has the words "an electronic sample" appended so as to distinguish it from that of the source text. Following similar reasoning, the author of the source text is not named here; rather, those responsible for creating an electronic sample from the source text are named. Note here that it is the policy of the BNC to name the organization, rather than the individual, responsible.

```
<titleStmt>
    <title> Wings &mdash an electronic sample </title>
    <resp>
        <role>  Data capture </role>
        <name>  Oxford University Press </name>
    </resp>
    <resp>
        <role>  Encoding, storage and distribution </role>
        <name>  Oxford University Computing Services </name>
    </resp>
    <resp>
        <role>  Text enrichment </role>
        <name>  Unit for Computer Research into the English
                Language, University of Lancaster </name>
    </resp>
</titleStmt>
<editionStmt n=1.0>
    1.0
</editionStmt>
<extent>
    37875 words
    460 kbytes
</extent>
```

Fig. 14. Non-composite written file description start.

There are several thousand written texts with identical statements of responsibility in the BNC. Consequently, actual headers use an entity reference which expands to the text shown here.

The edition statement and extent statement, also shown in Figure 14, follow the title statement. All texts in the initial release version of the BNC will be at revision 1.0. Should there be further releases, some – but possibly not all – of the texts in a given release will have a revision level greater than 1.0, signifying that their content has changed relative to that of the corresponding text in the initial release of the corpus. Such changes should be described by the texts' revision descriptions. (See 5.4.)

The extent statement gives the size of the text (without header or mark-up) in orthographic words, and in kilobytes. The latter Figure is intended to be useful for users who examine free-standing headers (see 8) prior to copying complete texts to local storage. Information about the range of pages captured from the source text appears in the source statement. (See below.)

The next element of the file description, shown in Figure 15, is the publication statement. As with the title statement, this information pertains to the electronic, not to the source, text, and so describes how the electronic text may be obtained, and the usage restrictions attaching to it. Although much of the material in the publication statement is identical for every text in the BNC, there is provision to insert usage restrictions specific to a particular text if necessary. (See also 3.4.)

The publication statement also contains two <**idno**> elements giving identifying numbers for the

```
<publicationStmt>
    <resp>
        <role> Archive site </role>
        <name> Oxford University Computing Services </name>
    </resp>
    <address> ... </address>
    <idno type=bnc3> A73 </idno>
    <idno type=bnc6> Wingss </idno>
    <availability status=restricted>
        <p> Additional restrictions relating to a particular
            work (if any) are summarized here.
        <p> Available only as part of the British National
            Corpus at nominal charge for academic research
            purposes throughout the EC ...
    </availability>
    <date>
        1993-03-17
    </date>
</publicationStmt>
```

Fig. 15. Non-composite written text publication statement.

```
<notesStmt>
    <p> Attributions on the epigraphs at the start of each
        chapter refer to characters in the text.
</notesStmt>
```

Fig. 16. Non-composite written text notes statement.

electronic text. The first of these consists of three characters, and is used in generating unique identifiers (values for *id* attributes) for elements of the text and its header, as described in 3.2. The second identifier is the six-character name used in creating references to material in the corpus. (See section 4.2.) For written texts, these names are generally derived from the title or author name for the text.

The file description provides for a notes statement. A possible use is shown in Figure 16. Here, a characteristic of the text which was noted during transcription, and which may be confusing to future users, is described.

The final element of the file description is the source statement, a bibliographic record for the source text. As Figure 17 shows, the information is recorded in a **<biblStruct>** element, one of a number of element types offered by TEI P3. Note that the **<biblScope>** element gives the starting and ending pages of the electronic sample; the start and end pages for the complete source text (if appropriate, and if known) are given as a note in order that users may know how great a proportion of the source text is contained in the electronic sample.

5.2 *The encoding description*

As shown in Figure 18, the encoding description for a typical corpus text is very short, all necessary declarations having been made in the corpus header. (See 4.2.) The relevant definitions are referenced via the *decls* attribute of the **<text>** element. (See 5.5.)

```
<sourceDesc>
    <biblStruct>
        <monogr>
            <author> Terry Pratchett </author>
            <title> Wings </title>
            <edition>   First paperback edition, published
                        1991, reprinted 1992
            </edition>
            <imprint>
                <publ> Corgi </publ>
                <date> 1991 </date>
            </imprint>
            <biblScope type=pages> 13-115 </biblScope>
        </monogr>
        <idno type=ISBN> 0 552 52649 5 </idno>
        <note> Source page range: 13-172 </note>
    </biblStruct>
</sourceDesc>
```

Fig. 17. Non-composite written text source statement.

```
<encodingDesc>
    <projectDesc>
        <p> See project description in corpus header for
            information about the British National Corpus
            project.
    </projectDesc>
    <editorialDecl id=a73ed000>
        <p> Any editorial practice specific to a single text is
            described here. All other practices are referenced
            through decls on the text tag or by default.
    </editorialDecl>
    <tagUsage gi=div1 occurs=12 ident=0></tagUsage>
    ...
    <tagUsage gi=p occurs=2308 ident=0></tagUsage>
    <tagUsage gi=q occurs=12 ident=0></tagUsage>
    ...
</encodingDesc>
```

Fig. 18. Non-composite written text encoding description.

A project description is given, taking the form of a human-readable pointer to information in the corpus header. The semantics defined by TEI P3 specify that information given in a text header overrides corresponding information given in the corpus header. Thus, although helpful to users "eyeballing" a text, giving a project description in the text header prevents SGML- and TEI-aware processing software from finding the fuller information in the corpus header. The problem is overcome by listing the *id* of the corpus header project description among the declarations on the **<text>** element, as shown in 5.5. This makes TEI-aware processors ignore the information in the text header.

The Figure also shows an editorial declaration. Even this should not be required, being necessary only if some editorial procedure specific to a single corpus text has been applied. (There are currently no corpus texts for which this is the case.) Explicit or implicit references from the **<text>** element to editorial declarations in the corpus header (see 4.2 and 5.5) should be sufficient.

The encoding description ends with a series of tag usage elements. For each type of element which is a descendant of the **<text>** element of a BNC text, a **<tagUsage>** element is given. It lists the number of occurrences of the element, and the number of these

```
<profileDesc>
    <textClass>
        <catref scheme=TA000 target=CA000>
        <catref scheme=TA001
            target='CA002 CA005 CA00G CA00H CA00P'>
        <catref scheme=TA003 target=CA00T>
    </textClass>
</profileDesc>
```

Fig. 19. Non-composite written text profile description.

where the element has an *id* attribute – presumably indicating that it is referenced by some other element. TEI P3 allows **<tagUsage>** elements to have content describing the circumstances and manner in which a particular element is used. This information is not provided here in the BNC, but instead is provided globally as tag set documentation. (See TEI P3).

5.3 *The profile description*

The profile description for a written corpus text consists of a sequence of **<catref>** elements, as shown in Figure 19. These elements point back to elements of taxonomies in the corpus header, and so categorize the text relative to the dimensions defined there. Decoding the description of the example text, it is a written text (first **<catref>**); it is from a book or periodical, it is imaginative, it is addressed to a wide audience, it is a beginning sample, and it was published between 1975 and 1993 (second **<catref>**); and it was chosen for inclusion in the corpus because of its circulation or influence (third **<catref>**). Some of the corresponding category definitions may be seen in Figure 9.

Currently, no provision has been made in the BNC header for classification information such as author age, author sex, author domicile, audience age, and so on. Some of this information, such as author sex, can be handled with further **<catref>** elements, while the remainder will be encoded by using **<particDesc>** elements to describe the author and the audience as participants in the interaction mediated by the text. (See 4.3 for an example of the use of **<particDesc>** in connection with spoken texts.)

5.4 *The revision description*

Figure 20 shows the final element in the text header, the revision description. During development of the corpus, the revision description lists processing steps. The information will not appear in the published corpus. Should it be necessary to revise a text within the corpus after the corpus has been published, the revision

```
<revisionDesc>
    <change>
        <date> 1993-03-17 </date>
        <by> OUP </by>
        <what> Passed to OUCS </what>
    </change>
    <change>
        <date> 1993-04-07 </date>
        <by> OUCS </by>
        <what> Passed to Lancaster </what>
    </change>
    <change>
        <date> 1993-05-30 </date>
        <by> UCREL </by>
        <what> Passed to OUCS </what>
    </change>
    <change>
        <date> 1993-06-15 </date>
        <by> OUCS </by>
        <what> Accession to corpus </what>
    </change>
</revisionDesc>
```

Fig. 20. Non-composite written text revision description.

```
<text decls=PD000>
    <div1 type=chapter>
        <p> ...
</text>
</TEI.2>
```

Fig. 21. Non-composite written text.

description for the text in the next published version of the corpus will describe the changes made.

5.5 *The text*

Figure 21 shows the start and end of the actual text. The **<text>** element has a *decls* attribute which references those declarations – sampling, editorial and so on – which apply to the text. In the case of this example text, just one declaration is required – that for the project description. (The reason for this is explained in 5.2.) In all the other cases where declarations might be required, the default declarations describe this particular text, and therefore need not be enumerated.

6. Text Header for a Composite Written Text

The second example is a short extract from *The Guardian*, a British national daily newspaper. The start of its header is shown in Figure 22. It is the practice of the BNC to partition newspaper material into texts which group a number of stories dealing with the same type of subject matter – here, world affairs. The example is atypical, containing just two articles – most newspaper-derived texts contain many more.

```
<TEI.2 n=GaW1dA>
<teiHeader type=text n=1.0
        creator=OUCS status=new
        date.created=1993-05-17 id=B9HTH000>
```

Fig. 22. Header start for composite written text.

```
<titleStmt>
    <title>
        The Guardian, edition of 1989-11-08 &mdash an
        electronic collection of material related to world
        affairs
    </title>
    <resp>
        ... as for first example text
    </resp>
</titleStmt>
<editionStmt n=1.0>
    1.0
</editionStmt>
<extent>
    850 words
    12 kbytes
</extent>
```

Fig. 23. Composite written file description start.

```
<publicationStmt>
    <resp>
        ... as for first example text
    </address>
    <idno type=bnc3> B9H </idno>
    <idno type=bnc6> GaWldA </idno>
    <availability status=restricted>
        <p decls=B9HPS000>
            Additional restrictions relating to a particular
            analytic text or texts (if any) are summarized
            here. The decls attribute cross-references the
            analytic texts affected. Further paragraphs may
            summarize different restrictions applying to
            different analytic texts.
        <p> ... common information as for first example text
    </availability>
    <date>
        1993-03-30
    </date>
</publicationStmt>
```

Fig. 24. Composite written text publication statement.

```
<sourceDesc id=B9HPS000>
    <bibl.struct>
        <analytic><title> Quote&hellip </title></analytic>

        Following encoded as &GuardnA in second bibl.struct

        <monogr>
            <title> &lsqb;The Guardian, electronic edition of
                    1989-11-08&rsqb </title>
            <imprint> Guardian Newspapers Ltd. </imprint>
            <biblScope type=pages> 23 </biblScope>
        </monogr>
        <series><title> The Guardian </title></series>
        <idno type=ISSN> 0261 3077 </idno>
    </bibl.struct>
</sourceDesc>
<sourceDesc id=B9HPS001>
    <bibl.struct>
        <analytic><title> Diary </title>
            <author> Andrew Moncur </author></analytic>
        &GuardnA
    </bibl.struct>
</sourceDesc>
```

Fig. 25. Composite written text source statements.

```
    <text org=compo decls='PD000 SD002 HN002'>
        <div1 decls=B9HPS000>
            <head> Quote&hellip </head>
            <p> ...
        </div1>
        <div1 decls=B9HPS001>
            <head> Diary </head>
            <head type=byline> Andrew Moncur </head>
            <p> ...
        </div1>
    </text>
</TEI.3>
```

Fig. 26. Composite written text.

6.1 *The file description*

The title statement for the text, shown in Figure 23 is very similar to that for the first example text, discussed in 5.2. The publication statement of Figure 24 is more interesting. As stated in 5.2, specific permissions information may appear in the publication statements of individual non-composite texts. The same is true for composite texts, but is complicated by the fact that each element of the composite may potentially have its own specific restrictions on usage. The example shows how, by using the *decls* attribute on a paragraph, it may be associated with a particular element (or elements) of the composite. The identifiers (*ids*) point to the bibliographic records (see below) for the elements in question. In the absence of a *decls* attribute, a paragraph applies to all elements of the composite text.

The file description ends with a structured bibliographic record for each element of (analytic text in) the composite. These are shown in Figure 25. Each record has an identifier (*id*) attribute, so that it can be referenced by permission information (see above), and from the relevant part of the body of the text (see 6.3). Where an analytic text has an attribution, as in the second case, this is given. The second bibliographic record shows how an SGML entity reference may be used to replace material common to many records. This greatly reduces header size in cases where a single monographic text contains many analytic texts, each with its own bibliographic record.

6.2 *The text*

The profile and revision descriptions for the composite written text are much as for the non-composite text discussed in 5.3 and 5.4 respectively, and so are not discussed here.

Fragments of the composite text are shown in Figure 26. The two analytic texts may be seen, each encoded as a <**div1**> element. (See also 10.) These elements have *decls* attributes which point back to the relevant bibliographic record in the text header. (See 6.2.)

The enclosing <**text**> element also has a *decls* attribute. As well as selecting the correct project description (see 5.5), these override the default declarations for sampling and for the editorial treatment of hyphenation. (See Figure 5 for the former; the latter is not among the editorial declarations shown in Figure 7.)

```
<TEI.3 n=026211>
<teiHeader type=text n=1.0
        creator=OUCS status=new
        date.created=1993-05-17 id=QA0TH000>
```

Fig. 27. Header start for spoken text.

7. Text Header for a Spoken Text

The third and final example is a spoken text transcribed from a cassette tape recorded by a volunteer picked using a demographic sampling method. The BNC also includes context-governed spoken material, which is not discussed in this paper. (Burnage and Dunlop, 1993) gives an overview of sampling methods for spoken material, which are fully described in (BNC, 1991a).

The start of the corpus text is shown in Figure 27. The text name, given by the *n* attribute to **<TEI.2>** is numeric for all spoken texts in the BNC. This is just a convention, serving to distinguish spoken texts from the alphanumerically-named written texts.

7.1 *The file description*

Figure 28 shows the initial elements in the file description for the spoken text. This information is similar to that in the written examples presented in 5.1 and 6.1, and so is not discussed here. The source description of Figure 29 is, however, quite different from that for a written text. It consists of a recording statement rather than a bibliographic record. As is the case for many header elements, TEI P3 provides for the recording statement either to be a sequence of paragraphs, or to be structured. The BNC has elected to use the former approach in this case, with the first paragraph giving the date and time of recording, and the second the recording method. A more structured approach involving the **<broadcast>** element (not shown in the example) may be adopted for broadcast material included in the BNC.

7.2 *The profile description*

The profile description for spoken text is, as Figure 30 shows, rather more complex than that for a written text. In addition to the category references which describe the text, text and setting descriptions are required further to describe the interaction represented by the text.

```
<titleStmt>
    <title> Spoken material from respondent Fred, sample
            026211 </title>
    <resp>
        <role> Data capture and transcription </role>
        <name> Longman Dictionaries </name>
    </resp>
    <resp>
        ... as for first example text
    </resp>
</titleStmt>
<editionStmt n=1.0> 1.0 </editionStmt>
<extent>
    992 words
    20 kbytes
</extent>
<publicationStmt>
    <resp>
        ... as for first example
    </address>
    <idno type=bnc3> QA0 </idno>
    <idno type=bnc6> 026211 </idno>
    <availability status=restricted>
        ... as for first example
    <date> 1993-05-04 </date>
</publicationStmt>
```

Fig. 28. Start of file description for spoken text.

```
<sourceDesc>
    <recordingStmt>
        <recording dur='12.16 mins'>
        <p> <date> 1992-03-15 </date>
            <time> 17:05 </time>
        <p> Recorded by respondent on Walkman compact cassette
            recorder; dubbed for archival to Digital Audio tape
            at 44.1 kHz sampling rate; redubbed for
            transcription to compact cassette.
    </recordingStmt>
</sourceDesc>
```

Fig. 29. Source description for spoken text.

The text description is provided by TEI P3 for use with any text, but is used by the BNC only in connection with spoken texts. Even here, some elements – **<domain>**, **<factuality>**, and **<purpose>** – contain default values, as the data collection methodology does not capture this information. The developers of other spoken corpora may wish to provide useful values for these elements.

```
<profileDesc>
    <textDesc>
        <channel mode=s>
        <constitution type=single>
        <derivation type=original>
        <domain type='not stated'>
        <factuality type=inapplicable>
        <interaction type=complete>
        <preparedness type=none>
        <purpose type='not stated'>
    </textDesc>
    <settingDesc>
        <setting>
            <place> Rushden, Northants, U.K. </place>
            <time> 17:05 1992-03-15 </time>
            <locale> Home </locale>
            <activity> Making tea/playing games </activity>
        </setting>
    </settingDesc>
    <textClass>
        <catref scheme=TA000 target=CA001>
        <catref scheme=TA004 target='CA00V CA00Y'>
        <catref scheme=TA005 target='CA01D CA01H CA01K'>
    </textClass>
</profileDesc>
```

Fig. 30. Profile description for spoken text.

```
        <text decls='PD000 SD003 NN001 QN001 HN002 AN001'>
            <u who=PA001> ...
            <u who=PA008> ...
            <u who=PA002> ...
        </text>
    </TEI.3>
</TEI.corpus.2>
```

Fig. 31. Spoken text.

The setting description describes one or more settings in which an interaction takes place. In the case of most spoken material in the BNC, a single <**setting**> element always suffices: precise information about the location of individual participants (for example "under the sink", "on the doorstep") is not available, and no recordings have been made of interactions in which participants are widely separated (telephone conversations). This situation may change if, for example, recordings of broadcast interviews in which interviewer and interviewee are in different studios are obtained.

The category references which end the profile description characterize the text as spoken (first <**catref**>); demographic, Midland region (second <**catref**>); and as produced by a male aged 56 or over in social class DE (third <**catref**>). (See also 4.3 and Figure 9.)

Information about participants in demographic spoken material is held in the corpus, rather than the text, header because it is common to a number of texts: the BNC demographic data collection methodology results in the same speakers appearing in many texts. This is not the case with context-governed material, in which participants (or participant groups) typically appear only in a single text. For this material (not shown in this paper), participant information appears in the text header profile description.

7.3 *The text*

Figure 31 shows the framework of the spoken text. The DECLS attribute of its <**text**> element overrides default declarations for project description (see 5.5), sampling, and for a number of editorial practices: normalization, hyphenation, quotation and analysis (see 4.3.). The defaults in the BNC favour written texts, resulting in a greater need to override them for spoken texts.

The body of the spoken text consists of a sequence of utterances. Each <**u**> element has a *who* attribute to identify the speaker. These attributes correspond to *id* attributes on <**participant**> elements in the corpus header. (See 4.3 and 7.2.)

8. Free-Standing Headers and the BNC

TEI P3 discusses the use of headers as free-standing bibliographic records. It is intended that, in addition to their use in conjunction with their associated texts, BNC headers should be usable in this manner. In particular, a corpus user should, by reference to the BNC corpus header and a collection of BNC text headers alone, be able to select texts which conform to some set of user designated criteria. (Imaginative written texts targeted at a wide audience and containing quotations, for example.) The advantages of this approach are twofold: firstly, the user saves a great deal of local storage through not needing the full corpus in order to make selections of this type; secondly, the user need not undertake the copyright responsibility defined by the BNC end user agreement (BNC, 1992b) for texts which are not of interest – only selected texts need be fetched from a central archive after they have been identified by reference to their headers.

9. The Automatic Generation of Headers

All of the information presented in BNC text headers, and much of the information in the corpus header, is derived from data stored in a relational database under the control of the Ingres database manager (Ingres, 1989). The headers are, in effect, database reports delivered in a format which conforms to SGML syntax and to TEI P3. The structure of the database (BNC, 1992b) is intended to eliminate duplication of data, even where duplicated information appears in headers. (For example, in the bibliographic records of composite source texts – see 6.1.)

Use of a database makes it possible to identify information which is duplicated, and so identify candidates for movement out of text headers into the corpus header. A case in point might be an author whose work appears in one or more books sampled for the corpus, and in newspapers or journals. Participant information for this author (see 5.3) could be centralized in the corpus header (4.3) rather than being duplicated in text headers. (However, it should be noted that TEI P3, while stating that it is intended that participant descriptions be useful for written, as well as for spoken, texts, propose no mechanism for linking elements of written texts to participant descriptions.)

The database can also help to identify elements which, because they have identical content in many headers, are candidates for replacement with space-saving entity references. (See 3.3 and 6.1.)

10. Grouping in Composite Texts

TEI P3 describes a <**group**> element, which allows the encoding of composite texts of arbitrary complexity. Unfortunately, this element was specified by the TEI after encoding of the composite texts in the BNC had commenced. Consequently, composite texts are represented in the BNC as <**text**> elements having the attribute *org=compo* (composite, rather than the default of sequential, organization), and containing a sequence of <**div0**> or <**div1**> elements. Those engaged in future corpus development projects should take advantage of <**group**>s where possible.

11. Summary and Conclusions

Experience in developing corpus and text headers for a large and relatively diverse corpus has shown that the model recommended by the TEI is adequate to the needs of such undertakings. Areas in which the TEI model was feared to be unnecessarily verbose – for example, the need to give full bibliographic records for each element of a composite text – have proved in the event not to present problems. However, one important area remains to be addressed: there is no mechanism allowing information in the corpus header to link together all texts sharing some feature in common. Such a feature would be useful to corpus users wishing to identify all texts by a given author, all editions of a particular newspaper, all conversations involving a particular participant, and so on. While some queries of this type can be satisfied by textual searches on fields in text headers, others currently require time-consuming examination of the text of large parts of the corpus. Work continues in co-operation with the Text Encoding Initiative to address this issue.

References

BNC, TGAW15. *Spoken Corpus Design Specification.* British National Corpus project document, 1991a. (*Note*: Copies of British National Corpus project documents may be obtained by sending electronic mail to the author at natcorp@vax.ox.ac.uk.)

BNC, BNCW08. *Written Corpus Design Specification.* British National Corpus project document, 1991b.

BNC, TGAP21. *Selecting Titles for the British National Corpus.* British National Corpus project document, 1992a.

BNC, TGBP05. *BNC Permissions Request.* British National Corpus project document, 1992b.

BNC, TGDW36. *The New BNC Database.* British National Corpus project document, 1992c.

Burnage, Gavin and Dominic Dunlop. "Encoding the British National Corpus". In *English Language Corpora: Design, Analysis and Exploitation.* Ed. Jan Aarts, Pieter de Haan and Nelleke Oostdijk. Amsterdam and Atlanta: Editions Rodopi, 1993, pp. 79–95.

Giordano, Richard. "The TEI Header". In this volume.

Goldfarb, Charles F. *The SGML Handbook.* Oxford: Oxford University Press, 1990.

Ingres. *Introducing Ingres for the UNIX and VMS Operating Systems.* Alameda, CA: Relational Technology Inc., 1989.

ISO. *ISO 8879:1986 Information Processing – Structured Generalized Markup Language.* Geneva: International Organization for Standardization, 1986.

ISO. *ISO 646:1991 Information Processing – ISO 7-bit Coded Character Set for Information Interchange.* Geneva: International Organization for Standardization, 1991.

Pratchett, Terry. *Wings.* London: Corgi, 1991.

Sperberg-McQueen, C.M. and Lou Burnard. *Guidelines for Electronic Text Encoding and Interchange (TEI P3).* Chicago, Oxford: Text Encoding Initiative, 1994.

TEI P3. See Sperberg-McQueen and Burnard.

PART III: ENCODING SPECIFIC TEXT TYPES

Computers and the Humanities **29**: 99–111, 1995.

Encoding Verse Texts

David Chisholm *
Department of German Studies, University of Arizona, Tucson AZ, 85721, USA
chisholm@ccit.arizona.edu

and

David Robey *
Department of Italian Studies, The University of Manchester, Oxford Road, Manchester, UK
e-mail: robey@vax.ox.ac.uk

Key words: SGML, verse, poetry, tagging, text encoding, TEI

Abstract

This article identifies problems and proposes solutions for encoding verse texts in SGML. It is organized around a series of distinctions and oppositions which the TEI Work Group on Verse regard as significant. These include examination of the formal properties which distinguish verse from prose, followed by discussions of (1) text-searching vs analysis, (2) markup vs algorithms, (3) markup vs transcription, (4) uniformity vs choice, (5) specificity vs generality, (6) metrical convention vs linguistic realization, (7) structural vs non-structural divisions and (8) fidelity vs interpretation. Using German and English verse forms as illustrations, the advantages and disadvantages of pre-line tagging, in-line tagging and feature structure analysis are discussed. We suggest that metrical and rhyme conventions always be tagged at the highest possible level of text divisions.

1. Introduction

This article discusses and illustrates the recommendations of the TEI Verse Work Group, and seeks to identify the main issues underlying the use of the Standard Generalized Markup Language (SGML) for encoding verse texts. The ideas and suggestions put forward here represent not only our own reflections, but also discussions with the other members of the Work Group on Verse and with members of the Committee on Text Analysis and Interpretation.[1] Our general and theoretical remarks are followed by some examples of marked up texts from the German and English verse traditions. These fragments do not include Document Type Definitions (DTDs), and have not been tested with an SGML parser. The essay does not aim at completeness, but is intended rather as a discussion – with illustrations – of various approaches to the encoding of texts of this kind.

Before the first meeting of the Verse Work Group all the relevant bulletin boards were circularized with a request for information about methods and standards from any colleagues who have been engaged in encoding verse texts. Only a very few answers were received.

* David Chisholm is Professor of German Studies at the University of Arizona. His interests include German lyric poetry and verse drama, metrics and versification, linguistic and computational approaches to literature, and phonological and prosodic aspects of literary style. His publications include "Computer-assisted Research in German Language and Literature" in the *German Quarterly* (1985), *Verskonkordanz zu Goethes "Faust, Erster Teil"* (with Stephen P. Sondrup, 1986), "Phonological Patterning in Twentieth Century German Verse and Prose" in *Descriptio Linguistica* (1986) and "Lexicality and the Versification of Johann Heinrich Voss" in *Insights in Germanic Linguistics* (1994).

David Robey is Professor of Italian at Manchester University and Dean of the Faculty of Arts. He has worked on Italian Renaissance Humanism, modern literary theory (editor and author with Ann Jefferson of *Modern Literary Theory: A Comparative Introduction*), and on the computer analysis of medieval and Renaissance narrative poetry. He is currently engaged in a metrical study of the *Divine Comedy*, and was Chair of the Verse Work Group of the Text Encoding Inititiative.

From this we concluded that, although a large number of verse texts now exist in machine-readable form, they have frequently been encoded in an ad hoc (and in many cases insufficiently considered) way, and that no substantial consensus yet exists concerning methods and standards among the scholars who have worked in this area. The Work Group's recommendations are therefore in many respects pioneering; it has had to try to decide the sorts of things that might interest encoders in the future, rather than formulating the established practice of the present. In view of the magnitude of this task, the few months it had at its disposal were were far from sufficient; there was no chance of producing as full a report as the task would ideally require. Our work has thus necessarily been open-ended, selective and tentative, and has concentrated as much on the attempt to identify problems as on the prescription of detailed encoding practices. As a result it seems appropriate to organize the pages that follow around a series of issues, expressed in the form of oppositions, rather than proceeding in order through a series of recommendations.

2. Verse vs Prose

The Work Group's subject comprises narrative and lyric poetry in fixed and free verse-forms; dramatic verse, which is dealt with elsewhere in P3, is excluded (see Lavagnino and Mylonas in this volume). What encodable features are specific to texts of this category? A major part of the answer is covered by the term "verse structure", in the sense of the set of formal properties that distinguish verse from prose. Thus the Work Group's main recommendations regard the encoding of meter and rhyme, as well as the characteristic hierarchical divisions that verse texts use. The term "verse structure" can also include typographical layout; this is especially important in the case of free verse, where, for instance, indentations, blank lines, blank spaces within the line, and page breaks can be used in a distinctively poetic fashion. Layout has not been extensively discussed by the group, however, and will not be considered further here, since adequate means of encoding it are provided in the parts of the Guidelines specifically concerned with typographical issues.

In addition, the Work Group has spent some time on aspects of the language and content of verse texts that are not parts of verse structure as defined above, but are still significant constituents of the texts' distinctive literary character; they include features of narrative structure, thematic patterns, rhetorical and stylistic analysis. While these aspects will be discussed briefly below, they have received a much smaller share of attention, since they are also the province of the other work groups concerned with literature.

3. Text Searching vs Analysis

We can distinguish two main uses of computerized verse texts. The first, text-searching, involves the production or use of tools for more or less conventional kinds of literary scholarship, tools such as concordances, indices, etc., and facilities for on-line searching. In this respect the computer makes an important but subordinate contribution to the scholar's work. This use will usually require only minimum markup of texts; it may be sufficient simply to tag the standard reference categories (book, canto, stanza, etc.) used for the text in question. Advanced concordancing and indexing may of course involve lemmatization, but the purely grammatical or lexical information that this process requires is the concern of a different work group.

The second main use of computerized verse texts, which we may call analysis, is more technical and systematic; it tends mostly to involve linguistic or statistical approaches to literature, notably for identifying and comparing literary styles and for solving questions of disputed authorship. This use may require very extensive markup, though often in categories of only limited interest to the broader community of potential students of the machine-readable text. The Work Group tried to cover both of these two kinds of use in its recommendations; the distinction between them is connected, however, to a further opposition which we discuss below, that between required and optional markup.

4. Markup vs Algorithms

It might be argued, when one tries to predict the future developments and related needs of verse-text encoding, that much of the analysis which currently requires extensive manual markup will in due course be carried out by electronic means. New parsers, notably, and new electronic dictionaries will permit automatic lemmatization, phonetic or phonological transcription, and labelling by semantic fields, to an extent that is not possible today. As resources expand and technology evolves, so we might expect that some of the suggestions made below for tagging systems will lose some of their relevance. For instance, the need for the kind of markup of stress and syllable structure that we discuss, in relation to meter and rhyming schemes, might be reduced in the future with the widespread availability of electronic dictionaries incorporating phonetic transcriptions of words. Indeed, the expectation that such resources will in due course become accessible may be one reason why the markup of verse texts seems not to have advanced very far in the scholarly community. However, there can be no question of replacing markup altogether by automatic processing. At the very least, markup will still be needed to record the results of such processing. But in any case, operations such as the analysis of meter must always entail an element of critical judgement that no program could ever perform. Electronic dictionaries and the like will substantially aid these operations, but never carry them out completely.

5. Markup vs Transcription

In some kinds of computer analysis of verse it may be necessary to work on a phonetic or phonological transcription, rather than, or as well as, a marked up version of the text.

The need for such a transcription to be encoded separately will vary from language to language. Italian and Spanish are sufficiently regular in their orthography to allow the transcription to be performed, within limits, by simple algorithms. The same is not true of English where, for instance, studies of sound repetitions may well require – in the absence of the sort of electronic look-up facilities described in the preceding paragraph – the previous encoding of a phonological transcription that will have to be manually produced. The Work Group has not itself made any recommendations on the subject of transcriptions, however, since they are covered by other parts of the TEI Guidelines: standard SGML entity names have been defined for the IPA character set, for the purposes of phonetic or phonological transcription; and the recommended procedures for text alignment may be used to link the transcription to the original poem.

6. Required vs Optional Markup

The distinction between required and optional markup is an issue which all work groups have had to confront. In our case, given that scholars concerned with verse encoding seem unable to reach any significant consensus as to good practice, it is perhaps appropriate to keep required markup to a minimum. This means that we should encode in TEI form the standard reference categories relating to the major structural divisions of the text (canto, stanza, etc.). To reintroduce the distinction made earlier, required markup is the minimum for purposes of text-searching, and does not comprise any of the additional categories that might be deployed for text analysis. Any user of a machine-readable verse text is likely to want to search it, and thus needs the standard reference categories to be encoded. Not all users will want to engage in the more specialist activities for which we have used the term analysis; if they do, the kinds of feature they will want to mark up are likely to vary significantly from case to case.

If the work in question is taken from a standard edition (which must be identified in the header), the reference categories employed by this edition should be used. If the electronic text represents a new edition of the work, the encoder should state in the Encoding Description which major divisions are interpretative or contentious and, if possible, any authority for them, such as another edition. In addition to this, and optionally, any other markup the encoder thinks will aid a significant number of researchers with varying points of view may be included if he or she so wishes. It is of course vital that the encoder should make clear, in the Encoding Description, the extent to which such markup depends on his or her theory.

7. Uniformity vs Choice

This takes us on to the important general point, that the peculiar issues involved in the encoding of verse texts can make the choice of tagging system an extremely contentious matter. For the minimum markup that we think should be required, it would clearly be inappropriate to leave the choice to individual encoders. In accordance with the preceding section, therefore, we have recommended a uniform system of markup for the standard reference categories of each text. Moreover, in view of their fundamental importance to almost any kind of verse analysis, we have also recommended that the uniform markup system be extended to all hierarchical divisions of verse texts, both below and above the level of the line. This uniform system is discussed further below. However, while we also make a variety of proposals below concerning the tagging of other features of verse texts, we have put these forward as suggestions, not as binding rules. The reason has not only to do with the absence of established practices, to which reference has already been made; it also concerns the pluralistic nature of literary studies as a whole. Analytical terminology always depends to a greater or lesser degree on theory, and literary or critical theory is a remarkably faction-ridden subject. For all features other than hierarchical divisions, therefore, it needs to be emphasized that the TEI Guidelines leave encoders the option to define their own tagging systems if they so wish.

The treatment of stylistic or rhetorical devices such as metaphor is a case in point. It might have been possible, for instance, to recommend a tagging system such as **<metaphor tenor=... vehicle= ...>** ... **</metaphor>**; but given the problems of definition involved, and the great richness of modern metaphor theory, it is clear that such a format would have seemed objectionable to some and excessively restrictive to many. Leaving the choice of tagging terminology to individual encoders carries with it a vital corollary, however: that the encoder be utterly explicit, in the Encoding Description, about the methods of tagging used and the criteria and definitions on which they rest.

8. Specificity vs Generality

For the verse line itself the standard tag **<l>** has been a long-standing feature of the Guidelines, but for the hierarchical divisions above and below the line a major issue arises as to the relative merits of a familiar, specific vocabulary, and a neutral, general system such as the **<div1>**, **<div2>** ... tags included in the Guidelines' recommendations for prose texts. The following hierarchy can serve as an example of the first, specific, alternative:

<poem>
<book>
<canto>
<stanza>
<line-group> (quatrain, tercet)
<couplet>
<l>
<part-line> (hemistich et sim.)
<foot>
<syllable>

There are a number of arguments in favour of this alternative, most obviously that of ease of use, at least for many kinds of poem. On the other hand it would be inappropriate for particular types of verse, especially since our recommendations cover both lyric and narrative genres. It would also be inappropriate for certain literary cultures; the TEI Guidelines cannot afford to be culturally or historically provincial, but must build into their recommendations the flexibility and neutrality that would allow them to handle little-known traditions (as far as Europe and America are concerned), such as classical Chinese poetry. Moreover, recommending the use of specific and familiar terms raises serious problems of definition, and risks antagonizing potential users by appearing to prejudge the way in which they should do their analysis.

For these reasons we have preferred to start with the numbered or unnumbered **<div>** hierarchy of elements recommended by the Guidelines for the encoding of prose texts. When this is used, the meaning of each element must be determined by the encoder and defined in the Encoding Description in the TEI Header and/or in the form of attributes for each tag.

If the *type* attribute is used as a vehicle for the more specific terminology – e.g. **<div2 type=canto>** – then at the cost of some extra length the advantages of the general and the specific are combined. Those who dislike the general part of the system can easily eliminate it for their own private use, since strictly speaking it need only be included in the text for purposes of interchange. Our recommendation is that the **<div>** system be used for the upper-level divisions of verse as well as of prose texts. For the lower-level groupings of verse lines, such as stanzas, the numbered or unnumbered **<lg>** tags should be used in preference to the **<div>** tags, which are best reserved for larger sections of text. If desired, however, the **<div>** system may be extended down to any level above that of the verse line (**<l>**), since there might well be circumstances where it is helpful to have two alternative systems of names. The availability of **<lg>** tags alongside **<div>** tags is particularly useful not only where the hierarchy of divisions extends beyond the legal limit of **<div7>**, but also where the hierarchical structure differs from one part of a given document to another. For instance, in a poem (**<div1>**) divided into books, some of which are sub-divided into sections and others not, the **<div2>** tag could be used for the books and **<div3>** for the sections; for the next level of subdivision, for instance into stanzas, the numbered or unnumbered **<lg>** tag should be used instead of <**div4**>, not only because of the greater appropriateness of the name, but also because (where there are no intermediate divisions between books and stanzas) the <**div4**> tag could not nest directly within <**div2**>.

Given the central status of the line in virtually any kind of verse analysis, our preference was that a distinct but analogous series of tags should be used to mark the divisions below this level: <**ldiv1**>, <**ldiv2**>, <**ldiv3**>, etc. For reasons of economy, however, P3 uses instead the <**seg**> tag, which serves to mark any phrase-level unit of text, and is available like <**div**> and <**lg**> in both numbered and unnumbered versions. As above, the encoder can attach the appropriate familiar and specific term to each level of the system either in the Encoding Description, or as a *type* attribute of each element. An illustration of the recommended scheme is therefore the following:

```
<div1 type=poem>
<div2 type=book>
<div3 type=canto>
<lg1 type=stanza>
<lg2 type=quatrain>
<lg3 type=couplet>
<l>
<seg1 type=hemistich>
<seg2 type=foot>
<seg3 type=syllable>
```

One major advantage of the numbered <**div...**>, <**lg...**> and <**seg...**> systems is that they offer a clear representation of the hierarchy of text divisions, and are thus, in our view, generally to be preferred to the unnumbered versions for the encoding of verse. The latter are obviously useful for any cases where there might be difficulties in employing a strictly numbered hierarchy. There is also a practical advantage to the numbered versions, that the *type* attribute only needs to be specified once in each case; where the unnumbered versions are used to represent more than one level in a hierarchy, the *type* attribute has to be specified each time the level changes. Note, however, that for segmentations of a syntactic as opposed to a metrical nature the Guidelines provide the <**s**>, <**cl**>, <**phr**>, tags, for sentence-type divisions, clauses and phrases respectively; these may be used in place of <**seg type=sentence**>, etc., below the level of the verse-line and above. The following is an example (from Byron's *Beppo*) of the combination of the <**lg**>, <**seg...**> and <**cl**> tags:

```
<lg1 type=stanza n=70)
    <lg2 type=quatrain>
        <l><cl><seg1 type=foot n=1>He was <seg1 n=2>a
          Turk,
          <seg1 n=3>the co<seg1 n=4>lour of <seg1 n=5>
            mahogany;
        <l><cl><seg1 n=1>And Lau<seg1 n=2>ra saw
          <seg1 n=3>him,
          <cl> and <seg1 n=4>at first <seg1 n=5>was
            glad,
        <l><cl><seg1 n=1>Because <seg1 n=2>the Turks
          <seg1 n=3>so much <seg1 n=4>admire <seg1
            n=5>philogyny,
        <l><cl><seg1 n=1>Although <seg1 n=2>their
          u<seg1 n=3>sage of <seg1 n=4>their wives <seg1
            n=5>is sad;
...
```

This seems awfully cumbersome, but one can envisage important uses of this kind of combination of tags for the analysis of the interrelations of syntax and meter.

9. Convention vs Realization

In the treatment of meter and rhyme there is a fundamental distinction between metrical convention and linguistic realization. (Linguistic realization may in its turn be distinct from a real performance of a text; the former can be represented in phonological, the latter in phonetic terms.) For the purposes of tagging metrical convention it should be sufficient to use *met* (for "metrical convention") and *rhyme* attributes for the <**div...**>, <**lg...**> and <**l**> elements, with, as their values, standard terms such as "sonnet", "canzone", "hexameter", "alexandrine", etc., and/or the "ABBA ABBA..." notation for rhymes, and/or a graphic representation such as "+", "–", "/", "|", "o" for prominent and non-prominent syllable positions, line endings, foot boundaries and optional syllables respectively. (See *Guidelines*, 260ff.) The exact format of these values is best left to the individual encoder, with the important proviso that the usage in question be clearly explained in the Encoding Description in the TEI Header (the Guidelines provide a structured means for doing this). The general principle should be to tag conventions at the highest possible level of the hierarchy of text divisions. At each lower level, the default value of the *met* and *rhyme* attributes is inherited from the parent element.

The tagging of the linguistic realization is made difficult, in the case of stress-patterns, by the fact that these may involve either quantity or pitch or volume or (conceivably) a combination of more than one of these; and that it may be necessary to distinguish between primary and secondary stress, and/or between word-stress, phrase-stress and metrical stress. Given the confusion that exists about the terminology normally used for this sort of phenomenon, it would be best for the TEI not to propose a fixed set of terms and notations, but once again to leave the detailed form of these to the individual encoder. Whatever forms are chosen, a convenient means of encoding them is as values of the *real* (for "linguistic realization") attribute of the **<lg>**, **<l>** or **<seg>** elements. Stress-patterns can thus be marked up through either pre-line or in-line tagging, as attributes of any relevant element in the hierarchy of divisions of the text. They also need only be specified where there is a clash with or deviation from the convention, since the default value of the *real* attribute is that of the relevant *met* attribute; i.e. where *real* attributes are given for some but not all of the segmentations of a given level of the text, their default value in the remaining segmentations at that level is the value of the applicable *met* attribute (but it would be wise for the encoder to make this doubly clear in the Encoding Description). An alternative employed below is the use of a **<clash>** element, though this is not included in the Guidelines.

The other main aspect of linguistic realization that may be encoded comprises the various types of rhyme (end-rhyme, internal rhyme, rich/normal rhymes, masculine/feminine rhymes), all considered here to the extent that they may be constitutive elements of verse structure and not optional stylistic devices. The conventions relating to these would be tagged at the highest possible level of the hierarchy of text divisions, as with the metrical conventions dealt with above, and using the *rhyme* attribute provided in the Guidelines. The linguistic realizations may be tagged at the appropriate lower level: the phonological form of the rhyme, its category or type (rich, masculine, etc.), choices of rhyme pattern (ABBA versus ABAB, etc.) within the chosen convention. (In some cases, obviously, there will be uncertainty as to whether a given phenomenon might be treated as convention or realization, an uncertainty which the individual encoder will have to resolve.) No specific provision is made in the Guidelines for the encoding of rhyme realization as opposed to convention; the choice of terminology and symbols can once again be left to the individual encoder with the usual proviso. Either pre-line or in-line tagging could be used, and is probably best effected by creating new attributes (e.g. *rhyme_real*) of the **<div...>**, **<lg...>**, **<l>** or **<seg...>** elements. Similar measures could be devised for the markup of other sound patterns, such as alliteration and assonance.

There are further means available in the Guidelines for marking up aspects of linguistic realization. A selection from the entities recommended for the transcription of the IPA character set may be used for the purposes of phonological representation; in particular the entities representing the suprasegmental symbols for primary and secondary stress provide an economical means for the in-line marking of vowel accentuation, as an alternative to the lengthier procedures described here. Note that information about the use of such entities must be included in the Encoding Description. Finally, P3 provides the empty tag **<caesura>** for the feature in question, and an attribute *enjamb* for the **<l>** element for lines where there is enjambement with the line following. Encoders interested in defining different degrees of enjambement may express the value of this attribute accordingly.

10. Illustration: The German Classical Distich

This unrhymed verse form, borrowed from Greek and Latin versification and adapted to the German language in the late eighteenth century, consists, in its German manifestation, of a two-line group (a Classical hexameter line followed by a Classical pentameter line) in which each line consists of six feet, and each foot consists of one syllable in a prominent position of the meter followed by either 0, 1 or 2 syllables in non-prominent positions. There are, however, limitations on the poet's choice of the number of syllables in certain positions of the line. The metrical pattern of this distich can be represented as follows:

```
         1 2   3 4   5 6   7 8   9 10   11 12
Line 1:  + –   o + – o + – o + – o + –   – +   –
Line 2:  + –   o + – o +     + – o + –   – +
```

where "+" stands for a syllable in a metrically prominent position, "-" for a required and "o" for an optional syllable in a non-prominent position. Note that in the so-called pentameter line (Line 2) the pattern stipulates that there be no syllables in positions 6 and 12; position 10 must be disyllabic in both lines.

The following is an example from the beginning of Goethe's seventh Roman Elegy:

```
+  –    +     – – +   –    – +    – +    –  –  + –
O  wie  fuehl ich in Rom mich so froh! gedenk' ich der Zeiten,
+  –    –    +  – –     +    + –     – + –     – +
Da mich ein  graulicher Tag  hinten  im Norden umfing ...
```

Since the two-line pattern is repeated throughout the poem, the metrical pattern for the distich can be encoded in SGML at the highest possible level in the hierarchy of text divisions, i.e. before the first line of the poem, so that it applies to the whole poem (or to a series of poems written in the same meter – e.g. all 20 of Goethe's Roman Elegies). Any deviations from or variations of this metrical pattern in the linguistic realization can be indicated, as we have said, either by "pre-line tags" or "in-line tags" within the body of the poem.

The following example shows the same two lines with a pre-poem declaration "at the top", and the pre-line tags to the left of each line. The attribute *metrical-unit* below refers to a recurring sequential pattern of stressed and unstressed syllables, for example an "iamb" in iambic verse, or a "trochee" in trochaic verse. The attribute *metrical-domain* indicates the number of lines over which the metrical pattern extends – in this case the two lines of the Classical Distich. Neither of these attributes are contained as such in the Guidelines, but are included here as examples of the user-defined modifications which the Guidelines allow. The value used here for the *met* attribute will have been explained in the Encoding Description of the TEI Header; this will have made clear, among other things, that the metrical pattern described repeats itself every two lines in the poem. (The lines below beginning with "<! - -" and ending with "- ->" are SGML comments.)

```
<text>
   <div1 n=poem id=re7 metrical-unit=foot metrical-domain
      =distich met=+–o+–o+–o+–o+– –+–/+–o+–o++
      –o+– –+/>
<! - - "o" represents an optional syllable in the metrical - ->
<! - - pattern. - ->
      <div2 n=distich>
         <l n=1 real=+–+– –+– –+–+– –+–> O wie
            fuehl ich in Rom mich so froh! gedenk' ich der
            Zeiten,
         <l n=2 real=+– –+– –++– –+– –+> Da mich ein
            graulicher Tag hinten im Norden umfing...
...
</text>
```

Using in-line tags, these two lines could be marked as follows, where the user-defined **<opt-syll>** ... **</opt-syll>** tags surrounding a syllable indicate that it is the linguistic realization of the optional syllable in the metrical pattern:

```
<l n=1>O wie fuehl ich <opt-syll>in</opt-syll>
   Rom mich <opt-syll>so</opt-syll> froh!
   gedenk' ich der Zeiten,
<l n=2>Da mich <opt-syll>ein</opt-syll>
   grauli<opt-syll>cher</opt-syll> Tag hinten
   <opt-syll>im</opt-syll> Norden umfing.
```

The problem of marking up optional non-prominent syllables in many positions of the line arises with a number of prevalent verse-forms in both the German and English traditions, e.g. folk poetry, knittelvers, strong stress meter, and old Germanic and Old English alliterative verse.

11. "Line Groups" vs "Stanzas"

A further problem in encoding verse texts arises from the difference between "stanzas" – i.e. recurring line-groups which are identical in meter (e.g. iambic tetrameter), rhyme pattern (e.g. abab) and number of lines – and other line-groups which vary in meter, rhyme pattern, and/or number of lines. We can simply refer to the latter as "line-groups" to distinguish them from "stanzas". A poem in "free rhythms" containing "line-groups" rather than "stanzas" is Goethe's "Ganymed":

```
<div0 type=poem>
   <lg1 type=line-group n=1>
      <l>Wie im Morgenrot
      <l>Du rings mich angluehst,
      <l>Fruehling, Geliebter!
      <l>Mit tausendfacher Liebeswonne
      <l>Sich an mein Herz draengt
      <l>Deiner ewigen Waerme
      <l>Heilig Gefuehl,
      <l>Unendliche Schoene!
   <lg1 n=2>
      <l>Dass ich dich fassen moecht'
      <l>In diesen Arm!
   <lg1 n=3>
      <l>Ach, an deinem Busen
      <l>Lieg' ich, schmachte,
      <l>Und deine Blumen, dein Gras
      <l>Draengen sich an mein Herz.
```

```
      <l>Du kuehlst den brennenden
      <l>Durst meines Busens,
      <l>Lieblicher Morgenwind,
      <l>Ruft drein die Nachtigall
      <l>Liebend nach mir aus dem Nebeltal.
   <lg1 n=4>
      <l>Ich komme! Ich komme!
      <l>Wohin? Ach, wohin?
   <lg1 n=5>
      <l>Hinauf, hinauf strebt's,
      <l>Es schweben die Wolken
      <l>Abwaerts, die Wolken
      <l>Neigen sich der sehnenden Liebe,
      <l>Mir, mir!
   <lg1 n=6>
      <l>In eurem Schosse
      <l>Aufwaerts,
      <l>Umfangend umfangen!
      <l>Aufwaerts
      <l>An deinem Busen,
      <l>Alliebender Vater!
   </lg1>
</div0>
```

By contrast, consider now the following poem by Goethe (given here with only a limited amount of markup) in which each of the three differing line-groups has its own definite metrical pattern and rhyme scheme (alternating 4- and 3-stress iambic lines with an ababcdcd rhyme pattern in the first group, trochaic tetrameter couplets in the second, and trochaic trimeter – with a dactyl in the even-numbered lines-in the third). The <**div1**> attributes *line-group-ct*, *line-ct* and *metrical-unit* are user-defined; as before, the lines beginning with "<! - -" are SGML comments.

```
<text>
   <div1 n=poem type=lyric line-group-ct=3 line-ct=20
      metrical-unit=foot>
      <head>Auf dem See</head>
      <div2 met=−+−+−+−+/−+−+−+ rhyme=ababcdcd
         line-ct=8>
         <l n=1>  Und frische Nahrung, neues Blut
         <l n=2 real=+−−+−+>  Saug' ich aus freier Welt;
         <l n=3 real=+−−+−+−+>  Wie ist Natur so hold
            und gut,
         <l n=4 real=−−−+−+>  Die mich am Busen haelt!
         <l n=5>  Die Welle wieget unsern Kahn
         <l n=6>  Im Rudertakt hinauf,
         <l n=7>  Und Berge, wolkig himmelan,
         <l n=8>  Begegnen unserm Lauf.
      <div2 met=+−+−+−+o rhyme=AAbb line-ct=4>
   <! - - Upper case letters represent feminine rhymes - ->
   <! - - and lower case letters represent masculine - ->
   <! - - rhymes in the rhyme pattern. - ->
         <l n=9 >Aug', mein Aug', was sinkst du nieder?
         <l n=10>  Goldne Traeume, kommt ihr wieder?
         <l n=11>  Weg, du Traum, so gold du bist;
         <l n=12>Hier auch Lieb' und Leben ist.
      <div2 met=+−+−+−/+−+−−+o rhyme=ABABCdCd
         line-ct=8>
         <l n=13>  Auf der Welle blinken
         <l n=14>  Tausend schwebende Sterne,
         <l n=15>  Weiche Nebel trinken
         <l n=16>  Rings die tuermende Ferne;
         <l n=17>  Morgenwind umfluegelt
         <l n=18 real=−−+−−+>  Die beschattete Bucht,
         <l n=19 real=−−+−+−>  Und im See bespiegelt
         <l n=20 real=−−+−−+>  Sich die reifende Frucht.
</text>
```

Since the three line-groups in this poem differ both in meter and rhyme pattern, the <**div**> tag is used to divide the poem into separate groups, each of which is preceded by a different declaration for the meter and the rhyme pattern. In addition, the pre-line tag is used here to mark those lines whose linguistic realization differs from the metrical pattern. Using in-line tags, the first line-group of Goethe's "Auf dem See" could be marked as shown below. In this example clashes between the metrical convention and its linguistic realization are marked with the user-defined tag <**clash**>. This tag can be used to mark a single syllable (e.g. "mich" in Line 4) or a string of syllables (e.g. "Saug' ich" in Line 2):

```
<text>
   <div1 n=poem type=lyric line-group-ct=3 line-ct=20
      metrical-unit=foot>
      <head>Auf dem See</head>
      <div2 met=−+−+−+−+/−+−+−+ rhyme=ababcdcd
         line-ct=8>
         <l n=1>  Und frische Nahrung, neues Blut
         <l n=2>  <clash>Saug' ich</clash> aus freier
            Welt;
         <l n=3>  <clash>Wie ist</clash> Natur so hold
            und gut,
         <l n=4>  Die <clash>mich</clash> am Busen
            haelt!
         <l n=5>  Die Welle wieget unsern Kahn
         <l n=6>  Im Rudertakt hinauf,
         <l n=7>  Und Berge, wolkig himmelan,
         <l n=8>  Begegnen unserm Lauf.
   ...
</text>
```

12. Pre-Line vs In-Line Tagging

There are a number of considerations involved in deciding whether to use pre-line or in-line tags. For lines containing one or more "clashes" between the abstract meter and its linguistic realization, the pre-line tags show the stress pattern for all syllables, whereas the in-line <**clash**> tags only mark those syllables in which clashes occur. The latter may thus be more economical, but by interfering with the flow of the text they make it less easily readable for the human user. More importantly, while the pre-line tags provide a potentially useful representation of the stress-pattern of the line as a whole, they do not indicate the exact positions where clashes occur in the linguistic realization. The <**clash**> tags have a significant advantage in this last respect; on the other hand they do not in themselves provide a means of representing the stress pattern of the line as a whole. Compare the pre-line and in-line tags for the first four lines from Goethe's "Auf dem See":

(a) Pre-line tagging:

```
<l n=1>  Und frische Nahrung, neues Blut
<l n=2 real=+--+-+>  Saug' ich aus freier Welt;
<l n=3 real=+--+-+-+>  Wie ist Natur so hold und gut,
<l n=4 real=---+-+>  Die mich am Busen haelt!
```

(b) In-line tagging:

```
<l n=1>  Und frische Nahrung, neues Blut
<l n=2>  <clash>Saug' ich</clash> aus freier Welt;
<l n=3>  <clash>Wie ist</clash> Natur so hold und gut,
<l n=4>  Die <clash>mich</clash> am Busen haelt!
```

But while the user-defined <**clash**> tag is an economical means of indicating the position in the line in which the clash occurs, for a fuller metrical analysis a more complex system of in-line tagging is required that numbers the syllables or feet in question – thus showing that the clashes occur in syllables 1–2 in lines 2 and 3, but only in syllable 2 in line 4 (if we assign lexical, rather than emphatic stress to "mich"). It would then be possible from this to generate automatically a representation of the stress pattern realized in the line as a whole.

For another example of in-line tags, and of a procedure for numbering the positions where clashes occur, let us turn to a well-known sonnet from the English verse tradition, by Shakespeare. As in the previous example, "clashes" between the metrical pattern and its linguistic realization can be marked with the <**clash**> tag.

```
<text>
   <div1 n=poem type=sonnet rhyme=ababcdcdefefGG
      met=-+-+-+-+-+o>
      <l n=1> Full many a glorious morning have I seen
   <! -- In line 1 "many a" functions as a disyllable -->
      <l n=2> <clash>Flatter</clash> the mountain-
         tops with sovereign eye,
      <l n=3> <clash>Kissing</clash> with golden face
         the meadows green,
      <l n=4> <clash>Gilding pale</clash> streams with
         heavenly alche<clash>my</clash>,
      <l n=5> Anon permit the basest clouds to ride
      <l n=6> With ugly rack on <clash>his</clash>
         celestial face,
      <l n=7> And <clash>from</clash> the forlorn world
         his visage hide,
      <l n=8> <clash>Stealing</clash> unseen to west
         with<clash>this </clash> disgrace:
      <l n=9> Even so my sun one early morn did shine
   <! -- In line 9 "even" functions as a monosyllable -->
      <l n=10>With all-triumphant splendour <clash>
         on</clash> my brow;
      <l n=11>But out, alack! he <clash>was</clash> but
         one <clash>hour </clash> mine,
      <l n=12>The region cloud hath mask'd him
         <clash>from </clash> me now.
      <l n=13>Yet him for <clash>this</clash> my love no
         whit disdaineth;
      <l n=14><clash>Suns of</clash> the world may
         stain when heaven's <clash>sun</clash> staineth.
</text>
```

As a means of indicating the exact metrical position where the clash occurs, there is the more informative, but also more cumbersome alternative of using the <**seg**> tag with the *n* and *real* attributes. This could be done as follows:

```
<div1 n=poem met=-+|-+|-+|-+|-+o>
   <l n=1> Full many a glorious morning have I seen
   <l n=2> <seg1 type=foot n=1 real=+->Flatter</seg1>
      the mountain-tops with sovereign eye,
   <l n=3> <seg1 n=1 real=+->Kissing</seg1> with
      golden face the meadows green,
   <l n=4> <seg1 n=1 real=+->Gilding</seg1> pale
      streams with heavenly al<seg1 n=5 real=-->
      chemy</seg1>,
```

The marking of the foot boundaries with the symbol | in the *met* attribute value of the <**div1**> element allows the human reader, or a software program, to isolate the correct portion of that attribute value as the default value for the same attribute on the <**seg1**> elements for feet, namely −+.

It might of course be possible for syllable tagging and numbering to be done automatically by a syllable parser or a program which identifies vowel nuclei and syllable boundaries and counts the former; this is, for instance, fairly easy in Italian. Where this can be done, such detailed tagging would be either much easier to effect or, perhaps, redundant.

13. Irregular Forms

Thus far we have looked at some relatively regular verse forms: the Classical distich, the Chevy-Chase Stanza (consisting of iambic tetrameter and trimeter lines), a trochaic tetrameter stanza, a variant of a trochaic trimeter stanza (in which the second foot of the even-numbered lines is a dactyl instead of a trochee), and an iambic pentameter sonnet consisting of three quatrains followed by a couplet (although it is printed as a group of 14 consecutive lines).

Let us turn now to some early nineteenth-century German poems which exhibit more intricate and unusual characteristics. The following poem is taken from Novalis' *Hymnen an die Nacht.* Visually this Romantic poem consists of one line group of 28 lines. The rhyme scheme, however, divides the poem into 7 four-line stanzas. Based on an analysis of its *rhythmic* structure, the poem can also be divided into *six* line-groups, each of which consists of one of patterns (a) and (b) below (where, as before, "o" represents an optional unstressed syllable). In this example, our markup shows not only the broad *conventions* chosen by Novalis (two-stress line, AbCb rhyme pattern), but also individual *rhythmic* characteristics unique to this particular poem by this particular poet. For the former we have used an attribute *stress-pat* at <**div1**> level, keeping the *met* attribute for the individual rhythmic characteristics at the level of <**div2**>; it could of course have been done the other way round. Note that we are treating the individual rhythmic characteristics as convention rather than realization, the difference between the two being marked where appropriate by the in-line <**clash**> tag.

(a) −+−+o
(b) −+−−+o

```
<text>
  <div1 n=poem stress-pat=−+−o+o rhyme−pat=AbCb
    metrical-unit=foot line-ct=28>
    <head>Hinueber wall' ich</head>
    <div2 n=line-group met=−+−+o line-ct=8>
      <l n=1> Hinueber wall' ich
      <l n=2> Und jede Pein
      <l n=3> Wird einst ein Stachel
      <l n=4> Der Wollust sein.
      <l n=5> Noch wenig Zeiten
      <l n=6> So bin ich los
      <l n=7> Und liege trunken
      <l n=8> Der Lieb' im Schoss.
    <div2 met=−+−−+o line-ct=4>
      <l n=9> Unendliches Leben
      <l n=10> <clash>Wogt</clash> maechtig in mir
      <l n=11> Ich schaue von oben
      <l n=12> Herunter nach dir.
    <div2 met=−+−+o line-ct=3>
      <l n=13> An jenem Huegel
      <l n=14> Verlischt dein Glanz -
      <l n=15> Ein Schatten bringet
    <div2 met=−+−−+o line-ct=3>
      <l n=16> Den kuehlenden Kranz.
      <l n=17> O! Sauge, Geliebter,
      <l n=18> Gewaltig mich an,
    <div2 met=−+−+o line-ct=2>
      <l n=19> Dass ich entschlummern
      <l n=20> Und lieben kann -
    <div2 met=−+−−+o line-ct=8>
      <l n=21> Ich fuehle des Todes
      <l n=22> Verjuengende Flut
      <l n=23> Zu Balsam und Aether
      <l n=24> Verwandelt mein Blut -
      <l n=25> Ich lebe bei Tage
      <l n=26> Voll Glauben und Mut
      <l n=27> Und sterbe die Naechte
      <l n=28> In heiliger Glut.
</text>
```

As mentioned above, the markup for this poem shows individual *rhythmic* characteristics unique to this particular poem. There is of course a general question as to whether text markup for scholarly interchange should be limited to broad formal *conventions* (e.g. meter, rhyme, stanzaic forms), or whether *individual* characteristics of verse texts may also be included (a step which often represents the foundation of a stylistic *interpretation).* Our approach would be to give the "editor" the freedom to include this type of markup, with the stipulation that it be clearly distinguished (either in SGML comments or in the header) from the markup of purely conventional or formal characteristics of a text. There are, of course, "borderline" cases in which there is ambiguity or uncertainty regarding the conventional characteristics. An example of this occurs in the following poem ("Das verlassene Maegdlein" by Eduard Moerike), where the underlying metrical structure could have more than one form:

> Frueh, wann die Haehne kraehn,
> Eh' die Sternlein verschwinden,
> Muss ich am Herde stehn,
> Muss Feuer zuenden.
> (first of four stanzas)

There are at least two possibilities for the metrical pattern of this stanza:

1) +−−+−−
   −−+−−+−
   +−−+−−
   −+− +−

2) +−−+− +
   +− +−−+−
   +−−+− +
   −+− +−

Such borderline cases are relatively infrequent in the German verse tradition. When ambiguity does occur, however, an "editorial note", using the **<note>** tag, can be included to indicate that the pattern indicated by the markup is not the only possible pattern for the verse text under consideration. (An ambitious editor could, of course, provide more than one markup for such texts.)

Our last example is from German madrigal verse, by Barthold Heinrich Brockes. The meter is consistently iambic, but both the line-length and the rhyme pattern are variable. Although most lines are rhymed, unrhymed lines ("orphans") may also occur. Since the line-length is variable in this verse form, the *iambic foot* is the only constant. It is therefore defined below as the basic metrical unit, using once again the *met* attribute; the value given to this (*met* = "−+/...") would have to be recorded in the Encoding Description of the TEI Header as standing for a variable number of iambic feet.

```
<text>
   <div1 n=poem type=madrigal-verse metrical-unit=foot
      met="−+/..." rhyme=variable>
      <head>Kirschbluete bei der Nacht</head>
<!--Only the first eight lines of the poem are given here.-->
      <l n=1> Ich sahe <clash>mit</clash> betrachten
         <clash>dem</clash> Gemuete
      <l n=2> <clash>Juengst</clash> einen Kirschbaum,
         welcher bluehte,
      <l n=3> In kuehler Nacht beim Mondenschein;
      <l n=4> Ich glaubt', es koenne nicht von groessrer
         Weisse sein;
      <l n=5> Es schien, als waer ein Schnee gefallen;
      <l n=6> Ein jeder, auch der kleinste Ast
      <l n=7> Trug gleichsam eine rechte Last
      <l n=8> Von zierlich weissen runden Ballen.
</text>
```

Using the **<seg>** tag, the first two lines could be encoded as follows:

```
<l n=1> Ich sa<seg1 type=foot n=2 met=-->he mit</seg1>
   betracht<seg1 n=4 met=-->endem </seg1> Gemuete
<l n=2> <seg1 n=1 met=+−>Juengst ein</seg1>en
   Kirschbaum, welcher bluehte...
```

14. Readability vs Technicality

The difficulties of marking up such complex and frequently overlapping structures are strong pointers in the direction of the alternative mode of markup contained in TEI P3, that of feature structure analysis (FSA) (see Langendoen and Simons in this volume). This undoubtedly constitutes a powerful and effective way of tagging metrical and rhyme conventions and their realization (and the relationship between the two), and is particularly appropriate for elements smaller than the line, when a complex segmentation is required; it would also be suitable for other features of the language of verse, such as metaphor. But it could be dauntingly difficult to read, perhaps far too much so for the average user in the field of literary scholarship. Moreover systematic pre-line or in-line tagging could, if required, be converted into FSA by fairly simple algorithms. Our consensus is to leave to the individual encoder the choice in this area among the three alternatives of FSA, pre-line and in-line tagging. At least for the foreseeable future we must always allow a form of markup that the non-computer-specialist scholar can easily manage. So far the TEI's Guidelines have been exceedingly daunting for all but experts, and dedicated experts at that. If the Guidelines are to succeed, they must where appropriate allow for the choice between technical sophistication and more simple forms of expression.

15. Structural vs Non-Structural Divisions

The recommendations discussed so far have all concerned features of verse structure. However, the Work Group also spent some time considering the encoding of features that are neither peculiar to verse nor in certain senses structural, in that they are not part of a system of hierarchical divisions, may overlap with one another, and/or may be discontinuous. For instance an encoder may wish to mark passages of text associated with particular characters, themes, images, allusions, topoi, styles or modes of narration; much of the computerized analysis of verse seems likely to require dividing texts up into blocks in this way. FSA offers one very powerful means of encoding such features, but with the attendant disadvantages already described. Another means is to use the **<note>** tag: **<note resp=dr>** theme of love begins **</note>** ... **<note resp=dr>** theme of love ends **</note>**. This tag can be appropriate for the encoding of analyses that might be regarded as matters of interpretation, as personal or controversial; the fact that the tag indicates the originator of the analysis is thus especially important, as a means of avoiding a spurious air of objectivity in the markup in question. One disadvantage is that it involves the interpolation in the original text of material which might inadvertently be left in when a simple markup stripping facility is used on the file. (We therefore recommend that where the **<note>** tag is used in this way, users' attention should be drawn to the fact in the Encoding Description; it would also be desirable to have tag-stripping software that included the possibility of removing such material.) A more important disadvantage is that it is cumbersome and that, since there are no rules for the syntax of its contents, these are less useful, potentially, than they otherwise might be as paramaters for further processing.

Where it is desirable to tag the sort of segments described above in a more rigorous and systematic way, the Work Group pressed for the institution of a new tag, for which, after some discussion, the term **<span>** has been used: e.g. **<span from=xxx to=xxx type=theme value=love resp=dr>**. The *from* and *to* attributes point to identified positions in the text; the *type* and *value* attributes can serve as parameters for further processing; the *resp* attribute indicates the originator of the segmentation and makes the point that it may be more a matter of interpretation than, say, a system of hierarchical divisions. The tag is an empty one, and may be placed within or outside the text. A list of some possible values for the *type* attributes would be: "character", "theme", "image", "allusion", "topos", "style", "narrative mode", the exact terminology to be determined by the encoder. Metaphors and other rhetorical devices could also be tagged in this way, where they stretch over a large number of words, and especially if they bridge hierarchical boundaries; an alternative solution would be to use FSA. When these last devices are restricted to specific, perhaps to single words, and no bridging of hierarchical boundaries is involved, they could be the subject of in-line tagging, as in the example given at the beginning.

For the encoding of more systematic features of the narrative structure of texts various options are available elsewhere in the Guidelines. The system of concurrent hierarchies could be used when the features in question could be expressed in a hierarchical form. For the treatment of time, use could be made of the **<timeLine>** tag proposed by the Work Group on spoken texts. Similarly, narrative voice could be tagged following the same Work Group's recommendations for the identification of speakers. All of these are topics which our Work Group recognized as potentially important for the encoding of verse, but which it could not treat as central to its concerns.

16. Fidelity vs Interpretation

It is always important to remember that, to a greater or lesser degree, markup represents an *interpretation* of a verse text, which is subject to revision by the user of that text. Take, for example, the following lines from an iambic pentameter sonnet by Keats:

And I have many miles on foot to fare
Yet feel I little of the cool, bleak air.

In the second line the word "I" is unstressed. But what about the first line? Here "I" could receive emphatic stress, but, since it is non-lexical, it could also remain unstressed, in which case the two lines could be marked up as follows:

And <clash>I</clash> have many miles on foot
to fare
Yet feel I little <clash>of</clash> the cool,
<clash>bleak</clash> air.

The difference in the interpretation of the stress level is significant, for it frequently reflects a difference in the interpretation of the *meaning* of a phrase or sentence. Cases such as this should be indicated by the "editor" (the person doing the markup), for instance using the proposed <**note**> tag.

One might go even further and say that an element of interpretation exists not only in the process of marking up a text but in the very act of encoding. Any encoding of a text must necessarily be selective; and since any act of selection is also an act of interpretation, all encoding must involve interpretation (see also the discussion by Greenstein and Burnard in this volume). However this abstract truth must not obscure a principle of equal if not greater importance, that of fidelity to the original text – a principle which concerns the entire scholarly community, but might be felt to have a special relevance to anyone concerned with literary analysis, and all the more so to those concerned with so complex a verbal medium as poetry. Scholarly analysts of verse texts are used to working with authoritative critical editions, and whether these exist or not, their custom is always to relate their analysis to specific printed texts or manuscripts. When using a machine-readable text, therefore, they will naturally expect it to constitute a faithful transcription of an identifiable original, at least of those aspects of the original that are relevant to their needs. The encoder therefore needs to think very carefully of the purposes to which his or her text is likely to be put. For the purposes of verse analysis, a faithful transcription will usually mean an exact reproduction of the linguistic form of the original, including orthography and punctuation, and of a few aspects of presentation such as italicization and, perhaps, page-breaks. In some cases, we have already noted, aspects of typographical layout, such as indentations, may also be relevant to verse analysis, and where appropriate these should be faithfully recorded as well. There are occasions, of course, when quite substantial modifications may legitimately be made in the process of encoding, for instance to modernize the spelling and punctuation of an early printed book or manuscript. It is vital, when this is done, that it be done systematically, in accordance with an explicit and justifiable set of principles stated in the Encoding Description. If more than one original, for instance two different printed editions of the same text, is used for encoding, the machine-readable version should show, in as much detail as feasible, its exact relationship to its different sources. On occasion the machine-readable text may itself claim to constitute a new edition of the work in question, in which case its claims to authority would have to be fully documented in the same way as for any scholarly edition. More discussion of fidelity and non-fidelity to a printed text and the means to deal with it appears in Ide and Véronis, in this volume.

Note

[1] The members of the Verse Work Group are David Robey (Chair), David Chisholm, Elaine Brennan, and Willard McCarty. The article draws on substantial contributions to discussion from all members of the Work Group, from the editors of the TEI Guidelines (Michael Sperberg-McQueen and Lou Burnard) and from the chair of the Committee on Text Analysis and Interpretation (Terry Langendoen). Robey is primarily responsible for the treatment of general issues, Chisholm primarily for that of individual instances of encoding practice.

References

Chisholm, D. "Phonological Patterning in English and German Verse: A Computer-assisted Approach". *Quantitative Linguistics*, 14 (1982), 114–46.

Sperberg-McQueen, C.M. "Text in the Electronic Age: Textual Study and Text Encoding with Examples". *Literary and Linguistic Computing*, 6, 1 (1991), 34–46.

Sperberg-McQueen, C.M. and Lou Burnard, eds. *Guidelines for Electronic Text Encoding and Interchange (TEI P3)*. 2 vols. Chicago and Oxford: Text Encoding Initiative, 1994.

Computers and the Humanities **29:** 113–121, 1995.

The Show Must Go on:[1] Problems of Tagging Performance Texts

John Lavagnino *
Department of English and American Literatures, Brandeis University, Waltham, MA 02254–9110, USA
e-mail: lav@binah.cc.brandeis.edu

and

Elli Mylonas *
Scholarly Technology Group, Brown University, Providence, RI 02912, USA
e-mail: elli_mylonas@brown.edu

Key words: SGML, tagging, performance texts, theater, TEI

Abstract

A dramatic work may be seen either as an event or as a text; the TEI guidelines make it possible to encode a dramatic work in either way, but do not attempt to solve the difficult problem of doing both at once. The basic element of a dramatic work, when seen as a text, is the speech; the guidelines also provide elements for encoding other familiar parts of dramatic texts (such as stage directions and cast lists), as well as for encoding analytic information on various aspects of texts and performances that is not normally included in printed dramatic texts. There are often other formal structures in dramatic works that intersect with the structure of speeches – metrical structures, for example; we discuss approaches for encoding these structures.

1. Setting the Stage

A dramatic work has a double existence: it is an event, a performance presented by actors before an audience, and it is also a text, a set of written instructions for staging a performance. An encoding of a dramatic work can represent one of these aspects, but it cannot readily represent both, because they call for very different perspectives on the work. A performance-centered encoding must represent a complex event unfolding in space and time, with overlapping speech, movement of actors, and manipulation of props, settings, and lighting; a text-centered encoding must represent the way instructions for an imagined performance are specified in writing, including features such as cast lists and speech headings that have no direct analogues in a performance. There may be no written script at all for a particular performance, or a performance may substantially diverge from the script that was used; but a written dramatic text almost always professes to be prescribing a way of staging a performance. That is true even when the performance is not intended to be staged, or would be very difficult to stage – as in closet dramas like Thomas Hardy's *Dynasts*, with its settings that include several large-scale land and sea battles, heaven, and the House of Commons. And it is true for texts that include lengthy passages directed to readers alone, such as the long novelistic stage directions in Shaw.

The approaches we need to take to describe a particular event, on the one hand, and an idealized and textualized event, on the other, are different enough that it is not possible to describe both simultaneously and do it well. (A distinction between performance-

---

* John Lavagnino is a graduate student in English and American Literature at Brandeis University. His fields of interest include Renaissance drama, modern literature, textual scholarship, and electronic textuality. He is Electronics Editor of *The Collected Works of Thomas Middleton* (forthcoming from Oxford University Press).

Elli Mylonas is a Lead Project Analyst for the Scholarly Technology Group at Brown University. Formerly she was the Managing Editor of the Perseus Project. Her areas of interest are Roman poetry, textual markup and SGML, and hypertext.

centered and text-centered approaches exists in other branches of literary study as well: for examples from criticism, see Issacharoff and Jones [1988] and Thompson and Thompson [1989]; for examples from textual editing, see Howard-Hill [1989].) Moreover, in formulating any encoding guidelines, there is a tension between standardizing texts and emphasizing their differences: between finding a common model to ease interchange and reuse, and respecting the details of our texts that deviate from such models. But there are cases when one model cannot encompass all the features of a single kind of work; the difficulty of encoding dramatic text and dramatic event at once is such a case.

In our work we have chosen to limit ourselves to encoding written dramatic texts, for the most part, though we do provide some features for encoding numerous aspects of performance – those traditionally represented in written texts, and a number of others that can be productively combined with an encoding of the written text. To encode drama as an event and not a written text, as a performance and not a script, we suggest the use of the TEI guidelines for transcription of speech (TEI P3 chapter 11, and Johannson's article in this volume), which provide mechanisms for representing the features normally minimized or omitted in written dramatic texts, such as intonation and overlapping speech.

All markup of written texts faces the choice between focusing on uninterpreted transcription of layout and typography, and interpretive translation of a printed representation into an electronic representation. The choice, we feel, has to be for the latter: in favor of encoding as translation, not as digital paper (Sperberg-McQueen, 1991). But the markup for drama that we propose goes beyond this. Although this tag set is designed primarily to describe the features of printed texts, according to TEI practice (TEI P3, p. 9), we also provide for enhancements to the text that will facilitate computer processing directed to ends other than simple display. A properly-encoded dramatic text will be usable for studies of differences between characters in their use of language – since the character speaking will be identified for all dialogue. It can also take into account differences in the use of verse forms or song. A text may include detailed specifications of the motion of characters onto or off the stage, so that analysis can turn on who was on the stage at each moment – for studies of the psychological dynamics of groups of different sizes, or of the casting requirements faced by dramatic companies. A text may incorporate information on not just one, but many different performances, and the differences among these performances can then be taken into account in any other kind of study. In itself, marking a text up in this way leads to deeper analytical insight on the part of the encoder, and the electronic text that is the product of these efforts can provide a springboard for others' scholarship.

2. The Play's the Thing

The higher-order structural units of drama are familiar to most of us: plays are divided into acts, scenes, stasima, episodes and other large divisions that are typically signaled both in printed form and in performance, and that are part of the way authors and audiences think about plays. The TEI **<div>** element family is appropriate for major structural divisions of this sort, and can be used to indicate any number of different types of division.

Below this level, however, it is not so easy to agree upon the structural elements common to all drama. We can certainly identify many elements that might appear: they include sentences, paragraphs, and metrical elements (lines and stanzas). We can distinguish between individual speech and choral speech, between action and commentary upon action, between dialogue and soliloquy, and between spoken and sung passages. But none of these distinctions is useful in every play, and together they still don't exhaust the possibilities of dramatic structures. It is necessary to find a structural "chunk" that is analogous to the paragraph, or even the sentence; that is characteristic of drama but not of other literary forms; and that can be identified in virtually all dramatic texts. We decided that the *speech* (encoded with the **<sp>** tag) is such an element, and that drama is best encoded, below the **<div>** level, as a sequence of speeches by different characters in turn. Printed dramatic texts typically make it very clear who is speaking which speech – because performers expect this as part of the instructions for their performance; indeed, speeches and their speakers are much more fully notated in most dramatic texts than stage action. Even as a unit for encoding performances **<sp>** works well, since we can still identify individuals speaking and what they speak; these distinctions may not always be so clear to an audience if many actions and many speeches are taking place at once, but the performers need to know. In fiction, by contrast, it is not always easy to tell who is speaking or to assemble the full text of what was said, so a speech element would be a poor building block; but it fits the conventions of drama.

A speech is spoken by a character (or characters – but this more general case is an uncomplicated extension of the simple case). As instruction for performance, this aspect of the speech is simple enough: the character in the representation must be indicated. For this purpose, a simple attribute on the speech is adequate. But printed texts are not that simple, because they sometimes vary the printed speech headings used for a particular character. One common reason is to modify the *reader's* experience so that it's more similar to that of the spectator. For example, at the start of Shaw's *Pygmalion*, a character appears whose first speech is headed "The Note Taker". Only after the dialogue has informed the reader (as, on stage, it informs the audience), late in the first act, that this man's name is Henry Higgins does his speech heading change. Disguises provide another reason why a speech heading might differ from speech to speech, if the reader is to be kept in the dark as the theater audience is, or, on the contrary, should be let in on the truth behind a transparent disguise. Finally, there are occasions in ordinary life that can involve a change in name or form of address, such as marriage and royal succession. For example, Coriolanus in Shakespeare's play is called Martius in the opening scenes.

To meet the requirements of both typography and analysis, speeches need two separate indications of their speaker: an embedded element that specifies the printed speech heading, and an attribute that identifies who is speaking, in a way that is constant for each character in the fiction, however disguised or variously described by speech headings. For *Pygmalion* we might say:

```
<sp who=Higgins>
   <speaker>The Note Taker</speaker>
   <p>Live where you like; but stop that
      noise. </p>
</sp>
```

Since the attribute value would be the same for all the speeches of Henry Higgins, one can study the language of Henry Higgins without having to know all the different headings that might be used for his speeches. In the electronic edition of the Oxford Shakespeare, by contrast, there is no equivalent of this *who* attribute, and consequently the documentation includes a table listing all characters who have more than one speech heading.

The <**speaker**> element is optional: in many plays speech headings are not varied in the ways detailed above, and in those cases the *who* attribute is quite sufficient. But when it is specified it does need to be an element and not an attribute, because the rendition may need to be encoded – for historical reasons, or to preserve information about an ambiguous original: when speech headings are abbreviated, as in many older plays, they are sometimes ambiguous and in need of interpretation, and an encoder may wish to record the original version. The right place to put this element in the hierarchy is not immediately obvious: our Working Group had some trouble deciding between a place outside and immediately before the <**sp**> element, and a place inside the <**sp**> element as the first contained element. The question might appear similar to the question of placement for a section heading – but where a section heading is clearly a part of the section, a speech heading is merely an identification of a speaker, needed only in the text of the drama: on stage there are no speech headings, there are only speeches. The best choice for the location of <**speaker**>, we finally decided, is inside, on the grounds that a speech heading without the subsequent speech has very little significance; they are not separable, as putting <**speaker**> outside would imply.

In the vast majority of cases, fitting a passage of dialogue into a speech element is not difficult. The optional speech heading may be followed by a sequence of paragraphs, in the case of prose drama, or verse lines, in the case of verse drama, or a mixture of the two. These sub-elements present no difficulties beyond those listed in chapter 6 of P3, "Core Elements Available in All TEI Documents" (P3, pp. 139–215). The more interesting and complex problems arise in thinking about how to relate the rest of a play's text to its dialogue – in thinking about the play as event rather than as sequence of words.

3. Taking Care of (Stage) Business

Dialogue, although it is the defining characteristic of dramatic texts, is not sufficient for describing all the performance features of a play. Other features, such as the cast list, initial setting, and stage directions, are conventionally used in printed texts to convey non-speech information to the reader. A researcher may want to extend these conventional features and add information about actors' entrances and exits, blocking, or other performance instructions, like lighting and properties. Such additional performance notes might, in the case of entrances and exits, apply to all productions of a play, or might take the form of notes describing a specific performance or series of performances by a particular ensemble.

The primary way to record information about a particular edition or performance is to use the **<performance>** element in the front matter. This element, which is optional and which may be repeated, provides a place to put a textual description of a particular performance, notes that are printed in a particular edition, or features like a cast list, as well as general information about the encoding conventions that apply to one performance or edition. If more than one version of a play is being encoded in a single electronic text, the documentation that is provided in the **<performance>** element and in the TEI header are extremely important. Without them, it is impossible to use the information correctly.

In print, cast lists are familiar and tractable things that describe performances – they list characters, roles and possibly the actors who played them. To encode the *information* that a cast list conveys and not merely its appearance, however, is a difficult task. This information constitutes a kind of database about the characters in the play: for each character, the cast list may specify a name, title, gender, station, profession, and legal or emotional relationship to other characters. It does this not merely by listing these attributes after the character's name: much may be implied by the formatting. In an electronic text, it is possible to record either the database information or the formatting. Doing both, however, is rather difficult: it ends up being similar to marking up a sentence to show, at one time, both how it is printed and the logical structure of the information it contains.

Some of the difficulties that can occur are: characters whose names are elided or omitted, indicated instead by roles ("Widow, his Mother"); the naming of multiple characters on a line ("Touchwood Senior, and his Wife, a decayed gentleman"); roles that apply to more than one character ("Wat and Nick, his bastards"); and larger groupings by family, gender, or other affinity. Finally, non-speaking roles may be omitted, and multiple cast lists may exist for a single play. These relationships can be indicated typographically, and understood by a human reader, but in an electronic text they need to be represented more consistently and explicitly to be useful.

MONTICELSCO, a cardinal; afterwards Pope PAUL IV

...

LODOVICO (Lodowick), in love with ISABELLA; later a conspirator in the pay of FRANCISCO.

ANTONELLI GASPARO	} his friends, later fellow conspirators

Our solution is to describe either the appearance of a cast list, or, by disambiguating elided or missing roles, to make the relationships and the true magnitude of the cast explicit. Both ends may be achieved at once, and the problem of multiple cast lists may also be circumvented, since more than one cast list is permitted using more than one **<performance>** element. If this type of information is available, then it is possible to study and analyze problems like role doubling and the total number of actors necessary for a performance.

```
<castList>
   <castItem>
      <role id="Mont">Monticelso</role>, <roleDesc>a
         cardinal; afterwards Pope </roleDesc>
         <role id="Pope">Paul IV</role>
   </castItem>
...
   <castItem>
      <role id="Lod">Lodovico</role><role
         rend="parens" id="Lod2">Lodowick</role
         >, <role Desc>in love with <name
         >Isabella</name>; later a conspirator in the pay
         of <name>Francisco </name>.</roleDesc>
   </castItem>
   <castGroup rend="braced">
      <castItem>
         <role id="Ant">Antonelli</role>
      </castItem>
      <castItem>
         <role id="Gasp">Gasparo</role>
      </castItem>
      <trailer>his friends, later fellow conspirators</trailer>
   </castGroup>
</castList>
```

Note that the first **<castItem>** contains two **<role>** elements which indicate the same person, whose name changes during the course of the play. Each of these **<role>** elements must have a unique *id* attribute; however, only one would be used as the target of the *who* attribute on **<sp>** and other elements. To indicate the relationship between Antonelli and Gasparo, their **<castItem>** elements are enclosed within a **<castGroup>** element. The **<castGroup>** specifies the large brace by using the *rend* (rendition) attribute and the description is tagged with a **<trailer>** element rather than a **<roleDesc>** element: as it is shared by both characters, it cannot go inside either **<castItem>**.

Actions occur on stage that are not spoken, and thus not printed as part of an actor's lines. When these are indicated in a printed text, and not left up to the director of the performance, actions are usually indicated using stage directions.

```
<sp>
  <speaker>Algernon</speaker>
  <stage type="movement">retreating to back of
    sofa</stage>
  <p>But why does she call herself little Cecily
    if she is your aunt and lives at Tunbridge
    Wells?
    <stage type="delivery">Reading</stage>
    <quote>From little Cecily with her fondest
    love. </quote></p>
</sp>
```

Printed texts often employ typographical distinctions between different types of stage direction, so that directions concerning the manner in which speeches are delivered look different from entrances and exits, or from scene settings.

> POGIO
> I'll leave you and go tell my Lord Vincentio.
> [Exit
>
> *Enter Benevenius with others, bringing in Strozza with an arrow in his side.*
>
> CYNANCHE (aside)
> See the sad sight! I dare not yield to grief,
> But force feign'd patience, to recomfort him.

But although a particular text will often apply its classification with great consistency, there is considerable variation in these classifications and their formatting across diverse places, eras, and languages. Moreover, although we can distinguish a number of different types of stage direction, they are often combined within single printed directions. For example, entrances, exits, other actions, and description may all be combined:

> Enter Lady Bracknell. The couples separate in alarm. Exit Merriam.
>
> They are interrupted by the entry of Louka, a handsome proud girl in a pretty Bulgarian peasant's dress ...

Two approaches to classifying stage directions are feasible. We can encode the visual appearance of stage directions as printed in the source – thereby preserving the source's rendition, but losing all possibility of processing the stage directions on the basis of their function. Or we can classify them functionally using a *type* attribute on the **<stage>** element, accepting that the values of this attribute cannot be fixed for all texts; this is the approach we have chosen because it is less ambiguous.

Even with a functional typology of stage directions, however, there is a need for a way to encode movement that is more precise and easier to process electronically, since stage directions can be ambiguous, or refer to multiple actions at once. The **<move>** element marks the motion of a character onto, off, or about the stage – either in a particular production, or in a general analysis of the play. In the latter case this might be seen as entirely interpretive, if often uncontroversially so; we introduced it because the alternative is to mark up the stage directions themselves, which again introduces the conflict between typography and analysis that we encountered with cast lists.

```
<stage type="exit">He goes into the inner room
  with Old Woman.</stage>
<move who="fergus oldwoman" where="off">
```

In the following, more complex example, the movements of the actors in a particular performance are encoded, going beyond the movements specified in Chekhov's stage direction.

```
<stage type="entrance movement">Two street
  musicians, a man and a girl, come in playing
  a violin and a harp.<move who="mus1 mus2"
  where="on lf"> Vershinin comes out of the
  house with Olga and Anfisa.<move who="ver
  olga anf" where="on mf"> They listen for a
  while in silence. Irina goes up to them.<move
  who="iri mf"></stage>
```

The **<tech>** element is another way to mark production information of a sort that does not traditionally appear in stage directions, even though both contain much the same kind of information. This includes detailed instructions for lighting and prop requirements, for example. Such information is part of the working documents used in theaters, but does not generally appear in printed texts. The content of **<tech>** elements will vary, depending on the practice of individual designers and theaters. We distinguish the **<tech>** element from traditional stage directions because, whereas the latter are directed to an imagined audience or reader as well as to the players, the former tend to be generated in the course of staging a play and are directed to the technicians and performers. Even though these are closely tied to a particular performance, we believe it is important to provide a way to encode them, because they do exist in many documents that are of potential significance.

4. The Play within the Play

As we discussed above, we identify the <**sp**> element as the basic unit within higher division levels. It is certainly not the only structure encountered within acts, scenes or other major divisions in dramatic texts; but it is common to substantially all dramatic texts, and is a defining feature. However, dramatic texts actually consist of multiple intersecting structures. What is necessary after speakers and speeches have been identified is a way to show other intersecting structures that contain speeches or parts of speeches, and how they fit together.

It is common in verse drama for metrical units and speeches to intersect – metrical lines may be split up among different speakers; larger structures like verses or strophes may be distributed among speakers. In the first case, a verse line can be distributed among two, three or more speakers, and it may even be interrupted by prose. For some encoders, it will be sufficient just to mark these lines as verse lines, and to ignore the fact that they are not *complete* metrical lines. An encoder is not required by the TEI guidelines to include a metrical analysis in an electronic verse text. However, these features and others that are not part of the basic tagset facilitate the interpretive act, and are necessary for many types of analysis that can be performed on the text. Including them substantially increases the value of the electronic text for many users.

The simplest way of marking overlapping lines is to state explicitly whether the line is complete or partial. The <**l**> tag which marks a line has a *part* attribute whose value may be *N* (the line is complete) or *Y* (the line is incomplete). By looking at this attribute, it is possible to tell whether a line is complete in itself, or whether it is only part of a logical metrical line. Another, fuller set of attribute values is also provided, which replaces the simpler *Y* value with *I*, *M*, and *F*. This set of attribute values is used to mark whether the partial line is the initial, medial or final part of a logical metrical line. The advantage of the second method is that it provides more information about the extent of the logical line regardless of which component partial line is encountered.

Here is an example from *The Roaring Girl* by Thomas Middleton and Thomas Dekker, scene 2, in which a verse line is interrupted by a speech in prose.

```
<sp>
    <speaker>Alexander</speaker>
    <l>"...That disease</l>
    <l>Of which all old men sicken, avarice,</l>
    <l part="I">Never infected me"&mdash;</l>
</sp>
<sp>
    <speaker>Laxton<speaker><stage>(aside)</stage>
    <p>He means not himself, I'm sure.</p>
</sp>
<sp>
    <speaker>Alexander</speaker>
    <l part="F">"For like a lamp</l>
    <l>Fed with continual oil, I spend and throw</l>
    <l>My light to all that need it, yet have still</l>
    <l>Enough to serve myself. ..."</l>
</sp>
```

Although partial lines may appear in many different configurations, they tend to come in sequence, with no partial line overlapping another or belonging to more than one logical line; and though a logical line may span several <**sp**> elements, the partial lines that comprise it will each fit within a <**sp**>. Other overlaid structures, like verses, strophes, and plays performed within the play do not fit so neatly within or around existing elements. This type of structure may begin in the middle of one speech and end in the middle of another, and it may be interrupted by intervening material that does not belong to it. For example, in Greek tragedy, choral stasima are clearly delimited from the episodes they separate. However, the strophic structure that makes up the choral ode need not coincide with speech elements, and strophes can be separated or even interrupted by tetrameter or trimeter passages. So, even if it is possible to use a <**div**> tag to indicate the stasimon as a whole, it is necessary to be able to show which fragments belong to particular strophes, and which fragments are external to the strophic structure but still within the <**div**>. Another such structure that appears in dramatic works from a wide variety of places and times is the play within the play, in which a mixing of dramatic levels rather than a clean separation is often found. In both cases, it can be difficult to decide to which level a particular piece of text belongs.

The parts of a superimposed or embedded structure may consist of fragments of several speeches, so it is not possible to use the <**sp**> element as a component part, as we do with lines when constructing logical lines out of partial lines. It has been necessary to create another type of tag to delimit the fragments of speeches that make up larger logical structures overlaid on the speech structure. These tags describe the type of overlaid structure – song, strophe, play – and they are contained within speech elements. Once subelements have been named and marked, it is necessary to indicate how these elements form larger structures. Two mechanisms are provided for this purpose: the linked-list method, which is simple to use, and the join element, which is more complex but has the merit of defining a virtual element.

We will show how to tag the following text using both systems.

> [Enter by Eisodos B a Chorus of Marathonian citizens.]
>
> *Chorus*
>
> Oh! Oh! What is this cry that has been raised near the altar? Of what disaster will it soon give proof?
>
> Str.
>
> [75] See the feeble old man lying spread upon the ground! O unhappy man,
>
> < >
>
> at whose hands have you had this wretched fall?
>
> *Iolaus*
>
> This man, strangers, dishonors your gods and drags me by force from the altar steps.
>
> *Chorus*
>
> [80] But you, old sir, from what land have you come to this people who dwell together in four cities? Have you left the shore of Euboea and put in from beyond the water with sea-going oar?
>
> *Iolaus*
>
> It is no islander's life that I live. [85] We have come to your land from Mycenae.
>
> *Chorus*
>
> What is the name the people of Mycenae call you?
>
> *Iolaus*
>
> You know, I'm sure, of Iolaus, the man who stood at Heracles' side. I am not unknown to fame.
>
> *Chorus*
>
> [90] I have heard of you before. But whose are the young children you lead by the hand? Tell us.
>
> *Iolaus*
>
> They are Heracles' sons, strangers, who have come as suppliants to you and your city.

Linked-list encoding uses *previous* and *next* attributes to point to the previous and next speech fragments in a chain, so that a linked list is formed. Separate linked lists are differentiated by assigning the same *name* attribute to each speech fragment in a chain. For example:

```
<div1 type="choral" id="1ch">
  <stage>Enter by Eisodos B a Chorus of Marathonian
    citizens.</stage>
  <sp>
    <speaker>Chorus</speaker>
    <p>Oh! Oh! What is this cry that has been raised near
      the altar? Of what disaster will it soon give
      proof?</p>
    <strophe id="1strA1" next="1strA2"> <milestone
      ed="p" unit="line" n="75"> See the feeble old man
      lying spread upon the ground! </strophe>
    <p>O unhappy man, <gap> at whose hands have you
      had this wretched fall?</p>
  </sp>
  <sp>
    <speaker>Iolaus</speaker>
    <p>This man, strangers, dishonors your gods and drags
      me by force from the altar steps.</p>
  </sp>
  <sp>
    <speaker>Chorus</speaker>
    <strophe id="1strA2" prev="1strA1" next="1strA3">
      <milestone ed="p" unit="line" n="80"> But you,
      old sir, from what land have you come to this people
      who dwell together in four cities? Have you left the
      shore of Euboea and put in from beyond the
      water with sea-going oar? </strophe>
  </sp>
  <sp>
    <speaker>Iolaus</speaker>
    <p>It is no islander's life that I live. <milestone
      ed="p" unit="line" n="85"> We have come to your
      land from Mycenae.</p>
  </sp>
  <sp>
    <speaker>Chorus</speaker>
    <strophe id="1strA3" prev="1strA2" next="1strA4">
      What is the name the people of Mycenae call
      you?</strophe>
  </sp>
  <sp>
    <speaker>Iolaus</speaker>
    <p>You know, I'm sure, of Iolaus, the man who stood
      at Heracles' side. I am not unknown to fame.</p>
  </sp>
  <sp>
    <speaker>Chorus</speaker>
    <strophe id="1strA4" prev="1strA3"> <milestone
      ed="p" unit="line" n="90"> I have heard of you
      before. But whose are the young children you lead
      by the hand? Tell us.</strophe>
  </sp>
```

```
<sp>
  <speaker>Iolaus</speaker>
  <p>They are Heracles' sons, strangers, who have come
    as suppliants to you and your city.</p>
</sp>
...
</div1>
```

The more complex, but also more intellectually satisfying method uses the **<join>** element defined in P3, Chapter 14, "Linking, Segmentation and Alignment" (P3, pp. 443–48). A **<join>** element identifies the type of overlaid structure that is being encoded, and lists the fragments which comprise it. This allows the program that is processing the SGML file to read in a set of **<join>** elements, and use that information to identify disjoint structures and piece them together as their fragments are encountered. This has the advantage over the simpler linked-list method that a program encountering any one fragment can immediately determine the extent of the whole overlaid structure. The linked-list encoding is easier to process, but only yields information about the whole structure after all its fragments have been encountered. The join encoding is more difficult to create and verify, but it includes in the document an explicit analysis showing what virtual elements exist, what their components are, and the order in which these occur – information that the linked-list encoding cannot provide without extra processing.

The text encoded by the join method looks like this:

```
<join id="1strA" type="Strophe" targets="1strA1 1strA2
  1strA3 1strA4">
<stage>Enter by Eisodos B a Chorus of Marathonian
  citizens.</stage>
<sp>
  <speaker>Chorus</speaker>
  <p>Oh! Oh! What is this cry that has been raised near the
    altar? Of what disaster will it soon give proof?</p>
  <strophe id="1strA1"> <milestone ed="p" unit="line"
    n="75"> See the feeble old man lying spread
    upon the ground!</strophe>
  <p>O unhappy man, <gap> at whose hands have you
    had this wretched fall?</p>
</sp>
<sp>
  <speaker>Iolaus</speaker>
  <p>This man, strangers, dishonors your gods and drags
    me by force from the altar steps.</p>
</sp>
<sp>
  <speaker>Chorus</speaker>
  <strophe id="1strA2"> <milestone ed="p" unit="line"
    n="80"> But you, old sir, from what land have you come
    to this people who dwell together in four cities? Have
    you left the shore of Euboea and put in from beyond the
    water with sea-going oar? </strophe>
</sp>
<sp>
  <speaker>Iolaus</speaker>
  <p>It is no islander's life that I live. <milestone
    ed="p" unit="line" n="85"> We have come to your land
    from Mycenae.</p>
</sp>
<sp>
  <speaker>Chorus</speaker>
  <strophe id="1strA3"> What is the name the people of
    Mycenae call you? </strophe>
</sp>
<sp>
  <speaker>Iolaus</speaker>
  <p>You know, I'm sure, of Iolaus, the man who stood at
    Heracles' side. I am not unknown to fame.</p>
</sp>
<sp>
  <speaker>Chorus</speaker>
  <strophe id="1strA4"> <milestone ed="p" unit="line"
    n="90"> I have heard of you before. But whose are the
    young children you lead by the hand? Tell us.</strophe>
</sp>
<sp>
  <speaker>Iolaus</speaker>
  <p>They are Heracles' sons, strangers, who have come as
    suppliants to you and your city.</p>
</sp>
...
```

Some of the most difficult overlaid structures to encode are overlapping and simultaneous speech. In performance, it is common to have actors interrupt one another or speak in unison, but this type of overlap is not usually represented in printed texts. Where overlaps are indicated, it is traditionally done using punctuation, stage directions and, in the most elaborate instances, detailed bracketing or layout features. A unique example is Samuel Beckett's *Play*, where passages that have to be spoken in exact relationship to one another are "scored" in an appendix. Using **<stage>** and **<rendition>** tags it is possible to convey temporal information to the same degree as in a printed text. This is not adequate, however, for encoding detailed time-based information of an actual performance. We did not create any ways of representing temporal information specifically for dramatic texts. Instead, we recommend that performances that require such tagging be considered as spoken texts, and encoded using the spoken text tags. These allow for very detailed markup of speaker, temporal information and other gestural and tonal features.

In this paper, we have focused on how to encode a printed dramatic text and its interpretation. We have tried to provide guidelines for encoding simple, basic features, and for conveying complex analytical information. We hope and recommend that encoders will try to encode as much information as is economically feasible for them: the more detailed the encoding, the more powerful and widely usable the text.

Note

[1] The work described in this paper is the outcome of the discussions of the Performance Working Group, whose members are Elli Mylonas (chair), Rosanne G. Potter, John Lavagnino, and Lou Burnard. The authors wish to thank the other two members for their contributions.

References

Howard-Hill, T.H. "Modern Textual Theories and the Editing of Plays". *The Library*, 6th ser., 11 (1989), 89–115.

Issacharoff, Michael and Robin F. Jones, eds. *Performing Texts.* Philadelphia: University of Pennsylvania Press, 1988.

Johannson, Stig. "The Encoding of Spoken Texts". In this volume.

Shakespeare, William. *The Complete Works.* Ed. Stanley Wells, Gary Taylor, John Jowett and William Montgomery. Oxford: Clarendon Press, 1989. (Electronic Edition)

Sperberg-McQueen, C.M. "Text in the Electronic Age: Textual Study and Text Encoding, with Examples from Medieval texts". *Literary and Linguistic Computing*, 6 (1991), 34–46.

Sperberg-McQueen, C.M. and Lou Burnard, eds. *Guidelines for Electronic Text Encoding and Interchange (TEI P3).* Chicago and Oxford: Text Encoding Initiative, 1994.

Thompson, Marvin and Ruth Thompson, eds. *Shakespeare and the Sense of Performance.* Newark: University of Delaware Press, 1989.

Computers and the Humanities **29:** 123–136, 1995.

Encoding Textual Criticism

Robin C. Cover *
6634 Sarah Drive, Dallas TX 75236, USA
e-mail: robin@utafll.uta.edu, robin@acadcomp.sil.org

and

Peter M. W. Robinson *
Centre for Humanities Computing, 13 Banbury Road, Oxford OX2 6NN, UK
e-mail: peterr@vax.ox.ac.uk

Key words: SGML, textual criticism, electronic text editions, text encoding, TEI

Abstract

This paper chronicles the work of the TEI textual criticism working groups through several phases, documenting how and why the design goals were shaped by the requirements of several distinct user communities and by the nature of the textual evidence itself. Encoding schemes for the representation of physical details of textual witnesses were unified with encoding schemes for critical editing practices when it was observed that the two phenomena were inextricably layered and linked within real texts. Rationale is offered for the development teams' adherence to exceedingly general design principles: (a) the requirement that the encoding notations be neutral in text-theoretic terms; (b) the need to accommodate dramatically different text-transmission phenomena and research goals within diverse text-critical arenas; (c) the need for commensurability of the text-critical markup with encoding notations used in closely related text-analytic research. The paper also assesses the results of the effort in terms of the encoding scheme's adequacy for several scholarly purposes: suggestions are made concerning the need for programmatic testing, for refinement, and for extension of the encoding model to support a broader range of text-transmission phenomena and research objectives.

The design of a generalized encoding scheme for representing transcriptional and text-critical information has proved to be a significant challenge to the TEI subcommittees and working groups charged with the design task. In the following article, we wish to document the progress and achievements of this particular TEI effort in its historical perspective. Firstly, we summarize what is necessary for support of the electronic text critical edition (section 1). Secondly, we sketch the special challenges – intellectual, technical, and political – this task has presented (section 2). Thirdly, we describe the rationale for current proposals in version 2.0 of the draft Guidelines, outlining the development of this draft (section 3). Finally, we review the adequacy of the current proposals and give examples of the outstanding problems and deficiencies in the current encoding scheme, which will form the basis for continuing TEI work (section 4).

* Robin Cover serves as humanities computing technical consultant for the CELLAR Project (Computing Environment for Linguistic, Literary, and Anthropological Research), sponsored by SIL's Department of Academic Computing. His research involves conceptual modelling and functional design specification for a multilingual object-oriented document processing system and integrated bibliographic database management subsystem.

Peter Robinson is Executive Officer for the *Canterbury Tales* Project, was chair of the TEI work-group on textual criticism, and is developer of the computer program *Collate*, widely used in the preparation of critical editions based on multiple witnesses. He acts as consultant to several publishers and critical edition projects.

1. Goals and Requirements of Encoding for Text Critical Work

A well-edited text is the foundation of many kinds of humanities scholarship. In the past thirty years, computers have commonly been used for a single, specialized purpose in the preparation and manipulation of scholarly texts: most often in typesetting, but also for 'one-off' concordance making, or statistical analysis.[1] Recent advances in computer storage and display are likely to extend the use of computers in text-critical work far beyond this. Scholars may come to read the texts themselves on the computer; they may research and teach them through the computer.

This has considerable implications for textual scholarship. The computer may itself become the primary means of presentation of certain texts, and preparation of these texts for the computer the end of textual scholarship. This does not mean that scholarly texts will no longer be printed or studied in book form. Rather, certain types of texts, especially those with complex witness traditions or those that are richly supplied with authorial manuscripts, are likely to be best studied through computer presentation rather than printed presentation. It is because these texts (the Bible; major works of classical, medieval and modern literature; see also section 2.2) are among the fundamental texts of our culture that computer methods offer such potential.

1.1 *The electronic edition*

Consider, briefly, the possibilities held out by computer presentation of scholarly texts. Because there is no theoretical limit to the amount of material the computer may hold, one may study not just a single printed scholarly edition but every scholarly edition ever made; every printing of the text; every manuscript of the text; every reference to the text in other sources. One may see both transcriptions of this material, or computer images of it. Variant versions may be collated by computer, with (for example) the differences found by the collation program highlighted in the computer display. Scholars might browse the collations to determine the exact support for any one reading. Or, they might submit the information about witness agreements and disagreements to a cladistic analysis program, or a database, to explore the relations between the manuscripts.[2]

Further, these editions will be fluid, evolving objects: they should absorb the continuing contributions of scholars, as emendation, annotation, import of additional source material, with all layers of editorial responsibility explicitly accessible. (See section 2.2 below.) Some scholars may use these editions as quarries, using computer retrieval methods to extract information about (for example) the text and its transmission. Others might use these as springboards, adding their own encoding of (for example) grammatical or lexical information. Although we may call these 'electronic editions', such collections are best thought of as resources libraries for the study of texts, mixing archival and reference matter, scholarly commentary and traditionally edited texts with powerful computer tools in ways hitherto impossible.[3]

1.2 *The need for descriptive, standard markup as provided by SGML*

Successful achievement of these electronic editions is dependent on their computer encoding. Without some system of indicating the status of particular readings in particular witnesses, or what readings in what witnesses correspond to what other readings in what other witnesses, or why this editor prefers that reading to this, electronic editions will be unusable because of the very mass of information within them. Because it is impossible to foresee the ways in which scholars might use these electronic editions, 'procedural' markup, as in traditional typesetting systems (instructing this character to appear thus on this page) is inappropriate. Procedural markup limits the way material may be viewed and handled, much as a printed book can only be read with the typesetting determined by the printer. 'Descriptive' markup, as provided by SGML, is particularly apposite, and offers a way past the single view of the text prescribed by its processing to the many views implicit in the text itself.[4] The essence of scholarly editing is the recording of exact detail. Descriptive markup provides means for representing this detail using a machine-independent notation.

As an instance of the superiority of descriptive over procedural markup, consider the possible markup for Middle English manuscript 'et9nal', with the superscript hook character (here rendered by a 9) indicating manuscript abbreviation of 'er'. Using the procedural markup common in typeset editions, one would indicate the expansion of the abbreviation by italic type: 'et*er*nal'. Using descriptive markup, as in SGML, one could use the <**expan**> tag to indicate the expansion, with the *abbrev* attribute to carry the abbreviation, thus:

et<expan abbrev='9'>er</>nal

Observe how a computer system might use the two encodings. With the procedural markup, if italic text is used in the printed edition only to indicate editorial expansions of abbreviations, then all expansions may be extracted without error. But if italic text is used for any other purpose whatever (emphasis, structural division, marking conjectures, etc.) then the search results will become unpredictable. But with descriptive markup and the SGML use of <**expan**>, one can be quite sure that the search finds expansions, and only expansions. Further, a search on the SGML encoding might extract much more than this. It might locate all cases where the abbreviation mark '9' appears. It might locate all cases where this abbreviation mark is expanded to *er*, and (perhaps most interesting) all cases where it is expanded to some other value, or not expanded at all, or where the editor indicates two or more possible expansions, or where it is subject to emendation.

Not only should markup be descriptive, it should be standard. Scholarly editing may require extremes of skill and time. It will be no service to future editors for this knowledge to be locked into an idiosyncratic and inaccessible encoding, no matter how powerful or well-conceived. Again, SGML provides the best platform for development of a standard means of encoding scholarly editions. If one multiplies the possible plethora of encoding schemes by the size of some of the textual traditions which might be encoded (6000 manuscripts for parts of the New Testament) the potential for anarchy is all too real. Without standard encoding schemes, the making of machine-readable texts may take scholarship backwards, into a confusion of encodings, and not forwards, into new clarity of vision.

This is not to say that SGML, as it is presently most widely implemented, is ideal for scholarly purposes. The restrictions in SGML on nesting and overlapping of elements may lead to inelegant encoding, though solutions to this are generally available (see, for example, the <**addSpan**> and <**delSpan**> elements). More seriously, it is a continuing difficulty that most current SGML applications do not implement the CONCUR feature, and thereby permit direct encoding of one and only one document structure. For virtually all scholarly texts edited from originary witnesses, there are at least two distinct structures which scholars may wish to record. The first structure is the 'canonical' ordering of the text, as defined by scholars for ease of reference across many different witnesses (thus verse 1 of chapter 1 of Mark). The second structure is the 'physical' ordering of the text as it appears in a particular witness (thus, line 1 of folio recto 1). Typically, the current TEI recommendations cope with multiple structures by the use of empty elements, for example recording page and line breaks with empty <**pb**> and <**lb**> elements. This wastes much of the theoretic power of the CONCUR feature, with the ability to validate and align various document structures.

Despite these problems SGML remains far the best choice for a descriptive markup language. Vigorously promoted commercial markup languages, such as Microsoft's *Rich Text Format* or Adobe's *Acrobat* (Microsoft, 1992; Warnock, 1992), are heavily biased towards procedural markup and are very far from suitable for scholarly encoding.

1.3 *The need for conformity to the TEI dialect of SGML*

Electronic editions must be useful not only to textual scholars, but to the whole intellectual community: to historians, linguists, philosophers, students, researchers, and readers of every background. Through document layering and versioning techniques, the reader should gain access to the edition he or she can best read: whether the text in translation; or in edited, regularized form; or in the transcription of an individual witness; or through an image of that witness. Through the developing marriage of SGML/TEI and hypertext, this can be achieved at little or no cost to the encoder, so long as standard SGML/TEI techniques are used. Similarly, the use of standard SGML/TEI encoding strategies will facilitate the use of these electronic editions alongside (for example) linguistic databases or historical data-sets encoded using SGML. Scholars from outside the text-critical arena will then be able to add their own markup to electronic editions using SGML/TEI structures, and use them seamlessly in their own environments, with their own software. (See section 2.2 for instances where text-critical knowledge is critically dependent on advances in other scholarly areas.)

This commitment to working within the TEI environment meant that, where possible, we should resist the tailoring of specific mechanisms for specific text-critical purposes, in favour of use (with adaptation, if necessary) of general-purpose TEI mechanisms available to all areas of the enterprise. In the sometimes frenetic atmosphere of TEI work, with different workgroups energetically adapting the same mechanisms for many different uses, this has created some problems. At times we have had to wait for the resolution of problems on a TEI-wide basis: thus, with the certainty and feature structure elements. At other times, we have had to attempt to convince others that problems which we face actually require a TEI-wide solution: thus, with attribution of responsibility. At all times, we have had to look over one shoulder, at how our work might impact on that of other workgroups, and over the other shoulder, at how their work might impact on ours.

1.4 *The need for encoding to cater to different schools of textual criticism*

Over the several millennia of textual criticism, scholars have developed many different ways of editing texts. Some prefer transcriptions of the original witness so faithful as to be nearly indistinguishable from it; others regularize in transcription; others prefer not to transcribe at all from original witnesses, but to edit from existing realizations. Other scholars present reconstructed texts of varying artifice, built upon recensionist, metrical, intuitive or other concepts applied to transcriptions themselves of differing principles. Even the editing of modern texts, surviving in well-documented authorial states, is a battleground of theories of imperfected authorial intention against actual published text.[5] For any text critical encoding to be successful, it could not be seen to favor any one school of text critical thought over any other. If it did this, it would fail and deserve to fail.

2. The Special Challenges to a Generalized Encoding Strategy for Transcription and Textual Criticism

In the paragraphs that follow, we supply an overview of the special challenges presented to members of the TEI design teams who have collaborated to devise generic and extensible encoding methods.[6] Familiarity with these considerations may assist readers in understanding why the designers of the TEI have resolutely determined to keep the approaches as generic and simple as possible: this purposeful generality affords the encoding mechanisms and generic processing software a much greater chance of "working" for the more complex textual environments within which the SGML formalisms have not yet been tested (e.g., complex multilingual text relationships; arenas involving heavy textual recension). Similarly, discussion in this section will enable reviewers to better visualize how both "transcriptional" and "text critical" knowledge about a text must be stored in ways that are completely compatible with other realms of knowledge (literary, linguistic and historical analysis) if text-analytic software designed to process TEI texts is to support an integrated analysis of the encoded information.

An instance of this preference for widely-applicable generic solutions rather than narrowly-defined specific solutions is our use of the <**app**> and <**rdg**> tags. These were first conceived as specialized elements for registering the alternative readings of different physical witnesses. Thus, the alternative readings 'experiment' and 'eryment' in the manuscripts Cp and Ra2 could be recorded as follows:

```
<app>
   <rdg wit="Cp">experiment</rdg>
   <rdg wit="Ra2">eryment</rdg>
</app>
```

When we came to consider how alternative readings in a single witness (whether arising from authorial revision, scribal tinkering or editorial intervention) might be encoded, we realized that the <**app**> and <**rdg**> elements could be used for this purpose, too. For example, D. H. Lawrence's alteration of 'galls' to 'dogs' in the manuscript of *Eloi, Eloi, lama sabachthani*, by striking through 'galls' and writing 'dogs' above it, could be registered as follows:

```
<app>
   <rdg hand="DHL"><del type="overstrike">
      galls</del></rdg>
   <rdg hand="DHL"><add type="supra-
      linear">dogs</add></rdg>
</app>
```

At various times, the merits of some specialized tag to register such authorial or other substitutions were canvassed. However, given the blurring of the line in many editions between reporting of variant readings in a single witness and in many witnesses, the power of the general-purpose <**app**> and <**rdg**> elements was persuasive.

2.1 *Implications of multiple tradents*

Constructing a tag set for textual criticism forced us to reckon not only with document versioning problems that are still being studied by hypertext theorists, but with the more complex textual layering that results from the large number of different individuals (some playing multiple roles) who participate in giving a transmitted text its various shapes: author, amanuensis, copyist, author-as-corrector, author-as-reviser, editor, reviewer, liturgist, commentator, redactor, modernizer, etc. We frequently find the work of several tradents upon the same physical carrier; more predictably, we face the subconscious and conscious intervention of scribes, priests, and courtiers who sought both to preserve written traditions and to update or explain the texts in order to keep them relevant within their communities.

Two practical problems emerged directly from the need to deal with multiple tradents in multiple roles: (1) the descriptions of tag usage and the applicable SGML attributes vary considerably across the range of tradents and their functions, confounding a single definition for tag and attribute usage; (2) the semantic relationships between tag names, attribute names and attribute values become complex and sometimes hard to manage when the focus changes within a tagging environment from one tradent or agent to another. For example, SGML attributes are sometimes used to name an analyst responsible for identifying or classifying a textual feature, for otherwise properly interpreting it, or for assigning a level of confidence to a critical judgment implicit in a markup act. However, since SGML attributes cannot themselves contain substructure and cannot be repeated within an SGML tag, multiple critical judgments by multiple tradents attached to a single textual object sometimes require that the attribute notation be abandoned in favor of semantically-equivalent SGML tags that can support a richer information structure. Observation of a new datum or the addition of a new analytical perspective may thus render obsolete one form of encoding as one is forced to adopt a different scheme.[7]

2.2 *The case of canonical and sacred texts*

While transcription tags are necessary for encoding all kinds of texts (letters, tax records, contracts, monumental inscriptions, deeds, ration lists, office documents, etc.) the requirements for text-critical tags may be illustrated within the arena of "classical" texts which have been extensively copied and transmitted. The richest of these for text-critical purposes are texts that found a canonical home in the scribal curriculum or in religious tradition several hundreds or thousands of years ago, with several attendant difficulties that translate into encoding requirements.

(1) Because many sacred and canonical traditions began in antiquity, they involve writing systems that have complex orthographic strata. The need to reckon with ambiguity (imperfectly defined writing systems), glyph polyvalence, and *scripta continua* within these orthographic strata greatly complicate the definition of "transcription" for general purposes. Whereas "transcription" for well-known alphabetic writing systems reduces to a simple algebra, "transcription" in several of the other relevant languages involves a multi-step process. The current TEI transcription tags are designed to work for Roman-based writing systems, but we anticipate the need for some modified definitions and strategies as more complex writings systems come into the TEI sphere of investigation.

(2) Owing to the high antiquity of many texts in the classical and canonical traditions, transmission of text across languages forms a vital part of those traditions. In addition to the customary practice of modernizing canonical texts through translation, we have interlinear and parallel versions (sometimes with extensive commentary) attested for texts before the common era. Frequently, since ancient texts are best preserved or only completely preserved in translations, the text critical encoding must provide for processes of retroversion through which successively older editions can be reconstructed. These mechanisms depend heavily upon the TEI encoding strategies developed for synchronization, segmentation and alignment – encoding strategies which are still under development at the time of our work.

(3) Also owing to the high antiquity of texts in the canonical and sacred traditions, encoders are faced with representing complex evolutionary processes that can be documented for these texts along their historical continuum and through their geographical spread. Because these texts were usually performed liturgically, ritually or in other ways supportive of the political processes for which they were composed, they were sometimes subject to programmatic redactional and recensional activity. Whereas transcription tags describe a text instance as a snapshot (synchronic description), the encoding mechanisms supporting text criticism must be diachronically expressive: they must be commen-

surate with and integral to the larger processes of modern literary-critical and linguistic analysis which are brought to bear upon the documentation of these textual "catastrophisms" within the slower evolutionary sweep.

(4) Finally, within the ancient canonical traditions, the dependence of text critical reasoning upon linguistic sciences (classical "philology") is quite marked. Where writing systems are poorly understood and written materials typically are in highly fragmentary state, clues from the linguistic and literary milieu are brought to bear more forcefully in text-critical argumentation. A textual datum that is merely permissible or simply not precluded by the paleography and orthography sometimes becomes probably or certain by virtue of literary and linguistic expectation. This consideration has made it necessary within the overall TEI design to ensure that the encoding strategies for transcription and textual criticism are commensurate with those of the literary and linguistic description. As outlined in 1.3 above, "The Need for Conformity to the TEI Dialect of SGML", applications processing the marked-up textual data must be able to appeal simultaneously to encoded analytical perspectives within several domains of knowledge.

2.3 *Transcription requires low-level attention to text detail*

Whereas historians, philosophers and literary critics typically investigate the higher cognitive and cultural issues within written "text", the task of transcription involves description of the written source at nearly the lowest levels: at the level of glyphs, characters, and syllabary-signs. Paleographers, epigraphers and archaeologists are all interested in the most minute details of writing, so that encoding schemes appropriate to their researches, in transcriptional terms, must inevitably reckon with character- or glyph-level annotation. In general, the older and lesser well-known the languages and writing systems are, the more important these paleographical and epigraphical considerations become. The TEI guidelines have attempted in some ways to provide for expression of character-level detail in the encoding, and indeed, the use of general strategies usually makes such representation possible. It remains to be seen, however, whether encoders will be able to accept the general mechanisms: these representations become extremely verbose and heavy with markup, and thus almost impossible to read, in any meaningful of the word, without specialized software.

For example, a recently released transcription of Hebrew biblical text from the Dead Sea Scrolls ("Qumran") corpus, published as an *editio princeps*, uses character-level sigla to indicate one of four levels of certainty regarding the transcriptions: a small superscript open circlet indicates a possible reading, a superscript dot indicates a probable reading, an in-line circlet indicates a doubtful character reading, while the absence of any character-level siglum indicates virtual certainty.[8] The general TEI strategy for encoding certainty about a reading is to store the (un)certainty data out of line in a separate **<certainty>** tag; this **<certainty>** tag contains a pointer to the text element. Thus, encoding character-level annotation for certainty (or for any paleographic feature) would require placing an **<anchor>** or other character-delimiting SGML tag into the text for each letter. To encode a single seven-letter Hebrew word from Exodus 12:7 in a sample Qumran text (HMZWZWT; English "doorposts") would require an encoding like this:

```
<seg type=wordFrag id=a1>H</seg><seg type=wordFrag
  id=a2>M</seg>
<seg type=wordFrag id=a3>Z</seg><seg type=wordFrag
  id=a4>W</seg>
<seg type=wordFrag id=a5>Z</seg><seg type=wordFrag
  id=a6>W</seg>
<seg type=wordFrag id=a7>T</seg><!-- out-of-line cer-
  tainty tags: --> <certainty target=A1 locus=‘#transcribed
  Content’ degree=probable given=“” assertedValue=“”
  desc=“”><certainty target=A2 locus=‘#transcribed
  Content’ degree=certain given=“” assertedValue=“”
  desc=“”><certainty target=A3 locus=‘#transcribed
  Content’ degree=possible given=“” assertedValue=“”
  desc=“”><certainty target=A4 locus=‘#transcribed
  Content’ degree=probable given=“” assertedValue=“”
  desc=“”><certainty target=A5 locus=‘#transcribed
  Content’ degree=possible given=“” assertedValue=“”
  desc=“”><certainty target=A6 locus=‘#transcribed
  Content’ degree=probable given=“” assertedValue=“”
  desc=“”><certainty target=A7 locus=‘#transcribed
  Content’ degree=possible given=“” assertedValue=“”
  desc=“”>[9]
```

Given the current density of mass storage, the markup overhead itself is not necessarily disturbing, especially if binary/compressed SGML representations are used: we are prepared to pay such prices for generality that truly works. But this example raises the matter of human readablity and of machine potential to render the text in real time. If the encoder wished to invent a proprietary character-level notation for the four levels of certainty in transcription, much of the bulk in this general encoding strategy could be reduced.[10] On the other hand, the integrity of the proprietary encoding could not be validated by SGML, and it would do nothing to alleviate the markup burden re-introduced for other reasons. The value of any similar "non-general" (non-SGML) solution would be compromised because **<anchor>** or **<seg>** tags must be inserted into the text at character level as hooks whenever *any other* kind of character-level description is needed in connection with the transcription (paleographic note, responsibility tag, reading or apparatus tag, etc.).

There is some disagreement among various TEI members about the relevance of the complexity factor that emerges when we attempt to reckon with transcriptional detail. Some maintain that character-level and word-level description are necessarily so complex that the human readability of the text in the normal linear sense is destined to become compromised when the SGML (inline) "markup" encoding strategy is used. Thus, they feel that text management and display software will be required in any case (e.g., for the management of IDs and IDREFs on hundreds of tags, and for filtering analytical detail). Furthermore, they argue that if concern for the visual complexity of a "raw" tagged SGML file is allowed to constrain the encoding model, expressiveness necessarily will be compromised: "We should design and encode for tomorrow's computers, not for yesterday's." These individuals tend to see the primary value of the TEI-SGML encoding as a validatable, internationally standard interchange format, and thus do not feel that a TEI-SGML text need be "simple" enough to be used "straight-out" within a real-time application.

Others within TEI feel that the complexity of encoding should not be so great that humanities researchers are required to use special data-tagging software and display software in order to manage the electronic texts. SGML encoding, they argue, is not just for interchange: text encoded in SGML should be manageable *directly* by hypertext and text-analytic applications, without conversion to a more compact local format: hence, visual and computational complexity beyond a certain level should not be tolerated. Accordingly, they maintain that character level annotation should be implemented using some indirect method (e.g., byte offsets into the text from one or a few fixed points) so that text will not become cluttered beyond recognition, or so complex that "plain" views of the base text cannot be constructed on the fly. Adjudicating between the desire for a simple, human-readable encoding with limited power of expression *versus* a more powerful encoding that obscures "the text" has presented a particularly difficult task for the TEI groups working on transcription and text criticism. This dilemma has, however, heightened our awareness of how similar the analytical concerns are to those of the AI ("Analysis and Interpretation") TEI subcommittees.

3. The Current Draft: Overview and History

3.1 *Strategy: The workgroup*

Provision of a single, standard system of descriptive markup capable of meeting every text-critical need of every scholar must, then, be the aim. But over the great range of texts and situations surveyed earlier in this article, the task is at least daunting and perhaps impossible. Of course, the question of whether a single encoding scheme could meet every text critical need will never be finally answered. Every new edition will test the encoding; as long as new editions are made (and one foresees no end to this) any encoding scheme must be provisional.

Thus, the workgroup faced an immediate contradiction. A standard encoding for text-critical work is needed, but in the face of the diversity of texts and their continual re-editing no standard scheme can ever be considered final. Development must proceed by gradual increments, and the history of our work (like that of any textual editor) is one of continual revision. We have tried to keep one eye on the parallel sets of TEI tags (core tags, analytical tags, segmentation and alignment tags) while keeping another eye on the future TEI goals of enhancing the expressiveness for physical description and for the embrace of more complex writing systems.

Our strategy was accordingly pragmatic. We could not hope to devise a scheme to satisfy every need. Instead, we would try to identify what is needed in as many domains as possible and seek to meet those needs. Accordingly, the membership of the textual criticism workgroup was chosen to give a deliberately varied range of expertise over text critical problems in different literatures.[11] In addition, an informal electronic discussion group ('TEXTCRIT', based on the Oxford Vax cluster) was set up in August 1991, moderated by Robinson. This was intended to allow any other interested scholars to contribute to the discussions leading to the drafting of the Textual Criticism section of the second version of the 'Guidelines' (P2). The comments of this group – always well-informed, and at times very lively – were invaluable in the early stages of our work.

Our work divided naturally into two areas. Firstly, we had to establish a scheme for transcription of individual witnesses, able to register deletions, additions, substitutions, damage, shifts of hand, abbreviation, etc. We called these 'transcription tags', using the term 'tag' loosely to signify any and all SGML mechanisms. Secondly, we had to establish a scheme for gathering together all the various readings in differing witnesses, in the manner of a traditional critical apparatus. We called these 'apparatus tags'. Observe that the two types of tags may overlap in use. A critical apparatus gathering the readings of many witnesses may need to employ 'transcription tags' to record the exact status of any one reading in any witness. A transcription of a single witness may also employ 'apparatus tags' to record variant readings, for example those of different editors or resulting from scribal substitutions within the transcriptions. Nor is there necessarily a clear division between a transcription of a single witness, which may incorporate reference to readings in other witnesses, and a synoptic edition which presents the evidence of many witnesses but keys these many witnesses to the base text of an individual witness. Accordingly, so far as is possible, we had to ensure not only that the transcription and apparatus tags were each adequate for their particular task but also that they could work together smoothly.

3.2 *The 'transcription tags'*

The group concentrated first on the definition of the transcription tags. The basis of the transcription tags was the set of 'editorial' tags available in all TEI documents and described in the first draft of the Guidelines (P1): the <**sic**> and <**corr**> tags, for correction of apparent errors; the <**norm**> tag for recording regularization of spelling; the <**add**> and <**del**> tags for expressing additions and deletions; the <**note**> tag for indicating annotation; the <**abbrev**> tag for recording abbreviation. As defined in P1, these seven tags were clearly not sufficient to meet the circumstances of text-critical transcription. How much of our special needs could be met by refinement of these tags; how many, and what, extra tags might be needed?

Our discussion was complicated by being one of many work groups interested in these tags. We had both to be aware of the definitions of these and new tags offered by other groups, and also of the impact our definitions and innovations might have on these groups. This has proved particularly difficult on the issue of expressing degrees of certainty. This is critical for our work and also for many other areas of the TEI. Therefore we could not develop something that worked just for us, but we have had to wait on the development of a TEI-wide solution. Similarly, we have become increasingly aware that feature structures might offer a means of coping with some of our most difficult problems. Again, we have had to wait on final resolution of feature structures. Accordingly, we are not able at this stage (July 1993) to do more than point out that feature structures may offer useful encoding strategies for some text critical material, without giving examples or further detail. Our discussion was also handicapped, in the early stages, by the possible overlap of our work with that of the workgroup responsible for the section 'Physical Description of Manuscripts'. A partial resolution of this overlap was achieved late in our work (see below).

Our first task, then, was scrutiny of what was available to us from P1. After much discussion, in the course of preparation of our first draft, completed by June 1992, we added the following tags to the group of seven P1 editorial tags:

<**addSpan**>: marks a longer sequence of added text, especially where that text crosses a structural boundary in the text being encoded;

<**delSpan**>: marks a longer sequence of deleted text;

<**omit**>: indicates a point where material has been omitted in a transcription;

<**orig**>: contains the original form of a reading, for which the regularized form is given in an attribute value;

<**expan**>: contains the expansion of an abbreviation;

<**damage**>: contains an area of damage to the text witness;

<**unclear**>: contains a character, word, phrase or passage which cannot be transcribed with certainty because it is illegible or inaudible in the source;

<**space**>: indicates the location of a significant space in the copy text.

Also, the P1 <**norm**> tag was renamed <**reg**>, various modifications of the attribute values of existing P1 tags were made (notably, the renaming of the *ed* attribute of P1 as *resp*), and the prose account of the tags attempted to clarify just how the various tags might work together. The new **<orig>** and **<expan>** tags were conceived as 'mirror tags' of their **<reg>** and **<abbrev>** tags counterparts, with attribute values and documentation reflecting this conception.

The re-activation of the 'Manuscripts' workgroup in the second half of 1992, under the chairmanship of Claus Huitfeldt and including two members – Peter Robinson and Michael Sperberg-McQueen – of the Textual Criticism workgroup, led to the complete reassessment of this first (June 1992) P2 draft. This draft in fact became the basis of the discussions of the manuscripts workgroup. The close scrutiny of the members of this group, whose experience ranged through historical texts (Donald Spaeth), medieval Latin philosophical materials (Dino Buzzetti), and modern philosophical writings (Alan Renear, Christian Kloesler, Claus Huitfeldt and Mary Keeler), showed up many gaps and opacities in the draft. For example, the draft did not contain adequate methods for registering document hands, and a need emerged for a more comprehensive scheme for assigning responsibility at the various levels of text creation, modification and encoding. Further, the fundamental shared interest of the two groups in primary source transcription led to the decision to amalgamate the transcription section of the textual criticism draft with the relevant work of the manuscripts group. In March 1993 and with the aid of a British Library grant, Peter Robinson, working in close consultation with Claus Huitfeldt, rewrote the whole section relating to primary source transcription. In the course of this rewriting, the following further tags were added:

<hand>: used in the header to define each distinct scribe or handwriting style;

<handShift>: marks the beginning of a sequence of text written by a new hand;

<supplied>: signifies text supplied by the transcriber or editor in place of text which cannot be read.

In addition, the attribute *hand* was added to many elements, so that it is possible to distinguish the agent responsible for a source feature (as given in the *hand* attribute of an addition) and the editor responsible for noting the feature (as given in the *resp* attribute of the element). Many examples were provided, and the prose attempted to specify more exactly the usage of each mechanism.

This March 1993 draft was subsequently printed in the papers for the May 1993 TEI review meeting, and was itself subject to further rigorous scrutiny. In particular, the examples given in the draft brought to light problems with expression of certainty, assignment of responsibility, and the interaction of tags and their attributes when nested within one another. We refer further to some of these difficulties in section 4.2 below.

3.3 *The 'apparatus tags'*

The writing of the second part of the draft, concerning apparatus tags, had a less eventful history. Firstly, the mechanisms provided in P1 were relatively more comprehensive than was the case for the P1 transcription tags. Secondly, these apparatus tags are very much the property of the textual criticism domain, and touch little upon other TEI areas, as did certain of the transcription tags. The methods for aligning apparatus fragments with a base text were somewhat altered. A 'location-referenced' method, which more closely mirrors many existing printed critical apparatus, was added and the 'single end-point' method given in P1 was dropped. The attributes of the apparatus elements **<app>**, **<rdg>** and **<lem>** were refined. Two new tags, **<witDetail>** and **<rdgGrp>**, were added. **<witDetail>** serves as a specialized note-carrier, permitting scholarly annotation within an apparatus of particular features in particular witnesses. **<rdgGrp>** permits grouping of variants because of a perceived affinity (as: all the readings exhibit a particular kind of variation).

We believe this system is capable of a level of encoding at least equivalent to that of a printed critical apparatus. For example, in Kane's edition of *Piers Plowman, A Text*, Kane prints the text of line 8 of the Prologue as follows:

Vnder a brood bank be a bo*ur*ne side

This line might be rendered using the **<div>** tag to identify the line and the **<expan>** tag to note the expansion:

```
<div type=l n=8>Vnder a brood bank be a bo
   <expan>ur</>ne side
```

Kane's apparatus for "bo*ur*ne" appears as follows:

bo*ur*ne] burne RDChVHLKWM; bo*ur*nis TUH2E (*a caret below* ur T); broke J.

Using the tags we recommend, the same information could be encoded as follows:

```
<app loc=8>
    <lemma>bo<expan>ur</>ne</>
    <rdg wit='RDChVHLKWM'>burne</rdg>
    <rdg wit='TUH2E' id=d8>bo<expan>ur</>
        nis</rdg>
    <rdg wit='J'>broke</>
</app>
```

and a separate **<witDetail>** element containing further information about the reading in the manuscript T:

```
<witDetail target='d8' wit='T'>
a caret below <q>ur</q>
</witDetail>
```

Close study of the March 1993 draft revealed areas of weakness in the proposed apparatus tags, as it did for the transcription tags. Notably, it was realized that a scheme for grouping variants as 'subvariants' – that is, variant forms witnessing a single 'substantive' reading, despite differences in orthography and even of language – was needed. This facility was added to the draft submitted to the May 1993 technical review meeting. Again, this feature has yet to be tested in serious work.

There is uncertainty, too, in the effects of use of the apparatus tags within a transcription, to indicate either variant readings (resulting from, for example, scribal substitution) or variant editorial interpretations. The effects of the interaction of apparatus and transcription tags and of the nesting of these tags, with possible inheritance of values down the hierarchy, remain to be tested in practice. For example: in the March and May 1993 drafts it was suggested that values for the *resp* and *hand* attributes on an outer **rdg** element might be inherited by elements within the **rdg** element. Thus:

```
<rdg resp=ETD>
    <corr>wright</>
</rdg>
```

is semantically equivalent to:

```
<rdg>
    <corr resp=ETD>wright</>
</rdg>
```

with the statement of responsibility for the correction inherited from the value of the *resp* attribute in the outer **rdg** element. However, the exact field of domain for the *resp* attribute varies from element to element (sometimes referring, as here, to the content of an element, sometimes to the value of an attribute of the element, as in the **<expan>** tag). At the least, correct application of these mechanisms will require considerable care.

This sketch of our work will show clearly enough that we proceeded by intense periods of revision separated by lengthy spaces of reflection and consultation. As we remarked earlier, no encoding scheme for text critical work can ever be considered final. Accordingly, our activity represents a series of attempts at finer-grained focus rather than a single act of definition.

4. The Adequacy of the Current Proposals and What Remains to Be Done

4.1 *The adequacy of the current proposals*

The workgroup chose to concentrate, in this phase of our work, on the comparatively simpler text-critical situations presented by medieval and modern Western European works: simpler, that is, compared to the complexities of the sacred traditions outlined in 2.2 above. The examples given in the March 1993 draft, drawn from modern authorial manuscripts for the transcription tags and from Chaucer's *Canterbury Tales*, illustrate this bias in our approach.

In these works, variation is typically expressed in an apparatus at the level of words, not individual graphemes. These are works in a single language, with Roman-based writing systems. Their apparatus rarely instance variants or subvariants from different languages or writing-systems, and commonly level out differences of spelling when reporting variation. Further, transcription of these textual materials is generally not concerned with character-level information, with the important exception of marks of abbreviation. Transcription is usually graphemic, not graphetic, representing a regularized orthography. Thus, work with these texts is not bound either, on the one side, by the need for the most exact recording of detail for each character in a transcription, or, on the other side, by the need to integrate millennia of commentary and transmission history, as is the case for the sacred texts discussed in 2.2. However, we believe the problems of registering fundamental text-critical information are common to both these texts and to sacred texts, and indeed to all texts whether in one witness or many, whether written millennia ago or today. Our hope in concentrating on medieval and modern Western European texts was that we might arrive at robust solutions to basic questions (how do we record a deletion? an addition? a substitution? a variant reading?). These solutions might then scale into more demanding text-critical environments, as those of sacred texts.

The TEI text-criticism working groups have been successful to the extent of developing basic encoding solutions. Thus, we have developed mechanisms which will enable effective SGML representation of existing scholarly texts of medieval or modern Western European tradition. They would permit capture, for example, of the Kane and Donaldson editions of Langland's *Piers Plowman* (as shown in the example above), and of Hans Walther Gabler's edition of Joyce's *Ulysses*. However, in accordance with our conviction that most important editions of the future will be in electronic form rather than printed form, we believe that a proper encoding scheme must be capable of far more than representation of existing printed editions. Here, too, extension of the capacity of the encoding to cope with many more situations than presently possible is important. We can feed the solution to problems arising from encoding sacred and other texts back into encoding of less complex texts, thereby enhancing the quality of these electronic editions further beyond what is possible for printed editions.

4.2 *Directions for future work*

Although formal provision for further TEI work remains unclear, the present authors feel that the TEI specification for transcriptional and text critical encoding could benefit from several kinds of additional collaborative work to test, enhance, revise, and document the recommended encoding strategies. Some of these opportunities are outlined below.

4.2.1 *Examples from different textual arenas*

In order to make the current encoding guidelines more accessible, TEI should develop tutorial and illustrative material drawing upon a wider body of literature – texts written in a variety of languages (including languages written in non-roman scripts), texts exhibiting longer and more complex recensional histories, texts representing several different literary genres, texts showing more complex layout structure as printed in aligned formats – so as to illustrate a greater variety of typical textual situations which face transcribers and textual critics.[12] Additionally, these sample materials should show the exact typography and structural layout within the copy texts in *literatim* format so as to portray the encoding strategies more clearly and realistically.

4.2.2 *Review and testing*

A stage of development which has hardly begun involves the testing of the transcriptional and text-critical encoding scheme. The true test of competency will be demonstrated when users show that they understand the documentation, and when they express that they find it acceptable (under usage) in terms of intellectual and clerical burden. Most critically, the adequacy of the scheme will be proven when testers reveal that they can apply the encoding constructs consistently. We expect that applications programmers writing for the TEI Guidelines will be required to reckon with a certain range of variability in the application of tags, but a certain threshold of predictable, uniform usage must be achieved in order to reward serious program development.

4.2.3 *Domain-specific term mapping*

During the preliminary stages of TEI work, the designers attempted to use neutral terminology and sometimes even *ad hoc* terminology so as to minimize the prejudicial influence of certain terms alternately sanctioned or proscribed within different text-critical schools. There is a need now to enlist the help of domain experts to map discipline-specific terminology onto the sometimes colorless TEI terms. The importance of this task should diminish in time as software developers, in collaboration with domain experts, design interfaces that mask complexities and potential ambiguities within the TEI text object name space.

4.2.4 *Recommended strategies for particular encoding problems*

A most critical task facing the TEI work force is designing and documenting *specific* recommended markup strategies for particular encoding problems within complex transcription and text-critical environments. The tag set itself is usable now for simple encoding tasks, but it is somewhat less usable, given the current documentation, for complicated situations that call for deep nesting, embedding, and other combinations of tag usage. That is: while a relatively rich inventory of tags and attributes is available for use, neither encoders nor software developers can be expected to intuitively interpret the "correct" meaning of every reasonable TEI-legal markup construct. In some cases, we have not even worked out for ourselves what it means (or should mean to an application) to use several tags in combination, and how to interpret the semantics when markup constructs (e.g., attribute values and tag names) appear to interact in unforeseen ways, and potentially, to conflict.[13]

Thus, collaborative effort should be directed toward the identification of a larger number of common textual phenomena which require multiple transcription and text-critical tags, and toward the design of recommended *encoding formulas* using the smaller constructs already available in the current tag set. To the extent that these transcriptional and text-critical situations have common names (e.g., "transposition", "paleographic confusion of glyphs and ligatured substrings", "haplography due to homoioarkton", "secondary change induced by rules of grammatical concord", "textual subvariants with masked accidentals", etc.), the recommended encoding solutions should be made accessible to users via keywords in the form of an index.

In designing these recommended markup strategies, the renewed effort should attempt to map the TEI encoding primitives onto the users' conceptual models of the features and phenomena implicit in the encoding tasks. It cannot be taken for granted – especially given the paucity of software tools designed to assist in text markup and to hide markup complexity – that users should be asked to adjust their text-theoretic frameworks and conceptual models of the problem domain to conform to TEI constructs. While it is desirable that encoders come to think in terms of the hierarchical and pointing methods used in SGML/TEI, it should not be necessary for users to undergo an entire methodological paradigm shift simply to use the tagset. To the extent that new methodological approaches are indeed required for sensible use of the TEI rules, the documentation of recommended strategies should ease the pain of transition for the textual scholars thereby affected, and likewise render the task of program specification clear for software designers.

4.2.5 *Greater expressiveness in recording controlled analytical and evaluative description of readings*

A limitation of the current encoding guidelines for text-critical work is that formal evaluation of readings and provision for detailed controlled analytical description are only thinly supported.[14] Further specification lay outside the timeframe and resources of the subcommittees, but we think that the most revolutionary forms of textual research facilitated by the SGML encoding of critical apparatus will be realized only when it is possible to supply more detailed analytical characterization of individual readings and their relationships to other readings in multiple relevant genetic and typological streams. While the rudiments for such description are present, they are not yet specified at a level that clarifies for working text critics or software engineers how the analyses might best be recorded, or how software might exploit these formal descriptions.

An example may be drawn from an appraisal of the *cause* attribute allowed for variant readings. Readings stored within a TEI apparatus share a common set of SGML attributes which permit classification of the reading and assignment of other useful descriptive information. The attribute most suitable for storing an evaluation of the reading (and thus for building a text-critical database) is the attribute *cause*. The *cause* attribute provides an opportunity for the text critic to nominate a keyword or to enter a brief comment which provides an evaluative statement about the variant: the underlying mechanism which produced the change, or probable scribal motivation, or particular scribal lapse, or other transmission phenomenon which best accounts for the origin of the reading vis-à-vis readings typologically anterior, etc. The keywords or comments stored in the *cause* attribute are based upon a user defined or domain-specific typology, and can be used in manuscript collation or other processing. Sample values for *cause* given in the P2 Guidelines include terms for textual phenomena that normally would be found in the vocabulary of most text critics: "homoioteleuton", "homoioarkton", "paleographic confusion", "haplography", "dittography", "false emendation" and so forth.

In support of a first-level evaluation, the *cause* attribute provides some expressive power. What it fails to support is the structure or potential structure for a more detailed evaluation of the kind many text critics would find natural, and indeed, perhaps more strongly motivated than mere first-level description. For example, if an investigator determines that a variant reading arose because of paleographic confusion, then it would normally be possible and desirable to specify precisely what character was mistaken for what other character, or which ligatured sequence or character substring was confused with which other sequence. If these pairs of readings were registered in the text-critical database via the TEI-SGML encoding, they could used in further research to study writing systems, scribal penchants, identification of individual scribes, etc. Or again, in the cases of homoioteleuton and homoioarkton, a paleographer may want to know which particular character sequences are most prone to producing a haplographic environment – differentially, as it may turn out, for different scribal hands and different sets of scribal eyes.

Because the data type of the value of *cause* is non-parsable and non-structurable "string data", the attribute is effectively a dead end in terms of supporting these finer nuances. Further TEI work is necessary to design alternative structured objects which would hold text-critical information of these "standard" types such that general software can support research based upon the controlled analyses.[15]

5. Conclusion

The preceding description of TEI guidelines for manuscript transcription and text-critical encoding represents a reflection on the ambition and scope of our enterprise rather than a simple measure of the present achievement. Our appreciation of the complexity of the problems has increased as we have sought to develop and test our encoding.

Despite our heightened appreciation for the scope of the task, we believe that many of the currently recommended mechanisms are robust and efficient. Based upon preliminary testing, we think they are indeed sufficient of themselves to enable useful work to be done now: they may provide encoding certainly equivalent to that of current printed editions. Yet we feel that the knowledge we have won, often by hard argument, of what we cannot yet do is our most valuable achievement. We understand much more clearly now than when we started what styles of encoding the electronic edition of the future will need, and we have a deeper sense of costs and benefits of the alternative strategies.[16] As we apply these TEI encoding guidelines to transcribed text and critical apparatus, we acknowledge that much work remains to be done.

Notes

1 For examples of these, see the reviews and references in Hockey (1980, pp. 144–67), Oakman (1980, pp. 113–38), Lancashire and McCarty (1988, pp. 108–10, 205). For earlier accounts of critical editing using the computer, see the papers in *La pratique des ordinateurs dans la critique des textes* (1979). An exemplary instance is Wilhelm Ott's TUSTEP suite of programs, described in Lancashire (1991, p. 407). Through these, a scholar may make indices, concordances and collations of scholarly texts, and also typeset the edition with complex critical apparatus. The hundreds of scholarly books produced with TUSTEP witness its success. However, TUSTEP sees the end of editing as the printed book and offers no access to the text in electronic form, as the starting point for further analysis.

2 A useful discussion of statistical methods for analysis of variant corpora is in Pierce (1989). For cladistic methods, see Lee (1989), and Robinson and O'Hara (1992 and 1993).

3 Electronic edition projects currently at various states of planning and execution include: Dante Gabriel Rossetti (Jerome J. McGann, University of Virginia); Shelley (Neil Fraistat and Donald Reiman, University of Maryland and New York Public Library); Yeats (Richard Finneran, University of Tennessee); the Canterbury Tales (Norman Blake and Peter Robinson, Universities of Sheffield and Oxford); Armenian sacred texts (Michael E. Stone, Hebrew University of Jerusalem).

4 For the distinction between descriptive and procedural markup, see Goldfarb (1990, p. 7). Our comments on "markup" as a means of structuring the textual information are framed within the context of an agreement that electronic editions must be easily interchangeable in order to be useful for collaborative research and electronic dissemination. Proprietary database solutions which employ no explicit markup whatever are potentially useful for modeling and implementation, but of themselves do not provide solutions for the "open" interchange format required by textual scholarship.

5 Examples of the range of editing strategies for medieval and modern European texts, from 'facsimile type' editions to fully modernized 'reading' editions, are usefully grouped in Appendix II of Greetham (1992). Greetham also discusses different theories of critical editing (1992, pp. 335–46); see also Shillingsburg (1986, pp. 31–43). Reynolds and Wilson (1991), and Kenney (1974) give convenient histories of textual editing of classical texts, as does Metzger (1968) for the New Testament.

6 A consistent criticism of earlier drafts of the TEI textual criticism chapters was that in attempting to accommodate multiple operational premises (potential use of particular existing software; focus on the production of printed critical editions; parsing in a single pass), the TEI had created a bewildering smorgasboard of encoding alternatives. Over time, different methods have been persistently and ruthlessly cut down by Occam's razor – the principled rule that the simplest "adequate" general solution is likely the best.

7 For another example: the tag **<note>** might be used to indicate a scribe "secundo manu" glossing a difficult word in the text; or an early commentator citing a parallel passage; or a later editor commenting on both these. All these are indeed "notes", but they are all different types of notes, all expressing a different relationship between the originator of the note and textual tradition. In the course of our design work, a profound problem has been the difficulty in providing for identification of tradents and their special roles for all tags that scholars might find susceptible to such qualification. One such limitation is illustrated in section 4.2 below.

8 See Skehan, Ulrich and Sanderson (1992), and especially the siglum list on page xi and accompanying explanation on page 4.

9 See the Oxford *DJD* volume cited in the previous note, page 32, line 22.

10 For example, we might use "?" suffixed to any romanized transliteration character to signify "doubtful", "*" to mean "probable", "!" to mean "certain", and "+" to indicate "possible".

11 Robert Kraft and Robin Cover provided contrasting experience on work with Biblical materials. Peter Robinson has worked with Middle English and Old Norse texts; Michael Sperberg-McQueen with Middle German; Ian Lancashire with Renaissance dramatic texts and Peter Shillingsburg with modern English prose texts. All members

of the group have substantial experience with computer treatment of texts, and Robin Cover and Michael Sperberg-McQueen have particular expertise with SGML markup.

12 Tutorial material of this type for scholars dealing with medieval and modern Western European tradition is provided in Robinson (1994).

13 To the extent that the same markup effect can be achieved in multiple ways, and that the "ways" are not always mutually exclusive under SGML constraints, it is indeed possible to encode conflicting analyses. Nonsense, of course, cannot be ruled out by SGML any more than honest mistakes, but conflict and ambiguity can be minimized by documenting recommended markup methods for particular encoding situations. Software applications, when they become available, can be expected to shoulder the burden of both preventing and flagging inconsistencies that are easily introduced when doing markup by hand.

14 In one sense, provision for evaluation and analytical description is *completely* supported: it it always possible to modify the TEI DTD, to design elaborate feature structure notations, and to use the all-purpose <**note**> – together yielding a limitless potential for complex description. In this section, we have in mind structured (SGML validated) support for analysis and evaluation directly within the context of the specific recommended tags and attributes documented in TEI P2, chapters 20 and 21.

15 Any number of alternative TEI strategies might be devised by a text critic to store the desired information in a "structured" manner: feature structure notation, general notes, compounded terms or multiple terms stored in the attribute value literal of *cause*="". For example, one could attach a note to a reading thus:

```
<note type='rdg.cause.paleographic.confus'
target="IDREF">presumedVorlageSubstring=""
resultantSubstring=""</note>
```

But these devices would all suffer from a common defect: they would be proprietary notations. Researchers designing and using these customized approaches will not have any guarantee, at least initially, that such encoding strategies developed outside the native "recommended" TEI Guidelines will be supported in TEI-commensurate applications which process the encoded data. Moreover, it is not clear that such custom solutions will optimally support the goals of information interchange: local centers most likely will be compelled to write custom software to process custom "TEI" encoding constructs, but the processing tools may not be easily exportable with the modified TEI data.

16 See for example the special issue of *Romance Philology* dedicated to electronic *ecdotique*, supervised by Charles B. Faulhaber and Jerry R. Craddock: *Romance Philology*, 45, 1 (1991). Its surveys and analytical essays represent a growing awareness on the part of textual scholarship that computer-assisted creation of text-critical databases and electronic editions will permanently change text-critical endeavor.

References

Gabler, H.W. *Ulysses: A Critical and Synoptic Edition*. Garland: New York and London, 1984.

Goldfarb, Charles F. *The SGML Handbook*. Oxford: Clarendon, 1990.

Greetham, D. C. *Textual Scholarship: An Introduction*. Garland: New York and London, 1992.

Hockey, S. *A Guide to Computer Applications in the Humanities*. London: Duckworth, 1980.

Kane, G. *Piers Plowman, The A Version*. Revised Edition. London: Athlone, 1988.

La pratique des ordinateurs dans la critique des textes. Colloques internationaux du Centre National de la Recherche Scientifique, n. 579 (Paris, 29–31 mars 1978). Paris: Editions du CNRS, 1979.

Lancashire, I. and W. McCarty. *The Humanities Computing Yearbook 1988*. Clarendon: Oxford, 1988.

Lancashire, I. *The Humanities Computing Yearbook 1989–90*. Clarendon: Oxford, 1991.

Lee, A. "Numerical Taxonomy Revisited: John Griffith, Cladistic Analysis and St. Augustine's Quaestiones in Heptateuchum". *Studia Patristica*, 20 (1989).

Metzger, B.M. *The Text of the New Testament*. Second Edition. Oxford: Clarendon, 1968.

Microsoft Product Support Services. "Rich Text Format (RTF) Specification". Application Note GC0165, June 1992.

Oakman, R.L. *Computer Methods for Literary Research*. Columbia: University of Southern Carolina, 1980.

Pierce, R.H. "Multivariate Numerical Techniques Applied to the Study of Manuscript Traditions". In *Tekst Kritisk Teori og Praksis*. Ed. B. Fidjestol *et al.* Oslo: Novus Forlag, 1988, pp. 24–45.

Reynolds, L.D., and N.G. Wilson. *Scribes and Scholars: A Guide to the Transmission of Greek and Latin Literature*. Third Edition. Oxford: Clarendon, 1991.

Robinson, P.M.W. and R.J. O'Hara. "Report on the Textual Criticism Challenge 1991". *Bryn Mawr Classical Review*, 3, 4 (1992), 331–37.

Robinson, P.M.W. and R.J. O'Hara. "Computer-Assisted Stemmatic Analysis". In *The Canterbury Tales Project Occasional Papers Volume I*. Ed. N. Blake and P. Robinson. Oxford: Office for Humanities Communication, 1993.

Robinson, P.M.W. *The Transcription of Primary Textual Sources Using SGML*. Oxford: Office for Humanities Communication, 1994.

Shillingsburg, P.L. *Scholarly Editing in the Computer Age: Theory and Practice*. Athens and London: University of Georgia, 1986.

Skehan, P.W., E. Ulrich and J.E. Sanderson, eds. *Qumran Cave 4, IV. Paleo-Hebrew and Greek Biblical Manuscripts. Discoveries in the Judean Desert, IX*. Oxford: Clarendon, 1992.

Sperberg-McQueen, C.M. and L. Burnard. *Guidelines for the Encoding and Interchange of Machine-Readable Texts Draft Version 1.0 (TEI P1)*. Chicago and Oxford: The Text Encoding Initiative, 1991.

Warnock, John E. "The New Age of Documents". *Byte*, 17, 6 (1992), 257–60.

Computers and the Humanities **29:** 137–148, 1995.

Speaking with One Voice: Encoding Standards and the Prospects for an Integrated Approach to Computing in History

Daniel Greenstein *
Department of History, Glasgow University, Scotland, UK
e-mail: digger@arts.gla.ac.uk

and

Lou Burnard *
Oxford University Computing Service, 13 Banbury Road, Oxford OX2 6NN, England
e-mail: lou@vax.ox.ac.uk

Key words: SGML, TEI, text encoding, history, historical documents, Sasines

Abstract

This paper focusses on the types of questions that are raised in the encoding of historical documents. Using the example of a 17th century Scottish Sasine, the authors show how TEI-based encoding can produce a text which will be of major value to a variety of future historical researchers. Firstly, they show how to produce a machine-readable transcription which would be comprehensible to a word-processor as a text stream filled with print and formatting instructions; to a text analysis package as compilation of named text segments of some known structure; and to a statistical package as a set of observations each of which comprises a number of defined and named variables. Secondly, they make provision for a machine-readable transcription where the encoder's research agenda and assumptions are reversible or alterable by secondary analysts who will have access to a maximum amount of information contained in the original source.

1. The Textual Trinity

The computer-aided management, analysis and reproduction of historical sources has developed along three parallel and, at present, frequently incompatible lines. If we ask the computer-aware historian what it is exactly that he or she uses the computer for, it is very likely that the response we receive will focus on one of three areas: printing, publishing, and word-processing; linguistic analysis and engineering; or data storage, retrieval, and analysis. We begin therefore by examining the processing techniques which characterize each of these three application areas, before proceeding to suggest that the existence of this so-called textual trinity may impose unnecessary constraints upon the future of computer-aided research. To focus discussion, we examine each processing technique with reference to one particular source – a seventeenth-century Scottish Sasine, or record of landholding and transfer. A facsimile of part of such a document is given in Figure 1.[1]

Sasines of this kind from the 17th century exist in abundance in various Scottish record offices; like other documents of the period they also show much variation. Thus, for many historians, a simple printed compilation might be a worthy aim, and one replete with learned footnotes an even worthier one. Either way, the computer will be the obvious tool to handle the

* Daniel I. Greenstein is a Senior Lecturer in Modern History at Glasgow University where he teaches and publishes in American urban and political history and culture, modern British education, and computer methods. Computing works include *A Historian's Guide to Computing* (Oxford, 1994).

Lou Burnard is Director of the Oxford Text Archive at Oxford University Computing Services, with interests in electronic text and database technology. He is European Editor of the Text Encoding Initiative's Guidelines.

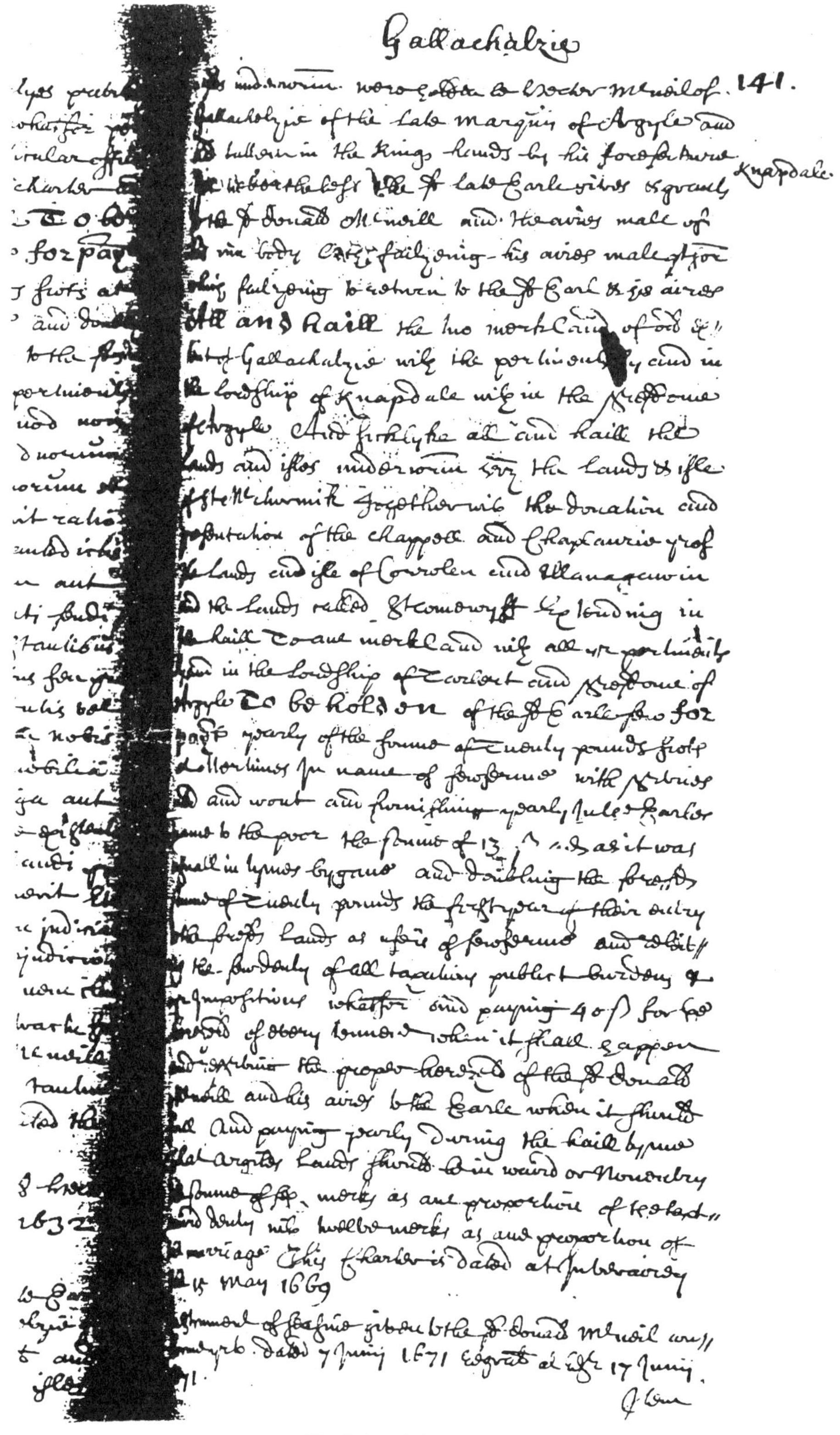

Fig. 1. Facsimilie of Sasine.

G320528 :Gallachalzie/140

Item instrument of Sasine given tha s[ai]d Hector Mcneill confirmed and dated 28 May 1632 [ms. illegible]; at Edinburgh upon the 15 June 1632

Item ane charter granted by ***Archibald late earl of Argyle*** to **Donald McNeill of Gallachalzie** wh[ich] makes mention that the lands [ms. illegible]; and Isles underwritten were [ms. illegible]; by ***Hector McNeill of Gallachalzie*** of the late Marquis of Argyle and held fallen in the kings hand by his Foresfeiture which nevertheless the s[ai]d late Earl yields and grants to the s[ai]d Donald MacNeill and the aires male of his ane body which failing his aires male q[ua]tsoe[ve]r which failing to return to tha s[ai]d Earl and his aires . [p.141]

All and hail the two merk land of old extent of Gallachalzie with the pertinents by and in the lordship of Knapdale within the sherrifdome of Argyll. And sicklike all and haill the lands and isles underwritten viz the lands & isles...

Fig. 2. Modernized reprint of Sasine.

drudgery of correcting errors, laying the text out neatly on the page and so forth. However, it is important to note that the production of a page like that shown in Figure 2 (the Sasine as it might be printed in an edited collection or critical edition) crucially depends on any number of interpretive acts, and is by no means a merely mechanical or even mechanizable process.

Even the most diplomatic of editions of a manuscript source such as this one necessarily enshrines in the authority of print one set of editorial assumptions about emphasis, illegibility, and even the interpretation of the letters of the text itself; a set with which other editors may wish to disagree or re-evaluate in the light of their own, perhaps more detailed or more specific knowledge.[2]

What is illegible to one editor may be perfectly plain to another, perhaps more conversant with Scottish legal practice; what one person regards as a standard abbreviation may require explicit expansion for another. Even experts may agree only that the decision as to whether a "u" or a "v" is intended at this point is not decidable.

For the historical linguist, the Sasine illuminates how vernacular Gaelic impinged upon English; for the historical geographer it provides valuable evidence for the evolution of place names. In such applications as these, the computer can be used to advantage but in a way rather different from that described above. The focus now is not on the orthography or presentation of the text but on its linguistic content.[3] We now present, as Figure 3, an extract from the same Sasine marked up in preparation for verbal analysis, using a standard concordance program such as OCP or TACT.

((Examples of TEI encoding applied to primary
historical sources: 17th c. Scottish Charters
Transcribed by Lorna Hughes
Encoded by Dan Greenstein and Lou Burnard))
<P 140>
<S G320528><N Gallachalzie>

Item instrument of Sasine given tha said %Hector_ Mcneill confirmed and dated 28 May 1632 ((illegible)) at #Edinburgh upon the 15 June 1632 Item ane charter granted by %Archibald_late_earl_ of_#Argyle to %Donald_McNeill of #Gallachalzie which makes mention that the lands ((illegible)) and /Isles
<P 141>
underwritten were ((illegible)) by %Hector_McNeill of #Gallachalzie of the late %Marquis_of_#Argyle and held fallen in the kings hand by his Foresfeiture which nevertheless the said late Earl yields and grants to the said %Donald_MacNeill and the aires male of his ane body which failing his aires male quatsoever failing to return to the said Earl and his aires All and hail the two merk land of old extent of #Gallachalzie with the pertinents by and in the lordship of #Knapdale within the sherrifdome of #Argyll And sicklike all and haill the

...

Fig. 3. Sasine marked up for verbal analysis.

Again, but perhaps rather more obviously than with the critical edition, the mark-up of the text is largely determined by the agenda of the analyst. Features of the text deemed of no relevance to his or her particular kind of research may be omitted from the transcription or included only partially.

In our example, parts of the text relating to proper names and currency measures have been identified with special markup codes. While this may gladden the heart of onomasticians and economic historians, clearly anyone interested in the lexical or linguistic structure of rights and obligations as specified in a pseudo-legal document will be out of luck. Of course, no-one could be expected to identify every textual feature which might conceivably be of interest; however with arbitrary codes such as those used here, it may be difficult or impossible to tell which features an analyst has chosen to encode, let alone those which he or she has passed over in silence.

There is also no guarantee that those features which are encoded will be encoded to everyone's satisfaction. It is entirely conceivable that two researchers interested in proper names may handle the expression "I went to Rochester to get some help" in rather different ways, one preferring to interpret Rochester as a place name, and the other as a personal name. Interpretations can conflict as well where analysts agree that a particular feature exists in a text but cannot agree where it begins and ends. Where, for example, does the personal name "Archibald, late earl of Argyle" begin and end in our Sasine? Determining the boundaries of the calendar date contained in the following expression is even more problematic:

> A fortnight after the Michaelmas faire in the twelfth year of the reign of our Gracious King James.

Preparing a document for linguistic content analysis shows how the research agenda not only determines which features are selected for encoding, but how the selected features are interpreted.

For the early modern historian, the Sasine is primarily of importance as neither a textual object nor a linguistic one, but rather as a means of constructing a real world system, the historical situation from which it emerged as an artefact. In conjunction with others, this Sasine might be used, for example, to determine the date at which standard taxation rates were adopted across Scotland, replacing a taxation system based on personal relations or patronage. Figure 4 shows such a database table, in which those parts of the Sasine relating (conjecturally) to land values and taxation have been re-expressed in terms of some standardized value.[4]

When completed, this table will allow us to determine whether any fixed relationship holds across whole areas in Scotland between the estimated value of land held by given individuals and the estimated value of taxes levied upon them. Here we see the same selectivity and the use of possibly contentious interpretions already implicit in the linguistic applications discussed above carried to their logical conclusion (or to a ridiculous extreme). Any features of the Sasine not considered relevant to the summary statement of land values and taxes paid are simply not present. Also missing from this record abstracted from our Sasine are the mathematical formulae used to standardize such radically different expressions of value as commodities (the two-merk land of old extent of Gallachalzie), obligations (the donation of the chappel and chaplainies), and currencies (13 shillings and 4 pence) before they could be included in the table.[5]

Of course, no-one would seriously regard such a bare abstraction as a faithful record of the original source, but from sheer expedience (consider the daunting bulk of many types of historical source materials) there is a natural tendency to confuse highly abstracted and possibly contentious interpretations of this nature with the source itself. Irrespective of what kind of processing is required by the historian, narrowly focussed research interests and assumptions inevitably impinge upon the creation of machine-readable textual transcripts and consequently the possibility of their later re-use.

This one example of how the same textual source is prepared very differently for computer processing, depending upon the particular processing aims in view, demonstrates how the textual trinity affects not only future prospects for computer-aided humanities research, but also the limitations of our current practices. Three problems in particular are worth emphasizing. Firstly, in pursuing a particular processing aim, the historian stores information in a way which optimizes only one kind of processing. The machine-readable critical edition is all but useless to both the historical linguist and the early modern economic historian. The inefficiencies are self-evident, especially when we consider the financial constraints under which most computer-aided research work is conducted and the high cost of creating machine-readable editions of large and important corpora.

Secondly, the meta-data that the historian brings to the interpretation of a textual source and which informs its transcription, is easily lost. In constructing the database table shown in Figure 4, the historian undoubtedly drew upon detailed expert knowledge of how best to interpret and equate early modern measures (whether currencies or commodities), and perhaps on machine-readable indices and translation tables of his or her own design. Likewise the publisher's expertise in early-modern paleography is lost to the secondary analyst and to other historians who may encounter and need to interpret documents which use orthographic and scribal conventions similar to those found in the

pid	date	trans_no	land_val	tax_due
M1	320612	T1	2678	34
M1	390523	T2	4576	22

..

Fig. 4. Sasine 'marked up' for database analysis.

Sasine. The point is that in preparing their texts for computer-aided processing, historians rely upon background knowledge which might be useful to other analysts whether or not they are interested in the initial document. This background information is lost owing to the exigencies of text-preparation.

Thirdly, while historians may not yet be the world's most prolific producers of machine-readable information, they will surely be amongst the world's most profligate consumers of the machine-readable texts that are created by others. Machine-readable administrative data is daily churned out in miles worth of magnetic tape by government agencies, hospitals, financial institutions, and industries. Consider also the machine-readable versions of reference and scholarly works daily being produced by publishing houses, even if the vast majority of these are intermediate steps in production of a printed text which are destroyed as soon as the text appears in print. Frequently, these data comprise ASCII text strings which may be more or less immediately amenable to publishing but to little in the way of analysis. A machine-readable edition of the diary of Philip Hone or Sidney George Fischer might be used to analyze networks of nineteenth-century U.S. urban elites, but only if the edition has been prepared in a way that can support both printed publication and database-style analysis. Alas, the mechanism for process-independent encoding of machine-readable data does not permit us to bridge this processing divide. And it is rather alarming to reflect that the machine-readable administrative data which are rapidly becoming the primary sources for administrative, political and diplomatic historians, are virtually inaccessible to the kinds of linguistic, content and database-style or statistical analysis which take up the lion's share of the space in our toolkit of computer-aided analytical techniques. More alarming still is the fact that these data which are the stuff of predictive measures as employed from econometrics to epidemiology, are not at all conducive to the kinds of statistical manipulations from which such measures are made.[5]

2. The Promise of Standardization

The foregoing discussion anticipates at least one solution – the development and widespread adoption of a standard markup language for encoding machine-readable data – a markup language which would make the same body of information comprehensible to different processing applications in a way which conformed to the processing applications' particular view of how data should and must be modelled. In addition, the markup language would enable researcher to document where and how their own research agenda determined how a text was interpreted for encoding purposes. With respect to the Sasine, then, our object is two-fold. Firstly, we require a machine-readable transcription which would be comprehensible to a word-processor as a text stream filled with print and formatting instructions; to a text analysis package as compilation of named text segments of some known structure; and to a statistical package as a set of observations each of which comprises a number of defined and named variables. Secondly, we require a machine-readable transcription where the encoder's research agenda and assumptions are reversible or alterable by secondary analysts who will have access to a maximum amount of information contained in the original source. In our view, the guidelines offered by the Text Encoding Initiative meet both of these criteria. To exemplify the point, the second part of this paper develops a small number of TEI solutions at some length, again with respect to the three very different processing aims which might determine how the Scottish Sasine is handled by a computer.

3. Applying the TEI Solutions

Before even considering how to ensure a machine-readable text's comprehensibility to different processing applications, agreement is necessary about how to describe the text itself. This is done in the TEI header, one of the very few required portions of a TEI-conformant text. A header for our sample Sasine is reproduced below:

```
<TeiHeader>
<fileDesc>
   <titleStmt>
      <title>Examples of TEI encoding applied to primary
         historical sources: 17th c. Scottish Charters
         </title>
      <respStmt><resp>transcribed by</resp><name>
         Lorna Hughes</name></respStmt>
      <respStmt><resp>encoded by</resp>Dan Green-
         stein and Lou Burnard</name></respStmt>
   </titleStmt>
   <publicationStmt>
      <release>Demonstrated at AHC Conference, Bologna
         1992</release>
   </publicationStmt>
   <sourceDesc>
      <bibl>Register of title deeds for Argyle, National
         Library of Scotland Mss. Advocates 31:2:3. </bibl>
   </sourceDesc>
</fileDesc>
   <encodingDesc>
   <editorialDecl>
      <normalization method=tags>
         <p>The following common scribal abbreviations
            are expanded:
            <list type=gloss>
               <label>sd<item>said</item></label>
               <label>wch<item>which</item></label>
            </list>
         </p>
         <p>Lineation of the original preserved.</p>
      </normalization>
   </editorialDecl>
</encodingDesc>
<revisionDesc>
   <change><name>LB</name><date>April 1993
      </date><what>Revised for CHum Publication
      </what></change>
</revisionDesc>
</TeiHeader>
```

The header comprises two principal sections. A file description describes the machine-readable text itself, stating, for example, its title, the name of the person or persons responsible for its creation, information about the place, date and circumstances of its publication, and so forth. In the file description one will also find bibliographic information about the source or copy text (where relevant). A second component of the header – the encoding description – makes explicit the editorial practices followed in creating it, defining, for example, any normalization system, policy with respect to abbreviations etc. The header also contains information tracing the machine-readable text's revision history, indicating, for example, who did what to the transcript and when. The encoding description is particularly important to the secondary analyst seeking to identify, assess, and perhaps undo some of the interpretive gestures made by previous researchers who have helped to encode the text.

Within the body of a TEI-conformant text, we may expect to find an initially bewildering variety of different tags. For simplicity of discussion, we begin by distinguishing the core elements from the rest. The term *core* is used by the TEI to identify a large but not unmanageable set of textual features which are found in almost every kind of text (as opposed to specialized features characteristic of certain kinds of text only). Many, but by no means all, core tags identify what are known in the language of diplomatics as a text's *external properties*, that is, features which require little or no previous knowledge of the text or the circumstances of its creation.[7] These are features which even a Martian could recognize, though not perhaps understand. Some examples are shown in the following example, which shows the start of our Sasine marked up using the TEI core tagset:

```
<body>
<pb n='140'>
...
<div type=sasine id=G320528 n='Gallachalzie/140'><head>
<lb> Item instrument of Sasine given tha &sd; Hector
<lb> Mcneill confirmed and dated 28 May 1632
<lb> &illegible; at Edinburgh upon the 15 June 1632 </head>
<lb> <p>Item ane charter granted by Archibald late earl
<lb> of Argyle to Donald McNeill of Gallachalzie
   <expan abbrev='wh'>which</expan>
<lb> makes mention that the lands &illegible; and
<lb> Isles
<pb n='141'>
<lb> underwritten were &illegible; by Hector McNeill of
<lb> Gallachalzie of the late Marquis of Argyle and
<lb> held fallen in the kings hand by his Foresfeiture
   <note place=rmargin resp=scribal>Knapdale</note>
<lb> which nevertheless the &sd; late Earl yields and grants
<lb> to the &sd; Donald MacNeill and the aires male of
<lb> his ane body which failing his aires male
   <abbrev type=susp expan='quatsoever'>qtsoer</abbrev>
<lb> which failing to return to tha &sd; Earl and his aires
<lb> <hi rend=inked>All and hail</hi> the two merk land
     of old extent
```

<lb> of Gallachalzie with the pertinents by and in
<lb> the lordship of Knapdale within the sherrifdome
<lb> of Argyll And sicklike all and haill the
<lb> lands and isles underwritten viz the lands & isles
<lb> of Stemchmirk together with the donation and
<lb> &illegible; of the chappel and chaplainies of
<lb> the lands and isle of Cowden and Allanagenein
<lb> and the lands called Steonewytt extending in ...

Our putative Martian would have no difficulty identifying, for example, the places in the text where a page or line break occurs: these have been represented in our example by the tags **<pb>** and **<lb>** respectively. It would also probably notice that the text is not a homogenous stream but consists of small chunks or paragraphs. We have marked the start of each such chunk with the TEI tag **<p>**. Our Martian might even surmise that the Sasine is part of a larger body of material. The tag proposed by the TEI to indicate any form of textual subdivision is **<div>**, and we have adopted it here on the grounds that we wish to regard the whole collection of Sasines as a single text, of which each individual document forms a part.[8] The **<div>** tag marks the beginning of each new Sasine in the text, and a **</div>** tag marks its end.

We do not here intend to describe the syntax of the TEI scheme in any detail, since many other detailed descriptions are already available.[9] We will, however, call attention to some aspects of it relevant to our general argument. Note for example the way in which the syntax allows us to distinguish clearly the textual transcription itself from additional information which is not explicitly present in the text by presenting such housekeeping information in the form of attributes, contained within particular start-tags, for example the identification and characterization of the **<div>** element. With *attributes,* the TEI scheme allows users to employ typologies which are relevant to their own disciplines, specialisms, or research projects. Here, we see how *attributes* are used to identify relevant textual subdivisions, thus mitigating against the imposition of particular names for them such as "section" or "clause". Hence we can identify this particular div as being a "sasine". We can supply as attributes both a unique machine-friendly identifier ("G320528") and a possibly non-unique person-friendly name or number ("Marquis of Argyle 2") for the sasine, enabling it to be cross-referenced by other elements. The *id* attribute has many applications, as we will demonstrate below, and is for that reason global – any tag may carry it. Not demonstrated here, but also globally available, are attributes to document the language of a particular element and its rendition.

However intelligent, our Martian is likely to lack wide experience of terrestrial paleography and diplomatic skills which are essential to much historical research. Consequently, it might not immediately notice that this Sasine includes an annotation, nor could it reasonably be expected to identify the abbreviations within the text. These are instances of core textual features whose identification requires a modicum of background knowledge about the text and the circumstances of its creation. To identify such features an interpretive act is necessary, but they are included with the TEI core because there is at least widespread agreement that they do exist in most kinds of text, although there may be controversy about whether or not a given instance has been genuinely so classed. The marked up text includes a **<note>** element, marking the existence, whereabouts, and authorship of a marginal comment which appears on the Sasine. It also demonstrates two complementary ways that the TEI provides for the handling of abbreviations – a notorious difficulty in manuscripts from this period. The first is to specify the expanded version of an abbreviation as the element's content, at the same time retaining the original form of the abbreviation as an attribute; see the treatment of "st" for example. The second does exactly the opposite; see the treatment of the abbreviation "qtsoer", for example.

Finally, note the two so-called *entity references* used here to indicate illegible portions of the text and the familiar abbreviation "said". We wish to note the advantages they offer the encoder wishing to defer a decision as to how a particular textual phenomenon should be encoded. Some abbreviations occur so frequently that they approximate to lexical or even graphemic status: (in Modern English "Mr" is a case in point). It may be that the scribal abbreviation for "said" is in this category; alternatively, it may be that we will wish to record each occurrence using the full-blown **<abbrev>** element discussed above. The entity reference "&sd" may be expanded by an SGML processor as "said" on one occasion, as "**<abbrev expan='said'>**sd.**</abbrev>**" on another, and as some machine-specific code representing the actual symbol in the text on a third.

It is often the case that the textual features whose existence our encoding is intended to flag will be simple consecutive sequences of words or phrases in the text. It is not, however, invariably so: and the TEI proposals therefore include a number of suggestions not only for ways of arbitrarily segmenting texts into smaller units, but also ways of recombining these arbitrary segments into meaningful analytic units of various kinds, irrespective of their physical sequence within the text.

This has a particular relevance when dealing with historical sources of information, for which such aggregation is often not only desirable, but may even be essential to an accurate analysis. A typical example is that of a geographical place name which cannot be interpreted correctly in isolation of temporal information. Thus, the expression "Germany" will have very different cartographic representations when it is used in conjunction with 1870, 1872, 1943, 1964, and 1993, respectively. Consequently, aggregation is necessary; it alone enables the researcher to combine a geographical place named somewhere in a text with the temporal information necessary to interpret it but which is available (perhaps implicitly) in a distant text segment.

As a simpler example, we consider the phrase "two merk land of old extent of Gallachalzie" in our Sasine. For the purposes of discussion, we will assume that at least one meaningful reading of these words would group "two merks of old extent" as one phrase, and "land of Gallachalzie" as another, and that it is this reading which we wish to encode. The problem is (of course) a generic one, for which the TEI proposes the following generic solution. Each fragment of the phrase must be identified as an <**s**> (segment) element and given an identifier.

```
<s id=s1>two merk</s>
<s id=s2>land</s>
<s id=s3>of old extent</s>
<s id=s4>of Gallachalzie</s>
```

Two methods may then be used to associate segments "s1" and "s3", and "s2", and "s4". The first makes use of two special attributes *next* and *prev*:

```
<s id=s1 next=s3>two merk</s>
<s id=s2 next=s4>land</s>
<s id=s3 prev=s1>of old extent</s>
<s id=s4 prev=s2>of Gallachalzie</s>
```

In the second method, the encoder simply creates a virtual <**join**> element, which does not enclose any part of the text, but simply exists to point at the two <**s**> elements and state that they are to be regarded as an instance of the element indicated by its *type* attribute:

```
<join type=measure parts='s1 s3'>
<join type=place parts='s2 s4'>
```

It is at around this point that encoders begin to worry that interpretation is taking over from transcription. As stated above, we are unconvinced that there can ever be a fundamental distinction between the two, other than that established by consensus. A neutral transcription is, we suggest, merely one in which the set of interpretative distinctions made happens to coincide with the set of such distinctions most people would wish to make most of the time; an analytic or interpretative transcription is one in which the set of distinctions made is peculiar to some specific analytic goal or agenda. It is hard to establish a more exact distinction, even with the aid of a Martian observer.

The point at which the consensus as to which textual features are actually present in a text breaks down is hard to define. For example, for many uses of the machine-readable Sasine, there is no need to postulate an analytic feature such as "cash value". It is hardly likely to be relevant to the production of a printed edition. Yet, if we wish to use the Sasine as evidence in a study of taxation practices in 17th century Scotland, some such element must be postulated. Even assuming that we are agreed on the necessity of including such an element within the encoded text, its internal structure is likely to be almost entirely different for different uses. For the historical linguist it might be sufficient simply to surround an expression of cash value with a begin and end cash value tag, or to analyze the language used to express cash valuation. For the economic historian a substructure composed of elements such as quantity, currency measure, denomination etc. would be essential. And even here, a substructure appropriate for cash values appearing in early modern historical sources would be utterly useless to the modern historian interested in cash values quoted on the New York Stock exchange say, in 1931.

In short, for analytic applications, the set of textual features which our markup must identify needs to be as open-ended as the number of different database table configurations which might be used to manage the data taken from a given historical source. To handle this situation, the TEI recommendations move "up a level". Rather than saying "the feature <**cashValue**> (or <**personalName**> or <**administrativeUnit**>) exists and has the following internal structure" it allows the encoder to provide a detailed formal *description* of each such textual feature, saying, effectively, "for my purposes, a feature exists which I will call "cash value" (or "personal name" etc), and I define it to have the following internal structure". Because this formal description uses SGML it has all the benefits of interchangeability associated with other parts of the TEI scheme; what is standardized, however, is not how the analytical features are conceived but how they are described in SGML. This formal description is expressed as a bundle of *feature structures*,[10] of which the following might be an example:

```
<fs type=cashValue>
    <f name=quantity><nbr value=2900></f>
    <f name=units><sym value=ecu></f>
    <f name=reliability><minus></f>
</fs>
```

For the purposes of analysis, we have decided that we wish to decompose the single notion "cash value" into three particular *features*. Each feature has a *name* ("quantity", "units" and "reliability" in the example above), and a value, concerning which we shall have more to say in a moment. This combination or bundle of features contains all we wish to record about "cash value" for this purpose; of course, other analysts might well decide to bundle other features together under this heading or type. Somehow, therefore, we will still need to specify what features are legal within our definition, and what it means if some feature of that definition is missing; that is the function of the *feature system declaration*, which is further discussed below (see also Langendoen and Simons in this volume).

The example above also demonstrates the range of different values which features may have, including number (the amount), symbol (i.e. the name "ecu" – drawn, we assume, from a closed domain of currency names) and Boolean plus or minus (cash values, according to this analysis, are either reliable or the reverse). If this description is starting to sound not unlike the traditional description of a database table, with its predefined columns each of a specific type, that is not entirely surprising. One of the things that the feature structure notation is intended to do is precisely to permit the encoder to embed within the text the database-like structure most appropriate to his or her particular analytical aims.

However, because they use SGML, feature structures can be used to build structures rather more complex than simple columns and rows. In the following example, we demonstrate both some more examples of different feature values and the crucial fact that one feature structure can itself form the value of some feature within another feature structure:

```
<fs type=payment>
    <f name=regular><plus></f>
    <f name=duedate><str>Mertimes</str></f>
    <f name=period><sym value='annual'></f>
    <f name=place target=P1></f>
    <f name=amount>
        <fs type=cashValue>
            <f name=quantity><nbr value=20></f>
            <f name=currency><sym value='pounds Scots'>
                </f>
        </fs></f>
    <f name=stdVal>
        <fs type=cashValue>
            <f name=quantity><nbr value=2900></f>
            <f name=units><sym value=ecu></f>
            <f name=reliability><minus><//f>
        </fs>
    </f>
    ...
</fs>
```

Note here that we have two occurrences of the feature structure called "cashValue". The first appears as the value for a feature called "amount", and the second as the value for a feature called "stdVal" (i.e. standardized value). These two features are themselves part of the large bundle making up the feature structure called "payment", along with several others ("regular", "duedate", etc.). This recursion (the ability to regard a feature value as itself a feature structure, containing values which are themselves bundles of other features, which...) gives this scheme much of its expressive power, as we shall see. Note also the use of the cross-referencing ability of SGML in the feature called "place": here the value has been specified simply as a *target* – in other words, the value for this feature is a pointer to some other SGML element somewhere in the same document with the identifier "P1". Again, any similarity to the characteristics which database cognoscenti might expect or require is entirely intentional.

As mentioned above, the TEI recommendations also provide the ability to define the whole of a "Feature System Declaration", or FSD, in which the analyst specifies, inter alia,

- names, descriptions and legal values for all features;
- constraints on which features may co-exist within a given feature structure;
- rules concerning the interpretation of any underspecifed feature structure, for example default or missing values for its constituent features.

Space precludes detailed discussion of this somewhat technical topic; we note here only its striking similarity to a database schema. In the not-too distant future, standard database and statistical packages should be capable of using a TEI-conformant FSD to construct tables like the following from the feature structure given above:

Table PAYMENT

PaytNo	Regular	DueDate	Period	Amt	StdAmt
1001	Y	Mertimes	Annual	P1	A1	A2

Table CASHVALUE

Key	Qty	Currency	Reliable
A1	20	PoundScots	Y
A2	2900	Ecu	N

Reinventing the capabilities of standard statistical or relational database models, while it may keep computer science departments in business, is not in itself particularly impressive. But feature structures are far more powerful than databases. They are, for example, far better at representing two notorious areas of difficulty for the traditional "atomic" valued database approach: features whose values are composite or ambiguous. The value of a feature may be a *conjunction* or a *disjunction* of one or more feature structures. Suppose, for example, that we wish to represent the fact that a payment has been made which is a combination of two cash values, using different currencies:

```
<fs type=payment>
    <f name=amount>
        <valGrp type=conj>
            <fs type=cashValue>
                <f name=quantity><nbr value=13></f>
                <f name=currency><sym value='shillings'>
                    </f>
            </fs>
            <fs type=cashValue>
                <f name=quantity><nbr value=4></f>
                <f name=currency><sym value='pence'>
                    </f>
            </fs>
        </valGrp></f>
    <f name=payee><str>the poor</str></f>
</fs>
```

The two "cash values" in this example are not independent feature structures as they were in the earlier example. Here they form the constituent components of a <**valGrp**> (value group) which is being supplied as the value of the "amount" feature. The whole "payment" feature structure represents the analysis "thirteen shillings and four pence payable to the poor".

Our second example illustrates the case where the value of a feature is understood to be *one or other* of a number of feature structures:

```
<fs type=persName>
    <f name=forename><str>Archibald</str></f>
    <f name=rank>
        <valgrp type=excl>
            <sym value=earl>
            <sym value=marquis>
        </valgrp></f>
    <f name=placeName><str>Argyle</str></f>
</fs>
```

Here, we know that there is a personal name "Archibald" referred to variously in the text as having a rank of "Earl" and "Marquis" (presumably Archie remained the Marquis until his father died, at which point he became the Earl). The <**valGrp**> tag enables us to express an interpretive gesture of a type which characterizes much historical research, in this case that a given object (a person named Archie) can also be known by one of two other names but not both (he can be either the Earl or the Marquis). Try designing that into a database table!

Just as important, the feature structure links a highly structured analysis of a text with the text itself using one of two mechanisms. In this way, it is very *unlike* a database where highly structured summaries (call them interpretations if you will) are entirely divorced from the textual information which underlies them. The TEI recommends two chief mechanisms for effecting this linkage. The first embeds the feature structure within the running text which it interprets:

```
...payt yearly of the summe of
<s>twenty pounds Scots
    <fs type=cashValue>
        <f name=quantity><nbr value=20></f>
        <f name=currency><sym value='pounds Scots'>
            </f>

        <f name=stdVal>
            <fs type=cashValue>
                <f name=quantity><nbr value=2900></f>
                <f name=units><sym value=ecu></f>
                <f name=reliability><minus></f>
            </fs>
        </f>
    </fs>
</s>
at Mertimes...
```

The second uses a neater referencing mechanism whereby the text that is to be interpreted is marked up as orthographic sentences which are pointed at by feature structure notations stored elsewhere in the file or even in another file entirely:

```
<s>payt yearly of the summe of</s>
<s analysis=SCL20>twenty pound Scots</s>
<s>at Mertimes</s>

<fsLib>
    <fs id=SCL20 type=cashValue>
        ...
    </fs>
</fsLib>
...
```

Together with the FSD, this mechanism for linking analysis to the text will in future enable the researcher to treat the two as a seamless whole, to speak with one voice.

4. A Vision of the Future

The feature structure, and the linkage it promises between a machine-readable text and database or statistical style computer processing brings us full circle back to the textual trinity with which we began. Three parallel developmental trajectories are joined. The time, effort, and expense involved in the creation of machine-readable data need no longer be dedicated to one particular processing aim. The fruits of our computer-aided research need no longer be constrained by the exigencies of our initial processing aims. Imagine, then, if you will, a machine-readable transcription of Sasines prepared for the purpose of creating a critical edition. The transcription uses many of the tags described above (divs, paragraphs, line, and page breaks), some of them possibly resulting from detailed analysis of the surface features of the text (for example the abbrev, expand, and note tags). Because all such features are explicitly tagged, converting them to the appropriate set of codes for ones favourite formatting system (be it TeX, Microsoft Word, or whatever) is a simple task. Because all the encoding in the text is done in the same way, filtering out any tags which are meaningless to the printing process is equally straightforward.

At the same time, the text is available for content analysis. Another piece of interchange software enables OCP, for example, to recognize the corpus as comprising a series of independent Sasines (each treated as a distinct **<div>** element) and to filter out entity references to illegible text portions, editorial notes, etc. Admittedly, the analyst may want to add an additional layer of markup to satisfy his or her own interpretive needs, for example, by encoding place names. A TEI-conformant editor enables the analyst to scroll through the Sasines as they appear in WYSIWYG fashion on the screen (i.e. with SGML tags suppressed from view). Our content analyst uses a mouse to highlight a place name, clicks, and a semi-intelligent interface responds with the question: "what feature are you highlighting?" It provides a user-defined list of optional responses: "place name", "currency measure", etc. The encoder chooses place name, the appropriate tags are inserted in the underlying transcription, and the editing continues. Undoubtedly, the analyst will want to use some of the segmentation and aggregation methods described above to create virtual elements such as "two merks of old extent" out of text segments which are physically separate from one another. The base text is still usable for printed production because the interchange program used for producing printed texts filters out unwanted place name tags; but it is also usable now for more advanced forms of content analysis.

Our database enthusiast can also turn to the text, in this case to pursue an investigation of Scottish taxation. No database-like analyses are as yet sustained by the Sasine, but the situation is easily rectified with a semi-intelligent interface similar to that just described. Highlighting a text segment with a mouse and clicking, the encoder is prompted: "what feature structure are you highlighting?" and is provided with a range of choices defined for the software by the user-designed FSD. The choices include, "cash value", "payment", etc. Upon choosing "cash value" the user is prompted to highlight any of the features allowed in the feature structure "cash value". Again, the angle-brackets are entered behind the scenes.

Notice, too, that however the machine-readable text is processed – by a wordprocessor, text-analysis package, or database management system – it is not irretrievably transformed by a single set of narrow research interests and assumptions. Features selected by the primary encoder for linguistic-content or database-style analysis can be ignored and others marked up in their place. Disagreement about the features that are encoded is also possible because the TEI recommendations readily support multiple and even competing interpretations of a text. The textual critic can therefore re-evaluate abbreviations where these were expanded "incorrectly"; the feature structure "cashValue" can be re-evaluated according to a different standard currency measure and/or re-worked to comprise a different array of features.

At last, the richly and fully encoded text can be used within any of the three processing environments. Assume access to an enormous terminal and we can have a quick look into four windows on the future. In the first is the encoded text itself, replete in all its ugliness with a plethora of angle brackets and their ungainly contents. In the second is the formatted text as it would appear in a printed critical edition. In yet a third window is a text as it might appear to a content analysis package consisting only of a series of divisions in which are embedded the occasional place name or currency measure. And in a fourth window is a database table whose few records show a highly summarized version of the financial information contained in the Sasine. At last we have found a single voice to express all that we want to say about our information source, and our transition from text to table is complete. Fantastic? Perhaps. But at this point in time we can say confidently that the markup language is there to sustain this level of interchange. What is required now is the software to implement it.

Notes

[1] Taken from a register of title deeds for Argyle, National Library of Scotland Mss. Advocates 31:2:3. The authors are deeply grateful to Lorna Hughes who has been particularly generous with her dual expertise in Scottish history and historical computation.

[2] See I. H. Kropac, "Medieval Documents", in D. I. Greenstein, ed., *Modelling Historical Data: Towards a Standard for Encoding and Exchanging Machine-Readable Texts* (St Katharinen, 1991), 111–16.

[3] Historians have made too little use of linguistic content analyses and stylistic measures which are so fruitfully exploited in other humanities disciplines. Fortunately there is at last some movement in this direction after a slow start. For an early discussion of how content analysis might be applied in history see T. F. Carney, "Content Analysis: A Review Essay", *Historical Methods Newsletter*, 4 (1971), 52–61. For substantive work see R. L. Merritt, "The Emergence of American Nationalism: A Quantitative Approach", *American Quarterly*, (1965), 319–35. More recent work includes P. Dawdler, "Les Déclarations des Droits de l'Homme: Une Approche Quantitative", Centre National de la Recherche Scientifique, IVe Congrès, History and Computing, Talence, 14–16 Septembre 1989: Volume Des Actes (Bordeaux, 1990), 65–73; P. Tavernier, "L'héritage de 1789 et de 1848 dans la Déclaration universelle de 1948", *Les droits de l'homme et la conquête des libertés* (Grenoble, 1988); M. Olsen and L-G. Harvey, "Computers in Intellectual History: Lexical Statistics and the Analysis of Political Discourse", *Journal of Interdisciplinary History*, 18 (1988), 456–8; D. I. Greenstein, *A Historian's Guide to Computing* (Oxford, 1994), chapter 5.

[4] Database and statistical processing is much more developed amongst historians than linguistic content analysis. For a brief review see L. D. Burnard, "Relational Theory, SQL and Historical Practice", in P. R. Denley *et al.*, eds., *History and Computing II* (Manchester, 1989), 63–71; L. D. Burnard, "The Principles of Database Design", in Sebastian Rahtz, ed., *Information Technology in the Humanities* (Chichester, 1987), 54–68; D. I. Greenstein, "Multi-Sourced and Integrated Databases for the Prosopographer", in E. Mawdsley *et al.*, eds., *History and Computing III: Historians, Computers and Data. Applications in Research and Teaching* (Manchester, 1990), 60–6 and "A Source-Oriented Approach to History and Computing: The Relational Database", *Historical Social Research*, 14:3 (1989), 9–16; P. Hartland and C. Harvey, "Information Engineering and Historical Databases", in P. R. Denley *et al.*, eds., *History and Computing II*, 44–62; C. Harvey and J. Press, "Relational Data Analysis: Value, Concepts and Methods", *History and Computing*, 4 (1992), 98–109; S. Pasleau, *Les Bases de Données en Sciences Humaines* (Liège, 1988). For the use of relational databases in medieval history see C. Bourlet and J-L. Minel, "An Expert System Decision Support System for a Prosopographical Database", in L. J. McCrank, ed., *Databases in the Humanities and Social Sciences* (Auburn, 1987); D. I. Greenstein, *A Historian's Guide to Computing* (Oxford, 1994), chapter 3.

[5] Amongst the most obviously contentious interpretions made when encoding machine-readable data are those concerned with the classification of occupational data. See M. B. Katz, "Occupational Classification in History", *Journal of Interdisciplinary History*, 3 (1972); D. J. Treiman, "A Standard Occupational Prestige Scale for Use with Historical Data", *Journal of Interdisciplinary History*, 7 (1976), 283–304; D. I. Greenstein, "Standard, Meta-Standard: A Framework for Coding Occupational Data", *Historical Social Research*, 16 (1991), 3–22. Coding notoriously fuzzy data including dates, place names, and currency measures is also problematic. See M. Thaller, "The Need for Standards: Data Modelling and Exchange", 5, and "A Draft Proposal for the Coding of Machine Readable Sources", 39, both in D. I. Greenstein, ed., *Modelling Historical Data*, pp. 1–64.

[6] See J. M. Clubb, "Computer Technology and the Source Materials of Social History", *Social Science History*, 10 (1986), 97–114; D. I. Greenstein, "Historians as Producers or Consumers of Standard-Conformant, Full-Text Datasets? Some Sources of Modern History as a Test Case", in D. I. Greenstein ed., *Modelling Historical Data*, 179–94; R. W. Zweig, "Virtual Records and Real History", *History and Computing*, 4 (1992), 174–82.

[7] See I. H. Kropac, "Medieval Documents".

[8] In fact, the TEI proposals for the encoding of corpora are rather more subtle than our simple example demonstrates, distinguishing for example between subdivisions of unitary texts (which are marked as **<div>**s) and composite texts or **<group>**s; a collection of Sasines would probably be better encoded using the latter method.

[9] The current Guidelines being one obvious example.

[10] At the time of writing, no public version of the TEI recommendations for the encoding of feature structures has appeared more recent than that published in P1. Our examples are based on TEI internal drafts for the relevant chapters of P2, and may therefore be inaccurate with respect to the final published version. Further and more detailed discussion of this mechanism is provided by the article by Langendoen and Simons in this volume.

Computers and the Humanities **29:** 149–158, 1995.

The Encoding of Spoken Texts

Stig Johansson *
Department of British and American Studies, University of Oslo, P.O. Box 1003, Blindern, N-0315 Oslo 3, Norway
e-mail: stig.johansson@iba.uio.no

Key words: TEI, SGML, text encoding, spoken texts, transcription, temporal alignment

Abstract

There is a great deal of variation in the encoding of spoken texts in electronic form, both with respect to the types of features represented and the way particular features are rendered. This paper surveys problems in the electronic representation of speech and presents the solutions proposed by the Text Encoding Initiative. The special tags needed for the encoding of spoken texts are discussed, including a mechanism for temporal alignment. Further work is needed on phonological aspects, parallel representation, and on the development of software which connects the systematic underlying representation with a workable format for input and display.

1. What Is a Spoken Text?

A text literally means "that which is woven" and characteristically refers to something more or less carefully composed in the written mode. A spoken text is a written or electronic representation of a stretch of speech which is treated for some purpose as a well-defined unit.

Some important categories of spoken material are:

– face-to-face interaction
– telephone conversation
– interview
– debate
– commentary
– demonstration
– story-telling
– public speech

In addition, we may distinguish between pure speech and various mixed forms:

– scripted speech (as in a broadcast, a performance of a play, or reading aloud)
– material spoken to be written (as in dictation)

Here we are mainly concerned with face-to-face interaction, the most ubiquitous form of speech – and, indeed, of language. This is also the prototypical form of speech in the sense that it has the characteristics which we associate particularly with speech: it is spontaneous, interactive, situation-dependent, multi-functional. If we can represent face-to-face interaction, we may assume that we have the main mechanisms needed for the encoding of spoken material. The examples will be limited to English, but the discussion and the proposals should be applicable more generally to the representation of speech in machine-readable form.

2. The Variety of Transcription Practices

Speech has been transcribed for a variety of purposes by different categories of people. Non-linguistic applications (focus on content) by:

– journalists and historians
– psychologists and social scientists
– transcribers of interrogations and court proceedings

* Stig Johansson is Professor of English Language at the Department of British and American Studies, University of Oslo. He is co-ordinating secretary of the International Computer Archive of Modern English (ICAME) and editor of the *ICAME Journal.* Recent publications include *Frequency Analysis of English Vocabulary and Grammar* (with Knut Hofland, Clarendon Press, 1989) and *English Computer Corpora* (with Anna-Brita Stenström, Mouton de Gruyter, 1991).

- transcribers of parliamentary proceedings and proceedings from conferences and meetings of various kinds

Linguistic applications (focus on language) by:

- lexicographers
- compilers of corpora for research on syntax and discourse
- dialectologists and sociolinguists
- psycholinguists
- students of child language and second language acquisition
- students of speech disorders
- phoneticians and phonologists
- engineers concerned with the transmission of speech

Transcription practice varies widely, both with respect to the types of features represented and the way particular features are rendered. In non-linguistic applications the transcription is usually heavily edited, so that the text differs minimally from an ordinary written text. In linguistic applications there may be a careful record of speech-specific features, such as: prosodic and paralinguistic features, speaker overlap, pauses, hesitations, repetitions, interruptions, and other disfluencies. For a survey of different transcription systems, see Johansson *et al.* (1991) and Edwards and Lampert (1993).

3. Other Special Problems in the Transcription of Speech

The lack of generally accepted transcription conventions is a challenge for the Text Encoding Initiative (TEI). There are many special problems in speech encoding. Speech varies according to a large number of dimensions, many of which have no counterpart in writing (tempo, loudness, pitch, etc.). The audibility of speech recorded in natural communication situations is often less than perfect, affecting the accuracy of the transcription. Then there are the disfluencies mentioned in passing in section 2. The transcriber must decide how to deal with all these things.

The very identity of a spoken text is a further problem. Where does it begin? Where does it end? What components does it have? Are non-vocal elements, such as gestures, part of the text?

Other problems are connected with the fact that speech is typically addressed to a limited audience in a private setting; writing, on the other hand, is characteristically public (but we have of course public speech and private writing). To fully comprehend speech, we need more knowledge of the context, while writing is typically designed in such a way that it can be interpreted more independently of the situation where it was produced. This must be taken into account by the transcriber, who needs to provide sufficient information on the speech situation.

4. Towards a TEI Model for Speech Transcription

In view of all these problems, it may seem to be a hopeless task to propose general guidelines for speech encoding. It is significant that speech was not considered in TEI P1 (Sperberg-McQueen and Burnard, 1990). The challenge is to propose conventions which are compatible with the general framework of the TEI proposals, without distorting the characteristics of speech while at the same time catering for the variety of needs of different users of spoken texts.

All texts, whether written or spoken, need a header providing documentation on the text. The header can be organized in basically the same manner for speech as for writing, with some modifications as shown below (4.1). To handle the actual text, it is necessary to use an additional tag set. The additional tag set contains tags for the units which are specific to speech. The most important special mechanism needed for speech encoding is the one for temporal alignment, synchronizing the various types of elements which make up a spoken text. TEI P3 presents a new explicit way of handling synchronization (4.4).

In the sections below I will show how some important areas of speech encoding are tackled in TEI P3; see further Sperberg-McQueen and Burnard (1994, pp. 297–320).

4.1 *Text documentation*

Because speech is more context-dependent than writing, there is typically a need for more documentation on spoken texts. We need to know whether the speech is spontaneous or scripted, we need to know about the recording and transcription of the material, about the setting and the participants, etc. Information on the setting and participants was often given in an introductory paragraph in conventional transcriptions, as in:

> A receptionist at a large business establishment in the Midwest. She is twenty-four. Her husband is a student. ... (Terkel, 1975, p. 57)

> Meeting: The President, Haldeman and Dean, Oval Office, September 15, 1972. (5:27–6:17 p.m.)
>
> On Sept. 15, 1972, the seven men arrested in connection with the break-in at Democratic National Headquarters in the Watergate complex in Washington were indicted by a Federal grand jury. Later that day, there was a meeting in the Oval Office where White House strategy on other investigations related to Watergate was the subject. It was at this meeting, John Dean later told the Senate Watergate committee, that he first spoke to the President about Watergate. ...
>
> This opens as Dean comes in the door.
>
> (*The White House Transcripts*, 1974, p. 57)

In the case of machine-readable transcriptions made for the purposes of linguistic research such information, as well as information on recording and transcription details, has generally been given in a separate document or included in a header section before the actual text (for examples, see Appendix 1 in Johansson *et al.*, 1991). The latter is the approach chosen by the TEI.

In the original proposal worked out by the TEI work group on spoken texts (see Johansson *et al.*, 1991) we proposed that, corresponding to the source description of a written text, there should be three major sections: a script statement (for scripted texts only), a recording statement (giving details on the recording), and a transcription statement (giving details on the transcriber and the transcription principles).

To harmonize the treatment of spoken and written texts, the original proposals were modified somewhat. If the transcription only exists in electronic form and has no previous source, it will be documented in the file description of the header. If there is a pre-existing written transcription, there will be documentation on this in the source description of the header (in the same way as for written source texts in general). Transcription principles will be recorded in the encoding description of the header, in the same way as editorial principles for texts in general. (On the TEI header, see Giordano in this volume.)

The script statement and the recording statement are included as optional elements in the source description, though parts of the recording statement were moved to another section of the header (see 4.2). As a result of these modifications of the original proposals, it is possible to cater for the special needs of speech encoding and at the same time preserve the same overall structure of the header as for written texts.

4.2 *Situational parameters*

The TEI work group on spoken texts proposed a fairly complex recording statement, containing information not only on such matters as the type of recording and the responsibility for the recording, but also on the setting and the participants (see Johansson *et al.*, 1991).

It is worth noting that the original proposals for written texts in TEI P1 provided no way of accommodating information on the setting and the participants. It was therefore necessary to propose additional elements in the header for spoken texts. Nevertheless, there are clearly cases of written texts as well where such information is highly relevant, e.g. letters and minutes from meetings. To provide a unified treatment of spoken and written texts, the information on setting and participants was included in a special section of the header called the "profile description" (while the information on the type of recording and the responsibility for the recording remains in the recording statement).

The profile description provides a large number of parameters according to which spoken and written texts can be classified. Using these parameters, it is possible to pick out texts with particular combinations of features, e.g. informal speech among particular types of participants (teenagers, men only, women only, etc.) or letters with particular types of senders or addressees. The parameters provide less detail in some respects than the original proposal from the spoken text work group, but on the other hand they cover a much wider range of textual features.

The unified treatment of spoken and written texts is in agreement with the studies of Douglas Biber (see especially Biber, 1988), which show that there is no single dimension which separates speech and writing. Some types of texts, e.g. prepared lectures, are close to writing; conversely, there are types of writing which are close to speech, e.g. private letters and electronic mail. The use of the same profile description facilitates the comparison of varieties across speech and writing.

There is no doubt that the profile description is an important enrichment of the traditional header which presents strictly bibliographic information only. It is a problem, however, that the profile description in TEI P3 is divided between the main file header and an additional tag set for the header.

4.3 *Basic units in speech transcription*

Although the header remains much the same for spoken and written texts, there is a need for an additional tag set to handle the actual text of speech. Most types of writing in our days are divided into easily recognizable parts, such as chapters, sections, paragraphs, and words. Headings, punctuation, and a variety of typographical devices further structure the written text. In speech there is basically a continuum, without a clear division into units. Nevertheless, it is necessary to have some sort of segmentation in order to study the text.

Conventional speech transcriptions divide the text up more or less as in writing, using paragraphs, sentences, and orthographic words. Such a transcription is no doubt often adequate, and probably preferable, if the focus is on content rather than on language. In many cases there is, however, a need for a transcription which is closer to the original spoken performance.

Linguists often prefer a division based on prosody, e.g. the tone units in the London-Lund Corpus (see Svartvik and Quirk, 1980) and the intonation units in the scheme set up for the Corpus of Spoken American English (see Du Bois *et al.*, 1990). A different sort of division uses "macrosyntagms", originally proposed for the analysis of a corpus of spoken Swedish. A macrosyntagm is defined in syntactic terms and corresponds roughly to an orthographic sentence in writing (see Loman and Jörgensen, 1971).

Most transcriptions of extended spoken texts, even those made by linguists, use the orthographic word as the unit below the prosodic or syntactic units mentioned above. A higher-level unit recognized both in conventional and more linguistically-oriented transcription is the turn or utterance, which represents the contribution of a single speaker at a particular point in a conversation. Turns may be grouped into speech events or discourse texts which represent some sort of natural unit, but frequently a spoken text is merely a grouping for convenience.

To cater for the various types of segmentation of spoken texts, TEI P3 includes the following elements:

<**text**> a transcription of a stretch of speech treated for some purpose as a well-defined unit
<**div**> a subdivision of a spoken text comprising one or more utterances treated as a unit for analytic purposes
<**u**> an utterance, i.e. a stretch of speech usually preceded and followed by silence or a change of speaker
<**s**> a subdivision of an utterance by prosodic or syntactic criteria

In addition to these units, which organize the primary linguistic material, there is a need for a number of additional tags to handle other sorts of features that need to be marked in spoken texts:

<**pause**> a pause either between or within utterances
<**vocal**> any vocalized but non-lexical phenomenon, for example a voiced pause or a non-lexical backchannel, appearing within or between utterances
<**kinesic**> any non-vocalized but communicative phenomenon, for example a gesture
<**event**> any non-vocalized, non-communicative phenomenon, for example incidental noise or some other event affecting the communication
<**writing**> a passage of written text revealed to participants in the course of a speech event

We can show the relationship between four of the key units using the features "eventive", "communicative", "anthropophonic" (for sounds produced by the human vocal apparatus), and "lexical":

	Eventive	Communicative	Anthropophonic	Lexical
Event	+	–	–	–
Kinesic	+	+	–	–
Vocal	+	+	+	–
Utterance	+	+	+	+

The differences are not always clear-cut. Among events we might include actions like slamming the door, which can certainly be communicative. Vocals include coughing and sneezing, which are usually involuntary noises. Equally, the distinction between utterances and vocals is not always clear (see further 4.3.4 below). Individual scholars may differ in the way borderlines are drawn and should declare their definitions in the file header.

4.3.1 *Higher-level units*

A spoken text in the context of the TEI, tagged <**text**>, is an electronic version of a speech event which is (1) internally cohesive, (2) describable by a single header, and (3) represents a single stretch of time with no significant discontinuities. In other words, there has to be some unity in terms of the recording and transcription of the speech event and with respect to the participants and the nature of the communication. The <**text**> tag can handle spoken texts of a variety of types, whether they have a well-defined structure and clear boundaries (such as a lecture or a debate) or form a mere grouping for the purposes of the analysis.

The other higher-level unit, tagged <**div**>, corresponds to the divisions used for written texts. Like the latter, it may have a type attribute specifying the type of unit. It could, for example, handle the exchanges and transactions used in the analysis of spoken discourse by the Birmingham group (Sinclair and Coulthard, 1975; Coulthard and Montgomery, 1981). As for divisions in writing, there may be several layers of embedding. Since the definition is not tied to any specific type of unit, it can handle a variety of groupings of utterances.

The elements <**text**> and <**div**> are defined differently for spoken and written texts. The definition is automatically adjusted when the additional tag set for spoken texts is invoked.

4.3.2 *Utterances and S-units*

Utterances form the core of any transcript of speech. An utterance is commonly defined as a "stretch of speech preceded and followed by silence or a change of speaker" (Crystal, 1991, p. 367). Utterances may vary in length from a whole lecture to a short one-word reply. What distinguishes utterances from texts and divisions is that they are tied to a single speaker (or, more rarely, speaker group).

Utterances are usually presented "drama style" in transcriptions for linguistic as well non-linguistic purposes:

> P – Hi, how are you? You had quite a day today, didn't you? You got Watergate on the way, didn't you?
>
> D – We tried.
> H – How did it all end up?
> D – Ah, I think we can say well at this point. The press is playing it just as we expect.
> (*The White House Transcripts*, 1974, p. 57)
>
> <1> Oh it's a funny old day today isn't it.
> <2> Hm, it's not cold is it? I <unclear>
> <1> Well I thought it was when I went out and exercise the dog before lunch. I went up to Jubilee Park and eh. I had a very brisk walk indeed and I was absolutely lathered by the time I got back to eat after half an hour. (Crowdy, 1991)

The TEI approach is to use the tag <**u**>, with a *who* attribute identifying the speaker, as shown by a re-coding of the first example above:

> <u who=P>Hi, how are you? You had quite a day today, didn't you? You got Watergate on the way, didn't you?</u>
> <u who=D>We tried.</u>
> <u who=H>How did it all end up?</u>
> <u who=D>Ah, I think we can say well at this point. The press is playing it just as we expect.</u>

The value of the *who* attribute will be an *idref* pointing to the speaker identification in the file header.

Utterances can be easily identified where speech proceeds in an orderly manner, without interruptions or overlap between different speakers. The latter is, however, very frequent in informal speech. The handling of speaker overlap will be dealt with in the section on temporal alignment (4.4).

As utterances may vary greatly in length, we need some way of subdividing them. The TEI does not opt for any particular subdivision of utterances. The general-purpose <**s**> element is provided for segmentation.Where utterances are segmented end-to-end, the <**s**>-element may be used, with an attribute defining the type of segment: <**s type=macrosyntagm**>, <**s type=toneunit**>, etc. If a particular type of <**s**> is used throughout a text, it is possible to specify this in the file header. Here is a re-coded version of our example above from the *White House Transcripts*:

> <u who=P><s>Hi, how are you?</s><s>You had quite a day today, didn't you?</s><s>You got Watergate on the way, didn't you?</s</u>
> <u who=D><s>We tried.</s></u>
> <u who=H><s>How did it all end up?</s></u>
> <u who=P><s>Ah, I think we can say well at this point.</s><s>The press is playing it just as we expect.</s></u>

Special problems arise where segments cross utterance boundaries, as can happen both with macrosyntagms and with tone units, when a speaker is interrupted and resumes after an intervention by the addressee. These cases can be handled by the general TEI mechanisms used for discontinuous elements (see the chapters on segmentation and alignment in TEI P3).

4.3.3 *Pauses*

Pauses have generally been transcribed by the use of punctuation marks or other symbols (e.g. periods or hyphens), the length of the pause often being shown by repetition of the symbol. Some transcriptions provide exact measures for long pauses. See the survey of conventions in Johansson *et al.* (1991).

In the TEI recommendations pauses are identified by the empty tag <**pause**>. Pause length may be shown by a *type* attribute (with values like: short, medium, long); alternatively, a *dur* attribute may be used to indicate length more exactly. In this way it is possible to cater for the various approaches used previously.

The empty tag <**pause**> is only used for silent pauses. It may occur within utterances, in which case it applies to the relevant speaker, or between utterances, where it applies to all the participants. The following example from the London-Lund Corpus (Svartvik and Quirk, 1980, p. 200) gives the original transcription, omitting most of the prosodic coding, and a re-coded version:

A there are cups . nescafe -
B shall we have a cup of coffee .
A yes certainly yes certainly . yes
B I see they're all (6 seconds untranscribable) - - -

<u who=A>there are cups <pause type=brief>
nescafe</u><pause type=unit>
<u who=B>shall we have a cup of coffee</u>
<pause type=brief>
<u who=A>yes certainly yes certainly <pause
type=brief> yes</u>
<u who=B>I see they're all <note resp=ed>6
seconds untranscribable</note></u><pause
type:threeunit>

As regards the editorial note, see further section 4.6.

4.3.4 *Vocals*

Transcriptions of informal speech frequently contain non-lexical or semi-lexical vocalizations, such as voiced pauses and backchannels. These may be transcribed as "words", either orthographically or phonetically; if so, projects frequently maintain a control list of permissible forms. Alternatively, they may be described, typically using some kind of parenthesis notation. The latter approach is characteristically used with non-verbal sounds, such as laughter or audible inhalation.

The TEI approach is to use the empty tag <**vocal**>, with a *desc* attribute describing the phenomenon. The attribute supplies a description of the phenomenon or provides a semi-lexical representation, for example:

description: burp, click, cough, exhale, giggle, gulp, inhale, laugh, sneeze, sniff, snort, sob, swallow, throat, yawn

semi-lexical: ah, aha, aw, eh, ehm, er, erm, hmm, huh, mm, mmhm, oh

As an example, consider the following extract from the London-Lund Corpus (Svartvik and Quirk, 1980, p. 152), presented with reduced coding, followed by a re-coded version:

A where do you come from - - .
B ((you mean)) where was I before
A *yes*
B *((history))* **(. giggles)**
A **m** -

<u who=A>where do you come from</u><pause
type=twounitplus>
<u who=B>you mean where was I before</u>
<u who=A>yes</u>
<u who=B>history<pause type=brief><vocal
desc=giggle></u>
<vocal who=A desc=m><pause type=unit>

We have not re-coded the double parenthesis notation (indicating uncertain hearing; see 4.6) and the asterisks (indicating speaker overlap; see 4.4). Note that a vocal can appear both within an utterance, in which case it applies to the speaker of the <**u**> which it is included in, and separately, in which case it requires a "who" attribute.

The distinction between vocals and utterances is not always clear, although for analytic purposes it will be convenient to regard them as distinct. Individual scholars may differ in the way the borderline is drawn and may prefer to regard some semi-lexical phenomena as "words" within the bounds of <**u**>. For example, the second vocal in our last example above might be represented as:

<u who=A>m</u>

This approach is of course only available where it is possible to transcribe, rather than describe, the vocal.

4.3.5 *Kinesics*

Gestures have an important function in spoken communication, but they are frequently left unmarked in transcriptions, as they are non-vocal and the transcription is generally made from an audio recording. Where they are marked, there is usually a description within parentheses in much the same way as for descriptions of non-lexical vocalisations. For examples of some ways in which kinesic features have been marked, see Johansson *et al.* (1991).

The TEI recommendations provide an empty tag <**kinesic**>, with a *who* attribute ascribing the gesture to a particular participant and a *desc* attribute describing the phenomenon. This is a simple concocted example, first represented as in a playscript and then re-coded according to the TEI approach:

Jane: Have you read Vanity Fair?
Stig: Yes.
Lou: (nods)

<u who=Jane>Have you read Vanity Fair?</u>
<u who=Stig>Yes.</u>
<kinesic who=Lou desc=nod>

In a case like this the verbal and the non-verbal response probably overlap in time. The way this is handled is deferred to section 4.4.

4.3.6 *Events*

Utterances, vocals, and kinesics can all be loosely described as events. In the TEI recommendations the notion "event" is used more narrowly and is reserved for non-vocal and non-communicative phenomena. These sorts of features correspond to stage directions in a play, and they are typically indicated by descriptions within parentheses in transcriptions of speech, as in the following example (from Atkinson and Heritage, 1984, p. xiii):

Jan: This is just delicious
((telephone rings))
Kim: I'll get it

In the TEI approach the empty tag **<event>** is used, with a *desc* attribute:

<u who=Jan>This is just delicious</u><event
desc='telephone rings'>
<u who=Kim>I'll get it</u>

It is envisaged that events as well as kinesics are only recorded in the transcription where their presence is felt to be of significance for the interpretation of the interaction.

4.3.7 *Writing*

Written text may appear as an important element in some speech situations, for example in a lecture or in a television broadcast. The TEI recommendations provide the tag **<writing>**, with a *who* attribute identifying the person who reveals or creates the writing and a *type* attribute categorizing the kind of writing in some way (e.g. overhead transparency, subtitle, etc.).

The case of writing could no doubt be handled in the same way as events, but it deserves a special tag, as it identifies something which is communicative and lexical (in other words, it is like **<u>**). This element is more marginal than those dealt with above, but there are circumstances where it may be crucial for the transcription.

4.4 *Temporal alignment*

The evolving of speech in time is regularly encoded as succession in space. Problems arise where the transcription must capture features which are simultaneous, e.g. overlapping utterances or overlap between utterances and non-vocal phenomena. Representing such overlapping features is perhaps the greatest challenge for the transcriber.

Overlap has most typically been shown by pairs of asterisks or by some kind of bracketing (sometimes combined with vertical alignment), as in:

A where do you come from - - .
B ((you mean)) where was I before
A *yes*
B *((history))* **(. giggles)**
A **m** -
(Svartvik and Quirk, p. 152)

Tom: I used to smoke { a lot more than this=
Bob: { you used to smoke
Tom: =but I never inhaled the smoke
(Atkinson and Heritage, p. x)

In both of these examples we have omitted some coding to focus on the point at issue. In the first example there is overlap between A's "yes" and B's "history" (the double parentheses indicating uncertain hearing) and between B's giggle and A's backchannel. In the second there is a case of overlapping utterances.

The mechanism we need must permit an explicit ordering of elements and must be general enough to handle overlap between the various types of features. The TEI work group on spoken texts (as reported in Johansson *et al.*, 1991) proposed that the various elements in a spoken transcription could be synchronized with reference to a "timeline". The gist of the proposals is outlined below.

The text has associated with it a timeline consisting of a series of points. Utterances and other elements of the text have start and end attributes referring to points in the timeline. Synchronization can also be shown by the insertion of special **<anchor>** tags, with a *synch* attribute pointing to the timeline. The latter is necessary where there is overlap in the middle of an element.

The timeline is outside the text and consists of a number of **<when>** elements. Using the timeline approach we can re-code the first two examples above as follows:

```
<timeline><when id=p1><when id=p2><when
   id=p3><when id=p4><when id=p5><when
   id=p6><when id=p7></timeline>
<u who=A start=p1 end=p2>where do you come
   from</u><pause start=p2 end=p3>
<u who=B start=p3 end=p4>((you mean)) where
   was I before</u>
<u who=A start=p4 end=p5>yes</u>
<u who=B start=p4 end=p5>((history))</u><
   vocal who=B desc=giggle start=p5 end=p6>
<vocal who=A desc=m start=p5 end=p6><pause
   start=p6 end=p7>
```

```
<timeline><when id=p1><when id=p2><when
   id=p3><when id=p4></timeline>
<u who=Tom start=p1 end=p3>I used to smoke
   <anchor synch=p2> a lot more than this</u>
<u who=Bob start=p2 end=p3>You used to smoke
   </u>
<u who=Tom start=p3 end=p4>but I never
   inhaled the smoke</u>
```

Note that the utterances in the last example could also be encoded as follows, with less interruption:

```
<u who=Tom start=p1 end=p4>I used to smoke
   <anchor synch=p2> a lot more than this
   <anchor synch=p3> but I never inhaled the
   smoke</u>
<u who=Bob start=p2 end=p3>You used to smoke
   </u>
```

Each point in the timeline has an *id* which is the target of the reference. The points may also have attributes specifying absolute time and relative time with respect to other points in the timeline.

While the original proposal from the work group only involved pointing from the text to the timeline, TEI P3 also proposes the alternative method of pointing from the timeline to the text. This has the advantage that the text is less cluttered by references to the timeline, but there is a need to insert <**anchor**> tags in the text where there is no available element to point to. A further possibility noted in TEI P3 is double linkage, with linking both from the text to the timeline and from the timeline to the text.

The timeline mechanism is flexible and can handle the various kinds of overlap in speech far more precisely than existing transcription schemes. It is a problem, however, that the coding becomes rather complex (a simpler, though less precise, way of marking overlap is also described in TEI P3; see Sperberg-McQueen and Burnard, 1994, pp. 313f., 436f.).

4.5 *Shifts*

The timeline is also invoked as a way of handling features like tempo, loudness, and voice quality. Such features have rarely been marked in a systematic fashion. Two approaches are illustrated in these examples:

A: they let us alone.
... <WH But we were scared,
And boy WH>,
did we ever get in trouble,
from Mel and Irvin.
(Du Bois *et al.*, 1990, p. 48)

m: wide	C *m* I'm getting *q* quite concerned
q: crk	about this *q#* -
q: gig	*q* really *q#* . *q* seriously - *q# m#*
q: lau	

(quoted from Boase, 1990, with reduced prosodic coding)

In other words, Du Bois *et al.* use labelled brackets to identify strings characterized by particular features (in this case: whisper). The second example shows the approach used at the Survey of English Usage, with an indication of the feature in the margin (in this case: wide pitch range, creaky voice, giggle, laughter) and of scope in the text (identified by pairs of letters, the one marking the end being followed by #).

To handle the types of features illustrated above, we can again make use of the timeline. The empty element <**shift**> is inserted at the point where there is a marked change in a feature. This is understood to apply for the relevant speaker until there is a new shift in the same feature for the same speaker, because the features dealt with here are characteristically tied to the individual speaker rather than to groups of participants.

Note that the strings between shift tags are not elements like utterances or segments. Nor are they co-extensive with other elements (though they may be so). We may have several independent shifts in an utterance, at different points. The nature of the shift is shown by attributes of the <**shift**> tag for *feature* and *new*, indicating the type of feature and the new state of the particular feature. The recommended features and values are taken from the transcription system of the Survey of English Usage (see Boase, 1990). The *new* attribute can in all cases take the value *normal*, which indicates that the feature ceases to be remarkable.

The first example above can be re-coded as follows (the <s> is not specified for *type* here; it is an intonation unit):

<u who=A><s>they let us alone.</s><pause type=long><shift feature=voice new=whisp>
<s>but we were scared,</s><s>And boy,</s>
<shift feature=voice new=normal><s>did we ever get into trouble,</s><s>from Mel and Irvin.
</s></u>

The location of the shift is shown by its place in the text. Where there is no risk of ambiguity, a shift back to normal may be indicated by a <**shift**> tag without attributes.

4.6 *Common elements and mechanisms*

Besides the specific tag set dealt with above, the representation of speech requires many of the common elements and mechanisms defined for TEI-conformant texts in general. There is a need to draw on the general mechanisms for character representation and shifting among character sets (including the International Phonetic Alphabet, in case a phonetic representation is called for); see the description of the Writing System Declaration in Gaylord (in this volume).

The ways of specifying reference systems and the devices for editorial comment apply both to spoken and written texts. The following examples illustrate some types of editorial comment needed in spoken texts:

P – What the hell do you think was involved?
D – I think DNC was planted.
P – You think they did it?
D – Uh huh
P – (Expletive deleted) – do they really want to believe that we planted that?
(*The White House Transcripts*, 1974, p. 58)

<1> Oh it's a funny old day today isn't it.
<2> Hm, it's cold is it? I <unclear> (Crowdy, 1991)

A there are cups . nescafe -
B shall we have a cup of coffee .
A yes certainly yes certainly . yes
B I see they're all (6 seconds untranscribable) - - -
(quoted from Svartvik and Quirk, 1980, p. 200, with reduced coding)

Note also the notation for uncertain hearing (double parentheses) in examples given previously from the London-Lund Corpus (4.3.4, 4.4). As in the examples above, editorial comment is typically shown by additions within parentheses. But parentheses are often used for other purposes in transcriptions, and there is clearly a need for more explicit mechanisms. These are provided by the TEI tags for editorial comment and textual criticism. Where there is no more explicit alternative, it is always possible to add an editorial note using the TEI <**note**> tag (as in the re-coded example in section 4.3.3).

Many of the common-core tags appear to be irrelevant for the representation of speech, e.g. the tags for print-oriented features like paragraphs, headings, lists, bibliographical references, and typographical highlighting. It may seem unnecessarily cumbersome to have all these tags available in speech transcription. However, as conventional transcriptions of speech are often reproduced more or less like ordinary writing and as written text may appear as an important element in some speech situations (4.3.7), we want to be able to use tags for print-oriented features also in the representation of spoken texts.

5. Remaining Problems

Using the TEI recommendations, it is possible to represent the types of features generally marked in speech transcriptions, and to do this in an explicit and systematic manner. The focus has been on the representation of texts to be used for discourse analysis and for lexical and grammatical analysis rather than for phonological studies. More work needs to be done on the phonological side.

There is also a need for mechanisms for parallel representation of spoken material, e.g. orthographic and phonological transcription, and for the specification of links between transcriptions and digitized recordings. It remains to be seen whether the alignment mechanism described in this paper can be extended to handle parallel representation.

One of the main guiding principles in existing transcription schemes has been the attempt to find a representation which is convenient to use (write and read) and reasonably easy to learn. The representation described here may not be easy to use directly. There is a need for supporting software which connects the systematic underlying representation with a workable format for input and display.

References

Atkinson, J.M. and J. Heritage, eds. *Structures of Social Action: Studies in Conversation Analysis*. Cambridge: Cambridge University Press, 1984.

Biber, D. *Variation across Speech and Writing*. Cambridge: Cambridge University Press, 1988.

Boase, S. *London-Lund Corpus: Example Text and Transcription Guide*. Survey of English Usage, University College London, 1990.

Coulthard, M. and M. Montgomery, eds. *Studies in Discourse Analysis*. London: Routledge & Kegan Paul, 1981.

Crowdy, S. "The Longman Approach to Spoken Corpus Design". Manuscript, 1991.

Crystal, D. *A Dictionary of Linguistics and Phonetics*. 3rd ed. Oxford: Blackwell, 1991.

Du Bois, J.W., S. Schuetze-Coburn, D. Paolino and S. Cumming. *Discourse Transcription*. Santa Barbara: University of California, Santa Barbara, 1990.

Edwards, J.A. and M.D. Lampert, eds. *Talking Data: Transcription and Coding in Discourse Research*. Hillsdale, NJ: LAwrence Erlbaum, 1993.

Gaylord, H. "Character Sets". In this volume.

Giordano, R. "The TEI Header and the Documentation of Electronic Texts". In this volume.

Johansson, S., L. Burnard, J. Edwards and A. Rosta. "Working Paper on Spoken Texts". Text Encoding Initiative, Spoken Text Work Group, 1991.

Loman, B. and N. Jörgensen. *Manual för analys och beskrivning av makrosyntagmer*. Lund: Studentlitteratur, 1971.

Sinclair, J. and M. Coulthard. *Towards an Analysis of Discourse: The English Used by Teachers and Pupils*. London: Oxford University Press, 1975.

Sperberg-McQueen, C.M. and L. Burnard, eds. *Guidelines for the Encoding and Interchange of Machine-readable Texts*. Draft version 1.0. Chicago and Oxford: Association for Computers and the Humanities/Association for Computational Linguistics/ Association for Literary and Linguistic Computing, 1990.

Sperberg-McQueen, C.M. and L. Burnard, eds. *Guidelines for Electronic Text Encoding and Interchange (TEI P3)*. Chicago and Oxford: Association for Computers and the Humanities/ Association for Computational Linguistics/Association for Literary and Linguistic Computing, 1994.

Svartvik, J. and R. Quirk, eds. *A Corpus of English Conversation*. Lund Studies in English 56. Lund: Lund University Press, 1980.

Terkel, S. *Working. People Talk about What They Do all Day and How They Feel about What They Do*. New York: Avon Books, 1975.

The White House Transcripts. Submission of Recorded Presidential Conversations to the Committee on the Judiciary of the House of Representatives by President Nixon. By the New York Times Staff for the White House Transcripts. New York: Bantam Books, 1974.

Computers and the Humanities **29**: 159–165, 1995.

E-Tif: An Electronic Terminology Interchange Format[1,3]

Alan Melby *
Department of Linguistics, Brigham Young University, Provo, Utah 84604, USA
e-mail: alan_melby@byu.edu

Key words: TEI, SGML, E-TIF, terminology interchange, translation

Abstract

This article begins by emphasizing the importance of terminology in this modern age of technical innovations and machine-based translation systems, establishing the need for a terminolgy interchange format, and distinguishing between lexicography and terminology. It then reviews previous attempts to establish terminology interchange formats and concludes with a forceful argument for a new system based on the TEI-based notions of elements and attributes.

1. The Importance of Terminology

The consistent use of terminology has always been important in technical writing and translation. For example, if a particular machine is called a "bottle inverter" in chapter one and a "jar flipper" in chapter three, serious confusion could result, especially if, elsewhere in the document, a "jar flipper" is a person who discards defective jars.

The volume of new technical text created each year is enormous. A frequently retold anecdote is that if one fills a Boeing 747 airplane with a paper copy of all the technical documents that relate to its construction, maintenance, and operation, the weight is such that the 747 cannot get off the ground.

Large quantities of technical text include large numbers of technical terms. Besides the need to use these terms consistently throughout a related set of documents, there is a growing need to translate technical documents. One translation equivalent must be identified for each technical term and used consistently throughout the translation process, even if several translators are each translating different parts of a document. This implies the need to provide each translator with the same bilingual terminology file.

2. The Need to Supply Terminology in Electronic Form

In the past, it was feasible to supply terminology files in the form of paper documents. However, paper as a medium is becoming problematical for several reasons. First is the growing use of terminology management software which allows the translator to access terminology files rapidly while translating. These software packages require the terminology file to be on disk in a certain format. If the translator is given a terminology file on paper there are only unpleasant alternatives: (a) keyboarding the terminological data into a terminology data base, which is too time consuming; (b) converting the data by scanning it and using OCR (optical character recognition) software, which is too error-prone and still requires manual reformatting according to the rules of the terminology management software; or (c) abandoning the use of the terminology management software and looking up terms on paper. As international trade expands and becomes more competitive, and as technology evolves ever faster, it becomes

* Alan K. Melby is Professor of Linguistics at Brigham Young University. He is involved in translation, technical communication, and computational language projects. He is the CEO of Linguatech International, the Chair of the Translation and Computers committee of the American Translators Association, and a member of the editorial board of *Machine Translation.* He serves as Chair of the Terminology Workgroup of the Text Encoding Initiative, and as a member of the U.S. tag of ISO TC 37. He is an accredited translator (French to English).

increasingly important to bring out foreign language versions of high tech products (such as photocopiers, computers, and software) at the same time as, or very soon after, the appearance of the source language version. This means that the translation (or, more broadly, localization) must be done faster, more accurately, and less expensively in order to remain competitive.

Another problem with terminology on paper is that new terms appear so often that the paper document must be reprinted very often, an expensive and non-ecological procedure. If only the changes are printed, the translator is confronted with the problem of consulting many updates in addition to the main (and outdated) version.

Another kind of problem with transmitting terminology on paper arises as more and more documents to be translated are transmitted in electronic form. Having the source text in electronic form suggests a whole new kind of translator tools, which are beginning to emerge. These new tools, which were foreseen over a decade ago (Melby, 1982), actively analyze the current segment of source text and highlights terms in the source text which appear in the terminology file, allowing the translator to insert the standard target term into the translation quickly and with unerring accuracy and consistency. Clearly, this new generation of translator tools requires terminology files to be in electronic form.[2]

When documents are created in electronic form and transmitted in electronic form, terminology files must be maintained in electronic form just to travel with the documents they apply to. When information is maintained in electronic form, a decision must be made as to its format, and terminological data are no exception. Therefore, we must consider the format of electronic terminology files.

3. The Need for a Terminology Interchange Format

If everyone used the same terminology management software on the same type of computer, all terminology files could be maintained in the format prescribed by that universal terminology management software package. However, as is usually the case in the software market, there are many competing packages, each with its own internal file format. And files that contain non-English characters are not easily transmitted from one computer to another (e.g., from an IBM-compatible to a Macintosh) without loss of information.

Indeed, terminology files currently exist in many different formats on many different computers. Looking at the public and non-commercial sectors of industrialized countries, there are national and international term banks such as Termium (a large English-French term bank maintained by the Canadian Government), Eurodicautom (a multilingual term bank maintained by the Commission of the European Union), multilingual terminology files maintained by the United Nations, and numerous monolingual and bilingual terminology files maintained by various standards organizations around the world (often in the form of word processing files). Looking at the private sector, we find that many large companies maintain their own terminology database, such as Siemens (the German industrial giant) and Xerox corporation, to name two out of hundreds. Also, we discover that many translation service bureaus have built up their own terminology databases. And, of course, many individual translators have a personal database built up over the years.

One way to allow interchange among all these terminology databases would be to write a two-way conversion program between each pair of formats. With just thirty-five different formats (there are probably many more than that), this approach would require over one thousand separate two-way conversion programs. Such a daunting task fills one with despair. However, if there were a common intermediate format for terminology files, the number of conversion programs required is reduced from over one thousand to just thirty-five (one between each format and the interchange format).

Thus, it becomes clear that an intermediate format is needed for terminology interchange. Such an interchange format could immediately be used within a large company. Ideally, terminology files would be consulted when a document is authored in order to ensure the consistent use of technical terms. New terms that are coined for use in a text would be added to the terminology file. Then, ideally, translation equivalents would be chosen for the new terms and added to the terminology file before documents are translated. Then, the terminology files would be consulted during the translation process, by either manual or automatic lookup. Translation in large companies is often done by a combination of in-house and independent translators, with independent translators usually being contacted through a translation service bureau. In any of these combinations, when several translators are involved, consistent use of terminology throughout a related set of documents becomes a significant issue.

So far we have emphasized the document production chain, including authoring and translation, within a company. There is also a need to maintain some consistency between companies. Computer software is a prime example. There are many companies that develop software for use with Microsoft *Windows*^{TM}. Since all *Windows* software products share a consistent user-interface, it is important to use the relevant terms consistently in the documentation for these products, including localized versions in other languages. To this end, Microsoft has published a book called a *GUI Guide* (*Graphical User Interface Guide*), with many terms in the "GUI" domain and their suggested equivalents in several languages. This is a positive step toward openness that benefits the end-user. But when the *GUI Guide* terms are distributed in electronic form, what format should be used? Similarly, many standards organizations define the basic terms in a given domain, but how is this terminological information to be distributed so that it is most easily used? Paper publication alone is no longer sufficient. All these trends point to the need for an electronic format for the interchange of terminology files.

Most of the rest of this paper will deal with the design and implementation of a proposed electronic terminology interchange format (E-TIF),.but first we will present a brief diversion to distinguish terminology from lexicography and thus explain what E-TIF is *not* claiming to do.

4. Lexicography Distinguished from Terminology

There are two distinct traditions, terminology and lexicography. First, terminology is concerned with particular domains of knowledge while lexicography is usually concerned with general vocabulary. Within a particular domain, one can normally identify well-defined concepts. People create these concepts because they are useful for clear, efficient communication within the relevant domain. Ideally, each concept is expressed as a single term in a given language. On the other hand, lexicography is not limited to a domain, preferring to identify typical uses of a word in the continuum of general vocabulary. With their basic orientation being different (terminology starting from concepts and lexicography starting from words), the two approaches have naturally developed along different lines.

A lexicographical entry in a dictionary treats a word, frequently called the headword. If there are two sets of meanings which are clearly distinct, such as the verb *to console* (i.e. to comfort and cheer up in a difficult situation) and the noun *console* (i.e. the keyboard, as on a pipe organ), they may be treated in consecutive entries, e.g. *console*(1) and *console*(2), called homonyms or homographs. Otherwise, many senses of a word will be treated in the same entry. For example, *foot* as a body part, *foot* at a measure of distance, *foot* as a part of a bed, and *foot* as a verb which means to pay the cost of something would all be treated in a single lexicographical entry. Lexicographical entries will often contain grammatical and etymological information pertaining to the word and may show inflected forms of the word.The entries are arranged in alphabetical order by headword, since the user will typically start with a word and want information about it.

On the other hand, a terminological entry will normally be limited to a single concept in a given domain or subdomain. Other senses will usually be treated in separate entries. A terminological entry will include the term used in one or more languages to express the concept. Of course, domains and thus concepts are not always identical across languages, so there may be a need for notes and provisos about equivalence and reversibility. There is typically less grammatical information in a terminological entry than a lexicographical one. This is natural since terms are principally nouns and noun compounds. Verbs, especially standard verbal phrases, will sometimes appear in terminological (strictly speaking, phraseological) entries, while adjectives, prepositions and other grammatical categories are relatively rare. Terminological entries are sometimes presented in a systematic order based on a view of how the concepts of a domain relate to each other, rather than in alphabetical order by the terms of one of the languages. However, in this case there will normally be an alphabetical index for the terms of each language with cross-references to the relevant entry or entries.

Given the above differences between terminological and lexicographical practice, it should not be surprising that the terminology interchange format described in this article does not claim to apply to lexicographical entries. Nevertheless, it should be possible to recast a domain-specific word-sense from a lexicographical entry as a terminological entry or to include a monolingual or bilingual terminological entry in a lexicographical entry. To facilitate such adaptation we have worked for maximal consistency between the encoding specifications for machine-readable dictionaries and terminology databases.

5. Previous Terminology Interchange Formats

Given the need for an electronic format for interchanging terminology files, and noting that the task is made more feasible by excluding the requirement that such a format be sufficient for lexicographical as well as terminological data, it would seem likely that efforts have already been made in this direction. And indeed, several such formats have already been developed.

Perhaps the best-known existing terminology interchange format is the international standard ISO 6156, usually called by its name, MATER, rather than by its number. MATER was a pioneering effort which began in the 1970s and culminated in the definition of an international standard in 1986. It is intended mainly for the interchange of data between mainframe-based term banks via 9-track magnetic tape. This orientation was a reasonable one at the time work on MATER began, since at the time microcomputers were relatively unknown and very limited, being mostly based on eight-bit processors and using the CP/M operating system. The first IBM PC did not even appear until 1981, at which time Apple computer had not yet introduced the Macintosh to replace the Apple II. By the time MATER became a standard, it had been overtaken by events. Terminology files were no longer restricted to mainframe computers.

In the early 1980s, work began on a proposal for a new terminology interchange format which came to be called MicroMATER (the name being intended to suggest an adaptation of MATER suitable for use with microcomputers). This work was even carried out with the cooperation of some of the designers of MATER. The principal aims of MicroMATER were to provide a flexible interchange format which would allow terminology files to be transmitted between various computer platforms (mainframes, minis, and micros) without loss of information and which could be inspected by a human and edited with a standard text editor at any point along the way. The MATER standard, unfortunately, was designed with the mainframe EBCDIC character set in mind, and could not be inspected and understood by a human, as it appeared to be mainly a sequence of numbers with pieces of text stuck together. The position and length of each field were defined by numbers in a header, which made it nearly impossible to edit with a text editor. MATER was intended to be created and read only by computer programs. MicroMATER was intended to created either by a computer program or by a human.

The results of the MicroMATER project were published (Melby, 1991), but by then, those involved in the MicroMATER project were already involved in developing a new terminology interchange format in cooperation with the Text Encoding Initiative.[3]

6. The Text Encoding Initiative as a New Framework

The Text Encoding Initiative had a tremendous appeal to the members of the MicroMATER project. One reason was that the Text Encoding Initiative (TEI) is based on SGML. But this was not the only reason. There is another, fairly recent SGML-based project to develop a terminology interchange format for use among several term banks in Norway, Denmark, and other nordic countries, hence its name, the Nordic Terminology Record Format (NTRF) (Hjulstad, 1991).

The main reason for joining with the efforts of the TEI was that many of the problems encountered in encoding other texts – such as character set problems, dealing with cross-references, showing the internal structure of a definition or other piece of text, including illustrations, interchange across 7-bit paths, and writing well-designed DTDs – also needed solutions for other types of text. By becoming a workgroup of the TEI, those of us who had worked on MicroMATER were able to interact with many others dealing with similar problems. It was hoped that association with the TEI would also effectively bring in more external review and further validate our conclusions. Not insignificant was the additional consideration that those who need a terminology interchange format will also be dealing with significant quantities of text and would hopefully look to the TEI for assistance in the world-wide shift from presentational to descriptive markup as that preferred for the master copy of a document from which all other forms are derived. Finally, we believe the future terminology management systems will be integrated with text management systems.

7. Design Considerations for a Terminology Interchange Format

When the Terminology workgroup (AI7) was formed within the TEI (March 1991), it was decided within the workgroup to totally reevaluate the design rather than simply adapt an existing format to the then-existing

TEI Guidelines (P1). In light of the fact that no previously proposed format had enjoyed widespread use, it was decided that, above all, it was necessary to develop a format which had some likelihood of broad acceptance and implementation. A terminology interchange format is only useful if it is widely used. A primary stumbling block would be the perception that the format was biased toward any particular school of terminological theory. Therefore, it must appear reasonably theory-neutral. Another obvious stumbling block would be if it could not adequately represent the information in a particularly terminology database. Thus, it must be flexible. And finally, it must not look so different from the way terminologists are used to looking at their data that it appears entirely too abstract and complex. Thus, it must appear as simple as possible.

Before going any further, the workgroup decided to examine the structure of as many existing terminology databases as possible. Upon examining over thirty of them, it was observed, as predicted, that although many field names were used identically across numerous databases, other field names were particular to just one or a few databases. Another problem was the sheer number of different field names, which amounted to several hundred. It was quickly concluded that it would not be feasible to devise a unique SGML generic identifier for each field name. Instead, after extended discussions, it was decided to use just a few broad generic identifiers, each with a *type* attribute to distinguish between various specific field names. Besides **<term>** and **<otherForm>**, which will be discussed next, it was decided to use only **<gram>** for grammatical information, **<descrip>** for definitions and other descriptive information, and **<admin>** for administrative information. Even within these broad classifications it was found that various databases disagreed. For example, although no one thinks that a definition or a contextual example is administrative information and no one thinks that responsible person or date of last change is descriptive, there is disagreement over whether subject matter domain is administrative or descriptive. In the end, it was decided to place all the possible values of the *type* attribute on the **<descrip>** and **<admin>** generic identifiers into one composite list, disallowing any distinction of meaning between use on **<descrip>** and **<admin>**, thus allowing users to decide whether a particular specific value applies to **<descrip>** or **<admin>**. This is not a problem for conversion software if it is designed to use one table of correspondences between **<descrip>**/**<admin>** tags and field names in the target database. By placing all possible values of *type* in a machine-readable list, those values can be validated by software, and the list can be modified without changing the DTD.

In parallel, an effort was made to develop a compendium of all the field names, which are called "data categories" or "data element types" within the terminology community, which could serve as a guide both to the person who is using the TEI-based Electronic Terminology Interchange Format (E-TIF) and to the person who is designing a new terminology database. This effort has subsequently developed from a project whose home was the Kent State Institute of Applied Linguistics into a work item of Technical Committee 37 of the International Organization for Standardization (ISO), which is slated to become international standard number 12 620.

Coming back to E-TIF, it was also necessary to decide on a structure for the interchange format. It was not sufficient to come up with a set of tags and an associated DTD which was flexible enough to describe the structure of any given terminology database.

This would make export routines very easy to write but import routines very difficult to write. Rather, it was necessary to decide on one structure into which any terminology database could be "poured" after a certain amount of manipulation.

The first level of structure was easy to agree on. Every terminology database is organized into entries, so we devised the **<termEntry>** tag. Unfortunately, the consensus stopped there. Some multilingual databases place each language section in a separate entry, while others combine them into one entry. Most databases are rather "flat", meaning that there is no explicit hierarchical nesting of information. Finally, after months of arduous discussions, the workgroup hit upon a new name for the structural element just smaller than an entry: a term information group **<tig>**. This name was neutral as to whether the entry was monolingual or multilingual and did not imply any particular theoretical bias since all entries contain terms and each term may have and almost always does have additional information associated with it.

The only artificial requirement we placed on a **<tig>** was that it could only contain one term. This restriction allowed the definition of an additional format called a flat format in which a **<termEntry>** consists overtly of just a list of elements with no explicit nesting at all. Many existing terminology databases can be represented in this flat format with little or no change except that each field becomes an SGML element and each record is enclosed in **<termEntry>** tags. Then a simple algorithm was devised that generated the implicit **<tig>** elements, one per term. When "terms" were present that did not really start a new term information group, typically synonyms or short forms, they had to be called an **<otherForm>**. This two-staged approach of converting an existing database first to a flat SGML structure and then to a more nested one with **<tig>** elements showing what items are grouped together has been acceptable to many persons considering the use of E-TIF.

There are several more complicated aspects to the flat/nested conversion, especially the introduction of the *group* and *depend* attributes which deal with discontinuous elements. The flat-to-nested conversion algorithm has been augmented to be sensitive to these attributes, which have the semantics of a TEI tree-traversing pointer. The interested reader is encouraged to study the chapter on terminological data in the TEI Guidelines for several examples of the use of *group* and *depend*.

In the TEI chapter, one will also see mention of a tag called **<ofig>** (**<otherForm>** Information Group). This can be used when an **<otherForm>** element, such as a synonym, has substantial information associated with it, such as a definition which applies to it and not to the primary term of the **<tig>**. There are no examples of its use in the chapter because it is seldom needed, and indeed, it is not clear that it would be desirable to use it in a fully normalized interchange format for "blind" interchange in which the source terminology data base is not known. Instead, such detailed information should probably be placed either in another **<tig>** or in another **<termEntry>** altogether with appropriate pointers back and forth.

A fully normalized structure is being defined as a subset of the nested format in which there is one **<termEntry>** per concept and one **<tig>** per term. Two examples of terminology data formats are included below, to illustrate the difference between conventional formats and E-TIF. Both examples have been excerpted from Chapter TE of TEI P3. The terminology data they contain come originally from ISO 472 (1988). The first format is similar to the ISO version, in that layout characteristics (bold, indent, blank lines) represent the structure inherent in the data. The second format, E-TIF, explicitly marks the hierarchical relationships among information segments according to the standard for fully normalized files (TEI P2, 1993).[2]

FORMAT 1

thermal degradation:
  The entirety of all deleterious chemical modifications of plastic at elevated temperature.
  NOTE - - It is essential to report the temperature and other environmental conditions at which the phenomenon is studied.
  See also ageing, degradation and deterioration.

décomposition thermique:
  Ensemble de toutes les modifications chimiques nuisibles d'une plastique à température élevée.
  NOTE - - Il est essentiel d'indiquer la température et les autres conditions d'environnement dans lesquelles le phénomène est étudié.
  Voir aussi vieillissement, dégradation et détérioration.

FORMAT 2

```
<termEntry id=te84.11>
   <admin type='domain'> plastics </admin>
   <ref type='bibliographic' target='ISO.472-1988'>
      p. 84</ref>
   <admin type='creation' date='1988' resp='ISO/TC 61,
      Plastics'>
   </admin>
   <ptr type='relatedTerm' target='te04.06'>

   <tig lang=en>
      <term> thermal degradation </term>
      <gram type=pos> n </gram>
      <descrip type='definition'> The entirety of all
         deleterious chemical modifications of plastic
         at elevated temperature. </descrip>
      <note> It is essential to report the temperature and
         other environmental conditions at which the
         phenomenon is studied. </note>
   </tig>

   <tig lang=fr>
      <term> d&eacute;composition thermique </term>
      <gram type=pos> n </gram>
      <gram type=gen> f </gram>
      <descrip type='definition'> Ensemble de toutes les
         modifications chimiques nuisibles d'une
         plastique &agrave; temp&eacute;rature
         &eacute;lev&eacute;e.</descrip>
      <note> Il est essentiel d'indiquer la temp&eacute;
         rature et les autres conditions d'environnement
         dans lesquelles le ph&eacute;nom&egrave;ne est
         &eacute;tudi&eacute;.
      </note>
   </tig>
</termEntry>
```

So far, the basic structure of <**termEntry**> and <**tig**> (see the chapter of P3 for details) has gained rather wide acceptance. The next step is to capitalize on that acceptance and encourage widespread implementation.

8. Acceptance of E-Tif

So far, E-TIF, as defined within the TEI, has been accepted by the American Translators Association (Terminology and Translator Workstation Committees), FIT (the international federation of translator associations), Infoterm (The International Information Centre for Terminology, headquartered in Vienna), ASTM (the American Society for Testing and Materials Committee on Terminology), the ESPRIT Translator Workbench II project and, significantly, LISA (the Localisation Industry Standards Association, which includes Microsoft, Apple, IBM, ICL, HP, DEC, and many others).

In addition, an even more nested version of E-TIF is well on its way to becoming an international standard alongside MATER. Currently a draft international standard version of E-TIF as ISO 12 220 is under consideration.

Notes

[1] This paper is based on work performed in the TEI work group on Terminology, whose members include Alan Melby, Brigham Young U. (chair), Sue Ellen Wright, American Translators Association and other affiliations, Greg Shreve, Kent State U., Gerhard Budin, Infoterm, and Richard Strehlow, ASTM and other affiliations.

[2] See "Base Tag Set for Terminological Data", in TEI P3 (1994), pp. 22–23.

[3] Portions of this chapter appear in the following work: Melby, Alan, and Wright, Sue Ellen. 1995. "Terminology Interchange." In: *The Terminology Handbook*, Sue Ellen Wright and Gerhard Budin, Eds. Amsterdam: John Benjamins.

References

Hjulstad, Havard. "Nordic Terminological Record Format (NTRF)". Oslo: Norwegian Council for Technical Terminology, 1991.

ISO. "Plastics – Vocabulary". In *ISO 472: 1988*. Bilingual edition. Geneva: ISO, 1988, p. 84.

Melby, Alan. "A Three-Level Design for Translator Tools". *Proceedings of COLING82*. Prague, 1982.

Melby, Alan. "MicroMATER: A Proposed Format for Exchanging Lexical/Terminological Data Files". *META: Translators Journal*, 36, 1 (1991).

Sperberg-McQueen, C.M. and Lou Burnard, eds. *Guidelines for Electronic Text Encoding and Interchange (TEI P3)*. 2 vols. Chicago and Oxford: Text Encoding Initiative, 1994.

Computers and the Humanities **29:** 167–179, 1995.

Encoding Dictionaries

Nancy Ide *
Department of Computer Science, Vassar College, Poughkeepsie, New York 12601, USA
e-mail: ide@cs.vassar.edu

and

Jean Véronis *
Laboratoire Parole et Langage, CNRS & Université de Provence, 29 Avenue Robert Schuman, 13621 Aix-en-Provence Cedex 1, France
e-mail: veronis@univ-aix.fr

Key words: encoding, TEI, dictionaries, SGML

Abstract

This article describes the major problems in devising a TEI encoding format for dictionaries, which, because of their high degree of structuring and compression of information, are among the most complex text types treated in the TEI. The major problems for this task were (1) the tension between generality of the description, in order to be widely applicable across dictionaries, and descriptive power, that is, the ability to describe with precision the particular structure of any given dictionary; and (2) the need to accommodate different views and uses of the encoded dictionary, for example, as printed object and as a database of information.

1. Introduction

Dictionaries are among the most complex text types treated in the TEI. Each dictionary entry is a highly structured object, in which a variety of abbreviatory and structural devices is used to present information compactly. Furthermore, the structure of dictionary entries is highly variable, both within and among dictionaries, to the point where it may appear at first that any piece of information can go anywhere in at least some dictionary. However, despite these variations, human readers are capable of interpreting dictionary entries, often without consulting the explanatory front matter. It is clear that there are some strong and consistent structural principles within dictionaries that an encoding format should capture. The first challenge for the TEI Dictionary Working Group[1] was to develop an encoding format both general enough to be common across different dictionaries and which at the same time captures these fundamental principles. This conflict between generality and descriptive power exists for many text types, but is severely exaggerated for dictionaries.

Other encoding problems arise from the fact that dictionaries, unlike other text types, are at the same time both text and database.[2] Dictionaries obviously look like texts and share many features with other types of texts. However, users typically do not read a dictionary linearly from A to Z as they do most texts, but access entries on the basis of a key (the headword) in order to retrieve various fields of information associated with that key (pronunciation, grammatical information, etymology, definitions, etc.). Electronic dictionaries now commonly available on CD ROM make this point even clearer: the user can retrieve all the words whose definition contains the word *x*, or all

* Nancy Ide is Associate Professor and chair of Computer Science at Vassar College, and Visiting Researcher at CNRS. She is president of the Association for Computers and the Humanities and chair of the Steering Committee of the Text Encoding Initiative.

Jean Véronis is Maître de Conférences in Computer Science at the Université de Provence and head of the Natural Language Processing Group of Laboratoire Parole et Langage.

the words matching given criteria (e.g., all the verbs in the nautical domain, appearing before 1900), etc. In addition, although the display on the screen still looks more or less like a text,[3] the internal representation is rarely that of a linear text.

As a result, dictionaries exhibit a strong duality between their surface structure (the text) and their deep structure (the information content). Much of the deep structure information is not explicit in the surface structure, but requires knowledge of the abbreviatory and layout conventions of dictionaries. For example, in the entry below, the surface structure – that is, the linear position of the various elements – does not explicitly provide the information that noun (*n.*) applies only to senses 1 and 2, while the pronunciation applies to all six senses.[4]

roughcast (ˈrʌfˌcɑ:st)*n.* **1.** a coarse plaster used to cover the surface of an external wall. **2.** any rough or preliminary form, model, etc. ~*adj.* **3.** covered with or denoting roughcast. ~*vb.* **-casts, -casting, -cast. 4.** to apply roughcast to (a wall, etc.). **5.** to prepare in rough. **6.** (*tr.*) another word for **rough-hew. --ˈroughˌcaster** *n.* [CED]

The duality in dictionaries creates a problem for encoding because there are two different views of the dictionary that users may want to encode. One user may want to encode the textual view and thus retain the surface structure, possibly in order to maintain fidelity to some existing or potential printed version. However, the kind of inferencing required to retrieve the deep structure information from the surface structure may be difficult, if not impossible, for a computer to accomplish.[5] Therefore, if the user is interested in the database view (perhaps in order to access and manipulate the dictionary with computer software) explicit encoding of the information given only implicitly in the surface structure is required. In some cases, users are interested in having access to both views simultaneously. Since the two views of the dictionary are often in conflict, their encodings are typically substantially different. Therefore, a second major challenge for the TEI Dictionary Working Group was to provide for encoding both views, either independently or simultaneously.

In this paper we focus on the two primary encoding problems for dictionaries, arising from the tension between the need for generality and the need for descriptive power on the one hand, and from the tension between the textual and database views of the dictionary on the other. We do not address here a number of other problems of dictionary encoding. The reader is referred to chapter 12 of TEI P3 (Sperberg-McQueen and Burnard, 1994), "Print Dictionaries",[6] (pp. 321–70) for a full description of the TEI dictionary encoding scheme.

2. Overview

The concern of the Dictionary Working Group was a description of the dictionary entry, since higher level elements (front matter, body, and back matter, and optional divisions and sub-divisions corresponding to sections for different languages in a bilingual dictionaries, common nouns and proper nouns, grammatical notes, various lists, etc.) are the same as those for many other text types.[7] In order to establish a sound working basis, the committee limited its scope to consider only western language dictionaries, and in particular limited itself primarily to modern, average-size dictionaries, which in themselves exhibit considerable variety in structure and content.

2.1 *Basic constituents*

There are several clearly identifiable kinds of information that appear in dictionary entries, such as information about the form of the word treated (orthography, pronunciation, hyphenation, etc.), grammatical information (part of speech, grammatical sub-categorization, etc.), definitions or translations in a target language, etymology, cross-references, related entries, usage information, and examples. The first step in the development of a DTD for dictionaries is the specification of a typology of atomic elements that appear in a dictionary entry and a suitable nomenclature for these elements. Atomic elements are those which constitute the basic, non-decomposable fields of information relevant in a dictionary entry. They contain no other dictionary elements; in TEI terms, their content is the same as the content of paragraphs (sequence of character data, possibly also phrase level elements[8]) – i.e., these elements have no internal structure. The identification of fundamental fields of information in dictionaries has received attention in the past, and although there is disagreement on some details, in general the fundamental fields of information in dictionaries were fairly well-established prior to the work within the TEI (see Danlex, 1987, and, in particular, Amsler and Tompa, 1988).

Some dictionary constituents are complex, comprising groups of atomic elements. For example, consider the definition below:

CRAWLER [krole] v.i. Nager le crawl. [PL]

This entry can be viewed as consisting of three distinct parts: (1) information about the spoken and written forms of the headword, (2) grammatical information, and (3) the definition. In many cases it is desirable to make these associations or groupings explicit; therefore, the Dictionary Working Group defined a set of bracketing tags to mark such logical relations. Correspondingly, the encoding for the entry above is[9]

```
<entry>
   <form>
      <orth>crawler</orth>
      <pron>krole</pron>
   </form>
   <gramGrp>
      <pos>v</pos>
      <subc>i</subc>
   </gramGrp>
   <def>Nager le crawl</def>
</entry>
```

The first piece of information consists of two subparts, marked by the tags **<orth>** and **<pron>**; the **<form>** tag identifies them as sub-components of a single logical constituent. Similarly, the **<gramGrp>** constituent[10] consists of two sub-components, the part-of-speech (**<pos>**) and subcategorization information (**<subc>**). The definition is a simple constituent, consisting only of the definition text itself and having no internal structure.

In addition to associating elements, bracketing tags are used to restrict (by means of their definitions in the DTD) the tags that can be nested inside them, thus enabling a tighter definition of allowed entry structure. In this way, these tags behave as a set of "labeled brackets"; for example, **<form>** is defined to contain **<orth>**, **<pron>**, **<hyph>**, **<syll>**, **<usg>**, **<lbl>** or another **<form>**, in any order. It may also contain, at any position, sequences of character data and other standard phrase-level elements (i.e., the elements defined by the parameter entity *paraContent* in TEI P3, chapter 3, p. 68), to allow for free text between elements where it is desired to include it. The DTD fragment defining **<form>** is

```
<!ELEMENT form- -   (orth|pron|hyph|syll|usg|lbl|form
                     |%paraContent)+                        >
```

The major constituents of dictionary entries identified by the Dictionary Working Group are referred to as "top-level constituents of entries" and listed in TEI P3, chapter 12, p. 333.

```
entry
|
+-homograph
  |
  +-sense
    |
    +-subsense
      |
      +-sub-sub-sense
        |
        ...
```

Fig. 1. Divisions and sub-divisions of dictionary entries.

2.2 *Hierarchical structure and scope of information*

The most pervasive and consistent structural property of dictionary entries is their hierarchical organization. For example, an entry often consists of two or more sub-parts, each corresponding to information for a different part-of-speech homograph of the headword. The entry for *roughcast* given above demonstrates this: it has three part-of-speech homographs (noun, adjective, verb). An entry (or part-of-speech homograph if the entry is split this way) may also consist of senses, each of which may in turn be composed of two or more sub-senses, etc. (see Figure 1).

Hierarchies can be very deeply nested in some dictionaries, in order to show that some elements are more closely related as well as to distinguish finer and finer grains of meaning, as in the entry below. In some cases, levels can be missing (e.g., the homograph level) altogether.

valeur [valœʀ] n. f. **A. I. 1.** Ce par quoi une personne est digne d'estime, ensemble des qualités qui la recommandent. (V. mérite). *Avoir conscience de sa valeur. C'est un homme de grande valeur.* **2.** Vx. Vaillance, bravoure (spécial., au combat). *"La valeur n'attend pas le nombre des années"* (Corneille). ◊ *Valeur militaire (croix de la):* décoration française...

...

II. 1. Ce en quoi une chose est digne d'intérêt. *Les souvenirs attachés à cet objet font pour moi sa valeur.* **2.** Caractère de ce qui est reconnu digne d'intérêt...

...

B. I. 1. Caractère mesurable d'un objet, en tant qu'il est susceptible d'être échangé, désiré, vendu, etc. (V. prix). *Faire estimer la valeur d'un objet d'art...* [DNT]

The hierarchical organization of dictionaries enables the factoring of information over certain levels of the hierarchy so that common information is not re-specified. That is, the scope of information spec-

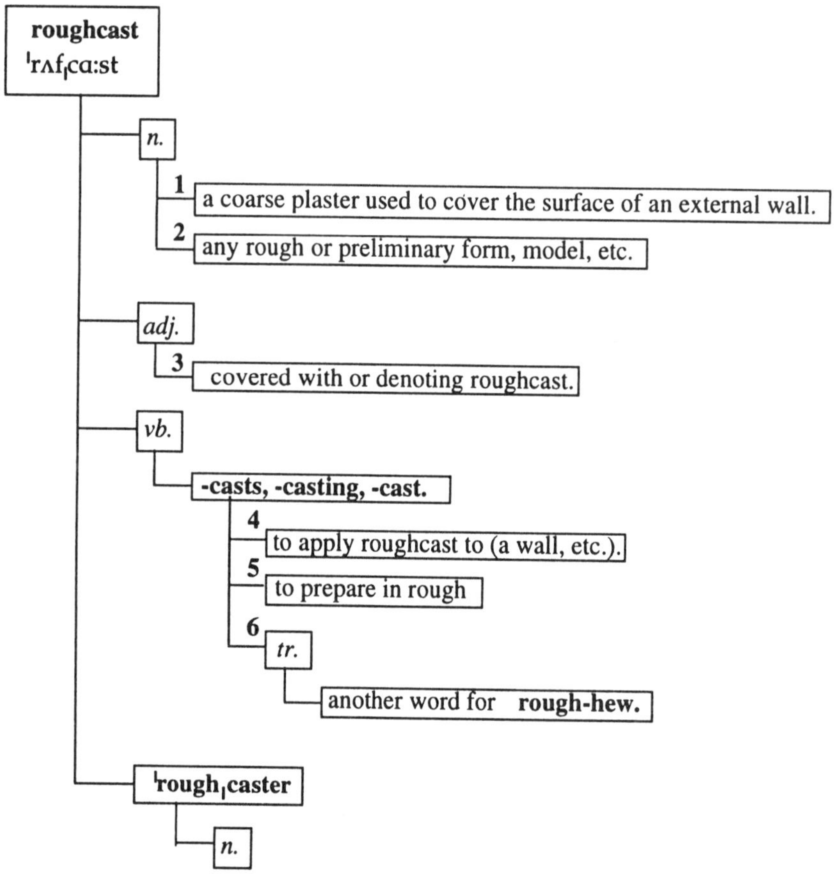

Fig. 2. Factoring and scope.

ified at one level in the hierarchy is that level plus any nested levels, as for variables in a block-structured language such as Pascal. Information such as pronunciation, orthographic form, part of speech, etc. is typically "factored out" at the head of an entry in order to make it clear that it applies to a number of senses. For example, in the entry for *roughcast* given earlier, the orthographic form and pronunciation apply to the whole entry, noun applies to the first 3 senses, etc. (see Figure 2).

Typical entries will therefore have simple structures like the following:

```
<!-- entry with two senses -->
<entry>
   <form>...</form>
   <gramGrp>...</gramGrp>
   <sense n='1'>...</sense>
   <sense n='2'>...</sense>
</entry>
```

```
<!-- entry with two homographs and two senses in
   each -->
<entry>
   <form>...</form>
   <hom n='I'>
      <gramGrp>...</gramGrp>
      <sense n='1'>...</sense>
      <sense n='2'>...</sense>
   </hom>
   <hom n='II'>
      <gramGrp>...</gramGrp>
      <sense n='1'>...</sense>
      <sense n='2'>...</sense>
   </hom>
</entry>
```

3. Handling Variation

On the basis of the structural principles outlined above, it would be fairly simple to write a DTD that describes dictionary structure. Such a DTD would nest homographs within entries, senses within homographs, subsenses within senses, etc. In addition, specific factored constituents would be allowed to appear at the appropriate levels in the hierarchy. So, for example, <**entry**> would be defined to contain <**form**> and one or more homographs (<**hom**>), <**hom**> would be defined to contain <**gramGrp**> and one or more <**sense**> tags, etc.

Unfortunately, the situation is not this straightforward. Dictionary structure is far more complex and variable than this simple scenario suggests. The following sections outline some of the problems encountered by the Dictionary Working Group in developing a DTD general enough to apply across the majority of dictionaries, while at the same providing some meaningful description of dictionary structure.

3.1 *Variation across dictionaries*

Although the principles of hierarchical organization and information factoring are a constant underlying the structure of almost all modern western dictionaries, there is still considerable variation in the structure of different dictionaries. The extreme variation in entry structure within and among dictionaries makes it very difficult to find a meaningful structural description that can apply across all possible dictionaries. For instance, different dictionaries place etymological information in different places, as in the following entries:

nougat (ˈnu:gɑ:, ˈnʌgət) *n.* a hard chewy pink or white sweet containing chopped nuts, cherries, etc. [C19: via French from Provençal *nogat,* from *noga* nut, from Latin *nux* nut] [CED]

NOUGAT n.m. (mot prov.). Confiserie de sucre, de miel et de blancs d'oeufs frais ou desséchés, additionnée d'amandes, de noisettes ou encore de pistaches. [PL]

In the *CED*, etymology is always at the end of an entry, whereas in the *PL* it is always at the beginning and follows grammatical information. Sample DTD fragments defining these two structures are as follows:

```
<!-- DTD fragment for CED entries (not TEI)                    -->
<!ELEMENT entry -- (form, gramGrp, ..., etym?)                  >

<!-- DTD fragment for PL entries (not TEI)                     -->
<!ELEMENT entry -- (form, gramGrp, etym?, ...)                  >
```

However, since the Dictionary Working Group was charged with defining a DTD applicable across dictionaries, it was necessary to allow all possible variants in the DTD. But simply to accommodate the two variants above, something like the following would be required:

```
<!-- DTD fragment for CED and PL entries (not TEI)        -->
<!ELEMENT entry --  (form, gramGrp,
                    ((etym?, ...)|(..., etym?))              >
```

Although this "merged" DTD is more general – i.e., it allows more possible structures – it is also over-generative for each of the two dictionaries. For example, if this DTD is used to validate the structure of the *PL*, it will allow an etymology to appear at the end as well as the beginning of an entry, thus permitting accidents and errors.

This is a small and simple example of the kinds of variation that exist among dictionary structures. Etymologies appear in still other locations within other dictionaries (see for example the entry *nougat* in the *PR* in the next section), and the same problem exists for almost all other kinds of dictionary constituents. A DTD that is flexible enough to allow for all potential variants must therefore be maximally general, allowing any constituent to appear anywhere, any number of times. Thus the definition for the entry element in the TEI dictionary DTD is

```
<!-- Fragment of the TEI dictionary DTD                 -->
<!ELEMENT entry --  (hom|sense|form|
                    gramGrp|usg|def|etym|eg ...)+        >
```

This definition allows for the nesting of <**hom**> and <**sense**> tags within <**entry**>, as well as the appearance of any top level constituent.[11] To serve the demand for maximum flexibility, these elements are allowed to appear in any order, any number of times. Thus the definition allows not only all possible variant structures, but several nonsensical structures as well.

3.2 *Variation within dictionaries*

The generality problem is compounded by the many exceptions that exist in dictionary entries, even within a given dictionary. In particular, top-level constituents may appear at any level in the hierarchy, depending on the scope over which the information applies. For example, in the entry below, pronunciation, which is usually given once at the highest level and factored over the entire entry, is given lower in the hierarchy, at the homograph level:

In addition, there is a well-developed "override" system in dictionary entries; for example, it is very common to give exceptions for a specific sense when factored information does not apply:

- pronunciation appears at the sense level in sense 3 of the word *conjure* in the *CP* because it has a different pronunciation from the other senses in the entry:

conjure (ˈkʌndʒə) *vb* **1.** to practice conjuring. **2.** to summon (a spirit or demon) by magic. **3.** (kənˈdʒʊə) to appeal earnestly to... [CP]

- The entry *heave* in the *CED* shows that inflected forms may apply to individual senses:

heave (hi:v) *vb.* **heaves, heaving, heaved** *or (chiefly nautical)* **hove** ... **5.** *(past tense and past participle hove) Nautical.* **a.** to move or cause to move in a specified way ... **b.** (*intr.*) (of a vessel) to pitch or roll... [CED]

- The *PR* sometimes specifies different etymological information for particular senses:

NOUGAT [nuga] n.m. - 1750; *nogas* plur. 1595; provenç. *nougo* "noix", d'un lat. pop. *nuca*, class. *nux* "noix" **1.** Confiserie fabriquée avec des amandes (ou des noix, des noisettes) et du sucre caramélisé, du miel. ... **2.** (1928) FIG ET FAM *C'est du nougat !* c'est très facile. ... **3.** (1926; *jambes en nougat* "fatiguées, molles" 1917) POP *Les nougats* : les pieds. ... [PR]

Variations in structure are due not only to the complexity of the entry content, but may also result from changes in editorial policy; this is particularly true for large dictionaries such as the *OED* or the *TLF* which were assembled over decades by ever-changing teams of lexicographers.[12]

The variability in entry structure within dictionaries leads to the need for even more generality in the dictionary DTD, since in effect any of the hierarchical levels (entry, homograph, sense, subsense, etc.) can contain any of the top level constituents. In terms of the DTD definition for these elements, this means that tags marking levels in the hierarchy (**<entry>**, **<homograph>**, **<sense>**) would have (virtually) the same content.

The Dictionary Working Group recognized a parallel between dictionary divisions and nested document divisions (volume, chapter, section, sub-section, etc.), which are treated in the TEI by providing a generic **<div>** tag which nests recursively and takes a *type* attribute describing the division type, rather than providing specific "hard-coded" tags such as **<chapter>**, **<section>**, etc. (TEI P3, p. 219).[13] The Dictionary Working Group considered providing a similar tag, **<ediv>** (for "entry division"), that would mark the hierarchy of levels in an entry corresponding to entry, homograph, sense, sub-sense, etc. All levels would therefore be defined to have the same content, as follows:

```
<!-- (not TEI)                                              -->
<!ELEMENT ediv -- (ediv|form|
                   gramGrp|usg|def|etym|eg...)+              >
```

The **<div>** solution is adopted in the TEI because it is felt that there is a wide (and possibly open) range of means and nomenclatures for dividing a document (e.g., "part", "section", "book", "act", "scene", "canto", etc.). However, the Dictionary Working Group felt that for dictionaries, there is substantial agreement on the nomenclature for entry divisions and, therefore, hard-coded tags such as **<entry>**, **<hom>**, and **<sense>** could be defined. Therefore, the **<ediv>** solution was rejected in favor of the following:

```
<!-- Fragment of the TEI dictionary DTD                     -->
<!ELEMENT entry -- (hom|sense|
                    form|gramGrp|usg|def|etym|eg...)+        >
<!ELEMENT hom --   (sense|form|
                    gramGrp|usg|def|etym|eg...)+             >
<!ELEMENT sense -- (sense|form|
                    form|gramGrp|usg|def|etym|eg...)+        >
```

Note that **<sense>** is defined to nest recursively, to allow for sub-sense nesting to any degree. In this case, the generic solution (analogous to **<div>**) was adopted to avoid the proliferation of nested tags for **<subsense1>**, **<subsense2>**, **<subsense3>**, etc. Also, it was felt that the proliferation of unique names for subsense levels severely complicates queries to a database corresponding to the encoded dictionary. (See section 4 below for a discussion of the dictionary as a database, and Ide *et al.*, 1993, for a discussion of the query problem.)

3.3 *Exceptions*

Although the dictionary DTD fragment given in the previous section is very general and allows for a wide variety of entry structures, it still imposes some regularities which, in exceptional cases, may be violated. For example, in the following entry it is necessary to include a **<pron>** element within a **<def>**, which is not permitted by the DTD fragment given above:

demi•god /ˈdemɪgɒd/ *n* one who is partly divine and partly human; (in Gk myth, etc) the son of a god and a mortal woman, eg *Hercules* /ˈhɜ:kjʊli:z/. [OALD]

In large, complex dictionaries such as the *OED*, unusual exceptions of this kind are fairly common. As a result, it is probably impossible to define a fixed structure that would enable absolute fidelity to the original structure of every printed dictionary. For such cases the only solution is a completely "free" DTD, which says effectively that any of the constituents of a dictionary entry (e.g., orthographic form, pronunciation, part of speech, definition text, usage note) can go anywhere within a given entry. However, it was felt that the "structured" DTD fragment given in the previous section captures some important regularities of entry structure and would apply in the vast majority of cases. The final dictionary DTD therefore provides two distinct elements for dictionary entries:

- **<entry>**, which captures the regularities of most conventional dictionaries;
- **<entryFree>**, which uses the same basic components as **<entry>** but allows them to be combined in any order or organization.

Both are included in a single dictionary DTD (rather than providing two alternative DTDs) in order to enable encoding both regular and non-regular entry structures within the same dictionary. However, this solution is not completely satisfactory, since in many cases deviant entries are very nearly regular except, say, for the structure of one sub-sense or the unusual placement of a single piece of information (as in the example above). The current solution forces relaxing the structural constraints on the entire entry to accommodate such situations. Unfortunately, SGML does not provide a mechanism that cleanly handles local irregularities.

3.4 *Generality vs. descriptive power*

The discussion above makes clear the tension between the generality of a DTD describing dictionary entry structure and its descriptive power – i.e., its ability to describe precisely the structure of a given entry. At one extreme, we could have a very tight DTD for a given dictionary that describes its entry structure perfectly – but such a DTD would not be applicable to multiple dictionaries, or even to all entries in the same dictionary. At the other extreme, we have **<entryFree>**, which places no restrictions at all on entry structure – but which, as a result, causes problems for validation, retrieval, and complex typographical display of dictionary entries.

The Dictionary Working Group ultimately adopted a compromise solution in which the content of the **<entry>** element was defined to capture some relevant commonalties of entry structure, although it is vastly over-general with respect to any particular dictionary. As a result, it is likely that in practical applications, the TEI DTD will need to be customized and in many cases, restricted, to enable validation, retrieval, etc. We recognize that the proposed scheme is not adequate for many applications, but hope that it provides a framework for dictionary encoding based on an analysis of general structural principles, together with (at least) a set of fragments which users may reassemble to suit their own needs.

The tension between generality and descriptive power is pervasive across the TEI, which has sought to develop a scheme which is broadly applicable and at the same time provides a set of precise encoding conventions for specific text types. The solution adopted in different cases varies across the TEI, depending on text type and the priorities and interests of various working groups. The over-generality problem is inherent in SGML, and no complete solutions are apparent, although some work on extensions to SGML (e.g., object-oriented) take steps in this direction.

4. Handling Multiple Views

4.1 *Users and views*

The dictionary encoding format being developed within the TEI is intended for use primarily by the following general groups:

1. Publishers and lexicographers, who are developing databases of lexical information to enable the manipulation, presentation, and use of this information in various ways, and to provide the potential to produce different types of dictionaries (for example, a full version, a concise version, and a pocket version) from the same data. A common format for dictionary data would enable them to check coherency across related dictionaries and exchange lexical data among different dictionaries, potentially by automatic means.
2. Computational linguists, who use printed dictionaries as a rich source of ready-made linguistic data, from which computational lexicons for natural language processing systems can be constructed. In the past decade, computational linguists have commonly analyzed typesetter's tapes for printed dictionaries to identify and extract different fields of information. Their goal is typically to represent this data in a lexical database, which contains the same kinds of information found in printed dictionaries as well as additional linguistic information. A common encoding format would enable com-

putational linguists to exchange data, in particular translated typesetter's tapes, and to more easily merge information from different sources.

3. Philologists and print historians, who want to study and compare historical dictionaries. They are potentially interested in all aspects of physical layout of dictionaries, including page breaks, hyphenation, etc. However, philologists are at the same time interested in the content, and may in fact be interested in the relations between content and printed rendering. They need a common encoding format to enable data sharing among researchers and the use of common software to process dictionaries.
4. Dictionary users, who want to be able to retrieve lexical information as they would from a database, but want the results to appear as in a printed book. The advantage of a common format for dictionary users is the potential for common software for processing dictionaries distributed in electronic form.

As pointed out in the introduction, there are at least two different views of dictionaries:

1. The textual ("surface structure") view – the one-dimensional sequence of tokens which comprise the original text. Here, for example, the particular form in which the domain name is given in a particular dictionary (e.g., as *nautical, naut., Naut.*, etc.) would be preserved.[14]
2. The database ("deep structure") view – this view includes the information represented in a dictionary, without concern for its exact textual form. Thus the only information preserved concerning domain may be *nautical*, whatever the form in which it appears.

Different groups of users are interested in one or the other, or in some cases both, of these views when encoding a dictionary. Publishers typically begin with the database view and generate a textual view (i.e., information reflecting editorial choices for a particular dictionary, such as the use of the abbreviation *naut.* for *nautical*, etc. and some particular printed rendering). Ideally, this translation is automatic, and therefore publishers need to retain only the database view. In some cases, publishers attempt to develop databases from dictionaries which originally existed in printed form. This typically involves a process of "up-translation" which starts by translating typesetter's codes into increasingly more descriptive field identifiers.

Computational linguists and philologists often begin with the textual view and analyze it to obtain the database view. Computational linguists may ultimately be concerned with retaining only the database view, or they may wish to preserve the textual view as a reference text, since information can be lost or misinterpreted in the translation process. Philologists potentially want to see the two views simultaneously, since they may well be interested in questions which span both of them. For instance, they may want to determine all the (potentially inconsistent) variant forms in which the domain nautical is used in a given edition of a dictionary. Thus they need to access the database and the textual views simultaneously.

General users of dictionaries are typically interested primarily in retrieval of information from the dictionary. Thus although (at least at present) they deal with the textual object, their view of the data is primarily the database view. For example, consider the rendering of the following headword:

thyr(é)ostimuline [tiʀ(e)ostimylin] ... [DNT]

The user interested in retrieving this entry will search for *thyrostimuline* or its variant, *thyréostimuline* – but not *thyr(é)ostimuline*! The textual view is concerned with the printed rendering, while the database view sees the information conveyed, often cryptically as in this example, by the rendering.

4.2 *Encoding the textual view: Recoverability*

When a text is encoded from a printed or electronic source (typesetter's tapes, etc.) the ability to recover the source text from the encoded version – that is, to distinguish what was in the source from the markup and potential additional information – is often imperative. There are a number of different ways to define what is to be recovered from a source text, (e.g., a facsimile of a particular printed version of a text, layout, typography, etc.). However, for many purposes (comparison and validation between the source and the encoded text, operations such as word counts, search, concordance generation, linguistic analysis, etc.), it is sufficient to recover the sequence of characters constituting the text, independent of any typographic representation.

Recovery is an algorithmic process and should be kept as simple as possible, since complex algorithms are likely to introduce errors. Therefore, an encoding scheme should be designed around a set of principles intended make recovery possible with simple algorithms. Processes such as tag removal and simple mappings are more straightforward and less error prone than, say, algorithms which require rearranging the sequence of elements, or which are context-dependent. For example, a simple way to recover the original character sequence would be to employ the following principles:

1. None of the original sequence of characters (with the possible exception of rendition text) should be deleted or altered.
2. The original data should not be given in attributes, but should always appear as tag content.
3. Apart from the original data, no other data should appear as tag content.
4. The original order of the data should not be changed.

This is obviously a simplification for the sake of illustration, but it reflects a strategy which, although not explicitly stated as a principle, is followed more or less consistently in TEI P3. In order to provide a coherent and explicit set of recovery principles, various recovery algorithms and a set of related encoding principles need to be systematically worked out, taking into account such things as the role and nature of mappings (tags to typography, normalized characters, spellings, etc. with the original, etc.), the encoding of rendition characters and rendition text, definitions and separability of the source and annotation (such as linguistic annotation, notes, etc.), linkage of different views or versions of a text, etc. The development of a precise recovery strategy remains as a work item for the TEI.

Dictionaries present special concerns for recovery, since they include rendition characters (commas, parentheses, etc.) and rendition text (for example, conjunctions joining alternate headwords, etc.). Rendition characters and rendition text are retained in a "strict" textual view encoding. That is, removing the tags should exactly reproduce the original sequence of characters in the printed original. For example,

pinna (ˈpɪnə) *n., pl.* **-nae** (-ni:) *or* **-nas**... [CED]

would be encoded as[15]

```
<!-- strict textual view: all rendition text kept -->
<entry>
   <form>
      <orth>pinna</orth>
      <pron>("pIn@)</pron>
   </form>
   <gramGrp><pos>n.</pos>, </gramGrp>
   <form type=inflected>
      <num>pl.</num>
      <form>
         <orth>-nae</orth>
         <pron>(-ni:)</pron>
      </form>
      or
      <orth>-nas</orth>
   </form>
...
```

A more relaxed textual view encoding might conceal rendition text that is systematically recoverable (for example, parentheses which consistently appear around pronunciation in a given dictionary). In this case, removing the tags should exactly reproduce the original sequence of characters minus rendition text. Consistent rendition practices can be documented in the TEI header for the document containing the encoded dictionary, for example, by noting conventions such as those followed in the pinna entry above:

- parentheses around pronunciation
- comma before inflected forms
- or between inflected forms
- brackets around etymology
- period after part of speech and inflection information

Since the rendition elements described above are algorithmically recoverable, the entry can be encoded as follows:

```
<!-- textual view – rendition text implicit -->
<entry>
   <form>
      <orth>pinna</orth>
      <pron>"pIn@</pron>
   </form>
   <gram>
      <pos>n</pos>
   </gram>
   <form type=inflected>
      <num>pl</num>
      <form>
         <orth>-nae</orth>
         <pron>-ni:</pron>
      </form>
      <orth>-nas</orth>
   </form>
...
```

4.3 *Encoding the database view*

Encoding the database view may involve modifying the original data in various ways; for example:

- normalizing *nautical*, *naut.*, *Naut.*, etc., to *nautical*;
- expanding *delay*, *-ed*, *-ing* to *delay*, *delayed*, *delaying*;
- expanding *thyr(é)ostimuline* [*tiʀ(e)ostimylin*] to *thyrostimuline* [*tiʀostimylin*] and *thyréostimuline* [*tiʀeostimylin*];
- adding person, tense, number for each of *sings*, *singing*, *sang*, *sung*;
- reorganizing the order of elements in an entry to show their relationship, as in

clem (kl3m) or **clam** *vb.* **clems**, **clemming**, **clemmed** or **clams**, **clammimg**, **clammed** ... [CED]

where it would be necessary to group *clem* and *clam* with their respective inflected forms.
- splitting an entry into two separate entries, as in

celi•bacy /ˈselɪbəsɪ/ *n* [U] state of living unmarried, esp as a religious obligation. **celi•bate** /ˈselɪbət/ *n* [C] unmarried person (esp a priest who has taken a vow not to marry). [OALD]

This entry might be split into an entry for *celibacy* and a separate entry for *celibate*.

The *pinna* example above is encoded as follows in the database view:

```
<!--Database view:                     -->
<!--abbreviated forms expanded         -->
<!--forms grouped together             -->
<!--pos moved                          -->

<entry>
   <form>
      <orth>pinna</orth>
      <pron>"pIn@</pron>
      <form type=inflected>
         <num>pl</num>
         <form>
            <orth type=lat>pinnae</orth>
            <pron>'pIni:</pron>
         </form>
         <orth type=std>pinnas</orth>
      </form>
   </form>
   <gramGrp>
      <pos>n</pos>
   </gramGrp>
...
```

Note the differences between this encoding of the entry and the textual view encoding given in the previous section. In particular, the various forms of the headword are grouped together and the full inflected forms are provided. These modifications make the data conform more exactly to what might appear in a database template, where all forms would appear in a set of sub-fields for word forms, and variants would be represented in their full forms, etc. All of this simplifies database operations, for example, by simplifying the retrieval of all variant forms, of a given form, etc.

4.4 *Encoding both views*

Modifications such as those which are often required for the database view may make it impossible to recover the exact character sequence of the printed original, where one exists. However, it is often desirable to have access to both views of the data, thus demanding an encoding which retains both. Therefore, the Dictionary Working Group developed not only a means to encode each view, but also a mapping between them that preserves their relations.

TEI P3 provides a set of general methods to map between different encodings (see TEI P3, chapter 14, "Linking, Segmentation and Alignment," p. 393). Showing the correspondences between two views of a dictionary by aligning two different encodings (preferably in two different SGML documents) is in most cases the preferred solution. However, in some instances the database and textual views of a dictionary differ in only a few entries or parts of entries. Therefore, the Dictionary Working Group developed some additional mechanisms for simultaneously retaining two views of dictionary data in the same encoding. These consist of a set of attributes which are used to retain information which would otherwise be lost or unavailable in one or the other views of the data. The following is a set of general principles for the simultaneous encoding of both views.

Principle 1: If the order of the data is the same in both the textual and database views,
- chose one "dominant" view, the textual or database;
- encode the dominant view as tag content, and include the non-dominant-view in attributes on the appropriate tags. The governing principle is that if the tags are removed, the sequence of characters of the dominant view should be obtained.

For example, if the encoder wishes to expand *delay*, *-ed*, *-ing* to *delayed*, *delayed*, *delaying*, an encoding with the textual view dominant would be:

```
<form>
   <orth>delay</orth>
   <form type=inflected>
```

```
    <orth norm='delayed'>-ed</orth>
    <tns norm='pst,pstp'></tns>
</form>
<form type=inflected>
    <orth norm='delaying'>-ing</orth>
    <tns norm='prsp'></tns>
</form>
```

The expanded forms are provided in the norm attribute on the appropriate <**orth**> tags. Note the use of the <**tns**> tag with null content, to enable the representation of implicit information with no print realization.

An encoding of the same information with the database view dominant would be as follows:

```
<form>
    <orth>delay</orth>
    <form type=inflected>
        <orth orig='-ed'>delayed</orth>
        <tns orig=''>pst</tns></morph>
        <tns orig=''>pstp</tns></morph>
    </form>
    <form type=inflected>
        <orth orig='-ing'>delaying</orth>
        <tns orig=''>prsp</tns>
    </form>
</form>
```

Here, the attribute *orig* is used to provide the original printed form of the information that appears in expanded form as tag content. Here, the fact that tense information is not provided in the print version is indicated by the null value for the *orig* attribute on the <**tns**> tag.

Additional attributes (*split, mergedin, opt*) provide means to capture the discrepancies between the textual and database views. See TEI P3, p. 365, for more examples.

Principle 2: If the ordering of elements conflicts, use alignment mechanisms to show the correspondence between the two encodings if they are kept in the same document (see TEI P3, section 14.4).

For example, if the original is only slightly modified, the <**anchor**> tag and the location attribute (TEI P3, section 14.3) can be used to associate the original position with the moved element, as in this example:

```
<entry>
    <form>
        <orth>pinna</orth>
        <pron>'pIn@</pron>
        <anchor id=p1>
        <form type=inflected>
            <num>pl</num>
            <form>
                <orth type=lat>pinnae</orth>
                <pron>'pIni:</pron>
            </form>
            <orth type=std>pinnas</orth>
        </form>
    </form>
    <gramGrp>
        <!- moved ->
        <pos location=p1>n</pos>
    </gramGrp>
...
```

5. Conclusion

Initially, the task of developing encoding conventions for dictionaries seemed to be one of the easiest for the TEI, since the problem had been addressed for individual dictionaries in the past and tags for basic dictionary components existed. However, the task of developing a format that could accommodate the full range of dictionary structures proved to be far more challenging than expected. One clearly valuable result of the work of the Dictionary Working Group is the deep analysis of the structure of dictionary entries it undertook in order to attempt to find a general solution, which goes far beyond anything that had been done in the past. This analysis provides useful input for the development of future dictionaries, as does the analysis of the divergent views and uses of encoded dictionaries, which are likely to become more database-like as they are increasingly published in electronic form.

In the course of dealing with this very difficult text type, the Dictionary Working Group tackled a number of encoding problems which proved to be pervasive across text types, and as a result, some of the work of this group has informed global TEI recommendations. In particular, the Working Group addressed the difficult issues of recoverability, as well as the tension between general solutions which allow for great variety in structure vs. the need to provide tighter structural descriptions for given texts. This last problem is one which remains outstanding not only for the TEI, but for SGML use in general. Some of the sources of the problem lie in the design of SGML itself, and modifications or extensions to SGML may be required to solve them adequately.

Notes

[1] The members of the TEI Dictionary Working Group were Robert Amsler, Susan Armstrong-Warwick, Nicoletta Calzolari, Carol Van Ess-Dykema, John Fought, Nancy Ide, W. Frank Tompa, and Jean Véronis. The authors would like to acknowledge the contribution of discussions with other committee members to the ideas in this paper. We also refer the reader to several related papers: Amsler and Tompa (1988), Calzolari (1990), Fought (1990), Fought *et al.* (1993), Ide and Véronis (1992), Ide *et al.* (1992), Ide *et al.* (1993).

[2] It should be noted that although a database can be made from the information in any text (such as the historical texts described in Greenstein and Burnard, 1995), a dictionary is intended to be a database from the start.

[3] However, nothing prevents a less linear display, and in the future we can expect that electronic dictionaries will be far more "hypertextual" in nature, allowing users to navigate through and among entries, and linking entries to sound, image, examples from corpora, etc.

[4] In this paper we will use the following abbreviations for dictionary names:

CED	*Collins English Dictionary*
CP	*Collins Pocket Dictionary*
DNT	*Dictionnaire de Notre Temps (Hachette)*
LDOCE	*Longman Dictionary of Contemporary English*
OALD	*Oxford Advanced Learner's Dictionary*
OED	*Oxford English Dictionary*
PL	*Petit Larousse*
PR	*Petit Robert*
TLF	*Trésor de la Langue Française*

[5] For example, consider the following entries in the *CED*:

dead man's handle or pedal...
confidence man or trickster...

In the first case, the word following *or* replaces the last word in the preceding phrase; in the second case, the word following *or* is a replacement for the entire preceding phrase. No simple algorithm could make these distinctions, since complex semantic knowledge, difficult to provide for computers, is required.

[6] The term "print dictionaries" is in part a historical artifact, since in the course of devising the scheme it became apparent that although the most familar form in which dictionaries exist is a printed form, dictionaries increasingly exist in an electronic form that is independent of a particular printed form. The TEI dictionary encoding scheme must necessarily apply to both.

[7] See TEI P3, chapter on "Default Text Structure for TEI Documents".

[8] In TEI P3, paragraph content is defined with the standard content models *paraContent* and *specialPara*.

[9] Note that in this and many of the following examples, we do not encode the *or* nor the parentheses around the pronunciations because they are automatically retrievable/generatable – see the discussion on rendition text in section 4.2 below.

[10] The original **<gram>** tag, in which only explicitly named tags such as **<pos>**, **<cat>**, etc. could appear, was changed to **<gramGrp>** to avoid conflict with the scheme adopted for encoding terminology (see TEI P3, chapter 13, "Terminological Databases"). **<gram>** is now an atomic tag for any grammatical information, which may take a *type* attribute to define precisely the kind of information involved. This change has the disadvantage of providing two alternative means to do the same thing, thus violating a principle of orthogonal design which the dictionary group had hoped to follow. However, this solution provides a means to encode types of grammatical information which are unknown or were unforeseen without extension to the current DTD.

[11] In the definition of the **<entry>** tag given on p. 328 of TEI P3, the top level constituents are represented by a parameter entity, *m.dictionaryTopLevel*. We have listed the constituents explicitly here for clarity.

[12] For example, the *TLF* was originally conceived to consist of some 40 volumes, but this number was drastically reduced after the appearance of the first six volumes, leading to substantial modifications to the format and structure of subsequent entries. See Martin (1994).

[13] The TEI also provides numbered divisions (**<div1>**, **<div2>**, etc.), thus allowing different levels to have different content models. See TEI P3, p. 220.

[14] To be precise, the textual view can be sub-divided into

- the *typographic view*, which is concerned with the two-dimensional, printed page, including information about line and page breaks and other features of layout. This view is effectively the output of the typesetting process, and represents the exact form of a given printing. For example, a domain indication in a dictionary entry may be broken over a line and therefore hyphenated (e.g., "naut-" "ical"); the typographic view of the dictionary preserves this information.
- the *editorial view*, which can be seen as the input to the typesetting process. The wording and punctuation and the sequencing of items are included in this view, but not the specifics of the typographic realization (for example, that a certain word was broken across lines, that a page ended at a certain point, etc.).

[15] There are several ways to encode transcriptions of International Phonetic Alphabet (IPA) characters in SGML. The TEI defines a set of entities for IPA transcriptions (see TEI P3, p.693). For the sake of brevity, the content of all **<pron>** elements in our examples consists of an ASCII transcription of the IPA representation, taken from the transcription scheme used in the electronic edition of the *OALD (OALD3e)*. It is up to the dictionary encoder to decide between the use of entities or a transcription scheme such as the one utilized here; in the latter case, a Writing System Declaration (see TEI P3, chapter 25 "Writing System Declarations") should be provided with the DTD.

References

Amsler, R.A. and F.W. Tompa. "An SGML-Based Standard for English Monolingual Dictionaries". In *Information in Text: Fourth Annual Conference of the UW Center for the New Oxford English Dictionary*. Waterloo, Ontario: University of Waterloo Center for the New Oxford English Dictionary, 1988, pp. 61–79.

Calzolari, N., ed. "Computational Model of the Dictionary Entry: Preliminary Report". Esprit Basic Research Action no. 3030. Pisa, Italy: CNR, Acquilex, April 1990.

Fought, J. and C. Van Ess-Dykema. "Toward an SGML Document Type Definition for Bilingual Dictionaries". TEI Working Paper no. TEI AIW20. Chicago and Oxford: Text Encoding Initiative, 1990.

Fought, J., M. Welser, H. Davenport and C. Van Ess-Dykema. "Extending SGML Concurrent Structures: Toward Computer-Readable Meta-Dictionaries". *Literary and Linguistic Computing*, 8, 1 (1993), 33–38.

Greenstein, D. and L. Burnard. "Speaking with One Voice: Encoding Standards and the Prospects for an Integrated Approach to Computing in History". In this volume.

Ide, N. and J. Véronis. "Print Dictionaries". TEI Working Paper no. AI5 D17. Chicago and Oxford: Text Encoding Initiative, 1992.

Ide, N. and J. Véronis. S. Warwick-Armstrong, and N. Calzolari. "Principles for Encoding Machine-readable Dictionaries". In *EURALEX '92 Proceedings*. Ed. H. Tommola, K. Varantola, T. Salmi-Tolonen and Y. Schopp. Tampere, Finland, 1992, pp. 239–46.

Ide, N., J. Le Maître and J. Véronis. "Outline of a Model for Lexical Databases". *Information Processing and Management*, 29, 2 (1993), 159–86.

Martin, R. "Présentation". (Numéro Spécial: Autour du T.L.F.). *Le Français Moderne*, 62, 2 (1994), 129–34,

Sperberg-McQueen, C.M. and L. Burnard. *Guidelines for Electronic Text Encoding and Interchange*. Chicago and Oxford: Text Encoding Initiative, 1994.

The DANLEX Group. *Descriptive Tools for Electronic Processing of Dictionary Data*. Lexicographica, Series Maior. Tübingen: Niemeyer, 1987.

Computers and the Humanities **29:** 181–190, 1995.

The TEI Hypertext Guidelines

Steven J. DeRose *
Electronic Book Technologies, One Richmond Square, Providence, RI, USA
e-mail: sjd@ebt.com

and

David G. Durand **
Department of Computer Science, Boston University, Boston, MA 02215, USA
e-mail: dgd@cs.bu.edu

Key words: TEI, Hypertext, HyTime compatibility, markup

Abstract

This paper describes the TEI guidelines' approach to describing hypertext features, the rationale that went into the design of the tagset, and the range of features included in the guidelines. It also discusses the relation and integration of TEI markup and the HyTime standard (ISO 10744).

1. Hypertext

The essence of hypertext lies in referring or "pointing" to things. There ought to be no restrictions on the kinds of "things", but in order to point between them at least the nature of the pointers must be established. On this there were no standards at the time the TEI hypertext committee began its work, although prior to even the first hypertext conference, the authors had argued that SGML is an effective means for representing hypertext documents portably (see DeRose and Durand, 1987; Coombs, Renear, and DeRose 1987; cf. Feiner, 1988). Soon after, others were making the same argument and building systems (see Hughes, 1988; Sperberg-McQueen and Burnard, 1989; Killough, 1990; and Mylonas et al., 1991).

A recently passed ISO Standard also adopts this point of view. ISO 10744 "HyTime" prescribes ways to represent hypermedia information in SGML, whether or not the data referenced by the hypertext links are encoded with SGML. HyTime is a highly general mechanism that is not optimized for any particular application of SGML, such as the TEI (see DeRose and Durand, 1994, for a detailed discussion of HyTime). Despite substantial differences in goals, the TEI and ISO hypertext efforts have both found SGML an effective technology for representing hypertext. Both groups share a conviction that the standardization and interchangeability of SGML provide the best hope for a standard format for the interchange of hyper documents. Through extensive interaction the HyTime and TEI hypertext committees have produced mechanisms that are almost identical in concept and structure; there are differences in syntax which reflect differing priorities, user communities and tool sets. Both systems provide "escape hatches" that permit taking advantage of each other's strengths when needed.

---

* Steven J. DeRose (Ph.D. in Computational Linguistics, Brown University) is now Senior System Architect at Electronic Book Technologies, the leading developer of SGML-based software for online delivery of electronic books. He served as director of the FRESS hypertext system project at Brown University, 1979–1982, and as a technical writer and design consultant for the CDWord Biblical hypertext project. He has published papers on descriptive markup, hypertext, natural language processing, artificial intelligence, and other topics. With David Durand he co-authored *Making Hypermedia Work: A User's Guide to HyTime*.

** David Durand is a graduate of Brown University, and Ph.D. student in computer science at Boston University, working on collaborative editing of hypertexts. He was a member of the TEI committees on Syntax and Metalanguage and on Hypertext. With Steven DeRose, he is co-author of the recent book *Making Hypermedia Work: A Users's Guide to HyTime.*

Cross-references have existed for millennia; what is new in hypertext is that computers can augment the usefulness and reliability of pointers, by allowing fast painless follow-up of references as well as verification of reference destinations. The most familiar precursors to hypertext links are footnotes (especially referential ones), bibliographies, indexes, "see also" notes, apparatus critici, and library catalogs. All of these depend on having a way to refer or point to data of interest. They may use footnote numbers, author names and titles, subject terms, page or section numbers, reserved symbols, ISBN numbers or library call numbers.

A primary goal of the TEI guidelines for hypertext has been to support the representation of such well-understood hypertext-like features, as well as to allow for computer-aided augmentation of the familiar operations scholars have traditionally performed with the aid of such tools. Where the tools can open new possibilities by virtue of computerization, so much the better. The committee felt that the encodings used must require relatively little adjustment where there is already an established practice, so an emphasis on pre-existing formal or "canonical" reference schemes is evident in the guidelines. A second major emphasis is on reliability. The most reliable pointing mechanism in SGML is the intrinsic one, using IDs and IDREFs; therefore the guidelines strongly encourage its use. The problem of inventing many unique identifiers for element IDs can be alleviated by the use of systematic naming conventions based, where possible, on reference systems already in common use.

A number of popular hypertext systems use a data model deemed inadequate for all but a few scholarly reference needs: this is the card-based or "chunky" hypertext model, in which documents must be fragmented into data atoms of uniform size and minimal internal structure. Since few documents have historically been structured in this manner, the TEI hypertext guidelines use the more flexible text-based or "creamy" approach to hypertext (historically, this more advanced model was the earlier one in the hypertext community as a whole – see Engelbart, 1968; Prusky, 1978). SGML's support for hierarchies of containment provides a natural means for expressing links to document portions of all levels and sizes; so for pointing into SGML documents the primary need is for naming conventions that facilitate unambiguous reference to the data elements SGML already supports. Chunky systems are easily handled as a special case of the more general model: their uniform data units and restricted pointers can easily be represented by the more flexible mechanisms used in the TEI.

2. Uses of Links

The notion of a link is a generalization of a formal property of cross-reference which is part of many common textual features. The range of possible link semantics that have been used in hypertext systems is quite large, and generally each mechanism has been designed with a particular use in mind. Nevertheless, the relatively limited choice of mechanisms in each system has led to different basic mechanisms to solve what are essentially the same problems.

Hypertext system designers often need to choose for their authors a specific model that satisfies trade offs between flexibility and system performance; however, the TEI's aims reflect the need for accurate description of pre-existing information structures. This strongly implies that no particular pre-existing model of hypertext should be unduly privileged. On the other hand, it does not mean that the TEI model should simply include every feature ever used in a hypertext system; rather it attempts to abstract fundamental mechanisms that can represent the wide variety of link behaviors and uses.

For example, the *type* attribute is available to record the semantics of links, but no attempt has been made to fix a vocabulary for such semantics. Such a vocabulary would be both difficult to compile and useless in practice, since this area is a research issue and remains in flux. In selecting what to represent, the goals were that all commonly used hypertext features should have elegant, simple representations, and that those common features of printed texts involving cross-reference and "hypertext-like" features should also have simple and elegant representations, using the same basic mechanisms.

In the following sections we will discuss the kinds of hypertext constructs addressed by the TEI guidelines. A more complete formal taxonomy of link structures and functions which addresses semantic issues is presented in DeRose (1989).

3. Cross-References

The cross-reference is the simplest sort of hypertext link, and the one that has most shaped the development of hypertext systems. To a reader it is a directive, indicating other text within the same document that may be of interest. When realized on a computer, a cross-reference acquires power through the speed and ease with which it can be followed; the machine can look up the referent automatically for the reader. This is the only sort of reference for which SGML itself provides direct support: the ID and IDREF features of SGML allow the text encoder to create elements that refer to other elements, and SGML validation includes checking such references to ensure that the destinations exist. This feature of SGML will, however, only check references within a document, so that inter-document cross-references do not have such direct support from SGML. HyTime provides one set of methods for handling this problem.

4. Alignment and Correspondence

The phrase "alignment and correspondence" is used as a cover term for the wide variety of instances in which several streams of data have a regular pattern of relationship that needs to be described, and that associates constituents of each stream with those of the other streams. There are two rather different ways that this can be done.

In grammatical tagging for linguistic purposes, single words of the text, "tokens", are generally associated with a fixed vocabulary of "types" which label individual occurrences of particular features. Such constructs are described in TEI P3, chapter 15 (Sperberg-McQueen and Burnard, 1994).

Parallel texts involve a different sort of alignment. A single text is connected with its translation into another language, or a commentary on its content. Such associations are "token to token" linkages between two or more streams of related instances in the document being tagged. Such sets of correspondences are known as correspondence groups, and marked by a **<LinkGrp>** tag. Each **<LinkGrp>** contains a series of **<link>** tags, each specifying a particular alignment of elements. This form of alignment is discussed in TEI P3, sections 14.1.3, 14.4.

Alignment and correspondence are often used in linguistic tagging. A brief example of the use of the **<LinkGrp>** tag to indicate alignment is presented in Langendoen and Simons in this issue.

5. Virtual Object Creation

Virtual objects are a way to represent situations where a single piece of data can appear at several places simultaneously. They can be thought of as a declaration of identity between two separate objects, with only one copy being stored. It is used to avoid duplication of data, particularly data that are repeated many times. For instance, grammatical tagging typically contains many redundant descriptions of verb-forms, parts of speech and the like: these can be represented by a single "template occurrence" which is referenced from the multiple places that it occurs within the text.

Another use of virtual objects is in the representation of "transclusion" or "quotation" links – these are hypertext structures that represent the inclusion of data at a point by reference to some location where the data themselves appear. In addition to its obvious use in representing quotations, this can be used to record temporal variation in a text, by having successive versions transclude portions of previous versions that remain unchanged in the new version. Such structures have been proposed and described by Ted Nelson (1987).

This form of link is described in TEI P3, Chapter 15. A brief example of its use for linguistic annotation is presented by Langendoen and Simons in this volume.

6. Intensional and Structure-Based Links (Virtual Links)

Intensional links (also sometimes called virtual links) are links whose destination is specified by some means other than a direct reference. This can occur in cases where there is no accepted reference system for a work being referred to: the reference may then need to be given in the form of a route to the target or a condition that the endpoint must satisfy. For instance, an intensional link might refer to the third paragraph of the second section of a particular file, or to all lines spoken by a particular character in a play.

Virtual links also provide a way to refer to documents that cannot be edited to contain the link-endpoint tags required for direct reference and to refer to information by a pattern that it must satisfy. They can also be used as an interface to or point of contact with more traditional database systems, in which the only form of access is by query rather than direct reference.

7. Computed Links

The most complex form of intensional link is so different in its effect that it has a separate name and treatment. Some hypertext systems (Hypercard notable among them) treat links procedurally: a link is a program in a general programming language (rather than a restricted query language) that determines its endpoint. This notion of linking is not well represented within the TEI, because of certain inherent difficulties. The use of a general programming language means that in principle, it is only possible to determine the behavior of the link/program by executing it. Thus no declarative solution of the sort intended by the TEI's use of SGML is possible. Additionally, the close integration in such programming languages between the primitive operations offered and particular features of the systems in which they operate make a meaningful declarative solution unlikely. For such links TEI allows the recording of the program and a specification of the system on which it was intended to run, but does not attempt to otherwise analyze such links.

8. Types of Reference

There are only a few general means of reference, all of which appear in both the TEI guidelines and HyTime. The first is via a formal name, unique in a given context. The second is via one or more numbers which can be treated as coordinates; a formal procedure can then interpret the coordinates and yield the location. The third method is via an intensional specification: a set of criteria is given such that all and only data objects meeting the criteria are "found". This is the method employed by full-text retrieval and other querying tools.

Brief examples may serve to clarify each of these types of reference:

1) The element with ID "figure27"
   The document "Euthyphro"
   The Biblical verse "John 1:1"
2) Chapter 3
   Chapter 3, section 4, subsection 1
   The rectangle from (x = 2, y = 4) to (x = 4, y = 5)
   The fourth through seventh words
   The section containing some (known) element
3) The title containing "Introduction"
   The chapter whose title contains "Heracles"

HyTime has introduced useful terms for each of these three sorts of reference: name-space addressing, coordinate addressing, and querying (in fact, the ISO improved the querying mechanisms in HyTime in response to requests from the TEI to accommodate scholarly reference methods).

While a description such as "Milton's allusions to the Psalms" is a legitimate (and indeed interesting) reference, it cannot be automated. HyTime can encode such references (as "biblocs") but they are not expected to be machine-processable. In the TEI, like HyTime, this type of reference is described as a link. Unlike HyTime, however, the TEI's bibliographic and text-critical elements provide a way to describe such a destination.

9. Querying Versus Direct Linking

In order to be followed automatically, cross-references need several basic support features, which can be combined to handle more complex references. Uniform formal names for document locations must be available. Counting is also necessary; the guidelines provide for counting SGML elements, word tokens, and characters. (Note that characters and bytes are different types of object. A character may be represented by several bytes, depending on the language and character encoding). Finally, a general query mechanism is required, which can find portions of a document matching certain criteria (specifically, criteria other than those of formal name or ordinal position).

Querying and searching in hypertexts are complex and difficult issues. In fact, a few early hypertext developers considered it anathema, likening searches to "gotos" in programming. But this has never been the dominant position; indeed Halasz (1987) made searching the first of his "Seven Issues for the Next Generation of Hypertext Systems" and stated that "search and query needs to be elevated to a primary access mechanism on par with navigation". Brown (1987, 1992), a strong opponent of searching, has recently changed his position and (at least once in the interim) the system he originated was successfully interfaced to a searching tool and applied to texts of scholarly interest (DeRose, 1990a, 1990b).

Query languages for SGML are hotly debated at present, and only a few implementations exist. It is known that traditional database search methods such as SQL are inadequate for SGML, in part because they are at best awkward in dealing with hierarchies, and in part because their interfaces are optimized for use on relatively flat, unordered tabular structures such as personnel records, and pessimized for polymorphous, deeply hierarchical structures such as documents (see, for example, Burkowski, 1991). Because the mechanisms for querying SGML are not well understood, the TEI guidelines provide only specific query types that are known to be useful and tractable. Despite the lack of a formal analysis to support the TEI's choice of query primitives, it seems to be a powerful set capable of expressing most queries of which the present authors are aware.

Descriptions of the general mechanisms provided by the TEI hypertext encoding guidelines follow. Complex issues of formal syntax and meaning dominate the guidelines; nevertheless, we emphasize that the simplest pointers are always the best: SGML IDs, followed by established canonical reference schemes (such as exist for most Classical texts). These methods are tried-and-true, and SGML IDs are inherently supported and validated by SGML parsers; thus, we encourage encoders to use them wherever possible.

An ID or canonical reference has one great virtue over all other methods: it persists despite changes to the document. Changing an ID requires specific manual intervention by the encoder, and even then an ordinary SGML parser can test and guarantee uniqueness for IDs. Also, a well-chosen ID or canonical reference is usually directly meaningful to the encoder: "John.1:1" is far clearer than "element 948". This reduces the probability of user error.

Why not use IDs everywhere? This would in many ways be ideal, but may be impractical in the real world. Many encoders work with limited computer resources, and may be unable to devote the effort and memory space required. Also, a text may well exist on a read-only medium such as CD-ROM, where the recipient cannot add IDs. Even should each recipient be capable of changing the document to add IDs, as soon as two copies exist they will diverge. This leads to problems of data integrity such as conflicting IDs which users must resolve by hand.

Because of such cases, the TEI guidelines provide many ways of referring to data elements that lack formal names. These mechanisms are designed so that encoders can maximize pointer reliability across document edits; with careful encoding, pointers can even retain their meaning despite translation, addition of critical apparatus, and other major changes.

10. The Basic TEI Link-Origin Elements

Although a link may point to anything, the origins must be encoded somewhere in or on SGML elements in documents. The guidelines provide six elements for this purpose that are distinguished along two orthogonal axes.

The first axis is the nature of the origin: *Ptrs* are references to points in a document (in SGML terms, they are "EMPTY" elements), whereas *refs* have scope (content, in SGML terms) which might be, for instance, a caption that a system could treat as a user-activated link traversal button. For example:

```
<p>This contention is supported by <ref target=sec37>
   Smith 1992, p. 20.</ref> But it is still
   implausible.<ptr target=cf234></p>
```

The second axis concerns the nature of the destination, for which three cases are distinguished.

The simplest method of specifying a destination uses SGML's intrinsic ID mechanism. These specifications use an SGML IDREF attribute, and are preferred whenever practical. They consist simply of a single attribute, as in the use of the *target* attribute in the **<ref>** immediately above. The primary strength of this method is that an SGML parser can validate and resolve such references; the primary weaknesses are that IDREFs can point only to entire elements, require an ID on the destination, and cannot express inter-document references. Here are two examples of ID-based links:

```
<ptr target=a27>
<ref target=a27>as shown by Smith.</ref>
```

Another method is needed to specify a destination where an IDREF cannot be used. Such cases arise because a destination is in another document, or has no ID attribute. The TEI extended location specification exists to support such cases in a compact and perspicuous manner. Its syntax permits destinations to be specified by naming a document, and then describing a position within it, via a set of coordinates – a method essentially similar to HyTime "location ladders". The position is usually a single SGML element, or a sub-string of a single text chunk within one. If extended location specifications are used, the **<xref>** and **<xptr>** tags are used:

```
<xptr from="ID (a27) CHILD (1 SEC) (2 P)">
<xref from="ID (a27) CHILD (1 SEC) (2 P)">
   as shown by Smith.</xref>
```

Yet more information is required to specify a destination that not only lacks an ID, but is not an SGML element or a sub-string of an element. In such cases two extended location specifications are required: one to specify the start of the destination and one for the end of the destination. Such a mechanism is required to address data that cross element boundaries, or multiple elements whose scope has no immediate containing element. For example, a reference to the last paragraph of one chapter and the first paragraph of the following chapter must be represented in this way. Such referents are sometimes known as *spans* in the hypertext literature; however, be careful of confusion: the TEI <**span**> tag is used for a related but different purpose in recording annotations. Pointers to *spans* have the forms shown here:

<xptr from="ID (a27) CHILD (1 SEC) (2 P)" to
="ID (a28) CHILD (5 SEC) (3 P)">
<xref from="ID (a27) CHILD (1 SEC) (2 P)" to
="ID (a28) CHILD (5 SEC) (3 P)"> as shown by Smith.</xref>

The full details of the pointing mechanisms are defined in the guidelines. The references for the examples at the beginning of the section on types of reference would have these forms:

1) The element with ID "figure27"
<ptr target=figure27>
The document "Euthyphro"
<xptr doc="Euthyphro" target="ROOT">
The Biblical verse "John 1:1"
<xptr target="REF (John 1:1)"
2) Chapter 3
<xptr target="CHILD (1 Book) (3 Chapter)">
Chapter 3, section 4, subsection 1
<xptr target="CHILD (1 Book) (3 Chapter)
(4 section) (1 subsection)">
The rectangle from (x=2, y=4) to (x=4, y=5)
<xptr target="SPACE (2 4) (4 5)">
The fourth through seventh words
<xptr target="TOKEN (4 7)">
The section containing some (known) element
<xptr target="ID (figure27) ANC (1 section)">
3) The title containing "Introduction"
<xptr target="ROOT PATTERN (Introduction)">
The chapter whose title contains "Heracles"
<xptr target="ROOT PATTERN
(Heracles)ANC (1 chapter)">

The strings in the *target* attribute of these examples show the range of complexity and sophistication possible in references creates by applying sequences of "location terms". Some of the extended location references use structural descriptions of the referenced nodes. Extended addresses can refer to the children (sub-elements) of an element by numerical position, to elements of a given element type, to ancestors of an element (elements at any level that contain it), and so forth. A few of these techniques are outlined in the next section.

11. Summary of Extended Location Pointer Terms

Many kinds of extended location specifications are provided for use in the extended location pointer forms, but one is recommended over all others: specifying the nearest ID in the ancestry of the destination element, and then a CHILD path down the layers of hierarchy to the destination itself. This is the most likely form to survive later editing. Consider the following (incomplete) sample document:

```
<book><chp id=baz><ct>Introde</ct>
<sec>My Squelchy Life
<artist>Brian Eno</artist>
<p>This song ...
</p>
<p> ...
</p> ....
</sec> ....
```

In this document the recommended extended location specification for an intra-document reference to the second paragraph would be:

<xref x.target="ID (baz) TREE (1 SEC) (2 P)">

Using element types in TREE specifications is called *qualifying* the tree specification, and is very important. Unqualified tree addresses are hard for people to understand and can easily become inaccurate. For example, the <**sec**> element in this example is the first <**sec**> element within its' containing <**chp**>; this is intuitive. However, if element types are ignored, it is the second element. In addition, SGML's rules for treatment of spaces and line-ends are difficult to understand – so much so that not all parsers handle them consistently. Since these rules determine whether spaces and line ends are ignored or whether they are text strings that are part of the containing element, this can lead to the presence of unexpected sub-elements or content portions, making seemingly reasonable counts incorrect. For these reasons the TEI guidelines recommend avoiding unqualified tree specifications, especially to address portions of #PCDATA within elements.

The terms in a location specification are drawn from a small list; in every case, they consist of a formal name followed by zero or more parenthesized parameters. They provide the basic ways of navigating around hierarchical structures that contain text, such as SGML:

<xref> and **<xptr>** also permit a doc attribute that can be used to name any external entity. When used, this means that the locater is to be interpreted beginning at (the rest of) that entity.

HERE no parameters; refers to the location of the locater element itself.

ROOT no parameters; refers to the containing document element.

ID the parameter is an SGML IDREF, whose referent is the resulting location.

REF the parameter is a canonical reference (such are commonly established for ancient texts; the syntax must be defined in the document's TEI header).

CHILD the parameters are used to step down the document tree, selecting a child node at each step, based on the child's ordinal position, attributes, and/or tag name.

DESCENDANT the parameters are used to step down the document tree as with TREE, but can search not only through direct children, but all descendants (this could of course have serious performance implications if specialized software is not available).

ANCESTOR the parameters are used to step up through the elements containing the current element, using constraints like those for TREE.

PREVIOUS Counts preceding siblings from the current element.

NEXT Counts following siblings from the current element.

PRECEDING Counts preceding element open tags from the current location.

FOLLOWING Counts following element open tags from the current location.

PATTERN Locates a string based on a pattern. TEI patterns are based on Unix regular expressions.

TOKEN the parameter specifies a range of words to be picked out from among those in the character content.

STR the parameter specifies a range of characters (not bytes) to be picked out from among those in the (parsed) character content.

SPACE the parameters are vectors (or points) in a coordinate space of any dimension.

FOREIGN the parameters are in some special notation, presumably to be interpreted by a special application.

HYQ the parameter is a HyTime Query language expression, (which of course can only be interpreted by HyTime-capable programs).

DITTO This is valid only in the *to* attribute, and indicates that the value of the *from* attribute should be used.

12. Referring to Non-SGML Data

Although any user of the TEI Guidelines is presumably using SGML, it is commonly necessary for SGML documents to refer to data in other formats, and vice versa. The case of non-SGML references into SGML encoded documents cannot be addressed by the TEI, but in the former case, the link origin looks exactly like any other. Two extended location specification types are provided for non-SGML data: SPACE and FOREIGN. The reader should bear in mind that the SPACE type is also intended for use to describe time-varying information (such as multimedia structures); for representational purposes we consider time as merely another dimension (HyTime uses the same method). It would be unusual to use SPACE and FOREIGN in combination with other specification types, but their usage is otherwise precisely analogous to other types.

Many recent operating systems and application programs provide a way to assign formal and unique identifiers to their documents (or portions of them). These can be used directly via the FOREIGN specification, permitting seamless support for current and future representations so long as they support the basic concept of unique identifiers.

13. Links that Cannot Be Stored at One of Their Ends

There are many cases where a link cannot, or ought not to, be encoded at one of its endpoints, but must be separately encoded from either or both of the points it connects. The most obvious example is a link that predicates an allusion between two published literary works. The works may be stored in a medium the annotator cannot modify; this is sufficient cause to provide for "out of line" links. But even when the annotator has a private and changeable copy of all involved documents it may be unwise to place the link directly inside either work: modifying a work opens the possibility of corrupting it. Permitting intentional changes also makes it difficult to detect unintentional changes, because straightforward (mechanical) comparison with a trusted original is no longer possible. Technical problems such as conflicts between the SGML IDs assigned to various annotators' links can also arise.

Fortunately it is not difficult to maintain links independently of the document to which they attach. For this purpose the Guidelines provide the <**link**> element; this is a grouping mechanism to connect a set of endpoints. A link predicates a relation between several destinations. A link specifies its endpoints with a list of IDs of elements representing the endpoints. If extended locations are needed to address the link ends, an attribute can be set to cause the endpoints to be evaluated. The elements designated as endpoints for an evaluated link must be pointers which indicate the endpoints. Following is a simple example of a <**link**>:

```
<link targets="line1 line2">
<l id=line1>Oh Rose, thou art sick</l>
<l id=line2>The invisible worm, </l>
```

Here is more complex example using evaluation:

```
<link targets="from1 to1" evaluate=one>
<xref id=from1 book=New.testament tgt="REF
   ('Matt 3:1')">
<xptr id=to1 book=Milton xid=ch.4>
```

This link could be used to assert a claim about a relationship between the two document locations it mentions. The actual assertion must be marked in another way, perhaps by encoding a *type* attribute on the link, or by placing the link in a context that makes its intention clear.

Because the guidelines place no limit on the number of endpoints that can be part of a single link, the same mechanism is used to predicate n-ary relationships. A targ order attribute on the <**link**> can be used to indicate whether the endpoints' order is meaningful – as in this example it certainly is.

It is frequently convenient to collect a large set of links in a single place (sometimes as a separate document and sometimes as a special section of a document). Such a group of links is often called a "web"; the Guidelines provide a <**linkGroup**> element that contains any number of <**links**>, generally related by common function. As with links, the meaning of the grouping must be extrinsically expressed, e.g. through a *type* attribute on the <**linkGroup**>. <**linkGroup**> elements are also one method used to mark the alignment of parallel texts.

14. Summary

TEI P3's support for hypermedia, for alignment and correspondence, and in general for managing the interconnection of data, all come down to the basic notion of reference, whether by name or by descriptor. A variety of mechanisms appropriate to hierarchical structures such as SGML and to other structures such as images and spatio-temporal objects, is provided in a simple syntax that allows creating compact, perspicuous, and robust links. The guidelines define the syntax and semantics of these extended location pointers; here we have described the rationale and recommended usage. While application programs that support these information structures will come and go with every passing year, the information structures themselves will remain, and remain useful. This is the major reason to choose abstract, generic descriptions such as SGML over concrete, specific ones such as a typesetting language. The same fundamental principles can now be applied to links, which are often as much a part of a document's meaning as the text itself.

References

Brown, P. J. "Turning Ideas into Products: The Guide System". In *Proceedings of Hypertext '87, Chapel Hill, NC, November 13–15, 1987*. Baltimore, MD: Association for Computing Machinery Press, 1987, pp. 33–40.

Brown, P. J. "UNIX GUIDE: Lessons from Ten Years' Development". In *Proceedings of the ACM Conference on Hypertext, Milano, Italy, November 30–December 4, 1992*. Baltimore, MD: Association for Computing Machinery Press, 1992, pp. 63–70.

Burkowski, Forbes J. "An Algebra for Hierarchically Organized Text-Dominated Databases". Manuscript. Waterloo, Ontario, Canada: University of Waterloo, Department of Computer Science, 1991. (Portions appeared as part of a paper presented at RIAO '91: Intelligent Text and Image Handling, Barcelona, Spain, April 1991.)

Coombs, James H., Allen H. Renear and Steven J. DeRose. "Markup Systems and the Future of Scholarly Text Processing". *Communications of the Association for Computing Machinery*, 30, 11 (1987), 933–47.

DeRose, Steven J. "Expanding the Notion of Links". In *Proceedings of Hypertext '89, Pittsburgh, PA*. Baltimore, MD: Association for Computing Machinery Press, 1989, pp. 249–57.

DeRose, Steven J. "Biblical Studies and Hypertext". In *Hypermedia and Literary Studies*. Ed. George Landow and Paul Delany. Cambridge: MIT Press, 1990a, pp. 185–204.

DeRose, Steven J. *CDWord Tutorial: Learning CD Word for Bible Study*. Dallas, TX: Dallas Theological Seminary, 1990b.

DeRose, Steven J. and David G. Durand. "Applications of Hypertext to Humanistic Analysis". Manuscript. July 22, 1987.

DeRose, Steven J., David G. Durand, Elli Mylonas and Allen H. Renear. "What is Text, Really?" *Journal of Computing in Higher Education*, 1, 2 (1990), 3–26.

DeRose, Steven J. and David G. Durand. *Making Hypermedia Work: A User's Guide to HyTime*. Dordrecht: Kluwer Academic Publishers, 1994.

Engelbart, Douglas C. and William K. English. "A Research Center for Augmenting Human intellect". In *Proceedings of the Fall Joint Computer Conference, 1968*. (Reprinted in *Computer-Supported Cooperative Work*, ed. I. Grief.)

Feiner, Steven. "Seeing the Forest for the Trees: Hierarchical Display of Hypertext Structure". In *Conference on Office Information Systems. March 23–25, 1988, Palo Alto, CA*. New York: ACM Press, 1988, pp. 205–12.

Halasz, Frank. "Reflections on NoteCards: Seven Issues for the Next Generation of Hypermedia Systems". Paper presented at Hypertext '87, November 13–15, 1987. (Reprinted in *Communications of the Association for Computing Machinery*, 31, 7 [1988], 836–55.)

Hughes, John. "Studying Ancient Greek Civilization Interactively–The Perseus Project". *Bits and Bytes Review*, 2, 1 (1988), 1–12.

International Organisation for Standardisation. *ISO/IEC IS 10744: Hypermedia/Time-based Structuring Language: HyTime*. 1992.

International Organization for Standardization. *ISO8879: 1986(E). Information Processing – Text and Office Information Systems – Standard Generalized Markup Language*. 1986.

Killough, Ronnie Lynn. "Hypertext Interchange with the Dexter Model: Intermedia to KMS". Master's Project. Department of Computer Science, Texas A&M University, 1990.

Langendoen, D. Terence and Gary F. Simons. 1994. "A Rationale for the TEI Recommendations for Feature Structure Markup". In this issue.

Mylonas, Elli, Gregory Crane, Kenneth Morrell and D. Neel Smith. "The Perseus Project: Data in the Electronic Age". In *Computing and the Classics*. Ed. J. Solomon and T. Worthen. University of Arizona Press, 1991 (forthcoming).

Nelson, Theodor H. *Literary Machines*. Edition 87.1. South Bend, IN: The Distributors, 1987.

Prusky, John. *FRESS Resource Manual*. Providence: Brown University, Department of Computer Science, 1978.

Sperberg-McQueen, C. M. and L. Burnard. *Guidelines for Electronic Text Encoding and Interchange (TEI P3)*. Chicago and Oxford: Text Encoding Initiative, 1994.

Appendix

TEI	HyTime
ptr link	clink ilink

linkGrp	a collection of ilinks. Not supported by a build-in HyTime construct.
location pointer specification	location ladder
ptr with doc and no location terms	nameloc of type "entity"

Chart 1. TEI-HyTime tag/form equivalents.

TEI	HyTime
tree, ancestor, descendent, previous, and next	treeloc, relloc (type and/or attribute filtering also require use of HyQ)
here	location source same as the id of the link
root	treeloc is among several ways of specifying this
canonical reference	Can be built with HyQ
token	dataloc with quantum=word
char	dataloc with quantum=str
pattern	HyQ, in conjunction with HyLex
preceding, following	not directly supported. Could be added with notloc.
ditto	ilink with two identical anchor elements
space	fcsloc
foreign	notloc

Chart 2. TEI-HyTime location equivalents.

The examples below illustrate various syntactic representations for a single, fairly simple kind of link. The destination is specified in steps, finding, in this order:

a) the element with ID attribute “a 25”,
b) within that element, the second child of type “CHAP” (assumed to be the third child overall, due to a title element),
c) within that element, the fourth child of type “SEC” (assumed to be the fifth child overall, due to a title element),
d) within that element, the fourth child of type “P” (assumed to also be the fourth child regardless of type),
e) within that element, the 5th word-token.

TEI P1 form

```
<xref target=“ID a25 TPATH CHAP=2/SEC=4/P=4 TOKEN 5”>
```

TEI P3form

```
<xptr target=“ID(a25) CHILD(2CHAP) (4SEC) (4 P) TOKEN(5)”>
```

Canonical HyTime form

```
<xref HyTime=clink linkend=step3>
<nameloc id=step1 HyTime=nameloc>
<nmlist nametype=element>a25</nmlist>
</nameloc>
<treeloc id=step2 locsrc=step1 HyTime=treeloc>
    <marklist HyTime=marklist>3 5 4</marklist>
</treeloc>
<dataloc id=step3 locsrc=step2 HyTime=dataloc
    quantum=word catsrc=nocatsrc catres=nocatres>
    <dimlist HyTime=dimlist>5</dimlist>
</dataloc>
```

Minimized HyTime form

```
<xref linkend=step3>
<nameloc id=step1 nametype=element namesrc=a25>
<treeloc id=step2 locsrc=step1><marklist>3 5 4
<dataloc id=step3 locsrc=step2 quantum=word>
    <dimlist>5
```

Chart 3. Syntax examples.

Computers and the Humanities **29:** 191–209, 1995.

A Rationale for the TEI Recommendations for Feature-Structure Markup[1]

D. Terence Langendoen *
Department of Linguistics, University of Arizona, Tucson, AZ 85721, USA
e-mail: langendoen@linguistics.arizona.edu

and

Gary F. Simons **
Summer Institute of Linguistics, 7500 West Camp Wisdom Road, Dallas 75236, TX, USA
e-mail: gary@sil.org

Key words: TEI, SGML, linguistic tagging, feature structure, features, lexical tagging, interlinear text analysis

Abstract

In this paper, we concentrate on justifying the decisions we made in developing the TEI recommendations for feature structure markup. The first four sections of this paper present the justification for the recommended treatment of feature structures, of features and their values, and of combinations of features or values and of alternations and negations of features and their values. Section 5 departs briefly from the linguistic focus to argue that the markup scheme developed for feature structures is in fact a general-purpose mechanism that can be used for a wide range of applications. Section 6 describes an auxiliary document called a "feature system declaration" that is used to document and validate a system of feature-structure markup. The seventh and final section illustrates the use of the recommended markup scheme with two examples, lexical tagging and interlinear text analysis.

One of the goals of the Text Encoding Initiative is to provide a markup scheme that will permit scholars to encode linguistic analyses of any text in any language to any desired degree of detail. We envision all sorts of ways of using the TEI recommendations for linguistic markup, ranging from making occasional notations about the grammatical analysis of selected words in a document to preparing a full-blown phonological, morphological, syntactic, and semantic analysis of an entire document. The mechanisms that we provide are designed to express the content of commonly used representations of linguistic analysis, including tree diagrams, feature-structure diagrams, and interlinear glossing. Thus the markup scheme can be used to represent explicitly the implicit linguistic structure of a text (with respect to a particular analysis). The result is a machine-readable and machine-interpretable version of an explicit analysis presented according to familiar human-readable and human-interpretable graphical and typographical conventions.

---

* Terry Langendoen is Professor and Head of the Department of Linguistics at The University of Arizona. He was Chair of the TEI Committee on Analysis and Interpretation. He received his PhD in Linguistics from the Massachusetts Institute of Technology in 1964, and held teaching positions at The Ohio State University and the City University of New York (Brooklyn College and the Graduate Center) before moving to Arizona in 1988. He is author, co-author, or co-editor of six books in linguistics, and of numerous articles.

** Gary Simons is Director of the Academic Computing Department of the Summer Institute of Linguistics, Dallas, TX. He served on the TEI Committee on Analysis and Interpretation. He received his PhD in Linguistics (with minor emphasis in Computer Science) from Cornell University in 1979. Before taking up his current position in 1984, he spent five years in the Solomon Islands doing field work with SIL. He is author, co-author, or co-editor of eight books in the fields of linguistics and linguistic computing.

In developing the recommendations for the markup of linguistic analysis and interpretation within the Text Encoding Initiative, we have chosen to concentrate on providing markup for the data structures that linguists typically use to represent the results of their analysis and interpretation, rather than providing markup for particular analyses and interpretations. In this way, we enable encoders to represent any analysis they wish, and do not force them to use the constructs of predefined analyses which may not be suitable for the material being encoded and which may not be easy to alter or extend. Markup is provided for two data structures in particular: feature structures and tree structures. In fact, the two data structures can be combined; any node in a tree can itself be a feature structure.

In this paper, we concentrate on justifying the decisions we made in developing the TEI recommendations for feature structure markup. It is not within the scope of this paper to give a formal definition of the markup scheme. (For that and for other details concerning feature-structure, tree, and other markup being recommended for linguistic analysis and interpretation, see TEI P3. [Sperberg-McQueen and Burnard, 1994]) The first four sections of this paper present the justification for the recommended treatment of feature structures, of features and their values, and of combinations of features or values and of alternations and negations of features and their values. Section 5 departs briefly from the linguistic focus to argue that the markup scheme developed for feature structures is in fact a general-purpose mechanism that can be used for a wide range of applications. Section 6 describes an auxiliary document called a "feature system declaration" that is used to document and validate a system of feature-structure markup. The seventh and final section illustrates the use of the recommended markup scheme with two examples, lexical tagging and interlinear text analysis.

1. Justification for Treatment of Feature Structures

Within linguistics, feature structures were first used by Roman Jakobson (1949) for the representation of phonemes (the distinctive or contrastive sounds in a natural language) as bundles of what he called distinctive features. Each feature represented an essential articulatory and acoustic property of a phoneme. So, for example, Jakobson considered the phoneme s/in English to be a bundle of distinctive features, such as [-grave], [+anterior], [voice], [+strident], etc. (In Jakobson's theory, the values are restricted to the binary values "+" and "−"; see section 2 for a discussion of the markup of these and other possible feature values.)

The use of feature structures quickly spread to other domains within linguistics. Chomsky (1965) extended Jakobson's distinctive feature theory to morphology and syntax, and developed the idea that a feature value within a particular feature structure could make reference to another feature structure. Subsequent developments in the theory of feature structures (within both linguistics and computer science) have led to the current situation in which feature structures, either by themselves or together with directed graphs (such as phrase-structure trees) in which feature structures are associated with the nodes in the graphs, can be used to express any linguistic analysis whatever. The ability of feature structures to serve as a general purpose linguistic metalanguage is what led us to use them as the basis of linguistic encoding.

To represent the structure that groups together a bundle of features and their values, we need a markup element that groups together (or, in SGML parlance, whose content model is a group of) features. We call that element **<fs>** (for "feature structure"), and the element that it groups together **<f>** (for "feature"). Leaving aside details that need not concern us here, the content of an **<fs>** is zero or more **<f>**s.

A linguistic analysis may consist of many different types of **<fs>** elements, each of which may group together different types of **<f>** elements. To distinguish among the different types of **<fs>** elements, we provide a *type* attribute, whose value is a string (such as "phonological structure" or "phrase structure") that specifies the feature-structure type. So, for instance, the markup of the distinctive feature analysis of a phoneme might look as follows:

```
<fs type="phonological structure">
   <f ... > ... </f>
      <!- -Representation for one distinctive feature- ->
   ...
   <f ... > ... </f>
```

```
    <!- -Representations for other distinctive features- ->
</fs>
```

One important reason to distinguish among feature structure types is that different types of feature structures will contain different types of features. However, given that we are proposing to use SGML attributes to distinguish among feature-structure types (and also to a considerable extent among feature types), it will not be possible to use an SGML validator to determine whether the appropriate types of features are being used as the content of a feature structure of a particular type. To enable an encoder to specify explicitly what feature types go with what feature-structure type, we provide recommendations for the creation of a special file called a Feature System Declaration, that specifies, among other things, the correlations between feature-structure and feature types (see section 6).

2. Justification for Treatment of Features

In this section we justify the approach taken to marking up features, that is, we explain why the **<f>** tag is defined as it is. The two main issue here are the treatment of feature names and the treatment of feature values. These two topics are covered in the following two subsections. Throughout the discussion we build on a single example, namely, an analysis of the word *Kind* 'child', occurring in the sentence *Das Kind war einsam*, 'The child was lonely', appearing in a modern German text. The feature-structure analysis that we want to represent may be diagrammed as follows:[2]

```
+---                                            --+
| category  = noun                                |
|                                                 |
| wordForm  = Kind                                |
|                                                 |
| proper    = -                                   |
|             +--                         --+     |
| agreement = | gender = neuter             |     |
|             | number = singular           |     |
|             | case   = nominative         |     |
+--           +--                         --+  --+
```

That is, the category feature has the value "noun", the wordForm feature has the value "Kind", the proper feature (for, "Is it a proper noun?") has the value "–" (or minus), and the agreement feature holds an embedded feature structure which groups the gender, number, and case features. The values for these represent neuter, singular, and nominative, respectively.

2.1 *Treatment of feature names*

SGML syntax suggests four alternatives for how the name of a feature might be marked up. The feature name could be: the name of an attribute of **<fs>**, the name of a tag embedded within **<fs>**, the content of a tag for feature name embedded in a general element for feature, or the value of an attribute of a general tag for feature. The following paragraphs consider the alternatives in turn and explain our reasons for rejecting the first three and favoring the last.

The attributes of an SGML element tag are very much like features. Could we use them to represent the features of a feature structure? For instance,

```
<fs   category=noun  wordForm=Kind
      proper=minus   agreement=???>
```

We immediately run into an insurmountable problem. Features must be able to embed feature structures as their values, but attributes do not allow tags to be embedded within them.

We could solve this problem by turning the attributes into tags. Thus each feature name would become a unique tag, as in:

```
<fs>
   <category>noun</category>
   <wordForm>Kind</wordForm>
   <proper>minus</proper>
   <agreement>
      <fs><gender>neut</gender>
         <number>sg</number>
         <case>nom</case>
      </fs>
   </agreement>
</fs>
```

The chief disadvantage of this solution is that it leads to an unbounded proliferation of tags. Every user of TEI markup would be required to modify the DTDs to add a new **<!ELEMENT ...>** definition for each needed feature. Note, too, that although embedding of feature structures within features becomes possible, it would only be allowed when the content model for a particular feature's **<!ELEMENT ...>** definition were written in such a way as to permit it.

To prevent the proliferation of tags, we need a single, general-purpose element to represent any feature. Its content model says once and for all that feature structures can be embedded within features. For this we have defined the <**f**> tag. Within the <**f**> tag, the name of the feature could be represented as the content of a tag for the feature name. For instance,

```
<fs>
   <f><fName>category</fName> ... </f>
   <f><fName>wordForm</fName> ... </f>
   <f><fName>proper</fName> ... </f>
   <f><fName>agreement</fName> ... </f>
</fs>
```

This was essentially the proposal in TEI P1. However, it turns out to be needlessly verbose. It also provides more power than we need, in that it suggests the possibility of embedded structure within the <**fName**> tag. In actual fact, no embedding is possible.

This leads to our final solution, namely, that a feature's name is the value of an attribute (called *name*) of the <**f**> tag. That is,

```
<fs>
   <f name=category> ... </f>
   <f name=wordForm> ... </f>
   <f name=proper> ... </f>
   <f name=agreement> ... </f>
</fs>
```

2.2 *Treatment of feature values*

Similarly, SGML syntax suggests three ways to markup the value of a feature. The feature value could be: the value of an attribute of the <**f**> tag, textual content of the <**f**> tag, or embedded tags in the <**f**> tag. The following paragraphs consider the alternatives in turn and explain our reasons for rejecting the first two and favoring the last.

The first possibility might be to treat *value* as an attribute of <**f**> analogous to the *name* attribute, as in:

```
<fs>
   <f name=category value=noun>
   <f name=wordForm value=Kind>
   <f name=proper value=minus>
   <f name=agreement value=???>
</fs>
```

This leads to the same dead-end as treating the feature name as an attribute name. The feature value must be able to embed a feature structure and this is impossible in the value of an attribute.

In order to allow feature structures to be the values of features, we must include the value of the feature as the content of the <**f**> tag. The simplest approach would be to treat values that were not feature structures as textual content of the <**f**> tag (that is, allow PCDATA or <**fs**> in the content model of <**f**>). For instance,

```
<fs>
   <f name=category>noun</f>
   <f name=wordForm>Kind</f>
   <f name=proper>minus</f>
   <f name=agreement>
      <fs><f name=gender>neut</f>
         <f name=number>sg</f>
         <f name=case>nom</f>
      </fs>
   </f>
</fs>
```

This solution falls short of being ideal in three respects. First, the content model for <**f**> exhibits the so-called "mixed content" problem. Although the SGML standard does not prohibit mixing PCDATA and tagged elements in the same content model, mixed content is known to pose problems for some processors and thus many practitioners advise against using mixed content models. Second, when the content model contains PCDATA, every space and line break within the contents of the tag is interpreted as part of the data; this makes it impossible to encode feature structures in "pretty-printed" indented formats that transparently reflect the structure of the embedded feature structures. Third, the markup treats all the textual content as the same kind of information, failing to distinguish symbols in closed sets (like noun) from arbitrary strings (like Kind) from universally defined concepts (like minus).

These problems are solved by requiring that all feature values be contained in tags. Therefore, the recommended markup for our example (following TEI P3) is as follows:

```
<fs>
   <f name=category><sym value=noun></f>
   <f name=wordForm><str>Kind</str></f>
   <f name=proper><minus></f>
   <f name=agreement>
      <fs><f name=gender><sym value=neut></f>
         <f name=number><sym value=sg></f>
         <f name=case><sym value=nom></f>
      </fs>
   </f>
</fs>
```

The content model for the definition of <f> in TEI P3 allows for the value of a feature to be any of the following:

(1) One of the universally defined feature values <**plus**> or <**minus**>. These are defined as empty tags (that is, they have no content or end tag).
(2) One of the (empty) tags for underspecified or uncertain values; <**any**> indicates that the value may be any valid value for the feature, <**default**> indicates that the value is the default value for the feature, and <**unknown**> indicates that the analyst does not know what the value is.
(3) A "typed" atomic value; namely, <**sym**> for a symbol drawn from a closed list, <**str**> for an arbitrary string, or <**nbr**> for a number.
(4) An embedded feature structure, that is, <**fs**>.
(5) Other kinds of structured values such as a list of values, or an alternation (disjunction) of values, or the negation of a value. The justification for our representation of such values is provided in the next section.

3. Justification for Treatment of Combinations of Features and Their Values

In this section, we justify the way in which we express the possibility that a feature may have more than a single value, or may have one of several alternative values. We also justify our method of indicating that a feature structure may have any of several different combinations of features. Finally, we justify our method of specifying that the value of a particular feature is other than some specified value.

Certain features that are used for linguistic analysis are understood to have more than one simple value. For example, a coordinate compound phrase such as *Bob and Carol* may be analyzed as having a members feature, whose value is a list of the phrases that are coordinated. Similarly, for a plural-referring expression, one may wish to provide an index feature, whose value is a set of numerical indices which abstractly indicate what things the expression refers to. One way of encoding such values would be to provide explicit tags such as <**list**> and <**set**> for enclosing their multiple values. For instance,

```
<f name=members>
   <list>
      <fs type=phrase>
         <f name=category><sym value=noun></f>
         <f name=barLevel><nbr value=2></f>
         <<f name=form><str>Bob</str></f>
      </fs>
      <fs type=phrase>
         <f name=category><sym value=noun></f>
         <f name=barLevel><nbr value=2></f>
         <f name=form><str>Carol</str></f>
      </fs>
   </list>
</f>
<f name=index>
   <set><nbr value=37><nbr value=128><nbr value=354></set>
</f>
```

However, such use of <**list**> and <**set**> tags, especially if <**list**> and <**set**> are permitted to nest within each other, provides for more descriptive power than is needed for linguistic representations. This is because whenever a list is contained as a value within another list of values, it does not do so directly but indirectly as the value of a feature within a feature structure in the original list. For instance, consider the coordinate compound phrase *Bob and Carol and Ted and Alice*, in which the members are the two compound subphrases *Bob and Carol* and *Ted and Alice* (one of eleven possible syntactic analyses of the whole phrase). The encoding of this would embed two <**list**>s (for the subphrases) within a <**list**> (for the whole phrase). However, the embedding is not direct; the members feature of the whole phrase would contain a list of two feature structures that would in turn have a members feature containing a list.

We conclude, therefore, that it is not necessary to provide a method of allowing a set or list to occur directly as an element of another set or list. We can then simplify the encoding of set and list values by providing the <**f**> tag with an attribute called *org* (for "organization"). Its possible values are drawn from "unit", "list", "set", and "bag", where a bag is defined as a collection of values that may contain repetitions but in which the order of the values is not significant. Thus, we encode the list and set values in our original examples as follows:

```
<f name=members org=list>
   <fs type=phrase>
      <f name=category><sym value=noun></f>
      <f name=barLevel><nbr value=2></f>
      <f name=form><str>Bob</str></f>
   </fs>
   <fs type=phrase>
      <f name=category><sym value=noun></f>
      <f name=barLevel><nbr value=2></f>
      <f name=form><str>Carol</str></f>
   </fs>
</f>

<f name=index org=set>
   <nbr value=37><nbr value=128><nbr value=354>
</f>
```

4. Alternation and Negation of Features and Values

In this section we justify our method of indicating that a feature structure may have any of several different combinations of features and that a feature may have any of several different combinations of values. We also justify our method of specifying that the value of a particular feature is other than some specified value.

4.1 *Alternation*

First, consider the problem of representing alternative values for a given feature, where we either do not know which value the feature has, or we wish to indicate explicitly that the structure containing that feature is ambiguous. For example, suppose that we wish to encode the fact that the case feature of the German noun *Kind* may have either the value "nom" or the value "acc" (where these values do not exhaust all the possible values for the case feature, so that the <**any**> tag cannot be used). One way that one might try to do this is simply to list both values, as in:

```
<f name=case><sym value=nominative><sym value=accusative></f>
```

However, this method of encoding multiple feature values has been reserved for the situation in which the feature is defined as taking a list or set of values, and we assume that "case" is not such a feature. Rather, we assume that "case" is defined as taking only a single value.

Thus it seems reasonable to define a tag which encloses the alternative values that a particular instance of a feature may have. The tag we have defined for this purpose is <**vAlt**> (for "value alternation"). Then the encoding of the case feature becomes:

```
<f name=case>
   <vAlt>
```

```
        <sym value=nominative>
        <sym value=accusative>
    </vAlt>
</f>
```

In addition to specifying alternations of values, one may also wish to specify alternations of features within a feature structure, as in encoding the grammatical structure of the English verb form *were*, which may be understood as having either second person or plural number. Since the potential content of this alternation tag must be different from that of the <**vAlt**> tag, we must give it another name, for example <**fAlt**> tag (for "feature alternation"), as follows:

```
<fAlt>
    <f name=person><sym value=second></f>
    <f name=number><sym value=plural></f>
</fAlt>
```

A more difficult problem is posed by the third-person German pronoun *sie*, which may be understood as having either nominative or accusative case and as having either singular number and feminine gender or plural number and any gender. How might one encode the grammatical structure of this word as a single feature structure? A first attempt, which makes use of both the <**vAlt**> and the <**fAlt**> tags, is the following:

```
<fs type='word structure' n=sie>
    <f name=category><sym value=pronoun></f>
    <f name=person><sym value=third></f>
    <f name=case>
        <vAlt><sym value=nominative><sym value=accusative></vAlt></f>
    <fAlt>
        <f name=number><sym value=singular></f>
        <f name=gender><sym value=feminine></f>
        <f name=number><sym value=plural></f>
        <f name=gender><any></f>
    </fAlt>
</fs>
```

However, since any number of features can combine to form a feature structure, this encoding does not make clear how many feature alternatives there are, and where one alternative ends and the next one begins.[3] One way to specify how many feature alternatives there are and where each one ends and the next one begins would be to insert a special empty tag at the points of demarcation. If we call that tag <**delim**> (for "delimiter"), the encoding of our example becomes:

```
<fs type='word structure' n=sie>
    <f name=category><sym value=pronoun></f>
    <f name=person><sym value=third></f>
    <f name=case>
        <vAlt><sym value=nominative><sym value=accusative></vAlt></f>
    <fAlt>
        <f name=number><sym value=singular></f>
        <f name=gender><sym value=feminine></f>
        <delim>
        <f name=number><sym value=plural></f>
        <f name=gender><any></f>
    </fAlt>
```

```
</fs>
```

This solution, however, does not identify the terms of the alternation (that is, the feature groups which are in alternation) as markup elements with which attributes (such as an *id* attribute, which is useful to indicate disambiguation) can be associated. To overcome these difficulties, we simply use untyped <**fs**> tags to enclose each group of features in the alternation. Our encoding for this example is as follows:

```
<fs type='word structure' n=sie>
   <f name=category><sym value=pron></f>
   <f name=person><sym value=third></f>
   <f name=case>
      <vAlt><sym value=nom><sym value=acc></vAlt></f>
   <fAlt>
      <fs>
         <f name=number><sym value=sg></f>
         <f name=gender><sym value=fem></f>
      </fs>
      <fs>
         <f name=number><sym value=pl></f>
         <f name=gender><any></f>
      </fs>
   </fAlt>
</fs>
```

Thus the content model for <**fAlt**> allows both <**f**>s and <**fs**>s; the alternation is among all the top-level elements occurring within the <**fAlt**>.

We face a similar problem of potential ambiguity when there is a value alternation for a feature that takes multiple values. For instance, consider the example given above of a feature named index which holds a set of numbers that give referential indices to the persons or things referred to by some expression. If we had a plural pronoun which ambiguously referred either to referents 37 and 52 or to referents 128 and 354, we might encode it as follows using a <**vAlt**> with the empty tag <**delim**> to delimit the terms of the alternation:

```
<f name=index org=set>
   <vAlt>
      <nbr value=37>
      <nbr value=52>
   <delim>
      <nbr value=128>
      <nbr value=354>
   </vAlt>
</f>
```

However, as explained above, we have not adopted such a <**delim**> tag. Our solution in this case is to normalize the complex <**vAlt**> into an <**fAlt**> by distributing the feature specification over both terms of the altemation. Our encoding for this example is as follows:

```
<fAlt>
   <f name=index org=set>
      <nbr value=37>
      <nbr value=52>
   </f>
   <f name=index org=set>
      <nbr value=128>
```

```
            <nbr value=354>
        </f>
    </fAlt>
```

4.2 *Negation*

Next, suppose that we wish to represent the value for a feature in a particular feature structure as being distinct from some specific value; for instance, that the value for case is distinct from "nominative". One possibility would be to provide a **<neg>** (for "negation") tag as part of the content model for feature values, so that it could be used as in the following example:

```
<f name=case><neg><sym value=nominative></neg></f>
```

However, there are a number of reasons not to specify distinctness from a particular value by means of a separate tag such as **<neg>**. First, it is not desirable to permit **<vAlt>** within the scope of such a tag. Second, there are other relations of distinctness that are useful to encode besides distinctness from a particular value. For example, for a feature that takes number values, it would be handy to be able to state that the value is greater than (or less than, or greater than or equal to, or less than or equal to) the value specified in the **<nbr>** tag. More importantly, for feature-structure values, one would like to be able to specify, among other things, that the feature value is any value that is subsumed by the one that actually appears, or is any value that the actually appearing value does not subsume.[4]

These considerations suggest that the specification for distinctness from a particular value should be expressed as the value of an attribute on the value tag itself. We name the attribute *rel* (for "relation"), and define the property of being distinct from the specified value as the "ne" (for "not equal") value for the *rel* attribute. Other relations appropriate for numerical and string values are "gt" (for "greater than"), "ge" (for "greater than or equal to"), and "It" and "le" for the "less than" and "less than or equal to" relations.

The default value for *rel* for value tags other than **<fs>** is "eq" (for "equal"); for **<fs>** values, it is "sb" (for "subsumes"). This means that when the desired feature value is the value actually specified, or in the case of an **<fs>** value, is any value subsumed by the specified value, the rel attribute can be omitted. Accordingly, our current example may be encoded as follows, and none of our preceding examples need altering to take into account the *rel* attribute.

```
<f name=case><sym rel=ne value=nominative>
```

Of course, this encoding by itself does not state what the possible values for the case feature are. To determine what they are, we need to supplement the feature-structure encoding with a feature system declaration (see section 6) which declares what the possible values of the case feature are. If they are declared to be the symbolic values "nominative", "genitive", "dative", and "accusative", then the above encoding is equivalent to the following:

```
<f name=case>
    <vAlt>
        <sym value=genitive><sym value=dative><sym value=accusative>
    </vAlt>
</f>
```

5. From Linguistic Markup to General Data Markup

As argued in section 1, feature structures are a fundamental mechanism for analysis in the field of linguistics, used not only in many subdisciplines of linguistics but also used across a wide variety of competing theories. In fact, "feature structures" have a much wider applicability than just linguistics. They can provide for the encoding of information of nearly any sort, since the data structure in question is the familiar and general one described by Knuth (1968) which consists of "nodes" (here called feature structures) and "fields" (here called features). About such structures, Knuth writes:

> ... the ideas we have encountered are not limited to computer programming alone; they apply more generally to everyday life. A collection of nodes containing fields, some of which point to other nodes, appears to be a very good abstract model for structural relations of all kinds; it shows how we can build up complicated structures from simple ones, and we have seen that corresponding algorithms for manipulating the structure can be designed in a natural manner. (p. 462)

A similar sentiment is echoed by Shieber (1986) who is writing specifically about the application of feature structures in the representation of grammatical formalisms. After explaining how six different formal approaches to grammar can be handled by the single computational model of unification of feature structures, he says:

> In fact, viewed from a computational perspective, it is not surprising that so many paradigms of linguistic description can be encoded directly with generalized feature/value structures of this sort. Similar structures have been put forward by various computer scientists as general mechanisms for knowledge representation (Ait-Kaci, 1985) and data types (Cardelli, 1984). Thus we have hardly constrained ourselves at all even though limited to this methodology. (p. 10)

Feature structures with features are essentially equivalent to many familiar schemes of data organization like records with fields, objects with attributes, frames with slots, property lists with properties, and even abstract data types with access functions. **<fs>** and **<f>** can thus be used to markup records, objects, frames, property lists, or instances of abstract data types, if such a perspective is more to the liking of the encoder. In fact, the tag names **<fs>** and **<f>** were deliberately chosen to allow the alternate reading of "field structure" and "field". For instance, the following might be the encoding of a bibliographic record:

```
<fs type=book>
   <f name=author><str>Goldfarb, Charles</str></f>
   <f name=year><nbr value=1990></f>
   <f name=title><str>The SGML Handbook</str></f>
   <f name=publisher><str>Clarendon Press</str></f>
   <f name=pubPlace><str>Oxford</str></f>
</fs>
```

We hasten to note that we have made no attempt in developing **<fs>** markup to include all the features of a database system. Rather, we have only sought to make the markup elements developed for linguistic markup as generally useful as possible. There are two aspects of the markup that particularly cater to the needs of more general use: (1) The **<fs>** element has a *type* attribute which makes it possible to distinguish different types of records or objects. (Note that the above example specifies type=book.) (2) An **<fsLib>** (for "**<fs>** library") element is also defined. Its content model allows a set of **<fs>** elements, permitting the encoder to encapsulate a whole data table (in which all the structures are of the same type) or even an entire database (containing structures of multiple types).

6. Justification for Feature System Declarations (FSDS)

One of the chief benefits of SGML markup is that the DTD (document type definition) provides formal documentation of the markup system used in an encoded document. SGML-aware software can in turn use the DTD to validate the tagging in the document. Much of this benefit is lost in the proposed mechanism for feature-structure markup. As explained in section 2, in order to avoid the proliferation of tags and the requirement that every user of feature-structure markup would need to define a customized DTD, a completely generic approach was devised. It treats all application-specific names as values of *type*, *name*, and *value* attributes. As a result the DTD for feature-structure markup can only validate the syntactic integrity of **<fs>** and **<f>** constructs, but it cannot validate their semantic integrity. In fact, it would not even be possible to write a customized DTD to fully validate a particular system of feature structure markup since there is no way in a DTD to specify how the value of an attribute should constrain the content model of its tag or the attribute values in embedded tags. Such capabilities would be needed, for instance, to ensure that only valid types of values were specified for each feature in a marked up document, or that all the features specified in any given feature structure were applicable to that type of structure.

To fill this gap we have devised an auxiliary document called a feature system declaration, or FSD. An FSD is an SGML-encoded document which provides a formal means for the developer of a particular system of feature-structure markup to specify the following:

1) a list of all the feature names with a brief prose description of what they represent;
2) a declaration of what values are valid for each feature;
3) a list of all the feature-structure types with a brief prose description of what they represent;
4) a declaration of what features are applicable to each type of feature structure;
5) a declaration of well-formedness constraints on feature structures which either require or prohibit cooccurrence of specified feature-value pairs.

We presume that application software will be developed that can parse the FSD and use the information in it to validate the integrity of every feature structure in a marked-up document.

An FSD fills another kind of gap. When linguists use feature structures, they typically specify the minimum set of features that distinctively encode an object or concept. Redundancy rules are used to define the appropriate values for the unspecified features. In order to make it possible for **<fs>** markup to follow this practice, an FSD also allows the designer of a system of feature-structure markup to specify:

6) a default value for each feature. The default may be a constant value, or it may be an expression that generates a value contingent on other feature values in the feature structure.

Application software that parses the FSD could use this information to generate the missing feature values in underspecified feature structures. Another aspect of underspecification is the **<any>** value of a feature. Application software can use the specification of feature value ranges in the FSD (number 2 in the above list) to expand **<any>** into a disjunction of the valid feature values.

We do not here explain the details of FSD syntax; the reader is referred to the chapter on Feature System Declarations in TEI P3 for the formal definition. However, an example is given below in section 7.2.

7. Using the Recommendations

We close by illustrating how the recommendations for linguistic markup can be used in practice. The first illustration demonstrates tagging all the words in a corpus for lexical category. The second demonstrates the encoding of an interlinear analysis of a text down to the morpheme level.

7.1 *Lexical tagging*

There are many different reasons why one may wish to mark up text for linguistic analysis. One, which motivated some of the very earliest schemes for linguistic markup like the one used for the tagged Brown Corpus (Kucera and Francis, 1967), is to provide enough information about the words in a text to at least partially disambiguate them. For instance, a given occurrence of the sequence *wash sinks* in an English text might be analyzed as a singular noun followed by a present-tense verb, or as a "bare" verb form followed by a plural noun. A text in which the words are marked up to indicate how they are to be grammatically interpreted could support more sophisticated methods of information retrieval and of text-to-speech mapping than one not so marked up. They could also be used in an effort to induce a grammar from textual material.

The tradition in linguistic lexical markup has been to associate mnemonic codes with each lexical item in the text, where the code picks out a unique grammatical analysis for the lexical item. All such coding schemes reflect to varying degrees the fact that lexical structure can be broken down into discrete bundles of information (what we have here called "features" and their associated values), but none of them are fully systematic in the way in which they analyze lexical structure. All of them also use rather primitive means of associating structural markup with text elements. For example, a passage containing the sequence *The wash sinks* may be encoded as follows, where "$" followed by a three-letter code provides grammatical information about the immediately preceding word.

```
The$DET wash$NNS sinks$VBZ
```

It is evident that this encoding, together with a code book that explains the coding scheme, provides enough information to determine that *wash sinks* in this case is a noun-verb sequence rather than a verb-noun one. It also provides some additional information, for example, that the noun is singular in number and that the verb form has an *-s* ending. However, the amount of detail that can be provided is limited by the encoding scheme, and any extensions to provide for a more detailed grammatical analysis of individual words would require that the entire coding scheme be revised. Moreover, the method of associating grammatical representations with individual words cannot be extended to provide for the encoding of higher levels of grammatical structure, such as phase structure. By using feature-structure representations, we are able to encode lexical structure in an easily extensible way, and also to embed them in larger structures of the same sort in the representation of multiword units. In this section, we take up first the problem of representing lexical structures as feature structures, and second the problem of associating those structures with text elements.

The grammatical structure of the verb interpretation of *sinks* may be encoded as follows (note that this provides considerably more information than is contained in the code "$VBZ"):

```
<fs type='word structure' id=vbidprx0sgp3>
   <f name=category><sym value=verb></f>
   <f name=mood><sym value=indicative></f>
   <f name=tense><sym value=present></f>
   <f name=auxiliary><minus></f>
   <f name=agreement>
      <fs type='agreement structure' id=sgp3>
         <f name=number><sym value=singular></f>
         <f name=person><sym value=third></f>
      </fs>
   </f>
</fs>
```

We may also assume that a feature system declaration has been provided that both legitimates this particular feature structure and specifies the value ranges of all the features mentioned in it.

Next, consider the problem of associating this particular feature structure with a textual occurrence of the word *sinks*. Clearly it would be undesirable to insert the feature structure next to the occurrence of the word in the text, since compared with the codes used for traditional text tagging, the feature-structure representations are very large. However, as the example indicates, each feature structure can be given a unique identifier (by means of the *id* attribute). This allows it to be pointed to from within a tag associated with a text element.

Thus, suppose we use the <**w**> tag (the "word" tag provided in the TEI analytic tag set) to identify the lexical items in our text, and that we assign each one a unique *id* attribute. Suppose also that we collect up a single instance of every lexical feature-structure representation that we require for marking up our text, and put them in a section of the document introduced by the <**fsLib**> (for "feature-structure library") tag.[5] Then one can use the *ana* attribute (for "analysis") on the <**w**> tag to point to the feature structure that represents its lexical analysis, as in the following example (which assumes that the 447th word of the text is *sinks* and is used as a verb).

```
<w id=w447 ana=vbidprx0sgp3>sinks</w>
```

Given that we have provided every segment with an *id* attribute as well as an *ana* attribute, we can also use the *inst* attribute on each <**fs**> in the feature-structure library to identify every lexical instance of that particular feature structure. So, for example, if the segments identified as "w35", "w292", "w447" and "w601" are all associated with the feature structure under discussion, we can make that fact explicit in the begin tag for that feature structure as follows:

<fs type='word structure' id-vbidprx0sgp3 inst='w35 w292 w447 w601'>

Just as we can have more than one lexical instance associated with a particular feature structure, so we can have more than one feature structure associated with a particular lexical instance. If we do, we would be explicitly representing lexical ambiguity. So, for example, if "nncmp1" is the value of the *id* attribute for the feature structure that represents the structure of a common plural noun, then our instance of the word *sinks* could be marked as ambiguous between these two interpretations as follows:

<w id=w447 ana='nncmpl vbidprx0sgp3'>sinks</w>

The method of relating lexical instances to lexical analyses by means of the *ana* and *inst* attributes on **<w>** and **<fs>** respectively, while superior to the method of including structural representations directly within texts, still has a number of drawbacks. It is quite cumbersome, it is very difficult to check for errors, and it may not be usable in a hypertext environment where the text and the feature-structure library are in different files.

A third method, which offers an easier approach to entering and editing relationships between text elements and structural elements and which may be used in a hypertext environment, employs the linking mechanism that has been provided for a variety of analytical purposes including the alignment of parallel texts. As with the method that uses *ana* and *inst* attributes as pointers, the linking mechanism requires that both the lexical instances and the feature structures be provided with unique identifiers. One may also identify the domains within which the links are being made; in the present case these would be the text containing the lexical instances whose analyses are being specified, and the feature-structure library which contains those analyses. The linking mechanism consists of a **<linkGrp>** tag whose content is a collection of **<link>** tags. The **<linkGrp>** tag has a *domains* attribute, which consists of a list of identifiers for the domains within which the links are being specified. For example, suppose that the text containing the lexical items whose analyses are being marked is a newspaper column whose begin tag is specified as follows:

<div3 type='column' id=nyt840404s2plc3n2>

Suppose also that the begin tag for the relevant feature-structure library is the following:

<fsLib id=enlxst2>

Then the **<linkGrp>** begin tag would be specified as follows:

<linkGrp domains='nyt840404s2plc3n2 enlxst2'>

The actual association of specific lexical instances with feature structures is specified by **<link>** tags which contain a *targets* attribute which in this case would contain two pointer values, the first to an element within the identified newspaper column and the second to an element within the identified feature structure library. Thus, to indicate that the segment identified within the text as "w447" has the analysis identified within the feature-structure library as "vbidprx0sgp3", one would provide the following **<link>** tag within the **<linkGrp>** tag mentioned above.

<link targets='w447 vbidprx0sgp3'>

All of the links provided within this particular **<linkGrp>** are one-to-one.[6] Thus each of the associations between a particular lexical instance and a particular feature structure are specified by a separate **<link>** tag. Lexical ambiguity may be indicated by separate **<link>** tags with the same first identifier for the lexical instance and different second identifiers for the feature-structure instances. In the case of the lexical instance identified as "w447", to say that it may be represented either as having the analysis identified as "vbidprx0sgp3" or as "nncmpl", one would provide both the preceding and the following **<link>** tags.

```
<link targets='w447 nncmpl'>
```

An important advantage of the linking mechanism is that no structural information needs to be recorded in the text itself, other than the identification of segments to be aligned with their analyses; nor does information about the text have to be represented in the begin tag of particular feature structures. To return to our hypothetical text whose 447th word is "sinks" used as a verb, we need only to provide a segment tag with a unique *id* attribute, as in:

```
<w id=w447>sinks</w>
```

Similarly, the begin tag of the feature structure for the relevant inflected form of the verb requires no *inst* attribute, as in:

```
<fs type='word structure' id=vbidprx0sgp3>
```

To represent the information that the segments identified as "w35", "w292", "w447", and "w601" are all associated with this particular feature structure, a **<linkGrp>** with at least the following **<link>** tags is needed:

```
<linkGrp domains='nyt840404s2plc3n2 enlxst2'>
   ...
   <link targets='w35 vbidprx0sgp3'>
   <link targets='w292 vbidprx0sgp3'>
   <link targets='w447 vbidprx0sgp3'>
   <link targets='w601 vbidprx0sgp3'>
   ...
</linkGrp>
```

As a result, when an analysis is changed or extended, no changes need to be made to the text (other than to add **<w>** tags with unique identifiers). Only the links need to be changed or extended, and feature structures changed or added.

Another important advantage of the linking mechanism is that it can be easily adapted to the situation in which one wishes to associate a variety of different types of information with a particular lexical instance. For example, suppose one also wished to associate with each lexical instance a pointer to a dictionary entry. Assuming that the dictionary containing the relevant entries has a unique identifier that can be pointed to from within the document containing the **<linkGrp>**, one would add that identifier to the list of identifiers in the value of its *domains* attribute. Then within each **<link>** in that **<linkGrp>**, appropriate reference would be made within the *targets* attribute to the identifier for the dictionary entry.

7.2 *Interlinear text*

Linguists, anthropologists, literary scholars, and others who deal with large corpora of foreign-language text, have traditionally used interlinear annotation as a mechanism both for developing and for presenting the morphological analysis and literal glossing of running text; see, for instance, Antworth (1993). As an example, consider the following sentence in the Eskimo language of northwest Alaska:

Akutchilighmik-uvva uqaaqtullangniaqtunga. 'I am going to tell a story about making Eskimo ice cream.'

(The digraphs *ng* and *gh* are used here to represent the "eng" and "dotted-g", respectively, of the standard orthography.) Consider that this sentence is the first sentence in a text that we want to analyze. An analysis of this sentence in interlinear format might look something like this:

1.	Akutchilighmik-uvva	uqaaqtullangniaqtunga.
	akut -chi-ligh-mik =uvva	uqaaqtu -llang-niaq-tunga
	akutuq -si -liq -mik =uvva	uqaaqtuq -llak -niaq-tunga
	icecream-RSL-GER -s.MOD=now	tell story-DUR -INT -ls.I
	about making Eskimo ice cream	I am going to tell a story

The first line gives the baseline text. The second line inserts morpheme breaks into the surface forms of the words; a hyphen breaks off a suffix and an equal sign breaks off an enclitic. The third line gives the underlying form for each morpheme. The fourth line gives a gloss for each morpheme; grammatical functors are glossed with technical abbreviations. The last line gives a gloss for each word.

In this example, there are structures at three levels; there is one sentence, two words, and many morphemes. In the encoding, these levels correspond to different types of feature structures. Thus, the sentence is encoded as an instance of <**fs type=sentence**>, and so on. The structure for the sentence has three features: "text" gives the text of the sentence in normal orthography, "translation" gives the free translation of the sentence, and "analysis" breaks the sentence into a sequence of analyzed words (that is, instances of <**fs type=word**>). The reference number for the sentence can be encoded as the value of the *n* attribute that is built into all TEI elements. The structure for the words also has three features: "form", "gloss", and "analysis". The sentence would then be encoded as follows (omitting for the moment instances of the <**fs type=morpheme**> tag, which encode the analysis of each word):

```
<fs type=sentence n=1>
   <f name=text>
      <str>Akutchilighmik-uvva uqaaqtullangniaqtunga.</str></f>
   <f name=translation>
      <str>I am going to tell a story about making Eskimo ice cream.</str></f>
   <f name=analysis>
      <fs type=word>
         <f name=form><str>akutchilighmik-uvva</str></f>
         <f name=gloss><str>about making Eskimo ice cream</str></f>
         <f name=analysis>...</f>
      </fs>
      <fs type=word>
         <f name=form><str>uqaaqtullangniaqtunga</str></f>
         <f name=gloss><str>I am going to tell a story</str></f>
         <f name=analysis>...</f>
      </fs></f>
</fs>
```

To handle the morphemic structure of the words, we encode the analysis of each word as a sequence of <**fs type=morpheme**> tags. These feature structures contain four features: "type" identifies it as a root, suffix, and so on (thus encoding the information carried by the hyphens and equal signs); "form" gives the surface form of the morpheme; "lexForrn" gives the lexical (or underlying) form of the morpheme; and "gloss" gives its gloss. "Type" is drawn from a small closed set so its values are encoded as symbols; all others come from open sets and are encoded as strings. The markup for the first word in the sentence is thus:

```
<fs type=word>
   <f name=form><str>akutchilighmik-uvva</str></f>
```

```
    <f name=gloss><str>about making Eskimo ice cream.</str></f>
    <f name=analysis>
       <fs type=morpheme>
          <f name=type><sym value=root></f>
          <f name=form><str>akut</str></f>
          <f name=lexForm><str>akutuq</str></f>
          <f name=gloss><str>ice cream.</str></f></fs>
       <fs type=morpheme>
          <f name=type><sym value=suffix></f>
          <f name=form><str>chi</str></f>
          <f name=lexForm><str>si</str></f>
          <f name=gloss><str>RSL</str></f></fs>
       <fs type=morpheme>
          <f name=type><sym value=suffix></f>
          <f name=form><str>ligh</str></f>
          <f name=lexForm><str>liq</str></f>
          <f name=gloss><str>GER</str></f></fs>
       <fs type=morpheme>
          <f name=type><sym value=suffix></f>
          <f name=form><str>mik</str></f>
          <f name=lexForm><str>mik</str></f>
          <f name=gloss><str>s.MOD</str></f></fs>
       <fs type=morpheme>
          <f name=type><sym value=enclitic></f>
          <f name=form><str>uvva</str></f>
          <f name=lexForm><str>uvva</str></f>
          <f name=gloss><str>now</str></f></fs>
    </f>
</fs>
```

The FSD (feature system declaration) for the above system of markup would contain an <**fsDecl**> for each of the three types of feature structures. Each <**fsDecl**> contains an <**fDecl**> for each of the features that can occur in that type of feature structure. These are very straightforward in this example. Worthy of special note is the <**fDecl**> for the "type" feature of morphemes; it specifies a closed list of the values that can occur in Eskimo words. Note, too, that the <**fDecl**> tags for the "analysis" features specify that the *org* attribute has the value "list". This is what allows the content of those features in the marked-up text to contain a sequence of values, rather than just a single value. The feature-structure declarations (extracted from the full FSD) for this example are therefore as follows:

```
<fsDecl type=sentence>
   <descr>Represents the interlinear analysis of a sentence</descr>
   <fDecl name=text>
      <descr>The text of the sentence in normal orthography</descr>
      <vRange><str rel=sb></str></vRange></fDecl>
   <fDecl name=translation>
      <descr>A free translation of the sentence</descr>
      <vRange><str rel=sb></str></vRange></fDcl>
   <fDecl name=analysis org=list>
      <descr>The analysis of the words in the sentence</descr>
      <vRange><fs type=word></fs></vRange></fDecl>
</fsDecl>
<fsDecl type=word>
   <descr>Represents the interlinear analysis of a word</descr>
   <fDecl name=form>
      <descr>The word form in the text without capitalization or punctuation</descr>
```

```
        <vRange><str rel=sb></str></vRange></fDecl>
    <fDecl name=gloss>
        <descr>A literal translation of the word</descr>
        <vRange><str rel=sb></str></vRange></fDecl>
    <fDecl name=analysis org=list>
        <descr>The analysis of the morphemes in the word</descr>
        <vRange><fs type=morpheme></fs></vRange></fDecl>
</fsDecl>

<fsDecl type=morpheme>
    <descr>Represents the interlinear analysis of a morpheme</descr>
    <fDecl name=type>
        <descr>The type of morpheme</descr>
        <vRange><vAlt>
            <sym value=root><sym value=prefix>
            <sym value=suffix><sym value=enclitic></vAlt>
        </vRange></fDecl>
    <fDecl name=form>
        <descr>The surface form of the morpheme</descr>
        <vRange><str rel=sb></str></vRange></fDecl>
    <fDecl name=lexform>
        <descr>The lexical (underlying) form of the morpheme</descr>
        <vRange><str rel=sb></str></vRange></fDecl>
    <fDecl name=gloss>
        <descr>A literal gloss of the morpheme</descr>
        <vRange><str rel=sb></str></vRange></fDecl>
</fsDecl>
```

Notes

[1] The initial feature-structure recommendations were formulated by the Analysis and Interpretation Committee at a meeting in Tucson, Arizona in March 1990, following suggestions by Mitch Marcus and Beatrice Santorini. The authors received valuable help in the further revision and refinement of the recommendations from Steven Zepp.

[2] Note that we are supposing that the source text does not contain any explicit linguistic analysis. If the source text were to contain this very feature-structure diagram, we might also want to add instructions for how to reproduce it graphically. Provision for this has not been made in the TEI P3 recommendations.

[3] In our example, an applications program (though not an SGML validator) could use the fact that the names of the features in the two alternatives are the same to infer what the alternatives are. However, the alternatives in a given feature alternation may involve features with different names.

[4] For discussion of subsumption, see Shieber (1986) and the relevant sections of TEI P3.

[5] This is one method that is recommended for gathering together feature structures. Another that ultimately will prove more useful for scholarly purposes is to provide them in publicly accessible documents that can be associated with one's text by means of hypertextual or other kinds of links. See the chapters on segmentation and alignment in TEI P3 for further discussion.

[6] This is not a necessary feature of the linking mechanism proposed in TEI P3. For instructions about how to state one-many and many-many linking relations, see the chapter on Segmentation and Alignment.

References

Ait-Kaci, H. *A New Model of Computation Based on a Calculus of Type Subsumption*. Doctoral dissertation. University of Pennsylvania, 1985.

Antworth, Evan L. "Glossing Text with the PC-KIMMO Morphological Parser". *Computers and the Humanities*, 26 (1993), 389–98.

Cardelli, L. *A Semantics of Multiple Inheritance*. Technical Report. Murray Hill, NJ: Bell Laboratories, 1984.

Chomsky, Noam. *Aspects of the Theory of Syntax*. Cambridge, MA: MIT Press, 1965.

Jakobson, Roman. "The Identification of Phonemic Entities". *Travaux du Cercle Linguistique de Copenhague 5* (1949), 205–13.

Knuth, Donald E. *The Art of Computer Programming. Vol. 1: Fundamental Algorithms*. Reading, MA: Addison-Wesley, 1968.

Kucera, Henry and W. Nelson Francis. *Computational Analysis of Present-day American English*. Providence, RI: Brown University Press, 1967.

Shieber, Stuart. *An Introduction to Unification-Based Approaches to Grammar*. Chicago: University of Chicago Press, 1986.

Sperberg-McQueen, C. M. and L. Burnard. *Guidelines for Electronic Text Encoding and Interchange (TEI P3)*. Chicago and Oxford: Text Encoding Initiative, 1994.

Computers and the Humanities **29**: 211–231, 1995.

Hierarchical Encoding of Text: Technical Problems and SGML Solutions[1]

David T. Barnard *
Department of Computer and Information Science, Queen's University, Kingston, Ontario, K7L 3N6, Canada
e-mail: barnard@queensu.ca

Lou Burnard **
Oxford University Computing Service, 13 Banbury Road, Oxford OX2 6NN, England
e-mail: lou@vax.ox.ac.uk

Jean-Pierre Gaspart †
Associated Consultants and Software Engineers sa/nv

Lynne A. Price ††
Frame Technology Corp., 333 West San Carlos Street, San Jose, CA 95110, USA
e-mail: lprice@frame.com

C.M. Sperberg-McQueen ‡
Computer Center, University of Illinois at Chicago, Chicago, Illinois 60680, USA
e-mail: u35395@uicvm.uic.edu

and

Giovanni Battista Varile ‡‡
Commission of the European Communities

Key words: TEI, SGML, encoding problems, hierarchical encoding

Abstract
One recurring theme in the TEI project has been the need to represent non-hierarchical information in a natural way – or at least in a way that is acceptable to those who must use it – using a technical tool that assumes a single hierarchical representation. This paper proposes solutions to a variety of such problems: the encoding of segments which do not reflect a document's primary hierarchy; relationships among non-adjacent segments of texts; ambiguous content; overlapping structures; parallel structures; cross-references; vague locations.

* David T. Barnard is Professor of Computing and Information Science at Queen's University. His research interests are in structured text processing and the compilation of programming languages. His recent publications include "Tree-to-tree Correction for Document Trees", Queen's Technical Report, and "Error Handling in a Parallel LR Substring Parser", *Computer Languages*, 19,4 (1993) 247–59.

** Lou Burnard is Director of the Oxford Text Archive at Oxford University Computing Services, with interests in electronic text and database technology. He is European Editor of the Text Encoding Initiative's Guidelines.

† Jean-Pierre Gaspart is with Associated Consultants and Software Engineers.

†† Lynne A. Price (Ph.D., computer sciences, University of Wisconsin-Madison) is a senior software engineer at Frame Technology Corp. Her main area of research has been representing text structure for automatic processing. She has served on both the US and international SGML standards committee for several years and is the editor of *International Standard ISO/IEC 13673* on Conformance Testing for Standard Generalized Markup Language (SGML) Systems.

‡ C. M. Sperberg-McQueen is a Senior Research Programmer at the academic computer center of the University of Illinois at Chicago; his interests include medieval Germanic languages and literatures and the theory of electronic text markup. Since 1988 he has been editor in chief of the ACH/ACL/ALLC Text Encoding Initiative.

‡‡ Giovanni Battista Varile works for the Commission of the European Communities.

1. Introduction

The straightforward way to use the Standard Generalized Markup Language (SGML)[2] is to define the content of a document as a number of components which in turn are defined by giving their components, and so on. The result of this approach is a hierarchical description of a document, in which the components are called elements. While this seems natural in many settings – a book has front matter, a body, and back matter, each of which can be described in more detail – it is too limiting for many documents of interest to participants in the Text Encoding Initiative (TEI). Many texts, or portions of texts, that are to be encoded using the TEI Guidelines can be viewed in more than one (hierarchical) way. One recurring theme in the project has been the need to represent non-hierarchical information in a natural way (or, at least, in a way that is acceptable to those who must use it) using a technical tool that assumes a single hierarchical representation.[3]

While some of the other papers in this volume address specific needs for non-hierarchical encodings, this paper explores SGML-based techniques for representation of data that is almost but not quite hierarchical in a notation for expressing a hierarchy.

Although some SGML constructs are common to more than one of the topics discussed, the sections of this paper are largely independent. The reader is assumed to be familiar with the general principles and use of SGML,[4] but not to be expert on the details.

The examples were inspired by discussions of TEI's metalanguage committee, often in response to specific problems identified by other committees and working groups in the project. The committee explored alternative encodings to understand the advantages and disadvantages of each. Rather than recommending a single approach to each problem, the committee concluded that working groups and individual researchers should make informed decisions about the techniques appropriate to individual requirements. Any more restrictive decision would force some TEI users to increase the encoding effort (perhaps prohibitively) with no immediate benefit.

The coding schemes shown below represent the committee's ideas on appropriate SGML mechanisms for logical problems; they do not necessarily reflect the views of the committee concerning the individual application areas. In the examples, especially, the focus is on markup problems; the examples in this paper are not intended as full analyses. Researchers working on hypertext encodings should also consult the paper by Steven DeRose and David Durand.[5] The examples and solutions described in this document are intended to be pedagogical; divergences in this document from the TEI guidelines or the HyTime standard should not be taken as rejections of those recommendations. In particular, some names are used for tags that are used in other ways or with other attributes in the TEI Guidelines; these are used in this paper as examples only.

The ideas presented in this paper have been influential in the work of the TEI to date. As can be seen from other papers in this volume, as well as in the Guidelines themselves, the committees and work groups of the TEI have made choices among the options described here while designing the TEI encodings for different kinds of texts.

In addition to their historical and pedagogical interest, the ideas presented here can serve as a model of the local extensions permitted by the TEI Guidelines. One of the features of the TEI encoding scheme is its extensibility,[6] which allows users to change existing features of the encoding scheme, or add new features to it, in controlled ways. Some of these local extensions may well involve dealing with other kinds of non-hierarchical structures than those already accommodated in the Guidelines, and users designing those extensions should find this paper to be of value.

In contrast with other papers in this volume which are about specific aspects of the content of the Guidelines, this paper is about SGML and the ways in which it might be used to accomplish some of the things accomplished in the Guidelines, or in extensions of the guidelines that others might wish to make.

2. Supplementing a Document's Hierarchy

An encoder often needs to indicate arbitrary segments whose boundaries do not reflect a document's primary hierarchy, or indeed, any hierarchical structure. This problem is illustrated by the frequent need to annotate a text with in-line comments such as the following:

- In an encoding of a particular copy of a work: "the passage is illegibly water stained".[7]
- In a transcript of an interview: "reply rendered inaudible by a passing truck".
- In a gestural transcription of a conversation: "Nino moved to the window".
- In minutes of a meeting covering tariff policy, foreign relations with Japan (including cultural exchange, economic cooperation, tariff policy, patent law), and wheat production (including a digression on wheat tariffs): "this section discusses tariffs".

The discussion of this problem is long because several SGML concepts are introduced in the discussion, and because the large number of situations that require non-hierarchical material suggests a large number of possible solutions.

2.1 *Boundary elements for arbitrary events*

The first solution introduces special elements into the document whose sole purpose is to mark the boundaries of such passages. While most SGML elements consist of content (in general, a combination of text and other elements) delimited by a start-tag at the beginning and an end-tag at the end, other SGML elements mark points in the text, but have no content. These elements have declared content EMPTY in the DTD. They provide information about the text but do not contain any text or other elements; this information is completely contained in the generic identifier and attributes in the start-tag, and the location of the element within the document hierarchy. Such elements have start-tags, but no end-tags.

For example, let us assume a detailed gestural transcription of an interview in which the structural markup is concerned only with the speeches made, but in which a general purpose **<action>** element is also used to describe the actions of the participants. Suppose, for example, that during the session Nino walked to the window, stood there, and, after a few minutes lit a cigarette, returning to the table before putting it out. Using the designations "passage A", "passage B" and so on to indicate the primary hierarchy of the transcript, the **<action>** element might be used as follows:[8,9]

```
<TEI.2>
...
<action start id=a237 person=nino desc='sits at table'>
   passage A
<action end id=a237>
<action start id=a238 person=nino desc='walks to window'>
   passage B
<action end actionId=a238>
<action start id=a239 person=nino desc='stands at window'>
   passage C
<action start id=a240 person=nino desc='smokes'>
   passage D
<action end actionId=a239>
<action start id=a241 person=nino desc='walks to table'>
   passage E
<action end actionId=a241>
   passage F
<action end actionId=a240>
   passage G
...
</TEI.2>
```

Here, actions have been arbitrarily numbered a1, a2, and so on. These action numbers are indicated by the value of the *id* attribute at the start of the action and the *actionId* attribute at the end. Custom application software can use this attribute to link the two ends of the action, recognizing, for example, that Nino was smoking throughout passages D-F. The application software can also assume that values for the *person* and *desc* attributes are specified at the start of the action.

The start and end of each action is indicated by the value of an *endpoint* attribute. Since the possible values of *endpoint* are predefined to be either "start" or "end", when the optional SHORTTAG feature is used, SGML allows the attribute name to be omitted from the start-tag. Thus, a tag such as:

```
<action end actionId=a241>
```

is an abbreviated form of the more complete:

```
<action endpoint=end actionId=e241>
```

The action element might be defined in SGML as follows:

```
<!ELEMENT action – O EMPTY >
<!ATTLIST action
   id ID #IMPLIED
   actionId IDREF #IMPLIED
   person NAME #IMPLIED
   desc CDATA #IMPLIED
   endpoint (start | end) #IMPLIED >
]>
```

The element declaration for *action* does not give a content model. Instead the declared content EMPTY indicates that the element is used as described above.

Note that *id* has the declared value ID and *actionId* has the declared value IDREF. The values of these attributes are SGML unique identifiers. SGML allows every element to be associated with a string of characters called a unique identifier. Only one element in a document instance may have a given unique identifier, regardless of its generic identifier. Thus not only must every two <**chapter**> elements, for instance, have different unique identifiers, but also the unique identifier of a <**chapter**> cannot be the same as that of a <**figure**>.

An element's unique identifier is specified as the value of an attribute whose declared value is ID. Since an element cannot have more than one unique identifier, an element can have only one *id* attribute. The SGML Standard recommends that the same name be used for the *id* attributes of all elements that have such attributes. A unique identifier is an SGML name. Under the reference concrete syntax, therefore, it starts with a letter, and may contain up to eight letters, digits, hyphens and periods. These restrictions are often modified. This paper, for example, assumes that the relevant SGML declaration increases the NAMELEN quantity to allow longer names. Elements may also have attributes that identify other elements through their unique identifiers. In particular, the value of an attribute with the declared value IDREF must be the same as that of the ID value of some element (the same one, a preceding one, or a following one); the declared value IDREFS means the value is a list of one or more ID values.

The *id* and *actionId* attributes declared above for the <**action**> element use this mechanism. While an SGML parser does not ensure that an *id* is specified whenever *endpoint* is "start", custom application software could do so. Custom software could also verify that the encoder honors other application conventions, such as specifying an *actionId* whenever *endpoint* is "end", specifying both a start and an end for each action, and not specifying more than one end for a started action.

At the expense of increasing the number of element types, this DTD can be modified so that SGML ensures that the right combination of attributes is specified at each end of the action. Here, instead of using a single <**action**> element type for both endpoints, there are separate <**actionStart**> and <**actionEnd**> element types:

```
<TEI.2>
...
<actionStart id=a237 person=nino desc='sits at table'>
   passage A
<actionEnd id=a237>
<actionStart id=a238 person=nino desc='walks to window'>
   passage B
<actionEnd actionId=e238>
<actionStart id=a239 person=nino desc='stands at window'>
   passage C
<actionStart id=a240 person=nino desc='smokes'>
   passage D
<actionEnd actionId=e239>
<actionStart id=a241 person=nino desc='walks to table'>
   passage E
<actionEnd actionId=e241>
   passage F
<actionEnd actionId=e240>
   passage G
...
</TEI.2>
```

2.2 *Typed boundary elements*

The method just described assumes that the kinds of action to be encoded (i.e., the possible values for the *desc* attribute) will not be known until the transcription is complete. When the possible event types are known in advance, they can be defined in the DTD as different generic identifiers:

```
<!ELEMENT (move|gesture|...) – O EMPTY>
<!ATTLIST (move|gesture|...)
   id ID #IMPLIED
   eventid IDREF #IMPLIED
   person (nino|lynne|lou|michael|pierre) #IMPLIED
   desc CDATA #IMPLIED
   endpoint (start | end) #IMPLIED >
```

This DTD fragment also assumes that the participants are known in advance and can be listed explicitly in the declared value for the attribute *person*. This allows the attribute name to be omitted when the value is given. Nino's walk to the window would therefore be encoded as:

```
<move start id=e238 nino desc='walks to window'>...
<move end eventid=e238>
```

2.3 *Concurrent markup*

SGML's optional CONCUR feature provides a different approach. Although most SGML document instances represent a single hierarchy, CONCUR allows the same data characters to be described in multiple hierarchies, presenting different views of a document. There is a separate DTD for each one; the first is known as the base document type declaration. When CONCUR is used, the generic identifier in a start-tag or an end-tag can be preceded by one or more document type names, separated by a connector and enclosed in group delimiters, to indicate that the tag applies only to the named DTDs. When a start-tag does not contain a document type name, it applies to all active views. For example, meeting minutes might be transcribed using one DTD for the text of speeches, and separate DTDs for the gestures of each participant. The DTD for Nino's possible movements might include declarations such as:

```
<!DOCTYPE nino [
<!ELEMENT nino (#PCDATA | move | gesture |...)+ >
<!ELEMENT move (#PCDATA) >
<!ELEMENT gesture (#PCDATA) >
<!ATTLIST (move, gesture,...) desc CDATA #IMPLIED>
]>
```

so that Nino's move to the window is bounded by:

```
<(nino)move desc='walks to window'>...</(nino)move>
```

where any speech or other gestures Nino made while he was walking are represented by the ellipsis.

In fact, CONCUR requires that all of the data characters be incorporated into each view. CONCUR by itself therefore does not support applications in which some data is present in some views only. For example, if the text of stage directions is to be omitted from a metrical view of a play, it is not sufficient to mark them up as:

```
<(drama)stagedir>exit</(drama)stagedir>
```

because even though the characters "exit" will only be considered content of the **<stagedir>** element in the dramatical view of the play, they will still be seen as data characters in other views (within the content of the containing element). Marked section declarations provide one way around this problem. For example, if the "metrical" DTD defines a parameter entity "%stagedir" to be "IGNORE", the markup:

```
<![%(metrical)stagedir[<(drama)stagedir>exit</(drama)stagedir>]]>
```

can be used. Here the parameter entity reference defines the effective status of the marked section to be "IGNORE" in the metrical view, and is the default "INCLUDE" in all other views.

This encoding assumes that no two gestures, movements, or other events can overlap or nest. If events may overlap or occur within each other, the illustrated element declarations must be revised appropriately to describe a suitable hierarchy. For example,

```
<!ELEMENT move (#PCDATA|gesture)+ >
<!ELEMENT gesture (#PCDATA) >
```

indicates that gestures may occur within movements, but does not allow the reverse. If there are no restrictions on the combinations of elements that may occur within each other, the gestural tags may all be defined as inclusion exceptions on the document type element and each other:

```
<!ELEMENT nino – O (#PCDATA) +(move | gesture |...) >
<!ELEMENT (move, gesture,...) – O (#PCDATA) +(move | gesture |...) >
```

Legibility or audibility information can be readily accommodated by CONCUR with a **<leg>** or **<aud>** DTD segmenting a document into segments of a given legibility or audibility. The DTD might look something like this:

```
<!DOCTYPE aud [ <!ELEMENT aud
    - - (clear | distorted | inaudible)+ >
<!ELEMENT clear - - (#PCDATA) >
<!ELEMENT distorted - - (#PCDATA) >
<!ELEMENT inaudible - - (#PCDATA) >
<!ATTLIST (distorted, inaudible) cause CDATA #IMPLIED >
]>
```

Here, the content model for **<aud>** requires every portion of a document to be coded as clear, distorted, or inaudible; the content models for **<clear>**, **<distorted>**, and **<inaudible>** prevent a single portion from belonging to more than one of these sections. A variation would provide a "DNA" option to be used when audibility does not apply (for example, to headings and annotations). Thus, interspersed among other markup, the encoded document could contain sequences such as:

```
<(aud)clear>...</(aud)clear>
<(aud)inaudible cause='truck'>...</(aud)inaudible>
<(aud)clear>...</(aud)clear>
<(aud)distorted cause='volume overload'>...</(aud)distorted><(aud)clear>...</(aud)clear>
```

There are limitations to this approach. First, it is necessary to define a different DTD for each type of coding (for example, for each participant in a conversation). Second, SGML parsers need not support the CONCUR feature and most currently available parsers do not. Third, there is the burden of additional markup to be inserted in the document; unfortunately the prefixing of tag names by DTD names is required for all tag names that do not occur in all the DTDs being concurrently processed, so that introducing a new concurrent variant can require adding a prefix to all existing tag names in a document.

2.4 *Separate analysis elements*

Even when CONCUR is not available, coding of independent passages does not need to be embedded in the existing hierarchy. In this next variation, the primary hierarchy contains the text of the transcription, indicating the boundaries of the desired segments. Relationships among these segments are indicated in a separate **<analysis>** element, which follows.[10] Where existing elements of the main hierarchy do not precisely define the desired segment, special segmentation elements (with the generic identifier <s>) provide additional markers.

Using this method, the document instance has three sections. The first is the transcription of the meeting, showing the segmentation of the text. Comments have been added to make the markup clear, but the comments are totally redundant and any processing software ignores them. More detail is shown here than in previous examples. In particular, the text is divided into paragraphs, which in turn are divided into segments to show the start and end of gestures as needed. When the paragraph boundaries do not coincide with the passages identified between gestures above, the passages are split into pieces:

```
<TEI.2>
...
<p>...
   <s id=s101><!- -Nino sits at table- ->passage A</s>
   <s id=s102><!- -Nino walks to window- ->passage B1</s>
</p>
<p>
   <s id=s103>passage B2<!- -Nino reaches the window- -></s>
   <s id=s104>
      <!- -Nino stands at window - - - ->passage C
      <s id=s105><!- -Nino starts smoking - ->passage D1</s>
</p>
```

```
<p>
   passage D2...
   <s id=s106><!- -Nino walks to table- ->passage E</s>
   <s id=s107><!- -Nino arrives at table- ->passage F1</s>
</p>
<p id=p235>passage F2</p>
<p id=p238>passage G</p>
...
</TEI.2>
```

In a separate section we define the gestures detected during analysis. A number of possibilities exist for for the representation of such abstract structures, many of which are described in chapters 14 to 16 of P3. In this example we use a simplified version of the "feature structure" analysis discussed in chapter 16 of P3. The elements **<fStruct>** and **<feature>** used here correspond with the **<fs>** and **<f>** elements discussed in that chapter. Here, the ordering of **<fStruct>** elements is irrelevant, because these gestures have not yet been related to the sequence of events marked in the text:

```
<analysis>
   <fStruct id=m1> <feature name=who>Nino</feature>
      <feature name=act>sits</feature>
      <feature name=loc>at table</feature>
   </fStruct>
   <fStruct id=m2>
      <feature name=who>Nino</feature>
      <feature name=act>walks</feature>
      <feature name=loc>table to window</feature>
   </fStruct>
   <fStruct id=m3>
      <feature name=who>Nino</feature>
      <feature name=act>stands</feature>
      <feature name=loc>at window</feature>
   </fStruct>
   <fStruct id=m4>
      <feature name=who>Nino</feature>
      <feature name=act>smokes</feature
   </fStruct>
   <fStruct id=m6>
      <feature name=who>Nino</feature>
      <feature name=act>walks</feature>
      <feature name=loc>window to table</feature>
   </fStruct>
</analysis>
```

The final section of the document encodes the relationships between the first two. Using *idref* attributes it connects the analyzed gestures with the actual text, using the unique identifiers that were assigned to the gestures in the analysis, and to the paragraphs and segments in the text:

```
<TEI.2>
...
   <alMap><!- - Nino sitting at table, passage A - ->
      <alPtr target=m1><alRange alStart=s101 alEnd=s102>
   </alMap>
   <alMap><!- - Nino walking to window, passage B - ->
      <alPtr target=m2><alRange alStart=s102 alEnd=s103>
```

```
        <!- - Note that Nino stops sitting as he begins walking. - ->
    </alMap>
    <alMap><!- - Nino at window, passages C, D - ->
        <alPtr target=m3><alRange alStart=s104 alEnd=s106>
    </alMap> <alMap><!- - Nino smokes, passages D-F - ->
        <alPtr target=m4><alRange alStart=s105 alEnd=p238>
    </alMap>
    <alMap><!- - Nino walks to table, passage E - ->
        <alPtr target=m6><alPtr alStart=s106 alEnd=s107>
    </alMap>
    <alMap><!- - Nino sitting at table, passage G - ->
        <alPtr target=m1><alRange alStart=p235 alEnd=p238>
        <!- - Note: fStruct from passage A reused - ->
    </alMap>
</alignment>
...
</TEI.2>
```

Although in this example, all the recorded events have separate start and end points, this approach applies equally well to instantaneous events that have a single time point. The <**alPtr**> element can provide the unique identifier of an element in the text as well as of an element in the analysis. Alignment mappings such as the following are then possible:

```
<alMap>
    <alPtr target=m17><alPtr target=p726>
</alMap>
```

This approach provides a more declarative interpretation of non-hierarchical material; it also automatically provides for discontinuous segments (such as sitting at the table, in this example). Its obvious disadvantage is the bulk and complexity of the markup.

In practice, subsequent work in the two groups responsible for linguistic analysis and hypertext resulted in a reasonably simple and more general mechanism for the encoding of this kind of standalone linking, using the same basic notion of an external element used to align text segments and their analyses. Other papers in this volume (notably those by Durand and DeRose, and Langendoen and Simons) and the relevant chapters of the Guidelines should be consulted for more detail.

2.5 *Discussion*

The relevance of these solutions to different situations depends on a variety of factors. The effort of encoding an analysis such as that in Section 2.4 is likely to be prohibitive if the primary purpose of the coding effort is to record the hierarchy of the text rather than the non-hierarchical material, but is to be expected if the focus of the research is the latter. How many types of annotations are to be made? Are the classifications known in advance? The answers to these questions help determine whether a general <**event**> tag or specific <**gesture**>, <**move**>, <**walk**>, <**set**>, elements are appropriate. Other considerations include the availability of CONCUR and the ease of developing custom applications. Users should choose one of the methods described above, or a variation, depending on specific circumstances.

3. Relating Non-Adjacent Text

Another problem of a non-hierarchic nature involves encoding relationships among non-adjacent segments of text.[11] Examples include:

- words rendered illegible by the stain on the right-hand side of a page;
- the finite verb *stellte vor* in the German sentence *Er stellte seine These den Kollegen hoffnungsvoll vor*,
- the discussion of tariffs in parliamentary minutes (assuming that the discussion wanders back and forth from one topic to another), and
- the root *ktb* in the Arabic word *al-kaatib*.

3.1 *Labeling related passages with unique identifiers*

The first solution uses a single SGML unique identifier to label all related passages. Most occurrences of this unique identifier appear as the value of an *idref* attribute, since it can be an *id* attribute only once. When the non-adjacent passages are elements of the document's natural hierarchy, the coding simply involves adding the attributes to the start-tags that would be used in any case. In the following sample, a topic is given an *id* and a full description the first time it occurs; thereafter, an *idref* attribute refers to the earlier labelling:

```
<!DOCTYPE TEI.2 system "tei2.dtd" [
    ...
    <!ELEMENT topic - - (#PCDATA) >
    <!ATTLIST topic
        id        ID      #IMPLIED
        full      CDATA   #IMPLIED
        topicid   IDREF   #IMPLIED
    >
]>
<TEI.2> ...
<topic id=tariff full='Tariffs on steel'>...</topic>
<topic id=wheat full='Wheat Crop Projections'>...</topic>
<topic topicid=tariff>...</topic>
<topic id=flag full='National Flag Month'>...</topic>
<topic topicid=tariff>...</topic>...
...
</TEI.2>
```

This coding artificially distinguishes the first occurrence of a topic from any others. Furthermore, since all attributes are optional, SGML does not enforce the intended use of the attributes. Both limitations can be avoided by defining a topic list as part of the document's front matter. This register contains the *id* attributes; the actual text contains *idref* attributes:

```
<!DOCTYPE TEI.2 system "tei2.dtd" [
    ...
    <!ELEMENT topic_declaration – O EMPTY >
    <!ATTLIST topic_declaration
        full   CDATA   #REQUIRED
        ID     ID      #REQUIRED
    >
    <!ELEMENT topic - - (#PCDATA) >
    <!ATTLIST topic topicid IDREF #REQUIRED >
]>
<TEI.2>
...
<front>
...
<topiclist>
```

```
    <topic_declaration id='tariff' full='Tariffs on steel'>
    <topic_declaration id='wheat' full='Wheat Crop Projections'>
    <topic_declaration id='flag' full='National Flag Month'>...
</topiclist>
...
</front>
<body>
    ...
    <topic topicid='tariff'>...</topic>
    <topic topicid='wheat'>...</topic>
    <topic topicid='tariff'>...</topic>
    <topic topicid='flag'>...</topic>
    <topic topicid='tariff'>...</topic>
    ...
</body>
</text>
</TEI.2>
```

Unique identifiers can also be used to indicate coincidental relationships determined by presentation rather than textual content. Here, CONCUR is used to identify the non-adjacent passages. CONCUR works well with unique identifiers, especially since an *idref* attribute must refer to a unique identifier defined in the same document instance. Thus, when CONCUR is being used, an *idref* attribute cannot refer to an element in a different view. For example, using "leg" to mean "legibility", "s" for "stain", "i" for "ink blot", "t" for "torn", suppose the purpose of the encoding is to indicate passages' legibility. The new DTD might be as follows:

```
<!DOCTYPE leg [
<!ELEMENT leg (#PCDATA | s | i | t)+ >
<!ELEMENT s (#PCDATA) >
<!ATTLIST (s, i, t) id
   ID #IMPLIED
      segid IDREF #IMPLIED >
]>
```

If "rhs.p23" is the unique identifier indicating "right-hand side of page 23", a typical document sequence might be:

... Random statistical quirk for the day: the word "no" appears 1344 times in the King James Bible, but the <(leg)s id=rhs.p23>word</(leg)s> "yes" appears only twice! (Grep for<(leg)s segid=rhs.p23> yourself if yo</(leg)s>u don't believe me). At<(leg)s segid=rhs.p23> first I thought thi</(leg)s>s was just a hilarious<(leg)s segid=rhs.p23> artifact of religious</(leg)s> dogma, so I chec<(leg)s segid=rhs.p23>ked Alice in Wonderlan</(leg)s>d – – "yes" appears onl<(leg)s segid=rhs.p23> y once! Curiouser </(leg)s>and curiouser. Well it<(leg)s segid=rhs.p23> turns out to be </(leg)s> a property of English (yes<(leg)s segid=rhs.p23>/no =.0</(leg)s>66 on average), and when you consider why this might be, it's undoubtedly due to the fact...[12]

A register of stains, similar to the above register of topics, can be used to provide more symmetric markup.

3.2 *Repeating related material*

A second solution is simply to gather the related segments in one place and repeat them. This solution is appropriate for short passages, such as relationships among discontiguous portions of a word. Thus the Arabic root mentioned above might be encoded as:

```
<word root=KTB>al-kaatib</word>
```

or

```
<word>
   <root>KTB</root>
   <form>al-kaatib</form>
</word>
```

The first variation emphasizes that *ktb* is the result of analysis rather than part of the text being lemmatized.

3.3 *Aligning non-adjacent passages*

The alignment map illustrated under Section 2.4 can also be applied to the problems described in this section.

4. Handling Ambiguous Content

The next problem addressed is that of encoding multiple analyses of the same content. Examples include:

- multiple parsings of the gross syntactic structure of the sentence "I saw the man with the telescope";
- the pagination of various editions of Shakespeare's *Hamlet*.

4.1 *Concurrent markup*

The first solution uses CONCUR. Each encoding (for the above examples, each edition, or each parse) is assigned a different DTD. Except for the declaration of the document element, these DTDs are essentially equivalent. Suppose the different editions of the play, for instance, are to be represented as a sequence of <**page**> elements. Within each <**page**>, the <**omitted**> element is used to indicate text that does not occur in the indicated edition. Using "F" to refer to the First Folio, "Q1" to the First Quarto, "Q2" to the Second Quarto, and "Ri" to the Riverside Shakespeare edition, the document instance set might be coded as follows:

```
<!- - Start document instance in all views: - ->
<(TEI.2)TEI.2><(f)f><(q1)q1><(q2)q2><(Ri)Ri>

<!- - Set up TEI encoding in the (TEI.2) view only - ->
<(f)omitted><(q1)omitted><(q2)omitted><(Ri)omitted>
<(TEI.2)teiHeader>...</(TEI.2)teiHeader>
</(f)omitted></(q1)omitted></(q2)omitted></(Ri)omitted>
<(TEI.2)text><(TEI.2)body>
<!- - Act 1, Scene 1 starts... - ->
<(TEI.2)div1 name='act' n='1'>

<!- - initial pagination for various editions - ->
<(F)page n='g5a'>
<(Q1)page n='3'>
<(Q2)page n='[3]'>
<(Ri)page n='234'>

<!- - Start text and indicate new pages as they occur - ->
... text of Hamlet...
</(F)page><(F)page n='g5b'>
... text of Hamlet...
</(Q2)page><(Q2)page n='4'>
```

```
... text of Hamlet...
</(Ri)page><(Ri)page n='235'>
... text of Hamlet...
</(F)page><(F)page n='g5b'>
... text of Hamlet (to end)
</(f)page></(q1)page></(q2)page></(Ri)page>
</(TEI.2)body>
</(TEI.2)text>
</(TEI.2)TEI.2>
```

The different DTDs can easily be defined using a common entity. For example, suppose the system identifier "page.dec" refers to a file with the declarations pertaining to **<page>**, **<omitted>**, and related elements. In addition this file can contain a declaration such as:

```
<!ELEMENT %version.name - - (page)* +(omitted) >
```

To define the individual DTDs, the prolog of the SGML document would repeatedly refer to this entity:

```
<DOCTYPE F system "page.dec" [<!ENTITY % version.name "F" >]>
<!DOCTYPE Q1 system "page.dec" [<!ENTITY % version.name "Q1" >]>
<!DOCTYPE Q2 system "page.dec" [<!ENTITY % version.name "Q2" >]>
<!DOCTYPE Ri system "page.dec" [<!ENTITY % version.name "Ri" >]>
```

A similar technique can be applied to ambiguous sentences. Here, however, there are no obvious meaningful names to assign the different DTDs; they can simply be called "a", "b", "c" and so on. One flaw in this method is that it limits the number of parses that can be encoded for a sentence to the number of DTDs that are defined. Furthermore, although the markup suggests a relationship between all components of one view, if a text contains more than one ambiguous sentence, there need be no special relationship between the particular parses coded under a particular DTD.[13]

4.2 *Repeated content*

Another way to represent the different interpretations is to repeat the ambiguous material, encoding a different analysis with each repetition. For example, the ambiguous sentence quoted above could be represented as:

```
<sentence>
   <parse>
      <s>
         <np>I</np>
         <vp>
            <vp>
               <v>saw</v>
               <np>the man</np>
            </vp>
            <pp>
               <p>with</p>
               <np>the telescope</np>
            </pp>
         </vp>
      </s>
   </parse>
   <parse>
```

```
      <s>
         <np>I</np>
         <vp>
            <v>saw</v>
            <np>
               <np>the man</np>
               <pp>
                  <p>with</p>
                  <np>the telescope</np>
               </pp>
            </np>
         </vp>
      </s>
   </parse>
</sentence>
```

This method works well unless CONCUR is used and the ambiguity is not common to all views. Since the repeated content is present in every view, this coding changes the content of views that do not have the ambiguity. In addition, of course, the encoding does not equate corresponding units (words, for example) of the different repetitions.

4.3 *Encoding application-specific analyses*

An element structure particular to the application can often be defined. The next encoding is based on a chart representation of two parses. In a chart, the words or tokens in a sentence are arranged on a line; arcs with endpoints between the words on this line represent the phrases formed by the words between their endpoints. The arcs are labelled with a marker indicating the phrase type.

One simple method of representing a chart in SGML is to number the words in the sentence. The points between words are then also numbered: the start of the sentence is 0 and the point after each word has the same number as the preceding word. EMPTY elements with attributes identifying the phrase marker and the endpoints then represent the arcs. The DTD might be:

```
<!DOCTYPE sentence [
<!ELEMENT sentence (text, parse*) >
<!ELEMENT text (#PCDATA) >
<!ELEMENT parse (arc)+ >
<!ELEMENT arc EMPTY >

<!ATTLIST arc marker (s, np, vp, pp, v, n, p) #IMPLIED
        s NUMBER #REQUIRED - - start of arc - -
        e NUMBER #REQUIRED - - end of arc - - >
]>
```

The sample sentence with its two analyses is then represented as:

```
<sentence>
<text>I saw the man with the telescope</text>
<parse>
<arc S s=0 e=7>
<arc NP s=0 e=1>
<arc VP s=1 e=7>
<arc VP s=1 e=4> <!- - saw the man - ->
<arc V s=1 e=2> <!- - saw - ->
<arc NP s=2 e=4> <!- - the man - ->
```

```
<arc PP s=4 e=7> <!- - with the telescope - ->
<arc P s=4 e=5> <!- - with - ->
<arc NP s=5 e=7> <!- - the telescope - ->
</parse>
<parse>
<arc S s=0 e=7>
<arc NP s=0 e=1> <!- - I - ->
<arc VP s=1 e=7>
<arc V s=1 e=2> <!- - saw - ->
<arc NP s=2 e=7> <!- - the man with the telescope - ->
<arc NP s=2 e=4> <!- - the man - ->
<arc PP s=4 e=7> <!- - with the telescope - ->
<arc P s=4 e=5> <!- - with - ->
<arc NP s=5 e=7> <!- - the telescope - ->
</parse>
</sentence>
```

Note that SGML's optional SHORTTAG feature was used in each <**arc**> start-tag above to omit the attribute name *marker* (and the separating equals sign) preceding the value of this attribute. This form of markup minimization can be used when the attribute's declared value is a name token group – an explicit list of possible values.

The above encoding does not express the relationship between words in the original sentence and the endpoints of the arcs. *id* and *idref* attributes can be added to the general method to add this information. The replacement declarations are shown below:

```
<!ELEMENT text (word)+ >
<!ELEMENT word (#PCDATA) >
<!ATTLIST sentence id ID #IMPLIED >
<!ATTLIST word id ID #IMPLIED >
<!ATTLIST arc marker (s, np, vp, pp, v, n, p) #IMPLIED
      s IDREF #REQUIRED
      e IDREF #REQUIRED >
```

Here, the *id* attribute for <**sentence**> represents the point before the first word and the *id* of each word identifies the point following it. The words themselves are good candidates for the ID values. Since the word "the" occurs twice in the sample sentence, different values must be chosen for each. The revised markup is:

```
<sentence id="s1">
   <text>
      <word id=I>I</word>
      <word id=saw>saw</word>
      <word id=the1>the</word>
      <word id=man>man</word>
      <word id=with>with</word>
      <word id=the2>the</word
      <word id=telescope>telescope</word>
   </text>
   <parse>
      <arc S s=s1 e=telescope>
      <arc NP s=s1 e=1>
      <arc VP s=I e=telescope>
      <arc VP s=I e=man>
      <arc V s=I e=saw>
      <arc NP s=saw e=man>
      <arc PP s=man e=telescope>
```

```
        <arc P s=man e=with>
        <arc NP s=with e=telescope>
    </parse>
    <parse>
        <arc S s=s1 e=telescope>
        <arc NP s=s1 e=I>
        <arc VP s=I e=telescope>
        <arc V s=I e=saw>
        <arc NP s=saw e=telescope>
        <arc NP s=saw e=man>
        <arc PP s=man e=telescope>
        <arc P s=man e=with>
        <arc NP s=with e=telescope>
    </parse>
</sentence>
```

Since the ID values have been chosen to indicate the marked phrase, the comments from the previous version have been omitted.

This solution is similar to the linguistic analysis tags described in the Guidelines. As is the case in the example, the <**fStruct**> element allows multiple analyses of the same content.

4.4 *Application-specific content*

Of course, any special notation expressed as a character string can be entered into an SGML document, although the SGML parser will not be able to validate the notation. The ambiguous sentence could be coded as follows:

```
<sentence>
    <text>I saw the man with the telescope.</text>
    <parse p='((1) (((2)(3 4)) ((5)(6 7))))'>
    <parse p='((1) ((2) ((3 4) ((5)(6 7)))))'>
</sentence>
```

Or:

```
<sentence>
    <text>I saw the man with the telescope.</text>
    <parse p='s(np(1) vp(vp(v(2) np(3 4)) pp(p(5)np(6 7))))'>
    <parse p='s(np(1) vp(v(2) np(np(3 4) pp(p(5)np(6 7)))))'>
</sentence>
```

4.5 *Ambiguities as non-hierarchical material*

The final suggestion for encoding ambiguities is simply to treat the alternatives as material that supplements the document's primary hierarchical structure, using one of the methods discussed in Section 2 above.

5. Overlapping Structures

Sometimes the boundaries of hierarchical units are not clear. Examples include:

- *She took advantage of Joan* (where *of* can be part of the single unit *took advantage of*, or part of the prepositional phrase *of Joan*)

- *Broadway Hit or Miss*
- Apo koinu constructions

Any of the methods discussed in Section 1 of this paper can be used to encode both relationships.

6. Synchronizing Parallel Structures

The next issue is encoding parallel texts in order to show corresponding segments. Examples include:

- translations, for example, into the nine languages of the EEC;
- manuscript variants (for example, of the Bible) or recensions;
- phonemic and orthographic transcriptions of the same content.

6.1 *Implicit parallelism*

As long as all versions of the text present corresponding constructs in the same order, all variations of a segment can be encoded as the subelements of a single unit. The DTD must be defined to show the alternative structures at the lowest level of the hierarchy. For example, the following declarations can be included in a DTD to indicate the corresponding phonemic and orthographic transcriptions of the words in sentences:

```
<!ELEMENT segment – O (phonemic, orthographic) >
<!ELEMENT phonemic – O (#PCDATA) >
<!ELEMENT orthographic – O (#PCDATA) >
```

The encoding of a particular sentence might begin like this:

```
<sentence>
   &lt;segment&gt;
      <phonemic> (phonemic transcription of 'the')
      <orthographic>the
   &lt;segment&gt;
      <phonemic> (phonemic transcription of'fat')
      <orthographic>fat
   &lt;segment&gt;
      <phonemic> (phonemic transcription of 'cat')
      <orthographic>cat
...
```

Note that end-tags for <**segment**>, <**phonemic**>, and <**orthographic**> are omitted above. SGML allows this form of markup minimization when a parser, following a strictly defined algorithm, can detect the end of the element without it, and the optional OMITTAG feature has been selected.

6.2 *Synchronizing with unique identifiers*

When the order of segments varies from one text to another, the correspondence can be indicated with *id* and *idref* attributes. In the following translation, successive phrases from the first language are numbered so they can be referenced in the other version:

```
<sentence>
   <translation German>
      <seg id=p1>Tor
```

```
        <seg id=p2>nach Durchfahrt
        <seg id=p3>bitte
        <seg id=p4>zumachen!
    </translation>
    <translation English>
        <seg id=p3>Please
        <seg id=p4>close
        <seg id=p1>the gate
        <seg id=p2>after passing through!
    </translation>
</sentence>
```

A more elaborate version of this same mechanism, allowing for one-to-many matching of segments, is found in the alignment mechanism of Chapter 14 of the Guidelines.

6.3 *Synchronizing with analysis elements*

The segments of parallel texts may appear in different orders without a one-to-one matching in the different versions. In this case, the <**alignment**> element illustrated in Section 2.4 can be used.

7. Cross-References

The next problem is how to refer to locations elsewhere in the same document or in a separate document. *id* and *idref* attributes provide a natural method of coding internal cross-references. For example, if a DTD contains the following declaration:

```
<!ATTLIST setting
    id ID #IMPLIED
    same IDREF #IMPLIED
>
```

a document instance might contain markup such as:

```
<act>
<scene><setting>A heath</setting>...
<scene><setting>A camp near Forres</setting>...
<scene><setting>A heath near Forres</setting>...
<scene><setting id=palace>Forres. The palace</setting>...
<scene><setting>Inverness. Macbeth's castle</setting>...
<scene><setting>Before Macbeth's castle</setting>...
<scene><setting id=within>Within Macbeth's castle</setting>...
<act>
<scene><setting same=within></setting>...
<scene><setting same=within>The same</setting>...
<scene><setting same=within>The same</setting>...
<scene><setting>Outside Macbeth's castle</setting>...
<act>
<scene><setting same=palace>...
```

As with all other *id* and *idref* attributes, the SGML parser verifies that the value of attribute *same* is always the value of an *id* attribute somewhere in the document instance. Aside from checking for errors, however, it does no special processing of the attribute. If, for example, the setting of Act II, Scene I is to be printed as "Within Macbeth's castle" by copying the text from the cross-referenced setting, it is the responsibility of application software to copy this text.

Since the value of an *idref* attribute must be the value of an *id* attribute elsewhere in the same document instance, *idref* attributes cannot be used for external cross-references. However, an attribute with the declared value NAME can be used to enter an ID value from another document. The external document can be identified by a second attribute of the same element. The declared value of this attribute can be ENTITY, to indicate that the external document is identified by the external identifier in an entity declaration, or it can be NAME or CDATA, to indicate that the external document is identified by a string that the application knows how to interpret. The use of the *entity* attribute is illustrated below:

```
<!ENTITY macbeth SYSTEM "macbeth.doc" SUBDOC>
<!ENTITY hamlet SYSTEM "hamlet.doc" SUBDOC>
...
<setting play=hamlet id=graveyard> and <setting play=macbeth
id=castle> have much in common
...
```

When the possible external documents are known in advance, a variation of this scheme can build the document identifiers into generic identifiers in the DTD. The above example could then be coded as:

```
<hamlet id=graveyard> and <macbeth id=castle>
have much in common...
```

8. Vagueness of Location

The final issue addressed in this paper is encoding segments with endpoints that are not well defined. Researchers may wish to encode details such as an echo of another text, which may begin and end gradually, so that the markup indicates a section that is certainly an echo, surrounded by a penumbra that may or may not represent an echo. Thus, the researcher tagging the document must be able to express opinions such as:

- "the passage begins somewhere along here"
- "the passage begins somewhere between these points"

8.1 *Precision attributes*[14]

Add a *precision* attribute to the element whose location is uncertain. The possible values of this attribute can be keywords such as "vague", "definite", "probable" or can be integers in which greater values indicate the tagger's greater confidence.

8.2 *Marking text ranges*

Mark both the start and end of the range of text where each endpoint of the passage may occur. The range can be marked by elements with declared content of EMPTY:

```
<echostart range=start>...<echostart range=end>
...
<echoend range=start>...<echoend range=end>
```

Alternatively, nested elements can be used:

```
<penumbra>
...
<echo>...</echo> ...
</penumbra>
```

or

```
<echo status=possible>
...
<echo status=certain>...</echo>
...
</echo>
```

9. Conclusions

The TEI metalanguage committee explored several practical problems of text encoding and illustrated SGML solutions that are compatible with TEI encoding. This paper has presented several techniques applicable to a range of issues and to classes of documents ranging from particular editions of historical works, through grammatical analyses, to transcripts of interviews and meeting minutes. Instead of recommending a particular approach, the paper has provided several possibilities, giving the reader criteria that can be used to select the variation must suited to requirements of particular projects. In the process of describing these techniques, the paper has introduced some constructs of SGML not covered in other TEI papers. The examples illustrate that SGML's flexibility allows it to capture the essential hierarchical nature of text while at the same time addressing properties that do not fit neatly into the hierarchy.

The ideas in this paper influenced the work of committees and work groups,[15] and can serve as useful background for researchers intending to extend the Guidelines for marking other non-hierarchic structures.

Notes

[1] This paper is derived from a working paper of the Metalanguage Committee entitled "Notes on SGML Solutions to Markup Problems" which was produced following a meeting of the committee in Luxembourg. The co-authors all participated in that meeting and provided input to this paper. Others serving on the committee at other times included David Durand (Boston University), Nancy Ide (Vassar College) and Frank Tompa (University of Waterloo).

[2] ISO (International Organization for Standardization). *ISO 8879–1986 (E). Information Processing – Text and Office Systems – Standard Generalized Markup Language (SGML).* Also *ISO 8879–1986:1986/A1:1988(E). Information Processing – Text and Office Systems – Standard Generalized Markup Language (SGML) Amendment 1.* [Geneva]: International Organization for Standardization, 1986 and 1988. See also Lou Burnard, "What Is SGML and How Does It Help?", in this volume.

[3] This is not precisely true, as will become clear below. SGML does have a method for representing concurrent hierarchies, but there was concern from the beginning of the project about the applicability of the CONCUR feature.

[4] Perhaps from reading Lou Burnard's paper in this volume.

[5] Steven J. DeRose and David G. Durand, "The TEI Hypertext Guidelines", in this volume.

[6] See Chapters 29 and, to a lesser extent, 28 of the Guidelines.

[7] Or more elaborately, the passage marked by straight lines in the left margin, the passage marked by wavy lines in the left margin, the passage underlined by hand with a simple straight line, the passage underlined by hand with a simple straight line which was later deleted by hand, etc., as in the transcriptions of Wittgenstein's manuscripts in the Norwegian Wittgenstein project. See Claus Huitfeldt and Viggo Rossvoer, *The Norwegian Wittgenstein Project Report 1988* ([Bergen]: NAVFs EDB-Senter for Humanistisk Forskning/Norwegian Centre for the Humanities, 1989), especially, pp. 201–236.

[8] This **<action>** element is similar to the **<milestone>** defined in the TEI Guidelines for segmentation of text according to pagination of multiple editions. However, **<milestone>** assumes a simple single-level segmentation of the text: the attribute values specified in any **<milestone>** element apply to all following text until the next **<milestone>** belonging to the same edition. Hence, no explicit end marker is needed and the *Id/idref* mechanism is not needed.

[9] Note that in the tag set for transcribing spoken text as actually published in P3, a different solution was adopted for this problem, involving the use of an empty "event" element synchronized by means of a mechanism similar to that described elsewhere in this article.

[10] This is essentially how most of the analytic elements discussed in Chapters 14 and 15 of P3 work.

[11] An equivalent facility is provided in P3 by the <**span**> element.
[12] Humanist 3.769, Tue, 21 Nov 89, posting from mike@tome.media.mit.edu (Michael Hawley).
[13] This method is further discussed in chapter 31 of P3.
[14] See also Chapter 17 of the Guidelines.
[15] And of the two editors, who were involved in these discussions.

Computers and the Humanities **00:** 233–242, 1995.

SGML/TEI Bibliography *

Robin C. Cover

Aberer, Karl; Böhm, Klemens; Hüser, Christoph. "The Prospects of Publishing Using Advanced Database Concepts." *Electronic Publishing: Origination, Dissemination and Design* 6/4 (December 1993) 469-480. ISSN: 0894-3982. Online document URL: ftp://ftp.darmstadt.gmd.de/pub/dimsys/reports/P-93-23.ps.Z.

Adler, Sharon C. "The Birth of a Standard (SGML)." *Journal of the American Society for Information Science* 43/8 (September 1992) 556-558. ISSN: 0002-8231.

Adler, Sharon C. "DSSSL — Document Style Semantics and Specification Language." *<TAG>* 1/8 (January 1989) 8-9.

Alschuler, Liora. *SGML: A User's Guide to Structured Information.* Van Nostrand Reinhold, [forthcoming] 1995. ISBN: 0-442-01858-4 (VNR); ISBN: 1-850-32197-3 (International Thomson Computer Press).

Amsler, Robert A.; Tompa, Frank W. "An SGML-Based Standard for English Monolingual Dictionaries." In *Fourth Annual Conference of the UW Centre for the New Oxford English Dictionary: Information in Text. Proceedings of the Conference.* Waterloo, Ontario, Canada, 26-28 October 1988. Waterloo, Ontario: University of Waterloo, 1988, pp. 61-79.

André, Jacques; Furuta, Richard Keith; Quint, Vincent (editors). *Structured Documents.* The Cambridge Series on Electronic Publishing. Cambridge/New York: Cambridge University Press, 1989. vii + 220 pages, with bibliographic references and index [193-213]. ISBN: 0-521-36554-6.

Angerstein, Paula. "An Introduction to the Document Style Semantics and Specification Language (DSSSL): A Description of the DSSSL Standard and on Its Status." *CALS Journal* (Spring 1993) 67-72.

Arbortext, Inc. *Getting Started with SGML: A Guide to the Standard Generalized Markup Language and Its Role in Information Management.* ArborText White Paper. Ann Arbor, MI: ArborText, Inc., 1995.

Association for Computers and the Humanities (ACH), Association for Computational Linguistics (ACL), and Association for Literary and Linguistic Computing (ALLC). *Guidelines for Electronic Text Encoding and Interchange (TEI P3).* Eds. C. M. Sperberg-McQueen and Lou Burnard. 2 volumes. Chicago, Oxford: Text Encoding Initiative, 1994. xxvi + 1290 pages.

Association of American Publishers. *Author's Guide to Electronic Manuscript Preparation and Markup.* 2nd edition, reprinted 1989. AAP, November 1987. ISBN: 1-55653-086-2.

Association of American Publishers. *The Markup of Mathematical Formulas.* 2nd edition, reprinted 1989. AAP, November 1987. ISBN:1-55653-083-8.

Association of American Publishers. *The Markup of Tabular Material.* 2nd edition, reprinted 1989. AAP, November 1987. ISBN: 1-55653-085-4.

Association of American Publishers. *Reference Manual on Electronic Manuscript Preparation and Markup.* 2nd edition, reprinted 1989. AAP, November 1987. ISBN: 1-55653-084-6.

Ballanti, Anna; Cork, Deborah; Dam, Lex van; Jonghe, Jurgen de; Herwijnen, Eric van; Nijdam, Marco; Samarin, Alexandre; Shave, Tony. "Text Processing at CERN. Part 1: Overview." *SGML Users' Group Bulletin* 3/2 (1988) 39-54.

Barnard, David; Burnard, Lou; Gaspart, Jean-Pierre; Price, Lynne A.; Sperberg-McQueen, C. M.; Varile, Giovanni Battista. "Hierarchical Encoding of Text: Technical Problems and SGML Solutions." *The Text Encoding Initiative: Background and Context*, Guest Editors Nancy Ide and Jean Véronis = *Computers and the Humanities* 29/3 (1995) 211–231. Also in this volume.

Barnard, David T.; Fraser, Cheryl A.; Logan, George M. "Generalized Markup for Literary Texts." *Literary and Linguistic Computing* 3/1 (1988) 26-31.

Barnard, David T.; Hayter, Ron; Karababa, Maria; Logan, George M.; McFadden, John. "SGML Based Markup for Literary Texts: Two Problems and Some Solutions." *Computers and the Humanities* 22/4 (1988) 265-276. ISSN: 0010-4817.

Barnard, David T.; Macleod, Ian A. *Maestro Working Paper 0: An Archive of Structured Texts.* Technical Report 89-262. Kingston, Ontario: Department of Computing and Information Science, Queen's University at Kingston, Kingston, Ontario, Canada, November 14, 1989. 10 pages.

Barnes, Julie A.; Mamrak, Sandra A. "A Model and Toolset for the Uniform Tagging of Encoded Documents." *Electronic Publishing: Origination, Dissemination and Design* 4/2 (June 1991) 63-85 (with 38 references).

* The following reference list has been extracted from a larger online bibliographic database covering SGML and structured document processing. Abstracts and other details are frequently omitted in the following list. The fuller online version is accessible via Internet WWW using any standard client software: http://www.sil.org/sgml/sgml.html.

Barron, David. "Why Use SGML?" *Electronic Publishing: Origination, Dissemination and Design* 2/1 (April 1989) 3-24. ISSN: 0894-3982.

Bauman, Syd. "Tables of Contents TEI-Style." *Electronic Texts and the Text Encoding Initiative [Special Issue] = TEXT Technology: The Journal of Computer Text Processing* 5/3 (Autumn, 1995) 235-247. ISSN: 1053-900X.

Bauwens, B.; Engelen, J.; Evenepoel F.; Tobin, C. "Structuring Documents: The Key to Increasing Access to Information for the Print Disabled." In *Computers for Handicapped Persons. 4th International Conference [Vienna, Austria, 14-16 September 1994], ICCHP '94 Proceedings*. Edited by Zagler, W. L.; Busby, G.; Wagner, R. R. Lecture Notes in Computer Science, No. 860. Berlin, Germany: Springer-Verlag, 1994, pp. 214-221. The article describes a European Union funded project within the Technology Initiative for Disabled and Elderly People (TIDE) Programme, and ICADD, the International Committee on Accessible Document Design. Within these projects, SGML plays an important role as an enabling technology to increase access to information for blind and partially sighted people.

Bauwens, B.; Evenepoel, F.; Engelen, J. J. "Standardization as a Prerequisite for Accessibility of Electronic Text Information for Persons Who Cannot Use Printed Material." *IEEE Transactions on Rehabilitation Engineering* 3/1 (March 1995) 84-89.

Becker, Dave. "UTF: an SGML Standard for the News Distribution Industry." *Seybold Report on Publishing Systems* 24/10 (January 30, 1995) 1, 7-17. UTF is the "Universal Text Format" representing an SGML application for the news distribution industry. Development of UTF is largely under the IPTC (International Press Telecommunications Council) and NAA (Newspaper Association of America).

Berglund, Anders. "SGML — What is It?" In *Proceedings of SEAS Anniversary Meeting 1985: User Friendly Computing* (Zurich 23-27 September 1985). Nijmegen: SHARE Eur. Association, 1985, 1:187-194

Blake, G. E.; Consens, M. P.; Kilpelainen, P.; Larson, P. A.; Snider, T.; Tompa, Frank W. "Text/Relational Database Management Systems: Harmonizing SQL and SGML." In *Applications of Databases. Proceedings of the First International Conference*. 1994 International Conference on Applications of Databases, ADB 94., Vadstena, Sweden, 21-23 June 1994. Berlin: Springer Verlag, 1994, pp. 267-280. ISBN: 3-540-58183-9.

Böhm, Klemens; Aberer, Karl; Hüser, Christoph. "Introducing D-STREAT: The Impact of Advanced Database Technology on SGML Document Storage." *<TAG>: The SGML Newsletter* 7/2 (February 1994) 1-4. ISSN: 1067-9197.

Böhm, Klemens; Aberer, Karl; Neuhold, Erich. "Administering Structured Documents in Digital Libraries". In *Advances in Digital Libraries*, edited by Adam, N. R.; Bhargava, B. K.; Yesha, Y. Lecture Notes in Computer Science. Berlin/New York: Springer Verlag, 1995, pp. 91-117 (with 29 references). Online document URL: ftp://ftp.darmstadt.gmd.de/pub/dimsys/reports/P-94-25.ps.Z.

Brown, Allen L., Jr.; Wakayama, Toshiro; Blair, Howard A. "A Reconstruction of Context-Dependent Document Processing in SGML." In *EP [Electronic Publishing] 92: Proceedings of Electronic Publishing, 1992* International Conference on Electronic Publishing, Document Manipulation, and Typography. Swiss Federal Institute of Technology, Lausanne, Switzerland. April 7-10, 1992. Sponsored by the Swiss Federal Institute of Technology and the Swiss National Science Foundation. Edited by Christine Vanoirbeek and Giovanni Coray. The Cambridge Series on Electronic Publishing. Cambridge: Cambridge University Press, 1992, pp. 1-25 (with 10 references). ISBN: 0-521-43277-4.

Brüggemann-Klein, Anne. *Compiler-Construction Tools and Techniques for SGML Parsers: Difficulties and Solutions*. Technical Report. Freiburg: Institut für Informatik, Universität Freiburg, May 29, 1994.

Brüggemann-Klein, Anne. *Formal Models in Document Processing*. Habilitationsschrift, vogelegt zur Erlangung der venia legendi für Informatik an der Mathematischen Fakultät der Albert-Ludwigs-Universität zu Freiburg i.Br. Freiburg, 1993. 110 pages, bibliography, index. Document URL: ftp://ftp.informatik.uni-freiburg.de/documents/papers/brueggem/habil.ps.

Brüggemann-Klein, Anne. "Unambiguity of Extended Regular Expressions in SGML Document Grammars." In *Algorithms — ESA '93: Proceedings of the First Annual European Symposium*. Bad Honnef, Germany. September 30 - October 2, 1993. Ed. Th. Lengauer. Lecture Notes in Computer Science, 726. Berlin: Springer Verlag, 1993, pp. 73-84. ISBN: 3540572732; ISSN: 0302-9743.

Brüggemann-Klein, Anne; Wood, Derek. "Deterministic Regular Languages." In *STACS '92: Proceedings of the 9th Annual Symposium on Theoretical Aspects of Computer Science*. Cachan, France, 13-15 February 1992. Ed. A. Finkel and M. Jantzen. Lecture Notes in Computer Science, 577. Berlin: Springer Verlag, 1992, pp. 173-184. ISBN: 3-540-55210-3.

Brüggemann-Klein, Anne; Wood, Derick. *The Validation of SGML Content Models*. Technical Report # 355. London, Ontario: Department of Computer Science, University of Western Ontario, London, Ontario, 21 March 1993. 15 pages, 13 references. ISBN: 0771415028.

Bryan, Martin. *SGML: An Author's Guide to the Standard Generalized Markup Language*. Wokingham/Reading/New York: Addison-Wesley, 1988. 380 pages. ISBN: 0-201-17535-5.

Buford, J. F.; Rutledge, L.; Rutledge, J. L. "Integrating Object-oriented Scripting Languages with HyTime." In *Proceedings of the International Conference on Multimedia Computing and Systems*. IEEE International Conference on Multimedia Computing and Systems, Boston, MA, USA, 15-19 May, 1994. Sponsored by IEEE Computer Society Task Force on Multimedia Computing. Los Alamitos, CA: IEEE Computer Society Press, 1994, pp. 425-434.

Burnage, Gavin; Dunlop, Dominic. "Encoding the British National Corpus." In *English Language Corpora: Design, Analysis and Exploitation.* Ed. Jan Aarts, Pieter de Haan and Nelleke Oostdijk. Amsterdam and Atlanta: Editions Rodopi, 1993, pp. 79-95.

Burnard, Lou (guest editor). *Electronic Texts and the Text Encoding Initiative.* A Special Issue [5.3] of *TEXT Technology: The Journal of Computer Text Processing.* Madison, SD: College of Liberal Arts, Dakota State University, [George M. and Merrill D. Hunter Electronic Publishing Center], Autumn 1995. ISSN: 1053-900X. This special issue (Autumn 1995) of *TEXT Technology* has contributions by: Eric Johnson; Lou Burnard [this entry, and the "Introduction"]; Jeffery Triggs; John Price-Wilkin; Susan E. Kruse; Laurent Romary, Nathalie Mehl, and David Woolls; James K. Tauber; Syd Bauman; C. M. Sperberg-McQueen.

Burnard, Lou. "An Introduction to the Text Encoding Initiative." In *Modelling Historical Data: Towards a Standard for Encoding and Exchanging Machine-Readable Texts.* Edited by Daniel Greenstein. Halbgraue Reihe zur Historischen Fachinformatik, Serie A, Historische Quellenkunden, edited by Manfred Thaller, Band (A) 11. St. Katharinen: [Published for the Max-Planck-Institut für Geschiche, Göttingen by] Scripta Mercaturae Verlag, 1991, pp. 81-91. iv + 223 pages. ISBN: 3-928134-45-0.

Burnard, Lou. "Rolling Your Own with the TEI." *Information Services and Use* [Workshop on Hypermedia and Hypertext Standards, Amsterdam, Netherlands, 22-23 April 1993. Sponsored by CEC.] 13/2 (1993) 141-154.

Burnard, Lou. "What is SGML and How Does It Help?" *The Text Encoding Initiative: Background and Context,* Guest Editors Nancy Ide and Jean Véronis = *Computers and the Humanities* 29/1 (1995) 41-50. Also in this volume.

Burnard, Lou; Sperberg-McQueen, C. Michael. *TEI Lite: An Introduction to Text Encoding for Interchange.* TEI Tutorial, TEI Document No. TEI U5. Oxford and Chicago: Text Encoding Initiative [ACH/ALLC/ACL], June, 1995. Extent: approximately 200K (HTML format). URL: http://www-tei.uic.edu/orgs/tei/intros/.

Carr, L. A.; Barron, D. W.; Davis, H. C.; Hall, W. "Why Use HyTime?" *Electronic Publishing: Origination, Dissemination and Design* 7/3 (September 1994) 163-178. ISSN: 0894-3982.

Carr, L.; Davis, H.; Hall, W. "Experimenting with HyTime Architectural Forms for Hypertext Interchange." *Information Services and Use* [Workshop on Hypermedia and Hypertext Standards, Amsterdam, Netherlands, 22-23 April 1993. Sponsored by CEC.] 13/2 (1993) 111-119 (with 4 references).

Cave, Francis. "Information Handling Techniques for the Office: Untangling the Standards Web." In *Information Handling Techniques for the Office: Full Text Rules OA (Office Automation)? Proceedings of the Institute of Information Scientists Text Retrieval '86 Conference* (London 1986). Edited by Susan Hills. London: Taylor Graham, 1987, pp. 100-110. ISBN 0-947568-33-6.

Chamberlin, Donald Dean; Goldfarb, Charles F. "Graphic Applications of the Standard Generalized Markup Language (SGML)." *Computers and Graphics* 11/4 (1987) 343-358 (with 6 references). ISSN: 0097-8493.

Chisholm, David; Robey, David. "Encoding Verse Texts." *The Text Encoding Initiative: Background and Context,* Guest Editors Nancy Ide and Jean Véronis = *Computers and the Humanities* 29/2 (1995) 99–111. Also in this volume.

Christophides, Vassilis; Abitebol, Serge; Cluet, Sophie; Scholl, Michel. "From Structured Documents to Novel Query Facilities." *SIGMOD Record* [1994 ACM SIGMOD International Conference on Management of Data, Minneapolis, MN, USA, 24-27 May 1994] 23/2 (June 1994) 313-324 (with 28 references).

Clark, Malcolm "A Note Comparing TEX to SGML." *SGML Users' Group Bulletin* 3/2 (1988) 67-68. ISSN: 0269-2538. The note is a response to the article of Lynne Price, "A Note Comparing SGML to Text Processing Macro Languages," *SGML Users' Group Bulletin* 2/2 (1987) 127.

Coombs, James H.; Renear, Allen H.; DeRose, Steven J. "Markup Systems and the Future of Scholarly Text Processing." *Communications of the Association for Computing Machinery* 30/11 (1987) 933-947. ISSN: 0001-0782. A landmark publication offering defense of descriptive and standard markup as a basis for document interchange. This seminal article is now reprinted in *The Digital Word: Text-Based Computing in the Humanities,* eds. George P. Landow and Paul Delaney (Cambridge/London: MIT Press, 1993) 85-118.

Cover, Robin. "SGML: Annotated Bibliography and List of Resources." *<TAG>* 5/3 (March 1992) 4, [1-12]; 5/4 (April 1992) 4, [13-24]; 5/5 (May 1992) 4, [25-36]. A three-part article covering SGML bibliography and resources in 10 major categories, including SGML software available on the Internet.

Cover, Robin; Duncan, Nicholas; Barnard, David. "The Progress of SGML (Standard Generalized Markup Language): Extracts from a Comprehensive Bibliography." *Literary and Linguistic Computing* 6/3 (1991) 197-209. ISSN: 0268-1145.

Cover, Robin; Duncan, Nicholas; Barnard, David. *Bibliography on SGML (Standard Generalized Markup Language) and Related Issues.* Technical Report 91-299. Kingston, Ontario: Queen's University, Kingston, Ontario, February, 1991. 312 pages. ISSN 0836-0227.

Cover, Robin; Robinson, Peter. "Encoding Textual Criticism." *The Text Encoding Initiative: Background and Context,* Guest Editors Nancy Ide and Jean Véronis = *Computers and the Humanities* 29/2 (1995) 123–136. Also in this volume.

Cruz, Gil C.; Judd, Thomas J. "The Role of a Descriptive Markup Language in the Creation of Interactive Multimedia Documents for Customized Electronic Delivery." In *Electronic Publishing '90: Proceedings of the International Conference on Electronic Publishing, Document Manipulation and Typography* (Gaithersburg, Maryland,

September 1990). Ed. Richard Furuta. The Cambridge Series on Electronic Publishing. Cambridge: Cambridge University Press, 1990, pp. 277-290. x + 298 pages, index. ISBN: 0-521-40246-8.

Derose, Steven J. "Markup Systems in the Present." In *The Digital Word: Text-Based Computing in the Humanities*. Edited by George P. Landow and Paul Delaney. Technical Communication and Information Systems. Cambridge/London: MIT Press, 1993, pp. 119-135. xii + 326 pages. ISBN: 026212176X.

DeRose, Steven J.; Durand, David G. *Making Hypermedia Work: A User's Guide to HyTime*. Boston/Dordrecht/London: Kluwer Academic Publishers, 1994. xxii + 384 pages. ISBN: 0-7923-9432-1. A very readable introduction to SGML is provided in Chapter 3 of this book (pages 35-61 = "Overview of SGML"). HyTime is an ISO standard (ISO/IEC 10744) and is an application of SGML for hypermedia and other time-based documents.

DeRose, Steven J.; Durand, David. "The TEI Hypertext Guidelines." *The Text Encoding Initiative: Background and Context*, Guest Editors Nancy Ide and Jean Véronis = *Computers and the Humanities* 29/3 (1995) 181–190. Also in this volume.

DeRose, Steven J.; Durand, David G.; Mylonas, Elli; Renear, Allen H. "What is Text, Really?" *Journal of Computing in Higher Education* 1/2 (Winter 1990) 3-26. ISSN: 1042-1726.

Dobrowolski, Andrew E. "Typesetting SGML Documents Using TeX." *TUGboat [issue = Proceedings of the 1991 Annual Meeting]* 12/3 (1991) 409-414.

Dunlop, Dominic. "Practical Considerations in the Use of TEI Headers in Large Corpora." *The Text Encoding Initiative: Background and Context*, Guest Editors Nancy Ide and Jean Véronis = *Computers and the Humanities* 29/1 (1995) 85-98. Also in this volume.

Electronic Book Technologies (EBT). *Guidelines for Electronic Text Encoding and Interchange*. Ed. C. M. Sperberg McQueen and Lou Burnard. Published for and copyright of the ACH/ALLC/ACL. Electronic Book Library, Volume 2. Providence, RI: Electronic Book Technologies, 1994. ISBN: 1-886034-00-1. This publication is an electronic edition of TEI P3, created with [EBT's] DynaText, offers many advantages over the original print edition. All cross references within the Guidelines have been converted to dynamic hypertext links. Each mention of an SGML tag is linked to a detailed glossary window. All technical terms are indexed for immediate search and retrieval.

Ellison, Paul A. "Introduction to SGML Concepts." In *Proceedings of the IEE Colloquium on 'Adding Value to Documents with Markup Languages'*. London, UK, 6-June-1994. IEE Colloquium Digest No.1994/142. London, UK: IEE, 1994, pp. 1/1-1/5.

Ellison, Paul A. "SGML and Related Information Standards." In *Document Exchange: The Use of SGML in the UK Academic and Research Community. Workshop Proceedings 5-7 March 1990*. [Loughborough]: Advisory Group on Computer Graphics, 1990, pp. 17-28 (1-12).

Ensign, Chet. *Managing Information in an Age of Change: SGML in Action*. Charles F. Goldfarb Series On Open Information Management. Englewood Cliffs, NJ: PTR Prentice Hall, [forthcoming Fall] 1995.

Exoterica Corporation. *The Compleat SGML*. CD-ROM. Ottawa, Ontario: Exoterica Corporation, August, 1993. This hypertext tool for Microsoft Windows (using an Asymetrix Toolkit) links the full online text of the *ISO8879:1986 SGML* standard with 2348 SGML test documents.

Exoterica Corporation. *Content Model Algebra*. Technical Paper ECM11-1091. Release 2. Ottawa, Ontario: Exoterica Corporation, 6 June 1991. v + 18 pages.

Exoterica Corporation. *Record Boundary Processing in SGML*. Technical Paper ETR13-1092. Release 2. Ottawa, Ontario: Exoterica Corporation, 22 October 1992. iv + 7 pages.

Exoterica Corporation. *Understanding the SGML Declaration*. Technical Report ECM03-1092. Release 2.2. Ottawa, Ontario: Exoterica Corporation, October 23, 1992. iv + 40 pages.

Fahmy, Eanass; Barnard, David T. "Adding Hypertext Links to an Archive of Documents." *Canadian Journal of Information Science* 15/3 (September 1990) 26-41.

Ferris, Ralph E.; Newcomb, Victoria Taussig (ed). *HyTime Application Development Guide*. Version 1.2. San Jose, CA and Rochester, NY: Fujitsu Open Systems Solutions and TechnoTeacher, Inc., May, 1995. 8 chapters, approximately 95 pages. Document URL: ftp://ftp.techno.com/pub/HyTime/ Application_Development_Guide.

Fought, John; Wesler, Marcia; Davenport, Heather; Van Ess-Dykema, Carol. "Extending SGML Concurrent Structures: Toward Computer-Readable Meta-Dictionaries." *Literary and Linguistic Computing* 8/1 (1993) 33-38 (with 8 references). ISSN: 0268-1145.

Fraser, Cheryl A. *An Encoding Standard for Literary Documents*. Masters Thesis. Kingston, Ontario, Department of Computing and Information Science, Queens University. April, 1986.

Gaspart, Jean-Pierre. "Use of the SGML Parser at the Office for Official Publications of the European Communities (OPOCE)." *SGML Users' Group Bulletin* 2/1 (1987) 29-36.

Gaylord, Harry. "Character Representation." *The Text Encoding Initiative: Background and Context*, Guest Editors Nancy Ide and Jean Véronis = *Computers and the Humanities* 29/1 (1995) 51-73. Also in this volume.

Gaynor, E. "Cataloging Electronic Texts: The University of Virginia Library Experience." *Library Resources and Technical Services* 38/4 (October 1994) 403-413.

Gennusa, Pamela L. "Advantages of an SGML Implementation for Management of an Electronic Text Database." *SGML Users' Group Bulletin* 2/2 (1987) 73-86.

Gennusa, Pamela. "President's Report: Recent Developments Regarding [SGML] Conformance Testing." *SGML Users' Group Bulletin Newsletter* 26 (February 1994) 2-4 [7]. ISSN: 0952-8008.

Giordano, Richard. "The Documentation of Electronic Texts Using Text Encoding Initiative Headers: An Introduction." *Library Resources & Technical Services* 38/4 (October 1994) 389-401 (with 10 references).

Giordano, Richard. "The TEI Header and the Documentation of Electronic Texts." *The Text Encoding Initiative: Background and Context*, Guest Editors Nancy Ide and Jean Véronis = *Computers and the Humanities* 29/1 (1995) 75-84. Also in this volume.

Goldfarb, Charles F. (editor). *Document Composition Facility [DCF]: Generalized Markup Language (GML) User's Guide.* First edition, July 1978. Document Number SH20-9160-0, corresponding to Program Number 5748-XX9. IBM Corporation, 1978. x + 166 pages. This publication represents one of the clearest and most accessible presentations of IBM's GML (Generalized Markup Language). Many of the specific markup constructs and notation conventions which were implemented in SGML were derived from analogues in IBM's GML.

Goldfarb, Charles F. "A Generalized Approach to Document Markup." *SIGPLAN Notices [= Proceedings of the ACM SIGPLAN SIGOA Symposium on Text Manipulation]* (ACM SIGPLAN SIGOA Symposium on Text Manipulation, Portland, Oregon, June 8-10, 1981) 16/6 (1981) 68-73.

Goldfarb, Charles F. *The SGML Handbook.* Edited and with a foreword by Yuri Rubinsky. Oxford: Oxford University Press, 1990. 688 pages. ISBN: 0-19-853737-1. The handbook contains the full annotated text of ISO 8879 (with amendments) and provides detailed commentary on the SGML standard.

Goldfarb, Charles F. "Standards — HyTime: A Standard for Structured Hypermedia Interchange." *IEEE Computer* 24/8 (August 1991) 81-84.

Gonnet, Gaston. *Examples of PAT Applied to the Oxford English Dictionary.* Technical Report OED-87-02. Waterloo, Ontario: University of Waterloo Centre for the New Oxford English Dictionary, July, 1987.

Gonnet, Gaston; Tompa, Frank W. *Mind Your Grammar: A New Approach to Modelling Text.* Technical Report OED-87-01. Waterloo, Ontario: University of Waterloo Centre for the New Oxford English Dictionary, February, 1987.

Goossens, Michel; Herwijnen, Eric van. "Scientific Text Processing." *International Journal of Modern Physics. C, Physics and Computers* 3/3 (June 1992) 479-547 (with 71 references). ISSN: 0129-1831.

Gordon, Thomas F. "The QWERTZ Synthesis of SGML and LATEX." *Computer Standards and Interfaces* 17/1 (January 1995) 25-33.

Graphic Communications Association. *GCA Standard 101-1983. Document Markup Metalanguage. Gencode and the Standard Generalized Markup Language (SGML).* Edited (in part) by Charles F. Goldfarb. Arlington, Virginia: The Graphic Communications Association, 1983. xxiv + 263 pages. ISBN: 0-89740-244-8.

Graphic Communications Association. *The SGML Source Guide. The Graphic Communications Association's Guide to Standard Generalized Markup Language (SGML) Systems, Software, Service, Consultants, Seminars and Resources.* Edited by Marion Elledge. Alexandria, VA: Graphic Communications Association, February, 1991. Form: 6" x 8", looseleaf, 105 pages. ISBN: 0-93505-13-2.

Greenstein, Daniel I. (ed). *Modelling Historical Data: Towards a Standard for Encoding and Exchanging Machine-Readable Texts.* Halbgraue Reihe zur Historischen Fachinformatik, Serie A, Historische Quellenkunden, edited by Manfred Thaller, Band (A) 11. St. Katharinen: [Published for the Max-Planck-Institut für Geschiche, Göttingen by] Scripta Mercaturae Verlag, 1991. iv + 223 pages. ISBN: 3-928134-45-0. The volume contains an edited collection of fourteen essays on various aspects of conceptual modelling and development of standardized encoding methods for representing knowledge in historical texts. The contributions are by Manfred Thaller, Lou Burnard, Daniel I. Greenstein, Hannes D. Galter, Ingo H. Kropač;, Donald A. Spaeth, Hans Jørgen Marker, Thomas Werner, Jan Oldervoll, and Kevin Schurer.

Greenstein, Daniel I. "Standard, Meta-Standard: A Framework for Coding Occupational Data." *Historical Social Research* 16/1 (1991) 3-22.

Greenstein, Daniel; Burnard, Lou. "Speaking With One Voice: Encoding Standards and the Prospects for an Integrated Approach to Computing in History." *The Text Encoding Initiative: Background and Context*, Guest Editors Nancy Ide and Jean Véronis = *Computers and the Humanities* 29/2 (1995) 137–148. Also in this volume.

Guittet, Christian. "Appendix — Introduction to SGML. Extract from FORMEX. Published by the EEC Office of Official Publications." *SGML Users' Group Bulletin* 1/1 (1986) 26-57.

Guittet, Christian (ed.) *FORMEX: formalisation de l'échange de publications électronique = Formalised Exchange of Electronic Publications.* Luxembourg: Office des Publications officielles des Communautés européennes, New Technologies — Project Management Department, 1985. Copyright ECSC, EEC and EAEC. ISBN: 92-825-5399-X The volume contains an introduction to SGML and implementation of the standard for electronic interchange of CEC and OPOCE documents.

Heath, Jim; Welsch, Larry. "Difficulties in Parsing SGML." In *Proceedings of the ACM Conference on Document Processing Systems, Santa Fe* (ACM Conference on Document Processing Systems, Santa Fe, New Mexico, 5-9 December 1988, sponsored by ACM SIGGRAPH, SIGOIS, and SIGIR). New York: Association for Computing Machinery, 1988, pp. 71-77. ISBN: 0-89791-291-8.

Herwijnen, Eric van. *The Annotated ISO 12083: Electronic Manuscript Preparation and Markup.* Geneva/Providence: ISO and Electronic Book Technologies, 1995. Supplies the annotated text of ISO 12083 as an electronic book for Microsoft Windows.

Herwijnen, Eric van. *Practical SGML.* 2nd edition. Boston/Dordrecht/London: Kluwer Academic Publishers, 1994. xx + 288 pages. ISBN: 0-7923-9434-8. This volume is one of the best introductory texts on SGML.

Hockey, Susan. "Developing Access to Electronic Texts in the Humanities." *Computers in Libraries* 13/3 (February 1993) 41-43.

Hockey, Susan. "Electronic Texts in the Humanities: A Coming of Age." In *Literary Texts in an Electronic Age: Scholarly Implications and Library Services*. Clinic on Library Applications of Data Processing, Graduate School of Library and Information Science, University of Illinois at Urbana-Champaign, April 10-12, 1994. Edited by Brett Sutton. University of Illinois, Urbana-Champaign, 1994, pp. 21-34 (with 39 references). ISBN:0-87845096-3. ISSN: 0069-4789.

Hockey, Susan; Walker, Donald. "Developing Effective Resources for Research on Texts: Collecting Texts, Tagging Texts, Cataloging Texts, Using Texts, and Putting Texts in Context." *Literary and Linguistic Computing* 8/4 (1993) 235-242.

Holstege, Mary Anne. *Marking and the Design of Notations*. PhD Dissertation. Technical Report No. STAN-CS-89-1270. Stanford, CA: Stanford University, Department of Computer Science, June, 1989. 239 pages.

Huitfeldt, Claus. "Multi-Dimensional Texts in a One-Dimensional Medium." *Computers and the Humanities [= Special Issue, Humanities Computing in Norway]* 28/4-5 (1994-1995) 235-241 (with 24 references). ISSN: 0010-4817.

Ide, N. "Encoding Standards for Large Text Resources; The Text Encoding Initiative". Proceedings of the 15th International Conference on Computational Linguistics, COLING '94, Kyoto, Japan, August 1994, pp. 574–578.

Ide, Nancy; Le Maitre, J.; Véronis, J. "Outline of a Model for Lexical Databases. *Information Processing and Management*, 29, 2, pp. 159–186.

Ide, Nancy; Sperberg-McQueen, C. M. "The Text Encoding Initiative: Its History, Goals, and Future Development." *The Text Encoding Initiative: Background and Context*, Guest Editors Nancy Ide and Jean Véronis = *Computers and the Humanities* 29/1 (1995) 5-15. Also in this volume.

Ide, Nancy; Véronis, Jean; Durand, David. "A Data Architecture for Multi-lingual Linguistic Corpora." Paper presented at ACH/ALLC '95, July 11-15, 1995. *ACH/ALLC '95: The 1995 Joint International Conference. Conference Abstracts, Posters and Demonstrations*. Santa Barbara: University of California/ACH/ALLC, 1995, pp. 60-62 [extended abstract].

Ide, Nancy; Véronis, Jean. "Encoding Dictionaries." *The Text Encoding Initiative: Background and Context*, Guest Editors Nancy Ide and Jean Véronis = *Computers and the Humanities* 29/2 (1995) 167–179. Also in this volume.

Ide, Nancy; Véronis, Jean; Le Maitre, Jacques. "Outline of a Database Model for Electronic Dictionaries." In *Intelligent Text and Image Handling: Proceedings of a Conference on Intelligent Text and Image Handling, "RIAO91"* Barcelona, Spain, 2-5 April, 1991 [Conference organized by the Centre de Hautes Etudes Internationales d'Informatique Documentaire (CID), Center for the Advanced Study of Information Systems, Inc. (CASIS). Sponsored by the Commission of the European Communities, Minister of Education and Sciences, Spain; Minister of "Industrie en Aménagement du Territoire", France; et al.] Ed. André Lichnerowicz. Amsterdam/London/New York/Tokyo: Elsevier, 1991, pp. 375-393 (with 25 references). Extent: xiii + 999 pages. ISBN: 0-444-89361-X.

Ide, Nancy; Véronis, Jean. "Toward a Comprehensive Set of Text Encoding Principles [Let's Not Rebuild the Encoding Tower of Babel]." In *Colloque International "Consensus ex Machina?". Abstracts.* International Joint Conference of the ALLC (Association for Linguistic and Literary Computing) and ACH (Association for Computers and the Humanities), Sorbonne, Paris, 19-23 avril 1994. Paris: Laboratoire "Lexicométrie et textes politiques" (INaLF, CNRS), and Ecole Normale Supérieure de Fontenay - Saint Cloud, 1994, pp. 109-110.

International Organization for Standardization (ISO). *ISO 639:1988 (E/F). Code for the Representation of Names of Languages*. First edition, 1988-04-01. Reference number: ISO 639:1988 (E/F). Geneva: International Organization for Standardization, 1988. iii + 17 pages.

International Organization for Standardization (ISO). *ISO CD 639/2:1991. Code for the Representation of Names of Languages: alpha-3 Code*. Geneva: International Organization for Standardization, 1991. iii + 52 leaves.

International Organization for Standardization (ISO). *ISO 8879:1986. Information Processing — Text and Office Systems — Standard Generalized Markup Language (SGML) [= Traitement de l'information, Systèmes bureautiques, Langage standard géneralisé de balisage (SGML)]*. First edition 1986-10-15; Reference No. ISO 8879:1986 (E). Geneva: International Organization for Standardization, 15 September 1986. With Amendment A1 (1988), ISO 8879 constitutes the core specification for SGML. A subset of SGML became a US FIPS (Federal Information Processing Standard) in 1988. The British Standards Institution adopted SGML as a national standard (BS 6868) in 1987, and in 1989 SGML was adopted by the CEN/CENELEC Standards Committees as a European standard, #28879. Australia has dual numbered versions of ISO 8879 SGML and ISO 9069 SDIF (AS 3514 — SGML 1987; AS 3649 — 1990 SDIF). The full text of this ISO standard with Amendment A is incorporated into the text Charles Goldfarb's commentary (*SGML Handbook*), and is available in electronic form on a CD-ROM disc published by Exoterica Corporation.

International Organization for Standardization (ISO). *ISO 8879:1986 / A1:1988 (E). Information Processing — Text and Office Systems — Standard Generalized Markup Language (SGML), Amendment 1 [Traitement de l'information, Systèmes bureautiques, Langage standard géneralisé de balisage (SGML), Amendment 1]*. Geneva: International Organization for Standardization, July 01 1988. 15 pages.

International Organization for Standardization (ISO). *ISO 9069:1988. Information Processing — SGML Sup-*

port Facilities — SGML Document Interchange Format (SDIF) [= Traitement de l'information — Bureautique — Format d'échange de document SGML (SDIF)]. First edition: 1988-09-15; Reference number ISO 9069:1988 (E). Geneva: International Organization for Standardization, 15 September 1988.

International Organization for Standardization (ISO). *ISO/IEC 9070:1991. Information Processing — SGML Support Facilities — Registration Procedures for Public Text Owner Identifiers [= Technologies de l'information, Facilités de support SGML, Procédures d'enregistrement pour identificateurs de propriétaire de texte public]*. Second edition, 15 April 1991; Reference number ISO/IEC 9070:1991 (E). Geneva: International Organization for Standardization/International Electrotechnical Commission, 15 April 1991. iv + 12 pages.

International Organization for Standardization (ISO). *ISO/IEC TR 9573:1988 (E). Information Processing — SGML Support Facilities — Techniques for Using Standard Generalized Markup Language (SGML)*. Edited by Anders Berglund. Geneva: International Organization for Standardization/International Electrotechnical Commission, December 09 1988. vi + 124 pages.

International Organization for Standardization (ISO). *ISO/IEC TR 10037:1991. Information Processing — SGML and Text Entry Systems — Guidelines for SGML Syntax-Directed Editing Systems*. Geneva: International Organization for Standardization/International Electrotechnical Commission, 15 March 1991.

International Organization for Standardization (ISO). *ISO/IEC DIS 10179.2:1994. Information Technology — Text and Office Systems — Document Style Semantics and Specification Language (DSSSL)*. Edited by Sharon Adler and James Clark. ISO/IEC 10179 was prepared by Joint Technical Committee ISO/IEC JTC 1, Information Technology. Geneva: International Organization for Standardization/International Electrotechnical Commission, 1994. viii + 142 pages.

International Organization for Standardization (ISO). *ISO/IEC DIS 10180:1991. Information Processing — Text Composition — Standard Page Description Language (SPDL)*. Geneva: International Organization for Standardization/International Electrotechnical Commission, 1991.

International Organization for Standardization (ISO). *ISO/IEC DIS 10743:1995. Information Technology — Standard Music Description Language (SMDL)*. Geneva: International Organization for Standardization/International Electrotechnical Commission, July 1995. [Was: ISO/IEC CD 10743:1991 (April 1, 1991).] Description from the 1991 CD version: SMDL "defines a language for the representation of music information, either alone, on in conjunction with text, graphics, or other information needed for publishing or business purposes. Multimedia time sequence information in also supported."

International Organization for Standardization (ISO). *ISO/IEC 10744:1992. Information Technology — Hypermedia/Time-based Structuring Language (HyTime)*. Edited by Charles F. Goldfarb (with assistance from Steven R. Newcomb). Geneva: International Organization for Standardization/International Electrotechnical Commission, 1992.

International Organization for Standardization (ISO). *ISO 12083:1993(E) Information and documentation — Electronic Manuscript Preparation and Markup*. First edition, 1994-01-15. Geneva: International Organization for Standardization, 1994. 96 pages.

International Organization for Standardization (ISO). *ISO/IEC DIS 13673:1993 Information Technology—Text and Office Systems — Conformance Testing for Standard Generalized Markup Language (SGML) Systems*. First edition. Geneva: International Organization for Standardization/International Electrotechnical Commission, 1993.

Johansson, Stig. "The Encoding of Spoken Texts." *The Text Encoding Initiative: Background and Context*, Guest Editors Nancy Ide and Jean Véronis = *Computers and the Humanities* 29/2 (1995) 149–158. Also in this volume.

Joloboff, Vania. "Document Representation: Concepts and Standards." In *Structured Documents*. Edited by Jacques André, Richard Keith Furuta, and Vincent Quint. The Cambridge Series on Electronic Publishing. Cambridge/New York: Cambridge University Press, 1989, pp. 75-105. ISBN: 0-521-36554-6.

Kaelbling, Michael J. "On Improving SGML." *Electronic Publishing: Origination, Dissemination and Design (EPODD)* 3/2 (May 1990) 93-98 (with 14 references). ISSN: 0894-3982.

Källgren, Gunnel; Eriksson, Gunnar; Höglund, Magnus. "Introducing the SUC: A Large Balanced Corpus, Linguistically Analyzed and Marked-up in Accordance with the Recomendations Issued by the Text Encoding Initiative." In *Colloque International "Consensus ex Machina?" Abstracts*. International Joint Conference of the ALLC and ACH, Sorbonne, Paris, 19-23 avril 1994. Paris: Laboratorie "Lexicométrie et textes politiques" (INaLF, CNRS), and Ecole Normale Supérieure de Fontenay - Saint Cloud, 1994, pp. 119-120 [partial abstract].

Kimber, W. Eliot. *HyTime and SGML: Understanding the HyTime HyQ Query Language*. Technical Report, Version 1.1. IBM Corporation, August 2, 1993. 40 pages. Document URL: ftp://ftp.ifi.uio.no/pub/SGML/HtTime/HyQ-1.1.Kimber.

Kimber, W. Eliot. *Practical Hypermedia: An Introduction to HyTime*. Charles F. Goldfarb Series On Open Information Management. New York: Prentice-Hall Professional Technical Reference, [forthcoming] 1995. Approximately 250 pages. ISBN: 0-13-309899-0.

Klensin, John C. "When the Metadata Exceed the Data: Data Management With Uncertain Data." *Statistics and Computing* 5/1 (March 1995) 73-84 (with 22 references).

Langendoen, D. Terence; Simons, Gary. "Rationale for the TEI Recommendations for Feature-Structure Markup." *The Text Encoding Initiative: Background and Context*, Guest Editors Nancy Ide and Jean Véronis = *Computers and the Humanities* 29/3 (1995) 191–209. Also in this volume.

Lavagnino, John. "Simultaneous Electronic and Paper Publication." *TUGboat: The Communications of the TeX Users Group [= Proceedings of the 1991 Annual Meeting]* 12/3 (December 1991) 401-405.

Lavagnino, John; Mylonas, Elli. "The Show Must Go On: Problems of Tagging Performance Texts." *The Text Encoding Initiative: Background and Context*, Guest Editors Nancy Ide and Jean Véronis = *Computers and the Humanities* 29/2 (1995) 113–121. Also in this volume.

Loeffen, Arjan. "Text Databases: A Survey of Text Models and Systems." *SIGMOD Record* 23/1 (March 1994) 97-106 (with 23 references).

Logan, Elizabeth (guest editor). *Structured Information / Standards for Document Architectures. = Journal of the American Society for Information Science* [Special Issue]. New York, NY: ASIS, [forthcoming] 1996. ISSN: 0002-8231.

Logan, Harry M. "Report on a New OED Project: A Study of the History of New Words in the New OED." *Computers and the Humanities [Proceedings of the Eighth International Conference on Computers and the Humanities]* 23/4-5 (1989) 385-395.

MacLeod, Douglas. "Building Buildings: An Analogy for a Language to Build Architectures." *<TAG>* 14 (May, 1990) 7-10.

Macleod, Ian A. (guest editor). *SGML Special Issue: Computer Standards & Interfaces*. Amsterdam: Elsevier Science Publishers B.V./North-Holland, 1995. ISSN: 0920-5489.

Macleod, Ian A. "A Query Language for Retrieving Information from Hierarchic Text Structures." *Computer Journal* 34/3 (June 1991) 254-264 (with 24 references). ISSN: 0010-4620.

Macleod, Ian A.; Barnard, David T.; Hamilton, D.; Levison, M. "SGML Documents and Non-linear Text Retrieval." In *Intelligent Text and Image Handling: Proceedings of a Conference on Intelligent Text and Image Handling, "RIAO91"*. Barcelona, Spain, 2-5 April, 1991. Conference organized by the Centre de Hautes Etudes Internationales d'Informatique Documentaire (CID), Center for the Advanced Study of Information Systems, Inc. Ed. André Lichnerowicz. Amsterdam/London/New York/Tokyo: Elsevier, 1991, pp. 226-244 (with 17 references). xiii + 999 pages. ISBN: 0-444-89361-X.

Maler, Eve; El Anduloussi, Jeanne. *Developing SGML Document Type Definitions*. Charles F. Goldfarb Series On Open Information Management. Englewood Cliffs, NJ: PTR Prentice Hall, [forthcoming] 1995. ISBN: 0-13-309881-8.

Mamrak, Sandra A.; Barnes, Julie. *Guidelines for the Preparation of SGML Document Type Definitions*. Technical Report OSU-CISRC-7/90-TR16. Columbus, Ohio: The Ohio State University, Department of Computer and Information Science, July, 1990. 21 pages.

Mamrak, Sandra A.; Barnes, Julie. *Guidelines for Specifying Data Representations in SGML Document Databases*. Technical Report, OSU. Submitted for publication in: *Electronic Publishing: Origination, Dissemination and Design*. Columbus, Ohio: The Ohio State University, Department of Computer and Information Science, October 12, 1989. 26 pages.

Matzen, Richard Walter. *A Formal Language Model for Detecting Ambiguity in SGML*. Ph.D. Dissertation. Oklahoma State University, Department of Computer Science, 1993. xii, 144 pages.

McFadden, John R.; Hayter, Ronald S. "Element Content vs. Mixed Content. Where it Matters." *<TAG>* 1/5 (1988) 12-13.

Melby, Alan. "E-TIF: An Electronic Terminology Interchange Format." *The Text Encoding Initiative: Background and Context*, Guest Editors Nancy Ide and Jean Véronis = *Computers and the Humanities* 29/2 (1995) 159–165. Also in this volume.

Mumford, Anne (editor). *Document Exchange: The Use of SGML in the UK Academic and Research Community. Workshop Proceedings 5-7 March 1990.* Loughborough: Advisory Group on Computer Graphics, 1990.

Newcomb, Steven R. "Multimedia Interchange Using SGML/HyTime. Part I: Structures." *IEEE MultiMedia* 2/2 (Summer 1995) 86-89 (with 2 references). ISSN: 1070-986X.

Newcomb, Steven R. "SGML Architectures: Implications and Opportunities for Industry." *<TAG>* 8/8 (August 1995) 1-5.

Newcomb, Steven R. "Standards. Standard Music Description Language Complies with Hypermedia Standard." *IEEE Computer* 24/7 (July 1991) 76-79. ISSN: 0018-9162.

Newcomb, Steven R.; Kipp, Neill A.; Newcomb, Victoria T. "The 'HyTime' Hypermedia/Time-based Document Structuring Language." *Communications of the Association for Computing Machinery* 34/11 (November 1991) 67-83. ISSN: 0001-0782.

Nicholas, Charles K.; Welsch, Lawrence A. "On the Interchangeability of SGML and ODA." *Electronic Publishing: Origination, Dissemination and Design* 5/3 (September 1992) 105-130 (with 15 references). ISSN: 0894-3982.

Nordin, Brent; Barnard, David T.; Macleod, Ian A. "A Review of the Standard Generalized Markup Language (SGML)." *Computer Standards and Interfaces* (Amsterdam, Netherlands: Elsevier Science Publishers B.V./North-Holland) 15/1 (May 1993) 5-19 (with 33 references). ISSN: 0920-5489.

O'Connell, Conleth S. Jr. *Supporting the Development of Grammar Descriptions for Multiple Applications*. OSU-CISRC-TR-7/90-TR20. The Ohio State University, Department of Computer and Information Science, July 1990.

Painter, J. Derek. "Marking up the Dictionary (The Oxford English Dictionary)." *Information Media and Technology* 21/2 (March 1988) 72-74. ISSN: 0306-2880.

Popham, Michael. "An Update on SGML." *Information Management and Technology* 27/6 (November 1994) 247-50, 262.

Popham, Michael G. "Use of SGML and HyTime in UK Universities." *Information Services and Use* [Workshop on Hypermedia and Hypertext Standards, Amsterdam, Netherlands, 22-23 April 1993. Sponsored by CEC.] 13/2 (1993) 103-109.

Poppelier, N. A. F. M.; Herwijnen, Eric van; Rowley, C.A. "Standard DTDs and Scientific Publishing." *EPSIG News* 5/3 (September 1992) 10-19.

Price, Lynne A. "An Alternate Representation of SGML Content Models." *SGML Users' Group Bulletin* 2/2 (1987) 125-126. ISSN: 0269-2538.

Price, Lynne A. "Graphic Representation of Content Models." *<TAG>* 10 (July 1989) 12-16.

Price, Lynne A. "A Parser Generator for SGML." In *PROTEXT IV. Proceedings of the Fourth International Conference on Text Processing Systems*. International Conference on Text Processing Systems, Boston, MA, USA 20-22 October 1987. Sponsored by INCA - Institute for Numerical Computation and Analysis. Ed. John J. H. Miller. Dun Laoghaire, Ireland: Boole Press, Ltd., 1987, pp. 118-23. ISBN: 0-906783-80-1.

Price, Lynne A. "The Problem with Ambiguous Content Models." *SGML Users' Group Bulletin* 3/1 (1988) 25-26.

Price, Lynne A.; Schneider, Joe. "Evolution of an SGML Parser Generator." In *Proceedings of the ACM Conference on Document Processing Systems, Santa Fe*. ACM Conference on Document Processing Systems, Santa Fe, New Mexico, 5-9 December 1988, sponsored by ACM SIGGRAPH, SIGOIS, and SIGIR. New York: Association for Computing Machinery, 1988, pp. 51-60. ISBN: 0-89791-291-8.

Price-Wilkin, John. "A Gateway Between the World-Wide Web and PAT: Exploiting SGML Through the Web." *The Public-Access Computer Systems Review* 5/7 (1994) 5-27.

Rath, Hans Holger. *Tabellen in SGML*. ZGDV-Bericht 75/93, Dipl.-Informatik Hans Holger Rath. Darmstadt: Zentrum für Graphische Datenverarbeitung e.V. [ZGDV], 1993. Extent: v + 77 pages, 47 references. Document URL: http://zgdv.igd.fhg.de/papers/ed/SGML-Tabs.ps.Z.

Rath, Hans Holger. *SGML — Eine Einführung*. ZGDV Technical Report. Darmstadt: Zentrum für Graphische Datenverarbeitung e.V. [ZGDV], 1993. 20 pages, 25 references. Document URL: http://zgdv.igd.fhg.de/papers/ed/SGML-Einf.ps.Z.

Raymond, Darrell R. *Lector — An Interactive Formatter for Tagged Text* Technical Report OED-90-02. Waterloo, Ontario: University of Waterloo Centre for the New Oxford English Dictionary and Text Research, August, 1990. 26 pages, 13 figures.

Reid, Brian K. "Scribe: Histoire et évaluation." In *Actes des Journées sur la Manipulation de Documents*. [Conference] La Manipulation de Documents, Rennes, 4-6 Mai 1983. Edited by Jacques André. Rennes, France: INRIA [Institut National de Recherche en Informatique et en Automatique], 1983, pp. 28-39 (with 17 references). ix + 286 pages. ISBN: 2-7261-0351-0. The article supplies an historical overview of the design, development, implementation, and early use of the Scribe document preparation system, many features of which were developed in in parallel with (S)GML beginning in 1975.

Reid, Brian Keith. *Scribe: A Document Specification Language and its Compiler*. Adviser: Robert F. Sproull. Ph.D. Dissertation. Pittsburgh, PA: Department of Computer Science, Carnegie-Mellon University, October, 1980. x + 148 pages. This dissertation and its related earlier work was highly influential in the United States, particularly within academic circles, in demonstrating the power of document grammars and descriptive markup principles.

Renear, Allen; Mylonas, Elli; Durand, David. "Refining our Notion of What Text Really Is: The Problem of Overlapping Hierarchies." In *Research in Humanities Computing*. Edited by Nancy Ide and Susan Hockey. Oxford: Oxford University Press, 1993, pp. xxx-xxx (16 pages, 23 references). See provisionally the URL: http://www.stg.brown.edu/resources/stg/monographs/ohco.html.

Robinson, Peter R. *The Transcription of Primary Textual Sources Using SGML*. Office for Humanities Communication Publications, No. 6. Oxford: Oxford University Computing Service, Office for Humanities Communication, 1994. vii+ 136 pages. ISBN: 1897791070.

Romary, Laurent; Mehl, Nathalie; Woolls, David. "The Lingua Parallel Concordancing Project: Managing Multilingual Texts for Educational Purposes." *Electronic Texts and the Text Encoding Initiative [Special Issue] = TEXT Technology: The Journal of Computer Text Processing* 5/3 (Autumn, 1995) 204-220. ISSN: 1053-900X.

Rubinsky, Yuri. "Standards for Hypertext Interchange." *SGML Users' Group Newsletter* 15 (January 1990) 14-15.

Rubinsky, Yuri. "SGML to Braille, Large Print, and Audio." In Part 4: Distinguished Seminar Series, *Annual Review of OCLC Research, 1994*. Dublin, OH: OCLC Online Computer Library Center, 1995, pp. 65-68. ISSN: 0894-198X. Online document URL: http://www.oclc.org/oclc/research/publications/review94/part4/sgml.htm.

Seaman, David M. "'A Library and Apparatus of Every Kind': The Electronic Text Center at the University of Virginia." *Information Technology and Libraries* 13/1 (March 1994) 15-19.

Simons, Gary F. "Conceptual Modeling Versus Visual Modeling: A Technological Key to Building Consensus." In *Colloque International "Consensus ex Machina?" Abstracts*. International Joint Conference of the ALLC and ACH, Sorbonne, Paris, 19-23 avril 1994. Paris: Laboratoire "Lexicométrie et textes politiques" (INaLF, CNRS), and Ecole Normale Supérieure de Fontenay - Saint Cloud, 1994, pp. 217-218 [partial abstract]

Simons, Gary. "Implementing the TEI's Feature-structure Markup by Direct Mapping to the Objects and Attributes of an Object-Oriented Database System." Paper presented at ACH/ALLC '95, July 11-15, 1995. *ACH/ALLC '95: The 1995 Joint International Conference. Conference Abstracts, Posters and Demonstrations*. Santa Barbara:

University of California/ACH/ALLC, 1995, pp. 111-114 [extended abstract].

Sklar, David. "Accelerating Conversion to SGML via the Rainbow Format." *<TAG>* 7/1 (January 1994) 4-5. ISSN: 1067-9197.

Smith, Joan M. *SGML and Related Standards. Document Description and Processing Languages*. Ellis Horwood Series in Computers and their Applications. New York/London: Ellis Horwood, 1992. xviii + 152 pages. ISBN: 0-13-806506-3.

Smith, Joan M. "The Standard Generalized Markup Language (SGML) for Humanities Publishing." *Literary and Linguistic Computing* 2/3 (1987) 171-175. ISSN: 0268-1145.

Smith, Joan M.; Stutely, Robert S. *SGML: The Users' Guide to ISO 8879*. Chichester/New York: Ellis Horwood/Halsted, 1988. 173 pages. ISBN: 0-7458-0221-4 (Ellis Horwood). ISBN: 0-470-21126-1 (Halsted).

SoftQuad, Inc. *The SGML Primer. SoftQuad's Quick Reference Guide to the Essentials of the Standard: The SGML Needed for Reading a DTD and Marked-up Documents and Discussing them Reasonably*. Version 3.0. Toronto: SoftQuad Inc., December, 1991. 36 pages.

SoftQuad, Inc. *The SGML World Tour*. Toronto, Ontario: SoftQuad, Inc., Spring, 1994. ISBN: 1-896172-01-6. This publication is a large and valuable library of SGML resources on CD-ROM.

Sperberg-McQueen, C. Michael. "Bare Bones TEI: A Very Very Small Subset of the TEI Encoding Scheme." *Electronic Texts and the Text Encoding Initiative [Special Issue] = TEXT Technology: The Journal of Computer Text Processing* 5/3 (Autumn, 1995) 248-265. ISSN: 1053-900X.

Sperberg-McQueen, C. Michael. "Specifying Document Structure: Differences in LaTeX and TEI Markup." *TUGboat [Proceedings of the 1991 Annual Meeting]* 12/3 (December 1991) 415-421.

Sperberg-McQueen, C. Michael. "The Text Encoding Initiative: Electronic Text Markup for Research." In *Literary Texts in an Electronic Age: Scholarly Implications and Library Services.*. Clinic on Library Applications of Data Processing, Graduate School of Library and Information Science, University of Illinois at Urbana-Champaign, April 10-12, 1994. Ed. Brett Sutton. University of Illinois, Urbana-Champaign, 1994, pp. 35-56. ISBN: 0-87845096-3. ISSN: 0069-4789.

Sperberg-McQueen, C. Michael. "Text in the Electronic Age: Textual Study and Text Encoding, with Examples from Medieval Texts." *Literary and Linguistic Computing* 6/1 (1991) 34-46. ISSN: 0268-1145.

Sperberg-McQueen, C. M.; Burnard, Lou. "The Design of the TEI Encoding Scheme." *The Text Encoding Initiative: Background and Context*, Guest Editors Nancy Ide and Jean Véronis = *Computers and the Humanities* 29/1 (1995) 17-39.

Sperberg-McQueen, C. M.; Burnard, Lou. "The ODD System of Tag Set Documentation." In *Colloque International "Consensus ex Machina?" Abstracts*. International Joint Conference of the ALLC and ACH, Sorbonne, Paris, 19-23 avril 1994. Paris: Laboratorie "Lexicométrie et textes politiques" (INaLF, CNRS), and Ecole Normale Supérieure de Fontenay - Saint Cloud, 1994, pp. 221-222 [partial abstract].

Tompa, Frank W. "What is (Tagged) Text?" In *Dictionaries in the Electronic Age: Proceedings of the Fifth Annual Conference of the UW Centre for the New Oxford English Dictionary*. St. Catherine's College, Oxford, 18-19 September 1989. Waterloo, Ontario: UW Centre for the New OED, 1989, 2:81-93.

Travis, Brian E.; Waldt, Dale C. *The SGML Implementation Guide*. Berlin/New York: Springer-Verlag, [forthcoming] 1995. ISBN: 0-387-57730-0.

Triggs, Jeffery. "Varieties of Electronic Experience: What Should an Electronic Text Be Like?" *Electronic Texts and the Text Encoding Initiative [Special Issue] = TEXT Technology: The Journal of Computer Text Processing* 5/3 (Autumn, 1995) 179-189. ISSN: 1053-900X.

Tucker, Hugh A.; Bogh, Torkil. *SGML & ODA. Standards for Document Processing and Interchange*. DS/INF 14, [1989]. Dansk Standardiseringsrad, 1989.

Vignaud, Dominique. *L'édition structurée des documents: SGML application à l'édition français*. Paris: Éditions du Cercle de la Librarie, 1989. ISBN: 2-7654 0420-8.

Vooren, Ludo van; Severson, Eric C. "SGML Architectural Forms." *<TAG>* 5/2 (February 1992) 1-3.

Walter, Mark. "OSU's Chameleon Architecture: A Grammatical Approach to Translation and DTDs." *The Seybold Report on Publishing Systems* 20/7 (December 24, 1990) [1,] 17-23. ISSN: 0736-7260.

Walter, Mark. "SGML For Journals: Toward Electronic Delivery." *Seybold Report on Publishing Systems* 21/18 (15 June 1992) 1, 3-13, 16-19.

Warmer, Jos; Egmond, Sylvia van. "The Implementation of the Amsterdam SGML Parser." *Electronic Publishing: Origination, Dissemination and Design* 2/2 (July 1989) 65-90. ISSN: 0894 3982.

Warmer, Jos; Van Vliet, Hans. "Processing SGML Documents." *Electronic Publishing: Origination, Dissemination and Design* 4/1 (March 1991) 3-26. ISSN: 0894-3982.

Weibel, Stuart L. "The CORE Project: Technical Shakedown Phase and Preliminary User Studies." *OCLC Systems and Services* 10/2-3 (Summer-Fall 1994) 99-102.

Weibel, Stuart L. "The Design and Implementation of XSCEPTER, an X-Windows Graphical User Interface to the CORE Project." In Part 2: External and Collaborative Research, *Annual Review of OCLC Research, 1994*. Dublin, OH: OCLC Online Computer Library Center, 1995, pp. 40-45. ISSN: 0894-198X.

Weibel, Stuart; Godby, Jean; Miller, Eric; Daniel, Ron. *OCLC/NCSA Metadata Workshop Report*. OCLC Conference Report. Dublin, OH: Office of Research, OCLC Online Computer Library Center, Inc., [March], 1995. The document includes a DTD for "the Dublin Core". Online document URL: http://www.oclc.org:5046/conferences/metadata/dublin_core_report.html.